S0-BCM-989

JOURNAL FOR THE STUDY OF THE OLD TESTAMENT
SUPPLEMENT SERIES
235

Sheffield Academic Press

Forming Prophetic Literature

Essays on Isaiah and the Twelve in Honor of John D.W. Watts

edited by

James W. Watts
and Paul R. House

Journal for the Study of the Old Testament
Supplement Series 235

Published by
Sheffield Academic Press Ltd
Mansion House
19 Kingfield Road
Sheffield S11 9AS
England

Typeset by Sheffield Academic Press
and
Printed on acid-free paper in Great Britain
by Bookcraft Ltd
Midsomer Norton, Bath

British Library Cataloguing in Publication Data

A catalogue record for this book is available
from the British Library

ISBN 1-85075-641-4

CONTENTS

ACKNOWLEDGMENTS

Many of the articles in this book were originally presented in 1994 and 1995 to the Society of Biblical Literature's Consultation on the Formation of the Book of the Twelve, a group which John Watts was instrumental in forming and leading. We are grateful to the members of that group for allowing their works to appear in this volume and to our other contributors who agreed to write on a fairly narrow range of topics for this collection. The book has benefited from the editorial help provided by James D. Nogalski, which we appreciate.

James W. Watts and Paul R. House

ABBREVIATIONS

AB	Anchor Bible
AOAT	Alter Orient und Altes Testament
ATD	Das Alte Testament Deutsch
BETL	Bibliotheca ephemeridum theologicarum lovaniensium
Bib	*Biblica*
BKAT	Biblischer Kommentar: Altes Testament
BZAW	Beihefte zur *ZAW*
CBC	Cambridge Bible Commentary
CBQ	*Catholic Biblical Quarterly*
ConBOT	Coniectanea biblica, Old Testament
DJD	Discoveries in the Judaean Desert
EvRTh	*Evangelical Review of Theology*
ExpTim	*Expository Times*
HAR	*Hebrew Annual Review*
HAT	Handbuch zum Alten Testament
HBT	*Horizons in Biblical Theology*
HKAT	Handkommentar zum Alten Testament
HSM	Harvard Semitic Monographs
HUCA	*Hebrew Union College Annual*
ICC	International Critical Commentary
IDB	G.A. Buttrick (ed.), *Interpreter's Dictionary of the Bible*
IEJ	*Israel Exploration Journal*
Int	*Interpretation*
JAOS	*Journal of the American Oriental Society*
JBL	*Journal of Biblical Literature*
JBR	*Journal of Bible and Religion*
JETS	*Journal of the Evangelical Theological Society*
JNES	*Journal of Near Eastern Studies*
JPTSup	*Journal of Pentecostal Theology*, Supplement Series
JSNTSup	*Journal for the Study of the New Testament*, Supplement Series
JSOT	*Journal for the Study of the Old Testament*
JSOTSup	*Journal for the Study of the Old Testament*, Supplement Series
JSS	*Journal of Semitic Studies*
KAT	Kommentar zum Alten Testament
LD	Lectio divina
MeyerK	H.A.W. Meyer (ed.), Kritisch-exegetischer Kommentar über das Neue Testament
NCBC	New Century Bible Commentary

OBT	Overtures to Biblical Theology
OTL	Old Testament Library
PRS	*Perspectives in Religious Studies*
ResQ	*Restoration Quarterly*
RevExp	*Review and Expositor*
SBLDS	SBL Dissertation Series
SBLEJL	SBL Early Judaism and its Literature
SBLMS	SBL Monograph Series
SBLSP	SBL Seminar Papers
SBS	Stuttgarter Bibelstudien
SWJT	*Southwestern Journal of Theology*
TLZ	*Theologische Literaturzeitung*
TynBul	*Tyndale Bulletin*
TZ	*Theologische Zeitschrift*
VT	*Vetus Testamentum*
VTSup	*Vetus Testamentum*, Supplements
WBC	Word Biblical Commentary
WMANT	Wissenschaftliche Monographien zum Alten und Neuen Testament
ZAW	*Zeitschrift für die alttestamentliche Wissenschaft*
ZTK	*Zeitschrift für Theologie und Kirche*

LIST OF CONTRIBUTORS

EHUD BEN ZVI is Associate Professor in the Division of Comparative Studies in Literature, Film, and Religion (MLCS) of the University of Alberta, Edmonton, Canada

DONALD K. BERRY is Associate Professor of Religion at the University of Mobile, Mobile, Alabama

DUANE L. CHRISTENSEN is Professor of Old Testament and Intercultural Studies at Patten College, Oakland, California, and Professor of Biblical Studies and Ancient Near Eastern History at William Carey International University, Pasadena, California

RONALD E. CLEMENTS was Professor of Old Testament at Kings College, University of London, London, England

KENNETH M. CRAIG, JR, is Assistant Professor of Religious Studies at Lees-McRae College, Banner Elk, North Carolina

RUSSELL FULLER is Assistant Professor of Theological and Religious Studies at the University of San Diego, San Diego, California

PAUL R. HOUSE is Professor of Old Testament Interpretation at the Southern Baptist Theological Seminary, Louisville, Kentucky

JÖRG JEREMIAS is Professor of Old Testament at Philipps-Universität, Marburg, Germany

JAMES D. NOGALSKI is Assistant Professor of Old Testament Interpretation at the Southern Baptist Theological Seminary, Louisville, Kentucky

MARGARET S. ODELL is Assistant Professor of Religious Studies at St. Olaf College, Minneapolis, Minnesota

PAUL L. REDDITT is Professor of Religious Studies at Georgetown College, Georgetown, Kentucky

THOMAS G. SMOTHERS is Professor of Old Testament Interpretation at the Southern Baptist Theological Seminary, Louisville, Kentucky

MARVIN E. TATE is Senior Professor of Old Testament Interpretation at the Southern Baptist Theological Seminary, Louisville, Kentucky

JAMES W. WATTS is Assistant Professor of Religion at Hastings College, Hastings, Nebraska

THE FORMATION OF A SCHOLAR

Paul R. House

Continuity, longevity, and creativity are scarce commodities in twentieth-century scholars and scholarship. They sometimes appear singly in an individual, and only more rarely as a group in an individual or family. John D.W. Watts has indeed embodied these desirable characteristics during his career. These qualities have not protected him from fallibility, but they have enhanced his ability to produce significant, serious, sustained scholarship during the most-recent four decades of his life. This brief essay will utilize these three ideals as signposts for a review and assessment of Watts's academic career.[1] Frankly, the assessment may be more gentle than some would like, but perhaps more vigorous than is normal in a festschrift. Certainly John Watts is not afraid of assessment, and stands ready to defend his positions to all who care to ask.

Continuity

Watts's family is the first and most foundational element in his career. His father, J. Wash Watts (1896–1975) taught Hebrew and Old Testament Exegesis for decades at New Orleans Baptist Theological Seminary. The elder Watts was a powerful force at the seminary, an observation that is borne out of my hearing him cited as a significant role model by a nationally-known New Orleans *alumnus* as late as 1992. He also wrote various popular and scholarly pieces, including his 1951 volume *A Survey of Syntax in the Hebrew Old Testament*, which reflect his commitment to both classroom teaching and scholarly research.[2] The

1. The writing of this essay has been made somewhat easier by the appearance of Watts's autobiographical article 'Amos: Across Fifty Years of Study', *RevExp* 92 (1995), pp. 189-93.

2. J.W. Watts, *A Survey of Syntax in the Hebrew Old Testament* (Nashville: Broadman, 1951).

younger Watts studied under his father at New Orleans, receiving his Master of Theology degree in 1944, having already earned a BA from Mississippi College in 1941. Watts credits his father with suggesting Isaiah 65 as the dissertation topic that completed his PhD from The Southern Baptist Theological Seminary in 1948.[3] This familial continuity is strengthened by the fact that James Watts, John's son, currently teaches Old Testament at Hastings College. Thus, three generations of the Watts family have dedicated themselves to teaching Hebrew scripture.

From his father and his other teachers (which included Ludwig Köhler, with whom he did post-doctoral studies at the University of Zürich), Watts gained a commitment to careful exegesis of the canonical biblical text and to analysis of that text's historical background. These interests have characterized Watts's writing throughout his career, even in the last decade when Watts has stressed a literary approach in his research. To these concerns Watts has added his own emphasis on specific biblical genres, especially the vision in prophetic literature. Because of this combination of methodological considerations, Watts has been able to produce writings that leaned towards historical criticism, rhetorical analysis, form criticism, and newer literary approaches. In other words, Watts's own approach to scripture has kept him in the mainstream of Old Testament scholarship for the bulk of his career.

Watts's first monograph illustrates his methodological interests. Published in 1958, *Vision and Prophecy in Amos* sought to establish the relationship between the notation in Amos 1.1 that says Amos 'saw' God's word, the visions recounted in Amos 7.1–9.10, and Amos's ministry.[4] Watts concludes that Amos's five recorded visions correspond to five reports the prophet gave about his ministry, the first three at Bethel when he was still welcome there, and the last two in Judah when he was no longer received at Bethel. Thus, Watts considers Amos 1–2 to be related to 7.1-4, Amos 3–6 to be connected with 7.4-6, Amos 7.7-9 to be the vision that prompts rejection and response in 7.10-17, Amos 8.1-2 to be the introduction to 8.3-14, and Amos 9.1-4 to be the vision that leads to the rest of the book. This strategy is also reflected in his

3. J.D.W. Watts, 'Amos: Across Fifty Years of Study', p. 189. This doctoral work was begun after Watts served as a naval chaplain in World War II. When the war ended Watts was ministering to troops slated to invade Japan.

4. Cf. J.D.W. Watts, *Vision and Prophecy in Amos* (Leiden: Brill, 1958).

popular treatments of Amos.[5] Watts explains the current order of the book by positing two separate collections of Amos' oracles, one a book of words (Amos 1–6) and one a book of visions (Amos 7–9), that were placed together by the prophecy's final editors. He considers the existence of two separate books evidence that prophecies are literary productions, 'not just transcripts of prophetic preaching'.[6] Watts's approach to genre, then, was already stressing that biblical prophecy, as it exists in the Hebrew Bible, is prophetic *literature* written to be read by later generations.

Watts bases his conclusions on Amos on careful textual analysis. This sort of care is evident in his next monograph, *Obadiah*, published in 1969.[7] Here Watts attempts to model for students how to do serious exegetical work. Again he chooses 'a vision' (Obad. 1) shaped as a literary whole as his subject, and again he focuses on a prophecy's possible cultic function. Watts pays close attention to Obadiah's similarity to Jeremiah 49, which indicates his interest in the connections between canonical prophecies.

Two works during the 1970s continued Watts's emphasis on visionary literature within the minor prophets. The first, a commentary of Zechariah, appeared in 1972.[8] Watts explores the visionary form here and also stresses the prophecy's theological concern with salvation and the emergence of the kingdom of God. This emphasis on theology is also reflected in a short volume on Old Testament Theology, a discipline Watts has addressed more in classes than in formal writing.[9] The second, a short treatment of six of the minor prophets, was published in 1975.[10] Like the Zechariah commentary, this book was intended for students and pastors more than for the academy. Still the volume reflects Watts's established penchant for careful readings of the Hebrew text, for treating prophecies as literary wholes, and for attempting to link the texts with

5. Cf. J.D.W. Watts, *Studying the Book of Amos* (Nashville: Broadman, 1965).

6. Watts, 'Amos: Across Fifty Years of Study', p. 190.

7. J.D.W. Watts, *Obadiah* (Grand Rapids: Eerdmans, 1969).

8. J.D.W. Watts, 'Zechariah', *Broadman Bible Commentary: Vol. 7* (Nashville: Broadman, 1972).

9. J.D.W. Watts, *Basic Patterns in Old Testament Religion* (Pasadena, CA: Jameson Press, 2nd edn, 1978).

10. J.D.W. Watts, *The Books of Joel, Obadiah, Jonah, Nahum, Habakkuk and Zephaniah* (CBC; Cambridge: Cambridge University Press, 1975).

their historical settings. These two efforts also helped facilitate Watts's interest in examining the minor prophets not just as separate entities, but as the Book of the Twelve.

After over thirty years of 'preparation', Watts used all the tools and expressed all the viewpoints reflected in his earlier writings in *Isaiah 1–33* (1985) and *Isaiah 34–66* (1987).[11] To these long-term concerns Watts added literary techniques that had begun to interest him in the late 1970's[12] and that were beginning to enter biblical studies in a significant way. Watts considers Isaiah a dramatic vision composed in twelve acts characterized by changing speakers. He concludes that the prophecy was written beginning in the eighth-century, but was added to for years and finally gathered and reshaped in 435 BCE as the complete book that is now canonical.[13] Watts suggests life settings that explain the twelve-act vision, so his literary approach does not cast off historical analysis.

Clearly, these books are similar to Watts's first two monographs in their insistence that prophetic literature is literature, that visions were given in specific historical settings, that careful translations of the Hebrew text are integral to the exegetical task, and that prophetic books were shaped and collected over a long span of time. They are similar to the commentaries written in the 1970's in their commitment to prophetic theology. Despite his determination to recover the prophets' original life settings, Watts's main objective in all these works is to examine and explain *the text itself.* He focuses on the shape of prophetic literature more than on the factors behind the formation of that literature.

In the 1990's Watts has continued his research in Isaiah by presenting papers on the book at Society of Biblical Literature (SBL) meetings. His more immediate concern, however, has been with the Book of the Twelve. Watts has been the initiator of the current SBL Consultation on the Formation of the Book of the Twelve. He presented a paper before that group in 1994 entitled 'Superscriptions and Incipits in the Book of

11. J.D.W. Watts, *Isaiah 1–33* (WBC, 24; Waco, TX: Word, 1985); and *Isaiah 34–66* (WBC, 25; Waco, TX: Word, 1987). The second volume was dedicated to his father and his son.

12. Watts, 'Amos: Across Fifty Years of Study', p. 191. In 1983 I took my first doctoral seminar under Watts, and this class focused on literary approaches to prophecy. I do not recall him discussing Isaiah to any great extent, but obviously he was already moving forward with the Isaiah commentaries that used literary principles.

13. Watts, *Isaiah 1–33*, p. xli.

the Twelve' that dealt with the close relation between the form and content of incipits and superscriptions in the Twelve, and how that relationship may help explain the process by which the twelve books became one. As could be expected, Watts links careful Hebrew textual analysis with genre studies and historical reflection in this paper. Methodological continuity has been maintained.[14]

Longevity

As the preceding survey indicates, one mark of Watts's longevity is reflected in his having published works in five different decades. He has been able to sustain a research and writing schedule that has not lessened over time. What is remarkable is the fact that these commitments have been kept in the midst of an extremely taxing teaching schedule that did not allow him a true sabbatical until very late in his career.

Following World War II, Watts was appointed a missionary to Europe by the Foreign Mission Board of the Southern Baptist Convention. He was assigned to the fledgling Baptist Theological Seminary located then in Rüschlikon, Switzerland. He served there from 1949–1970, acting as Dean from 1958–1963, then as President during 1964–1970. After spending two years as Visiting Professor at Southern Seminary, he completed his missionary teaching career in Serampore, India from 1972–1975. All the writing done during this period of time took place in stimulating surroundings in the presence of interested students. On the other hand, it was also done while lecturing, administrating, helping raise four children, and serving a denomination, all without extensive time for research.

Watts returned to the United States in 1975. He taught at Fuller Theological Seminary from 1976–1981, then returned to Southern Seminary in 1982, and continues teaching there. While at Fuller, Watts was appointed Old Testament Editor for the Word Biblical Commentary. This set has not yet been completed, a fact that continues to necessitate Watts's longevity. This assignment also helped Watts shape Old Testament studies through the supervision of a major commentary series. At Southern Seminary, Watts has directed and taught a number

14. Watts's desire to treat the Twelve as a whole is reflected in the fact that when asked recently to consider writing a commentary on one minor prophet he responded by saying he would only consider an invitation to write on the Twelve as one book.

of doctoral students. Three of these persons, myself, Ken Craig, and Don Berry, have contributed articles to this volume. Working with such students finalizes Watts's longevity.

Creativity

John Watts's creativity is evident in his writing. Happily, it stems from his willingness to apply tested techniques to new situations, not from a compelling urge to be trendy, or on this week's 'cutting edge of scholarship'. His work on Isaiah proves this point. Watts's analysis of the text revealed changing speakers that created movement, or plot, in the prophecy. His convictions about the vision genre led him to his conclusions about how Isaiah could be collected over three centuries and still have canonical status. His emphasis on history did not allow him to adopt a reader response approach to the prophecy, nor to explain the text as if it were written by a single author. Rather, his new reading of Isaiah came about as a result of established methodological considerations developed over several decades' time.

Watts may be remembered most for what he attempted in Isaiah. His approach broke molds of prophetic analysis that he had a hand in forging. He demonstrated conclusively that Isaiah has changing voices, and that the book, therefore, must not be read as a flat, one-dimensional document, but as a multi-faceted literary work whose artistry is comparable in quality to its theology. His treatment of Isaiah helps readers conceive of God, Israel, and the prophets as living personalities relating to one another, not figures from the past poorly presented by redactors. Watts senses the life in the text.

Assessment

As promised earlier, this section is predisposed towards kindness to the one honored by this volume. Still, as one of Watts's students I find it hard to believe he would expect no critique at all. One of his best pedagogical traits has been a willingness to hear his ideas disputed. Therefore, perhaps it is appropriate to offer the following four observations.

First, the whole of Watts's methodological convictions deserves praise. His literary and exegetical conclusions are generally well stated, and they are always grounded in serious consideration of the Hebrew text. His linkage of genre analysis, textual studies, and theology ought to be adopted by more writers.

Second, Watts's emphasis on prophecy as literature has been needed for decades. Scholars ought to stress that what we have received is a text, explain that text, and offer historical background that illuminates, not destroys, that text. Examining the text itself will lead to new *and* accurate understandings of biblical passages. This approach will guard against overly-speculative historical hypotheses on the one hand, and overly-tribalized reader-response commentaries on the other.

Third, despite my admiration for Watts's exegetical and literary skills, his work does contain one flaw that is typical of many form-critical studies. Where Watts's treatments of Amos and Isaiah are weakest is in their reconstructions of the prophets' *Sitz Im Leben*. Were Amos's first three visions and their succeeding statements *ever* acceptable at Bethel? Does the two-book approach to Amos explain adequately why editors would not integrate their contents? Should one identify the servant in Isaiah's servant songs as Cyrus, Darius I, or Zerubbabel? I do not think so, but it would have been out of character for Watts not to make the attempt to decide these matters. He would have been on firmer ground, however, to continue to stress what the text itself clearly divulges about the historical situation.

Fourth, it is interesting that Watts has not yet engaged in canonical analysis. After all, his emphasis on text, literature, history, and theology provides the material for this possibility. Perhaps Watts's specific commentary-oriented writing assignments never left enough time for him to decide in print how to integrate theological and exegetical data into canonical criticism. This 'lack' is a pity, for his gifts imply he could have helped Old Testament Theology break out of at least one or two of its methodological impasses and could also have aided canonical criticism in its infancy.

Conclusion

Hopefully, these essays on Isaiah and the Twelve capture the spirit of Watts's career. Certainly the contributions by his son and his students reflect continuity. The articles by his veteran colleagues suggest longevity, and the papers by the participants in the Consultation on the Formation of the Book of the Twelve demonstrate useful creativity. Regardless, Watts's life and work merit recognition. His teaching, writing, and editing have the marks of distinction. I am grateful to know him and to have benefited from his example of what a teacher and scholar can achieve over time, regardless of strenuous circumstances.[15]

15. This essay has not evaluated all of Watts's writings. It has focused on the heart of his publications, which is his analysis of prophetic literature. Perhaps the best of the rest of his work is 'Deuteronomy', *Broadman Bible Commentary: Volume 2* (Nashville: Broadman, 1970). This commentary allows Watts to develop his views on Deuteronomy's influence on prophetic literature and on scripture as a whole. Again, I wish Watts had been afforded enough time to use his ideas on Deuteronomy, Isaiah, and the Twelve to write a volume on prophetic theology. Perhaps he will still do so.

ISAIAH: METHOD AND INTERPRETATION

John Watts's two-volume commentary on Isaiah represented one of a number of attempts in recent years to read the book of Isaiah as a unified work of one sort or another. This trend marks a sharp break with past critical interpretations which divided the book into two, three or more pieces and analyzed them separately.

The three essays in this section all address the issue of Isaiah's 'unity' in various ways. Marvin Tate surveys the recent history of the interpretation of Isaiah and evaluates Watts's commentary within the context of this larger interpretive trend. Ronald Clements demonstrates how certain themes and metaphors unify the book, yet simultaneously resist reduction to prosaic formulas. Thomas Smothers illustrates how the theme of Yahweh's 'plan' serves to illuminate the details of a problematic passage and fit the Oracles against the Nations in Isaiah 13–23 into the message of Isaiah as a whole.

THE BOOK OF ISAIAH IN RECENT STUDY

Marvin E. Tate

In the mid-1980s, John D.W. Watts published an innovative commentary on the Book of Isaiah (*Isaiah 1–33* in 1985 and *Isaiah 34–66* in 1987). It appeared in the early tide of a major revision of Isaianic studies, a tide which is still running and is probably yet to reach its crest. His work is innovative in several respects. First, he sets as his primary goal an interpretation of 'the Book of Isaiah' and directs attention to Isaiah as a literary unit: 'a work of literature presented to a literate people'. In his commentary, Watts attempts to move away from 'the fragmentation of the book under analytic procedures' (1985: xliii) and to focus on it as it exists in its present form.

Second, Watts assumes a date for the completion of the book of ca. 435 BCE, arguing that it was addressed to the diverse Jewish community in Jerusalem at this period (1985: xxx). In his work, he says that the book was intended to address such issues as:

a. the syncretistic religious life of the people,
b. the exiles still in foreign lands,
c. fragmentation in the Jewish community,
d. Israel's role among the nations.

He summarizes the issues as being

> the bedrock questions of what Judaism was and should become...the nature and role of Jerusalem, of the *Golah*, the 'dispersion' in Babylon, Egypt, and elsewhere, and of the people of the land in Judah and former Israelite territories (1985: xxxi).

He adds a note that the foundation laid by Ezra and Nehemiah was probably not strongly in place. Isaiah has little use for priestly solutions although the book affirms the central role of the Temple.

Third, Watts defines the genre of the Book of Isaiah as a 'Vision' in dramatic form. The term 'Vision' (*ḥᵃzōn*) is taken from Isa. 1.1, 'The

Vision of Isaiah, Son of Amoz', which Watts understands as the book's title. He argues that 'vision' is a prophetic genre especially suitable for Isaiah and the Book of the Twelve (along with the terms *dābār*, 'word', and *massā'*, 'burden'). Further, he argues that 'the Vision' of Isaiah lends itself to dramatic form, 'suited to the artificial setting of a stage' (1985: xlv). In his translation he assigns various sections of the text to different speakers, especially to Yahweh, the Heavens, and the Earth, with chorus sections focused on fundamental points (for example, 8.8-10; 10.21; 14.31; 28.5-6; 42.10-12). Watts comments:

> This commentary understands the Vision to be a sort of drama in which Yahweh and his aides (Heavens and Earth, 1.2) are the principal characters... The 'horizons' of the drama are set in one dimension by historical references to eighth-century kings with the prophet Isaiah and by references to the Persian era in the latter part of the book. Another dimension includes observations and speeches from the throne room of Heaven as Yahweh and his court view three centuries of Palestinian and Mesopotamian history. The genre of vision requires an implied 'stage setting' from which Yahweh and his aides can see and relate to mundane events in Jerusalem, in Babylon, and other places (1985: xlix).

In keeping with this approach, Watts divides the Vision into twelve acts with multiple scenes and episodes in each act. The acts are as follows:

Act I:	Like a Booth is a Vineyard (chs. 1–6)
Act II:	The Gently Flowing Waters (chs. 7–14)
Act III:	Opportunity and Disappointment (chs. 15–22)
Act IV:	The Impact of Tyre's Fall (chs. 23–27)
Act V:	Requiem for the Kingdom of Judah (chs. 28–33)
Act VI:	From Curse to Blessing (chs. 34–39)
Act VII:	Good News for Jerusalem (chs. 40.1–44.23)
Act VIII:	Cyrus, the LORD'S Anointed (chs. 44.24–48.22)
Act IX:	The Servant of Rulers (chs. 49.1-52.12)
Act X:	Restoration Pains in Jerusalem (chs. 52.13–57.21)
Act XI:	Zion's Light Shines (chs. 58–61)
Act XII:	For Zion's Sake: New Heavens and New Land (chs. 62–66)

Watts adopts a literary approach, which seeks to interpret the 'finished product', in other words, the works of authors/ editors/ composers who chose and artistically arranged material drawn from the history of Israel from ca. 750 BCE to ca. 435 BCE, with special emphasis on the ministry of Isaiah of Jerusalem. He does not seem to allow for a distinct prophetic persona during the Babylonian exile responsible for the proclamation in chs. 40–55 (usually referred to as Second Isaiah or Deutero Isaiah or

Exilic Isaiah) or for a Trito Isaiah in Jerusalem after 539 BCE responsible for chs. 56–66. He assumes an author in a group ca. 435 BCE, who identified (1) with Isaiah, a prophet who worked in Jerusalem from ca. 700 to 750 BCE, (2) with the exilic 'servant' of chs. 42–48, (3) with the suffering Jerusalem 'servant' of chs. 49, 50, 53, and 61.1-4, (4) and with the community 'servants' in 55.1-6. He does not elaborate very much on the identity of the 'author', the nature of the group, or how the scroll of Isaiah emerged, except to suggest that the group espoused four basic views:

1. A new era (or creation) had begun with the destruction of the old order by the Persian Empire.
2. In the new order, the people should rally to Zion, coming from all over the earth to be taught God's word and worship—a vision of the City of God.
3. Israel should recognize Persian power as God's way for her and should oppose any move against Persia or Persian authority.
4. Apostate worship, especially of idols and pagan cults, is to be condemned; Yahweh continues to search for an attentive and responsive people, who are willing to be his faithful 'servants' (1985: xxxi-xxxii).

One should not assume, however, that Watts proposes to neglect history; if anything, he is too much concerned with the correlation of texts and historical events. For example, those who are familiar with the usual interpretations of Isaiah may be intrigued by Watts's correlation of the fall of Tyre in ch. 23 with the eschatological content of chs. 24–27, including the understanding of Leviathan in 27.1 as a symbolic reference to Tyre (1985: 348-49). The identity of the servant in 42.1-4, 6-9 as Cyrus (1987: 110, 118-19) will not be too surprising in the light of 44.21–45.17 (and probably 41.25), but some readers, at least, will be shocked to find the servant in 49.5-6, 52.13, and 53.11 identified as the Persian King Darius I, with Artaxerxes I identified with ch. 61 (1987: 114, 117, 119, 187, 222-33, 302). Zerubbabel is interpreted as the faithful teacher and leader in 50.4-9 and as put to death in ch. 53 but vindicated by Darius in 50.10–51.2 (Darius is also the speaker in 51.4-8). In connection with 49.5-6, Darius is defined as the promised 'beacon light to the nations whose fate is now bound up so closely with the Persian Empire' (1987: 187). I would venture to say that most readers are unlikely to be persuaded by this use of history in the interpretation of the texts. However, Watts's general position receives support from two recent monographs on Second Isaiah. R.G. Kratz has devoted attention to Cyrus in a redaction-historical investigation of chs. 40–55. He argues that a Cyrus redactional expansion layer added to the basic document of Second Isaiah, which is found mostly in chs. 40–48, (and dated ca. 539 BCE), reflects the early reign of Darius I (ca. 520–510 BCE), and adds the proclamation of divine deliverance through Cyrus to the basic layer (plus a 'Zion expansion' primarily in chs. 49–54). The first two servant poems, and possibly the third, were added to the content and served to make Cyrus servant, shepherd, and anointed of Yahweh, to deal with Israel and the nations. A. Laato concentrates in his monograph on the 'Servant of Yahweh' and Cyrus in chs. 40–55. He argues that both the Servant and Cyrus share an 'exilic messianic program' (1992: 282) which was derived from the reign of Josiah and his shocking death. Laato, however, does not identify the Servant with Cyrus. Cyrus creates the political framework for the return of the exiles, but the Servant (loyal/prophetic Israel) actually leads the people back and carries out the restoration of a New Zion (1992: 282-83). Incidentally, Laato argues that the redaction of chs. 40–55 was complete by ca. 539 BCE: 'the end of the Babylonian period did not mark the beginning of the redaction process but in fact marks its end' (1992: 283).

In summary, it may be said that legitimate caveats can be lodged against some aspects of Watts's commentary; indeed, there is considerable justification for referring to its 'many idiosyncratic features' (Williamson 1994: 17), especially in Vol. II. However, these caveats should not be allowed to obscure its innovative character and the author's courage to make new proposals. He had the vision and the skill to grasp the large body of material in Isaiah in a new way. His work can not be properly understood without a review of the context of Isaianic study in recent years. With some overgeneralization, the phases of Isaiah study may be treated as threefold: the one-prophet interpretation, the three-book interpretation, and the one-book of Isaiah interpretation. In the material which follows, I will discuss these phases briefly but sufficiently to provide the context for Watts's work.

The One-Prophet Interpretation

This is the traditional approach to Isaiah and assumes that Isaiah of Jerusalem (ca. 750–700 BCE) was responsible for the entire book. The book is not divided into multiple parts from different historical periods and read as if from different authors. Isaiah is taken as the one prophet whose words are in the book. In a few cases, contemporary interpreters who advocate the one-prophet reading allow for the theoretical possibility of some non-Isaianic material added at a later date: for example, the explicit references to Cyrus in 44.28 and 45.1. Allowance may also be made for the book to have been written by Isaiah's disciples (8.16) 'fairly soon' after he died (A.E. Hill and J.H. Walton 1991: 320, who add that regardless of when, 'what was written represents faithfully what Isaiah said').

I will make no attempt to trace out in detail the nature and history of this approach. It is still alive in current study, represented by two recent commentaries on Isaiah. J.N. Oswalt argues for the unity of the composition of the book and calls for a 'rebirth of attempts to interpret the book as a whole' (1986: 23). He also contends that 'the essential content of the book has come to us through one human author, Isaiah the son of Amoz' (1986: 25). However, Oswalt does allow for the alteration of the chronological order of materials in Isaiah from that in which they were originally delivered and for the addition of editorial or transitional content, added 'either by Isaiah himself or by those working with him' (1986: 26). He thinks it probable that the Book of Isaiah is an anthology of varied content, which does not require 'tight structural connections between various segments of the book' (1986: 26 n. 8).

Oswalt's reasons for maintaining the authorship of Isaiah are familiar in this interpretative tradition. Stylistic differences are not precise and may be accounted for by different periods and contexts of the prophet's career. A thematic unity of the book is essential; issues raised in chs. 1–39 require the material in chs. 40–55 in order to be valid for that post-monarchical day already anticipated in chs. 1–39. Critical scholars have been unable to agree on the date and authorship of the different sections of Isaiah and 'the results of these inquiries have devalued the religious message of the book' (1986: 24). Oswalt argues that the paucity of concrete historical references in chs. 40–66 is due to the fact that the content actually stems from Isaiah of Jerusalem (against B.S. Childs's suggestion that such references have been expunged in order to bring the total work under the rubric of Isaiah). It is clear that Oswalt's fundamental reason for his approach is theological (see 1986: 25) and is postulated on the defense of specific prophetic prediction. However, Oswalt's defense of the one-prophet approach to the book should not be allowed to blind readers to the over-all merit of his commentary. He is a well-informed scholar whose work is often very helpful in dealing with linguistic questions and matters of content in the text.

Essentially the same judgement is appropriate for the recent commentary on Isaiah by J.A. Motyer, a one-volume work with a stronger emphasis on literary matters than that of Oswalt. Motyer defends Isaianic authorship for the entire book, using arguments like those of Oswalt and others before them both. He does, however, place more stress on the case for a Palestinian milieu for *both* chs. 40–55 and chs. 56–66. In his opinion, the case for a Babylonian context for chs. 40–55 is unfounded and the Palestinian context points to the work of Isaiah prior to the Exile. He emphasizes the lack of explicit indications of the circumstances of the exiles: chs. 40–55 'bear no relation to what we know of the actual experiences of those who were transported to Babylon... The prophet is not offering reportage but using conventional stereotypes' (1993: 28). He thinks that sections like 43.14–48.22 which have a Babylonian orientation lack 'eyewitness participation' and represent prediction rather than presupposition. The detail expected of an eyewitness is 'simply not there—observations about the city, the ways its life is ordered, the structures of its society, the feel and smell of the place' (1993: 28). Unlike some one-prophet interpreters, Motyer does not allow the mention of Cyrus in 44.28 and 45.1 to be a later addendum.

Motyer takes note of Watts's proposal regarding the Book of Isaiah and rejects it, preferring to view the book as originating from an 'organizing mind' (Isaiah's) at the beginning rather than from an anonymous editor and a company of disciple-preachers in the fifth-century. Motyer is committed to the concept of verbal inspiration in which God superintends the human words of the prophets so that they are 'the very words of God himself' (1993: 31). He argues that if one assumes that Isaiah had this conviction (as Motyer does), he would hardly have left his message 'partly written and mostly oral, to the changes and chances of history' (cf. Isa. 8.16-20). As already noted, Motyer gives commendable attention to literary matters in Isaiah and sometimes uses rhetorical criticism to good advantage. He is aided in this aspect by postulating that the book is the product of one 'organizing mind', even if this is supported by shopworn appeals to verbal inspiration. For good or bad, the works of Oswalt and Motyer are testimony to the ongoing presence of the one-prophet interpretation.

The Three-Book Interpretation

In one form or another this has been the dominant mode of interpreting Isaiah since the publication of B. Duhm's commentary in 1892 and is so widespread as to require little comment here regarding the basic arguments (see Seitz 1991: 1–35). This approach magnifies the differences between the various sections of Isaiah and works with the basic assumption of three discrete works in the book: chs. 1–39, 40–55, 56–66. In general, these sections have been considered as independent compositions, relating to three different historical contexts, and at least three major prophets. First Isaiah (chs. 1–39) has been treated as a unit built around the prophetic ministry of Isaiah of Jerusalem; chs. 40–55 have been assigned to a prophet in the Exile (commonly termed Deutero/Second Isaiah); chs. 56–66 have been treated as derived from a third prophet (Trito/Third Isaiah) in a nonexilic/post-exilic Palestinian setting. The common treatments of these sections in introductions and commentaries separate them and discuss the sections independently. For example, the fourth edition of the widely used Old Testament introduction by B.W. Anderson deals with the 'Book of Isaiah' as the first 39 chapters ('The genuine writings of Isaiah', 1986: 321-22), while Second Isaiah (chs. 40–55) is discussed 113 pages later (1986: 468-502). Third Isaiah (chs. 56–66) is given very brief analysis on the following pages (1986: 502-504) under the rubrics of 'The Continuing Isaiah Tradition' and 'The Disciples of Second Isaiah'. The treatment of chs. 56–66 contiguous to Second Isaiah represents a change in the 1986 edition of Anderson's book from earlier editions which had Third Isaiah after Chronicles. Of course, Anderson's superbly written book is designed to treat Old Testament literature in a historical framework and the separation of the sections of Isaiah is understandable. Nevertheless, it is illustrative of the widespread practice of the three-book interpretation. Some major introductions in this tradition tend to discuss the three books seriatim but discretely (for example, see the introductions of O. Eissfeldt, G. Fohrer, R. Rendtorff, and A. Weiser; J.A. Soggin discusses Deutro-Isaiah after Zechariah, and W.H. Schmidt puts Second Isaiah and Third Isaiah after Ezekiel).

Second Isaiah

The adoption of the three-book approach by scholars did not mean that a consensus emerged on matters of interpretation regarding the books.

In fact, the contrary is so evident as to suggest major defects in the underlying assumptions. In some respects there has been greater agreement about chs. 40–55 than about 1–39 and 56–66. The postulate of a reconstructed exilic prophet, known by the ciphers Deutero-Isaiah or Second Isaiah, and functioning in a Babylonian context from ca. 550 to 540 BCE has been widely accepted. The assumption that 40.6-8 represents some sort of call experience is frequently made. J. Smart wrote eloquently of the pastoral element in Second Isaiah, noting that in most prophetic literature this element has 'left only a slight residue in the records':

> But in Second Isaiah the intimate concern of the prophet as pastor of his people comes clearly into the foreground and attains decisive expression. The broken and discouraged Israelites knew in him a man of God who moved through their midst with a word that was bread to the hungry—bread, milk, wine, water (cf. 55.1, 10, 11)—all that was needful to sustain life (1965: 13; see also G. von Rad 1965: 249-50)

The questions of genre and unity in Second Isaiah are commonly resolved in favor of small units of content (salvation oracles, disputations, trial speeches, eschatological hymns) combined into larger units by thematic and kerygmatic bonds (Melugin 1976: 175).

The division of chs. 40–55 into two large units seems reasonable: chs. 40–48 (the servant and Cyrus); chs. 49–55 (the servant and Zion). Of course, smaller divisions of these larger units can be recognized (Clifford 1993: 491). The interpretation of the so-called 'Servant Songs' (42.1-4, 5-9; 49.1-6; 50.4-9; 52.13–53.12) has been problematic, although there now seems to be a near consensus that whatever the origin(s) and history of these sections, they must be understood at present in the context of Isaiah 40–55 and not extracted out and read together as a separate unit (T.N.D. Mettinger 1983; P. Hanson 1995: 40-41). This has important implications for the understanding of the servant concept in Second Isaiah, mandating that the servant is in some sense Israel and moving toward freedom from the confusing quest for an individual who can be identified as the servant.

It should be noted, however, that the largely uncontested unity of Second Isaiah is being questioned in more recent study. The questions of a redaction history and the possibility of a more complex unity have been raised. H.-J. Hermisson (1989: 287-312) reviews works of some scholars who question the unity of chs. 40–55, especially K. Kiesow, R.P. Merendino, and J. Vermeylen. He recognizes the minority position of such approaches in scholarship devoted to Second Isaiah, particularly compared to scholars who have concentrated on the final form of the composition. Nevertheless, he ventures to examine some assumptions regarding Second Isaiah and to set forth a programmatic discussion of criteria which may apply in a redactional analysis. For example, he notes that the unity of chs. 40–55 is not easily based in the nature and function of a prophet—prophetic biography and a history of book composition by a supposed exilic prophet are excluded as a legitimate basis for unity. He argues that tensions in the text and differences of subject matter point to a complex history of composition, which begins with the oldest collection (before 539 BCE) and is then combined with two later layers of redaction: (1) a *qarob* ('near') layer, which stresses the nearness of the deliverance of Yahweh and seeks to stimulate flagging faith (for example, 46.8, 12-13; 48.17-19; 51.1-2, 4-8; 54.11-17) and (2) an anti-idol layer (for example, 44.9-20; 46.5-7), combined with bits and pieces of other texts (including the lengthy section in 48.1-11). H.G.M. Williamson (1994: 24-27) has reviewed Hermisson's work and made a tentative response to it. He doubts that the *qarob* layer is really theologically incompatible with Second Isaiah (as assumed by Hermisson on the basis that it contains an incoherence with other content which indicates a different literary hand) and argues that Hermisson is wrong in the case of 51.4-8 ('righteousness' and 'salvation' may be future in Second Isaiah's scheme of things). Also, he thinks that the rejection of biographical development in the context of Second Isaiah is pushed too far. Williamson argues that it is reasonable to assume that such a prophet as Second Isaiah has been supposed to be would have encountered opposition from the beginning of his message of salvation and of the coming of the glory of Yahweh (note 40.27-31). He argues that 49.1-6 is a hinge between the two halves of the work (chs. 40–48 and 49–55) and shows development in the speaker's understanding of the task of the servant (1994: 25; Hermisson accepts the traditional servant poems—42.1-4; 49.1-6; 50.4-9; 52.13–53.12—as a component part of the oldest collection).

Williamson is very forthright about his own adherence to the work of a single prophet, apart from a few minor glosses and additions. I am rather sure, however, that he will have to deal more fully in the future with the challenge of what he now calls 'the isolated opinion of individual scholars' (1994: 26). The monograph of R.G. Kratz, already referred to above, argues for five redactional layers in chs. 40–55, plus a number of later small additions (the foundational layer, the Zion expansion, the Cyrus supplementary layer, an 'idol layer,' and the Servant-Israel layer). More recently, J. van Oorschot has published a literary and redaction history investigation of Second Isaiah. Time and space exclude a full review and critique of his work in this article, but he finds a basic redactional layer in the following passages (divided into A, words of disputation; B, judgement speeches; C, words of salvation): A—40.12-31; B—41.1-4, 21-29; 43.8-13; 45.20-25; C—41.8-16; 43.1-7, 16-21; 44.2-4, 24-28; 45.1-7, 11-13; 46.9-11. In the second place, he isolates a 'first Jerusalem redaction,' which includes a prologue in 40.1-5, 9-11 and an epilogue in 52.7-10, plus 47.1-15; 48.20-21; 49.14-23; 51.9-10, 17-19; 52.1-2. These passages, of course, focus on Jerusalem/Zion, the return of the exiles, and the world-encompassing salvation work of Yahweh. Oorschot divides the remainder of the material in chs. 40–55 into five additional redactional layers, which I will not take the space to list here.

Redactional analyses of scholars like those of Hermisson and Oorschot often seem excessively subjective and circular; the evidence is sliced extremely thin. However, there are two factors of importance to remember in regard to Second Isaiah. First, R.E. Clements comments that if the 16 chapters usually ascribed to Second Isaiah are the work of one person, 'they stand unique within the otherwise intricate web of prophecy and prophetic interpretation which constitute the remainder of the book' (1985: 110-11). There would be no other such solid block of material in Isaiah. Of course, this may be the case, but the assumption raises questions. Second, bits and pieces of evidence in isolation may have little significance, but the whole is greater than the parts and the cumulative force of the arguments is considerable (a point made by Williamson, 1994: 29). Thus it is probable that Second Isaiah is the product of a redactional history. If this conclusion is justified, it diminishes the likelihood that chs. 40–55 stem from one exilic prophet like that described by J. Smart above. It is not impossible, of course, that a single prophetic person was responsible for a core of the material in these chapters and for subsequent modification and additions, but it is much more probable that more than one person was involved.

First Isaiah

The situation in Isaiah 1–39 in the three-book approach may be described as chaotic, though improving. The problem does not lie in the larger groupings of content, which are usually accepted (chs. 1–12;

13–23; 24–27; 28–32; 33–35; 36–39). However, the simplicity disappears when attempts are made to understand the logic of the arrangement of these chapters into independent compositions. Complicated analyses of the content, such as G. Fohrer's separation of Isaiah's preaching into seven minor collections (each in three parts: body, fragments, and promises as in 1.2-26; 1.29-31; 2.4 respectively) plus later passages and complexes of tradition, are difficult to accept at face value. Soggin deplores Fohrer's analysis as 'tiresome for anyone working with it, whether it is correct or not' (1980: 258). Fohrer's work, however, is symptomatic of the difficulties of the three-book approach. In his highly regarded commentary on chs. 1–39, H. Wildberger works out a scenario for the development of these chapters which is similar to that of Fohrer's but considerably less complex and more unified.

The problems are multiple: Is Isa. 1.1 a superscription for the entire book? For ch. 1 alone? For chs. 2–12? For chs. 1–39? How does it relate to the superscription in 2.1? Why is the supposed call of Isaiah in ch. 6? Does 6.1–9.7 form a separate unit inserted between 5.25-30 and 9.8–10.4—with perhaps an original order of 5.25; 9.8–10.4; 5.26-30? Why do Babylon and the Medes have major roles in chs. 13–23 (see 13.17-22; 14.14-27)? How do chs. 24–27 (usually dated to the post-exilic period) relate to chs. 13–23 and to 28–35? Indeed, do chs. 28–32, or 28–33, or 28–35 form a defined unit?—or only a loose collection? Why do chs. 12 and 35 have so many parallels with Second Isaiah? Are chs. 36–39 borrowed from 2 Kgs. 18.13–20.19 (usually assumed in the three-book approach) and how do they function in chs. 1–39? Attempts to correlate the material in chs. 1–39 chronologically in relation to historical events has not worked very satisfactorily (B. Duhm dated the materials over a period of seven centuries, from Isaiah in the eighth century to as late as the second century BCE).

Recent redactional approaches to chs. 1–39 have been more ordered in their analyses. Two recent commentaries on chs. 1–39 may be used to illustrate this point. R.E. Clements argues that the present form of these chapters was not designed to preserve the words of Isaiah alone but rather to present the message of the prophet as interpreted in the light of the subsequent history (1980: 2-3). This is especially noticeable in the oracles relating to Babylon in chs. 13–14, in 36–39, and of course in chs. 24–27 and 34–35 (which contain no words attributed to Isaiah). The primary collection of Isaiah's prophecies are found in chs. 2–12, since ch. 1 ('for the most part built up from authentic prophecies of Isaiah') serves as a summary of Isaiah's preaching and 'a guide to the way the book as a whole [chs. 1–39? chs. 1–66?] is to be read' (1980: 2).

Clements argues that there are traces of earlier collections in chs. 1–39 and that there is no reason to doubt an extended process of transmission history. The process of collection probably began with Isaiah himself, justifying the portion of the prophet's memoir (6.1–8.18) in the center of a larger collection in 5.1–14.27, which contains 'an overwhelmingly large preponderance of authentic prophecies.' Other collections are found in 2.6–4.1 and in chs. 28–31 (threatening judgement on Judah and Jerusalem).

Clements is skeptical of the idea of a 'school' or organized body of Isaiah's disciples based on 8.16 (and frequently postulated). But the prophet did not work alone and there were hearers and followers who established his prophecies in writing after his death so that others could know and reflect upon his words. By whom and where this took place are matters of conjecture, apart from the probable thesis of the development of a major form of the book during the reign of Josiah (640–608 BCE). In this regard, Clements adopts a modified form of the thesis of H. Barth (1977) who argues for an 'Assyrian Redaction' of Isaiah's prophecies during the time of Josiah. Barth's thesis is that the primary point of the redaction was that Yahweh, the God of Israel, would shortly overthrow the Assyrians as a world power. The placement of the redaction in the time of Josiah is indicated, on the one hand, by the fact that Assyria has not yet fallen (thus prior to 612–609 BCE) and, on the other hand, by its strong expectation of an imminent breaking of the Assyrian grip (cf. 10.24-27; 30.27-33).

Clements disagrees with Barth on some matters (for example, 9.3-7 [Heb. 8.23c–9.6] belongs to Isaiah) and prefers to refer to a Josianic Redaction in which he puts the following passages: 7.20-25; 8.9-10; 10.16-27, 33-34; 14.24-27; 17.12-14; 28.23-29; 29.5-8; 30.27-33; 31.5, 8-9; 32.1-5, 15-20. In addition, Clements judges it probable that chs. 36–37, dealing with Jerusalem's deliverance from Sennacherib, belong to the same basic circle responsible for the Josianic Redaction (1980: 5-6). Subsequent redactional history must be presupposed for other parts of chs. 1–39, especially in the period after 587 BCE, to deal with the fulfillment of the judgement prophecies of Isaiah (for example, 2.18-19; 5.14-17; 6.12-13; 8.19-22; 17.7-9; 22.4-8a, 8b-11, 24-35; 32.9-14), the preservation of the hope bound up with the Davidic monarchy, and the future of Jerusalem (32.1-5, 15-20; 11.1-5). A further stage extended into the fifth century (for example, chs. 24–27 and 34–35). However, Clements resists stretching the redactional history into the Hellenistic era (1980: 7-8).

The second commentary is that of C.R. Seitz on chs. 1–39 (1993a). As in the case of Clements, Seitz is influenced by the work of H. Barth. However, he adjusts Barth's thesis of an Assyrian Redaction in two important ways: (1) the date is moved closer to Isaiah's actual ministry, probably to the time of Manasseh's reign, and (2) emphasis is shifted away from the figure of Josiah to that of Hezekiah (1993a: 101-102, 195). Seitz places great emphasis on the interpretation and function of chs. 36–39 in the context of the book, rejecting the theory that these chapters were simply borrowed from 2 Kgs. 18.13–20.19. From this position Seitz proceeds to anchor the literary structure of chs. 1–39 around the polarity of the reigns of Ahaz (chs. 7–8) and Hezekiah (chs. 36–39). These reigns present contrasting pictures: Ahaz's refusal to ask for a sign marks his reign as characterized by a lack of faith, while Hezekiah's willingness to heed the words of Isaiah and to pray to Yahweh results in deliverance from the Assyrians. Isaiah confronts Ahaz, but he cooperates with Hezekiah—because of the unwillingness and willingness of the respective kings (1993a: 195). Hezekiah reestablishes the strength of the house of David from the weakness left by Ahaz and saves Zion.

In relation to Hezekiah, one of Seitz's most interesting sections is his interpretation of ch. 39.1-8. He notes that the usual reading of these verses presents a radically different presentation of Hezekiah from that in chs. 36–38. Isaiah rebukes Hezekiah for allowing a Babylonian delegation to see everything in the royal palace and storehouses (39.3-7). Isaiah informs Hezekiah that everything seen by the envoys will be carried away to Babylon, along with some of the royal sons (39.5-7), a threat to the continuation of the Davidic line. Hezekiah's reply in v. 8 ('The word of the LORD which you have spoken is good. For he was thinking to himself that peace and security would last in his lifetime' REB) has often been taken as a selfish response regarding his own welfare and as disregard for future consequences. Seitz appeals (as did Ackroyd 1987: 152-71) to the account of this incident in 2 Chron. 32.30-31, which includes the event in Isaiah 39 among the successful deeds and piety of Hezekiah (in contrast to the negative evaluation of Hezekiah's behavior in 2 Chron. 32.25, followed by his submission in

v. 26). On this basis, Seitz argues that Hezekiah's display of his treasures was a sign of divine blessing and the ignominious failure of the Assyrian assault against Zion (1993a: 265). The envoys are 'from a distant land', which is Babylon, and thus the Babylonians are introduced as the successors to the Assyrians and as the protagonists in chs. 40–55. According to Seitz, Isaiah's response to Hezekiah should be read as a prophetic announcement of future divine action and not as a judgement determined by Hezekiah's actions. Also, Hezekiah's response should be read as an affirmation of the prophetic word (it is 'good') and an acceptance of the well-being granted by God in his own days, along with a future which he cannot control.

> He hears the divine word of coming judgment, but in the end he can say without a hint of gloating or selfish disregard, 'There will be peace and security in my days.' The king's actions—never condemned by the prophet—merely point to days beyond his knowing, days to come (v. 5) (1993a: 266).

Seitz also argues that the real addressee of the prophet is the reader, who is reminded that God has not forgotten his plans for judgement (expressed in the preaching of Isaiah), but they are not plans that concern Hezekiah.

The interpretations of both Clements and Seitz are a welcome relief from some of the critical commentaries on chs. 1–39 of the past. We can look forward to more work by both scholars. In his review of Seitz's commentary (*JBL* 114 [1995]: 503-4), Clements observes that dealing only with chs. 1–39 is 'slightly anomalous' since the work assumes a relationship with the 'content and context of the later sections' of the book of Isaiah (particularly in regard to a 'Babylonian redaction' of 1–39). Both Clements (1980: 2) and Seitz (1993a: 4-7; also, 1993b: 260-63) defend the legitimacy of writing a commentary on chs. 1–39 as a unit (Seitz also sets forth the case for a 'significant division' at chs. 33/34; see 1993a: 241). However, both scholars eschew treating First Isaiah as an independent book and work with the assumption that chs. 1–39 are constituent parts of the book of Isaiah as a whole. Thus in some respects they may belong better to the one-book category than the three-book approach.

H.G.M. Williamson's work on Isaiah has been referred to above. It is a major contribution to the attempt to reconstruct the historical development of the book of Isaiah, especially First Isaiah. He assumes that there was a sort of major first collection of Isaiah's prophecies (but not necessarily the *ipsissima verba* of the prophet himself) before the fall of Jerusalem in 587 BCE (following in general H. Barth and R.E. Clements). This material was very influential in the ministry of Second Isaiah among the Babylonian exiles. This prophet considered

> the earlier work as in some sense a book that had been sealed up until the day of judgement should be passed and the day of salvation had arrived, which day he believed himself to be heralding... and... that in order to locate his message in relation to the earlier and continuing ways of God with Israel he included a version of the earlier prophecies with his own and edited them in such a way as to bind the two parts of the work together... (1994: 240-41).

It is not surprising, in the light of these statements, to find that Williamson is concerned with influence and borrowing going from Proto-Isaiah to Second Isaiah *and* redaction by Second Isaiah of the Proto-Isaiah material in order to adapt it to a new context.

Williamson argues that Second Isaiah's interest in Proto-Isaiah was focused on the Zion tradition and the need to reinterpret the tradition in the context of the fall of Jerusalem and the reality of exile. For Second Isaiah, there were elements in this stream of tradition which could still speak 'eloquently to the despair of the people' (1994: 242). For the prophet, Jeremiah and Ezekiel were too contemporary: 'It is in Isaiah alone that the larger sweep of God's dealings with Zion in both judgement and mercy is to be found' (1994: 242). Of course, there were other elements which were useful for Second Isaiah, and Williamson pursues some of these in chapters 3–4 of his book. In chapter 5, he makes much of Isa. 8.16-18; 8.1-4; 30.8 and their references to writing, inscribing, and 'binding up' prophetic testimony as a 'witness' for the future. In the light of such passages, Second Isaiah understood his ministry 'as an opening of a book long sealed up' (1994: 113), working with the literary deposit of Proto-Isaiah. Williamson's basic hypothesis is that Second Isaiah redacted the work of Proto-Isaiah in such ways that the two works could be read as one—his own work in Isaiah 40–55 being a continuation of what became First Isaiah after the redactional work. Second Isaiah (chs. 40–55) never existed as an independent work apart from some literary form of First Isaiah.

Williamson argues that some sections of Isaiah 1–39 belong to redaction later than that done by Second Isaiah (for example, ch. 1 is an introduction to the book added later; also chs. 24–27; chs. 34–35; chs. 36–39). The major Second Isaiah redactional sections of chs. 2–39 are found in 2.2-4; 5.24-29; 8.21-22; 11.11-16; 12; 13.1–14.23; 33 (at least in part). Chapter 33 served as 'the point of original connection between the literary deposit of Isaiah of Jerusalem and the material which Deutero-Isaiah added to it in chapters 40 and following' (1994: 238). It should be noted that Williamson finds the redactional hand of Second Isaiah both in the composition of new passages (as in 11.11-16) and in the relocation of material from elsewhere in the earlier literary deposit (for example, 5.25-29). Williamson's work is not yet complete, and we do not know in detail how he will work out the problems of Isaiah 56–66 and the final form of the book.

C.R. Mathews (1995a) also argues that chs. 34–35 are redactional in First Isaiah and later than Second Isaiah, in agreement with O.H. Steck (see below). However, because of her different approach, she rejects his proposal concerning the relationship between ch. 34 and ch. 35 (1995a: 260). Steck assumes that 34 was a component part of Proto-Isaiah, with 35 written as a bridge to Second Isaiah. Mathews concludes that both 34 and 35 are later additions from the time of Third Isaiah. She begins her analysis with the observation that ch. 34 seems to appear in an *inappropriate context* since one would expect to find it among the oracles against the nations in chs. 13–23. Why is the oracle against Edom separated from the other such oracles? She concludes that the Edom oracle functions differently in the larger context of the book (1995a: 252). Chapter 35 also seems out of context and invites consideration of its function in the book (1995a: 253).

Mathews argues that ch. 34 should be understood with ch. 63.1-6 (also dealing with Edom) and that the two passagers belong to the same context. She reads 63.1-6 as a depiction of the Divine Warrior's last stop on his way to Zion for works of both judgement and vindication (1995a: 255-60). She thinks the same basic patttern is present in chs. 34–35. Unlike Steck, who argues that the transformation of the wilderness in ch. 35 is the transformation of ruined Edom so that the exiles might pass through that land on their way home, Mathews (more cogently) thinks that ch. 35 speaks metaphorically of the wilderness of Zion; thus ch. 35 contrasts with ch. 34, which treats Edom as a typical or representative enemy (1995a: 256). Mathews bases part of her case on Ezekiel 35–36, where a pair of passages (or 'diptychs') with a similar pattern is found: oracle against Edom in ch. 35 followed by an oracle *to* the mountains of Israel in ch. 36. The multiple lines of evidence lead her to postulate that

'Isa. 35 was composed out of materials from Deutero- and Trito-Isaiah to serve as a mate of Isaiah 34' (1995a: 261).

In passing, I would suggest that Mathews's study leads to the possibility of an Edom redaction in the book of Isaiah. If this should be the case, perhaps a rough pattern of redactional development for the book of Isaiah may be emerging: (1) an Assyrian-Josianic redaction, (2) a Babylonian-Second Isaiah redaction, (3) a Third Isaiah-Edom redaction, and (4) an eschatological (or visionary) redaction of the post-exilic 'Isaianic Community.'

Third Isaiah

This section of Isaiah has been the source of perennial questions. The problem of the unity or disunity of chs. 56–66 is a natural outcome of the disparate nature of the content. Some passages are recognizably similar to Second Isaiah (chs. 60–62; 57.14-21; 66.7-16) while other passages are different (for example, chs. 56; 57.1-13; 58; 59; 63.7–64.12). Is this material all, or substantially, from one prophet? If the content is essentially from one prophet, is the prophet Second Isaiah? Or should we think of a Third Isaiah? Questions of historical context also arise. Does the material in these chapters belong to the period shortly before Nehemiah (ca. 450 BCE, so Duhm)? Or do they have a Jerusalem setting of 520–500 BCE, perhaps originating from Second Isaiah or one of his disciples? Or should divergent contexts be assumed, dating from the seventh to the third centuries?

The more-or-less mainstream answers to these questions are well known and need not be rehearsed in detail in this article. The defense of the substantial unity of Third Isaiah is frequently linked with the literary and stylistic analysis of K. Elliger (1928), who argued that Third Isaiah was probably a disciple of Second Isaiah. This disciple was responsible for the collection and supplementation of the oracles of Second Isaiah in chs. 40–55 and was contemporary with Haggai and Zechariah in the time of temple rebuilding. Elliger argued that only limited sections of chs. 56–66 are secondary: 56.3-8; 57.13c, 20; 58.13; 59.5-8, 21; 60.12, 17b; 65.20b; 66.17, 18-22, 23. It is worthy of note that Elliger was opposing, on the one hand, commentators who held that there is no significant break between Second and Third Isaiah (chs. 40–66 were attributed to a single author, perhaps in two different settings), and, on the other hand, those interpreters who advocated the view that chs. 56–66 are from different authors and divergent historical contexts (Seitz, 1992: 502).

Elliger's approach has not met with general approval among Isaiah interpreters. Most regard the postulate of a single author as implausible (Emmerson 1992: 55, 58). Soggin remarks that 'Trito-Isaiah is a book of a composite kind if ever there was one', observing that the majority of scholars consider it an anthology with about twelve passages (1980: 336). O. Eissfeldt argues that Elliger's stylistic arguments do not possess the validity he afforded them:

> If we consider the contexts of the individual sections, they do not appear to belong to the same period any more than they are products of the same poet (1965: 344).

He continues by saying that 'the opposite view cannot be proven either' and notes the lack of substantive 'allusions to concrete events which make possible the precise dating of one or another of the sections' (1965: 344). He points out that mention of the temple in chs. 56–66 is not decisive since it is not certain whether or not the references refer to a rebuilt temple after 520–515 BCE or to an earlier or to a later situation (56.7; 60.14, 15—finished? 61.4—unfinished? 64.10-11—destroyed? 66.1-3—built or unbuilt?).

> We are here in the realm of poetry, and poetry often rises above actual conditions and does not permit a prosaic and historical interpretation of its utterances (1965: 344).

He argues that attempts to date the texts on the basis of the history of religion and thought are misguided because of the insufficiency of data and because the phenomena of worship referred to in chs. 56–66 are not limited to one period: 'Here, as often elsewhere, we have to lay our main stress upon the understanding of the content, and be satisfied with recognizing possibilities as far as the dating is concerned' (1965: 344).

The difficulties of a history of religion approach have not deterred scholars from taking it. The best known of these in the case of Third Isaiah is that of P. Hanson (1979: 32-208; also 1995) who deals with Isaiah 56–66 as a major part of a wider socio-historical analysis of the early post-exilic Israelite community. Hanson's well-known thesis is that the early post-exilic community was divided between the 'visionaries', who were the followers of the oracles of Second Isaiah, and a pro-temple hierocratic leadership represented by Haggai, Zechariah 1–8, and later by Ezra. (Hanson's analysis also includes Ezekiel and Chronicles.) The hierocratic leaders were supportive of the Persian installed government. The visionaries maintained an eschatological ideal against the uneschatological perspective of the hierocratic group. Hanson makes much of the polemic passages which reveal internal division (for example, 65.8-16 and 66.5, and the framework of ch. 57, which is found in vv. 1-2 and 19-21). He attempts to deal with the content of chs. 56–66 along contextual-typological lines, moving toward a more apocalyptic eschatology than that in Second Isaiah: chs. 60–62 and 57.14-21 describe the ideal community envisioned by the disciples of Second Isaiah; 63.7–64.11 form a communal lament in which the prophet appeals to God in behalf of the people; the ideal is undetermined in 58.1-12; 59.1-20; growing tension appears in 65.1-25, which widens the schism and increases vindictiveness (66.1-16); controversy and expulsion are found in 59.9–57.13, and the conflict grows acrimonious in 66.1-6. Hanson rejects the search for authorship and does not attempt redactional reconstruction of Third Isaiah. His approach is often cited, and the stimulus and originality of his work is commended, but his thesis has met with widespread rejection (see Emmerson 1992: 81-97).

A surge of literature on Third Isaiah along tradition history and redaction history lines has emerged and is continuing to appear. I will survey only a few of the scholars involved, and that very briefly. The analysis of Claus Westermann in his commentary on Isaiah 40–66 (1966) can serve as an anchor point (Seitz calls it 'a model of form and tradition critical analysis', 1992: 505). Westermann assumes that chs. 60–62 are the nucleus of Third Isaiah's work; it is set in the framework provided by chs. 59 and 63–64 (which are communal laments—the nucleus in 60–62 gives God's answers to the supplications in the frame passages). He deduces that Third Isaiah was a prophet, a definite person, of the post-exilic period, whose purpose was to continue and revitalize Second Isaiah's message for a small group of people suffering from disillusionment and loss of hope (61.1-3 and 62.1, 6 reflect the persona of the prophet). The message of this prophet was 'salvation and nothing but salvation' (1966: 296). In keeping with this criterion, Westermann assigns 57.14-20; 65.16b-25 and 66.6-16 to Third Isaiah. All other parts of chs. 56–66 belong to editorial activity and modification of one type or another. He divides the contents into four strands: (1) the nucleus in chs. 60–62 (plus 57.14-20; 65.16b-25; 66.6-16 and perhaps 58.1-12; (2) 56.9–57.13; 57.21; 59.2-8; 65.1-16a; 66.3-5, 17—stressing cleavage between the devout and the wicked; (3) 60.12; 63.1-6; 66.6, 15-16; 66.20, 22-24—modifying the friendly attitude of Third Isaiah toward foreign nations; (4) 56.1-2, 3-8; 66.18-19, 21 (and perhaps

66.1-2)—additions at the beginning and end of the book.

More recently, S. Sekine (1989) has subjected chs. 56–66 to a rigorous, complex, and detailed redactional investigation. As in the case of Westermann, he isolates the work of Third Isaiah in chs. 60–62 and argues that 56.1-8 and 66.18-24 form a redactional bracket for the present form of the text. In his analysis, he divides the content of chs. 56–66 into two basic redactional layers. The first is supplemented by a series of redactional passages and, in its combined form, is found in the following sections: 57.13b-15, 18-21; 58.1-2; 59.15b-21; 60.1-22; 61.1-11; 62.1-12; 63.11a; 64.4a; 65.1, 16b-23, 24, 25; 66.5-6, 17, 18-24 (references are to the MT). The second layer is divided into seven sections: (1) 56.1-5 + 58.3-14; (2) 56.9-57.13a; (3) 59.1-15a; (4) 63.4b-8; (6) 65.2-16a; (7) 66.1-4. Also, in a long excursus, he argues that there are major weaknesses in Elliger's methodology and arguments. Sekine's recognition of the bracketing passages in 56.1-6 and 66.18-24 seems sound, but his separation of the redactional layers involves much subjective judgement—too much to be very persuasive for many people. However, in my opinion, Sekine's inclusion of material from chs. 56–59 and 65–66 in the foundational layer of Third Isaiah is a positive step.

Very recently, P.A. Smith has devoted a monograph to the structure, growth, and authorship of chs. 56–66. He finds the work of Third Isaiah (active in the early post-exilic period) in 60.1–63.6. A second Third Isaiah, who worked after Third Isaiah until the time when the rebuilding of the temple was complete in 515 BCE, is responsible for 56.1-8; 56.9–57.21; 58.1–59.20; 65.1–66.17 (1995: 204-207). Chapters 56–66 are rounded off by an appendix in 66.18-24, which is later (mid-fifth century at the earliest) and offers a vision of a new heavens and new earth focused around the worship of Yahweh by all mankind. The lament in 63.7–64.11 is exilic and quoted as appropriate for the context between 60.1–63.6 and 65.1–66.17. However, most of Third Isaiah should be understood as relating to the historical background of 538–515 BCE, between the first return and the rebuilding of the temple, and not during the time of Ezra and Nehemiah. Smith offers a simpler form of redactional development than scholars like Sakine and Lau.

O.H. Steck has given major attention to a redactional analysis of Third Isaiah (1991). In his opinion, the core and oldest component of chs. 56–66 is 60.1-62.9. Isaiah 62.10-12 is isolated as a separate layer of redaction, somewhat later than the other material in chs. 60–62, and this is a very important redactional unit for Steck. He finds no major influence from chs. 1–39 in the material in 60–62 except for 62.10-12, which he correlates with his earlier work on Isaiah 35 (1985). As already noted above, he argues that ch. 35 was written to form a bridge between First Isaiah and chs. 40–55, perhaps being written when the two books were put together. Steck argues that the parallels (especially between 35.8-10 and 62.10-12) indicate that the form of Second Isaiah when these two passages were written included most of chs. 60–62, and that before being joined with First Isaiah (whatever its exact extent), chs. 40–62.10 formed a discrete unit. Steck continues his redactional analysis of chs. 56–66 by isolating layers in chs. 56–59; 63.1-6 and 56.1-8; 63.7–66.24.

Steck's treatment is important also because of his conclusion that Third Isaiah in the 'great-book' of Isaiah is a product of scribal prophecy, which continues and expands a previous literary corpus. The material did not evolve from a prophet working orally, or from a series of such prophets in different contexts. It is literary work (and never existed as a separate work), continuing and expounding earlier prophecy: chs. 60–62 are a direct continuation of chs. 40–55, to which the other material in chs. 56–66 has been added in three redactional stages, and all the content should be understood in the context of the development of the book of Isaiah (1991: 44-45).

This important shift in approach is also present in the recent work of W. Lau (1994). Lau offers an elaborate redactional analysis, which follows in general the commonly accepted pattern in Third Isaiah: chs. 60–62 constitute the work of 'Third Isaiah'. The remainder of the material represents the work of three 'tradent-circles' plus some individual pieces (I—57.14-21; 66.7-14a; 65.16b-25; II—66.18-24; 57.3-13; 66.1-4, 5-6, 14-17; 65.1-7, 8-12, 13-16a; III—59.1-21; 56.9-12 and 57.1-2; 58.1-14; the individual pieces are: 56.1-8; 63.1-6; 63.7–64.11). Lau tries to dissect the redactional layers along the lines of a continuation of the basic message of chs. 40–55 and the context of sociological and theological conflict in the post-exilic community. I doubt that his precise textual surgery will persuade very many to agree with him in details, but his insistence on the nature of Third Isaiah as 'scribal prophecy' is interesting. He contends that the scribal prophets are really 'authors' and not mere redactors (1994: 7-21). These scribal prophets-authors-tradents reflected upon, continued, and re-interpreted earlier prophetic messages for new contexts. They were engaged in literary endeavors and did not present their messages orally, as seems to have been the case with pre-exilic prophets such as Amos and Isaiah of Jerusalem. As mentioned earlier, this approach seems increasingly popular for Isaiah 40–55 as well. The 'exilic prophets' may well become 'authors', whose pens were mightier than spoken words.

The One-Book Interpretation

The one-book approach constitutes a paradigm shift in Isaiah studies. As I commented at the beginning of this article, John Watts's commentary is representative of the new paradigm. Of course, some scholars were already into this mode of interpretation before Watts's commentary appeared. An important anchor point is found in B.S. Childs's treatment of Isaiah (1979: 311-38). Childs reviews the historical approaches to Isaiah and notes the problems which these studies 'raised without clear-cut resolutions', but refuses to use the failure as an indictment of the critical approach (1979: 323). He seeks a more 'radical hermeneutical solution' (1979: 324) with his proposals regarding the 'canonical shape of the Book of Isaiah' (1979: 325). In this regard, he begins with the peculiar absence of historical context in Second Isaiah, which lacks the expected indications (such as superscriptions) of independent writings. He notes the specific references to Cyrus (44.28–45.1) but says that the historical detail is minimal and argues that Cyrus has become more of a 'theological projection' (1979: 326) than a historical figure. In chs. 40–55, the theological context overshadows the historical.

The message of Second Isaiah has been placed within the context of eighth-century Isaiah and converted into a prophetic word directed to the future (1979: 325); a message originally designed for a specific exilic context has become 'fully eschatological', relating to the redemptive plan of God for Israel and the nations. He postulates a deliberate blurring of historical matter in chs. 40–55 in order to transform them into prophecy suitable for later generations of Israelites (1979: 327). Childs proposes that the solution to the long-standing problem of the 'former things' in Second Isaiah (see 41.21-23; 42.9; 43.9, 16-19; 48.3) can be solved by understanding the 'former things' as a reference to the prophecies of First Isaiah, which are being confirmed in a new context. He raises the question as to whether or not Second Isaiah ever circulated apart from being 'connected to an earlier form of First Isaiah' (1979: 329). He continues, but does not work out in detail, his analysis and suggests that Third Isaiah is dependent on Second Isaiah; both Second and Third Isaiah 'perform a similar function in relation to First Isaiah' in canonical perspective regardless of differences in the history of transmission (1979: 334). The final form of Isaiah is that of literature 'severed...from its historical context' and provided with 'a completely new and non-historical framework' which renders its message in ways accessible for all future generations. The differences in Childs treatment will be obvious immediately to any reader who compares it with the usual historical-critical introductions.

R.F. Melugin's work (1976) appeared earlier than Childs's introduction and has been cited frequently for its quality and for the prescient statements in the conclusion. He declares that although chs. 40–66 'manifest a literary integrity of their own...the fact remains that these chapters are somehow related to the whole of Isaiah' (1976: 176). He expresses the opinion that our understanding of the message of chs. 40–55 will continue to be incomplete until their relationship with the entire book is established. Chapters 40–66 were never meant to stand alone or as a separate work, and the situation toward which the speeches are directed is poorly defined. He accepts the sixth century setting as a correct 'scholarly reconstruction' but notes the small amount of specific historical information in the content. He assumes that the historical markers of a prophetic book had been in the material at an earlier stage, but that they were largely obliterated when the material was placed in the context of the book of Isaiah. This was done in order to establish continuity between the judgement in Isa. 1.4-9; 22.1-14; 30.13-14, understood in connection with the deliverance of Jerusalem from the Assyrians, and the final judgement which was delayed until the Babylonian exile. The sparing of Hezekiah in ch. 39 was understood by the redactor as a sparing of sinful Judah and a delay of the full judgement announced by Isaiah of Jerusalem. In chs. 40–55, of course, the delayed punishment is at an end and the glorious future is at hand.

The one-book interpretation received strong support from R.E. Clements in his well-known 1982 article. His major thesis is that the conjunction of chs. 40–55 with earlier chapters in Isaiah was 'a deliberate step taken by the scribal redactors of the book' (1982: 128). He argues for a strong thematic connection (the fate of Jerusalem and the Davidic dynasty) between the first two major parts of the book. The situation with chs. 56–66 is not so clear, but it is reasonably sure that they are a 'carrying-forward' of the message of the unnamed prophet of chs. 40–55 (1982: 123, 128). The overall structure of the book of Isaiah 'shows signs of editorial planning and...at some stage in its growth attempts were made to read and interpret the book as a whole'

(1982: 121). This is demonstrated by 'interim summaries' in the earlier parts of the book which presuppose chs. 40–66 (for example, ch. 35; 11.12-16; 19.23; 27.12-13. and 18.7 linked with 45.14), and even more by the complex structure of chs. 1–35 which shows dependence on subsequent chapters (1982: 121-23). In a later article, he takes the position that 'from the time of their origin' chs. 40–55 were intended to continue and supplement a collection of sayings from Isaiah of Jerusalem (1985: 101), and that chs. 40–55 'should no longer be regarded as the self-contained and independent body of material that it has so widely been thought to be in recent years' (1985: 106). Concomitantly, the reconstructions of the 'life and times' of a prophet called Second Isaiah become highly problematic.

In addition to the work of Childs, Melugin, and Clements in moving toward a one-book interpretation, mention, at least, should be made of the significant contributions of P.R. Ackroyd, R. Rendtorff, M.A. Sweeney, and B.W. Anderson. I will pass on, however, to a survey of the three main routes followed by the one-book interpretation: (1) thematic and intertextual continuities; (2) redactional analysis; (3) literary reading. The survey which follows is necessarily as abbreviated and incomplete as that of the one-prophet and three-book interpretations.

Thematic and Intertextual Continuities

The discovery of thematic continuities is a staple feature of the one-prophet approach. It has also become a major factor in the tradition historical and redactional approaches of other scholars. Some of the verbal-thematic features are commonplace. For example, the 'Holy One of Israel' is found thirteen times in the first part of Isaiah, thirteen in the second, and in 60.9, 14, plus a variation in 57.15 (the expression is found four times outside of Isaiah: 2 Kgs 19.22; Jer. 50.29; 51.5; Ezek. 39.7; cf. 'the Holy One' in Job 6.10; Hos. 11.9; Hab. 1.12; 3.3). The first appearance of this expression in Isaiah is found in 1.4. Other important thematic elements include Zion/Jerusalem (see Seitz 1991), the glory of Yahweh, righteousness, and the remnant concept. R.J. Clifford (1993) proposes that the unity of the book is manifest in its use of cosmogonic language, especially that of creation. W. Lau (1994: 320-21) isolates four content themes functioning in chs. 56–66: the Zion tradition; the servant of God tradition; the Holy One of Israel; the exodus tradition. These themes are found also in other sections of Isaiah (for the servant in chs. 1–39, see Isa. 20.3; also see W.A.M. Beuken 1990; for exodus in chs. 1–39, see 11.10-16). R. Rendtorff (1993: 149-55) calls attention to the words 'comfort', 'iniquity', and 'glory' in ch. 40 and shows that these ideas link up with the other two main parts of Isaiah ('comfort' relates to 12.1; 49.13; 51.3, 12; 52.9; 61.2; 66.13; 'iniquity' links to 1.4; 22.14; 30.13; 40.2; 59.2, 3a, 12, 20; 64.5, 6-7; 'glory' in 40.5 is related to 6.3; 35.2; 59.19; 60.1; 66.18). He says that 'the central themes of ch. 40 are therefore found in the first and third parts of the book as well' and concludes that the links are of such a nature as to indicate, in some cases at least, that they have been 'deliberately forged in order to connect the three parts' (1993: 155). All thematic elements must, of course, be evaluated individually in terms of tradition history and redaction analysis. Their relative importance varies one from another, but their cumulative force serves to create strong bands of unity between the subsections of major parts and between the parts themselves.

P.T. Willey has made an intertextual study of the figures of the servant of Yahweh and 'Daughter Zion' in Second Isaiah. She describes these as 'geopolitical figures that span the length of Second Isaiah' (1995: 209). Zion is a city in chs. 40–55, but the city is personified as a woman with children (49.14-26; 51.1-8; 54.1-17). The servant is identified with Israel/Jacob, and the two figures are intertextually related: the addressees in Second Isaiah are the masculine singular Israel/Servant, the feminine singular Zion, and the addressees tying all the sections together are designated by the masculine plural 'you'. She notes that in chs. 49–54, the Servant and Zion appear in contiguous but separate sections (Servant, 49.1-13; Zion, 49.14–50.3; Servant, 50.4-11; Zion, 51.17–52.12; Servant, 52.13–53.12; Zion, 54.1-17), with Zion and the plural 'you' appearing together in 51.1-16.

In pursuing her intertextual project, Willey seeks texts outside Isaiah which may correlate with the Zion and servant texts in Second Isaiah. In this regard, she devotes attention especially to the Daughter Zion contexts in Lamentations 1–2 and 4–5, with some attention to Jeremiah 2–3 and Nahum 2.1 (Eng. 1.15). She attempts to relate the Servant of Yahweh with the 'self-identified male figure' (a *geber*) in Lamentations 3, 'who contemplates his own sufferings in many of the same terms in which Daughter Zion had described herself in Lamentations 1 and 2' (1995: 296). The figure in Lamentations 3 is a male counterpart to Daughter Zion, who embodies the suffering of the community, in a pattern similar to that of Daughter Zion and the Servant in Second Isaiah: 'the servant acts the role that the *geber* prescribes' (1995: 299), especially in Isaiah 50 and 53. Willey's informative and provocative project is still under way. I hope she will address the Daughter Zion content in Third Isaiah (62.11) and in First Isaiah (1.8; 3.16, 17; 4.4; 10.32; 16.1; 37.22). Incidentally, she incorporates into her article a skilled and succinct explanation of intertextual theory (1995: 273-78).

Redactional Analyses

Strictly speaking, redactional analysis seeks to isolate indications of redaction in received texts and to trace the history of the redactional process through its expansion by additions and on into the formation of larger complexes, and finally into the present literary form of the texts. Form criticism, tradition history, and rhetorical criticism are closely related to redactional analysis, as are literary criticism and historical criticism. Actually, the various methodologies should be and are often molded into a synthetic whole in the exegesis of biblical texts.

I have already surveyed recent redactional studies of various sections of Isaiah. The practitioners of redactional analysis sometimes seem to fragment, even atomize, biblical content with hyper-subtle argumentation in ways that rival the worst features of old time source and form critics. Their excessive and dense verbiage is certainly wearisome for those who try to read their works! Nevertheless, there is an innate thrust in redaction criticism which pushes it toward wholeness; in the case of Isaiah toward the 'Great Isaiah' or the 'Isaiah Book' (Steck's terms). Sooner or later the redaction critic working in Isaiah must move beyond the component sections to analyze the whole book.

R. Rendtorff offers the interesting judgement that there are two basic approaches to the analysis of the composition of Isaiah, both legitimate. A diachronic reading seeks the stages by which a composition reached its final form, while synchronic reading deals with the structure and meaning(s) of the whole composition (1991: 16-17). He admits to oversimplifying the complex character of the problems but insists on the difference between the two forms of study. This is a helpful distinction, although most redactional work on Isaiah has elements of both approaches. For example, Steck's work would surely be classified as primarily diachronic, but he shows great sensitivity to literary matters and seeks for larger literary contexts.

Literary Readings

Thematic and redactional studies overlap with this approach. The scholars doing literary readings use other critical methods to a greater or lesser degree, but their emphasis is on reading the texts with understanding and involvement, with only a secondary concern for historical matters. The interpretations in this approach may contain little of the history of the process of the development of the text. I will discuss briefly three recent examples of this approach.

The title of E.W. Conrad's *Reading Isaiah* (1991) is significant since Conrad's first chapter is called 'Choosing Reading Strategies'. His strategy assumes that the text of Isaiah is 'something as a whole and seeks to discover what that whole is' (1991: 29). He says he is not interested in relating parts of the text to historical backgrounds external to them or to the history of their development but 'to the literary world of the text itself' (1991: 30). His process of reading involves the examination of 'rhetorical techniques and patterns that suggest unity' (1991: 30). Among the readings in his book, two seem especially interesting. First, he has a fairly extensive discussion of the function of 'The Lord's Plan' in the book of Isaiah, and second he seeks to define the major characteristics and concerns of the implied community of the book, although this is not worked out very fully.

P.D. Miscall offers as 'a reading of the text of Isaiah both as a whole and in its parts and, as much as possible, according to the order of the book' (1993a: 9). Miscall expresses his dependence upon and appreciation of John Watts's commentary, adopting his descriptive term 'vision' (Isa. 1.1) and making some use of his description of the book of Isaiah as drama.

> Isaiah presents his vision as a quasi-drama. The book is dominated by dramatic speeches... The characters are not presented as distinct and historical individuals, they are constructs in the grand poetic work of Isaiah (1993a: 15).

In his commentary, Miscall does not make as much use of intertextuality and free reading styles as in another work where he defines intertextuality in terms of displacement, decentering, and dispersal.

> Instead of borrowing and influence, instead of a stream of tradition that flows on and into texts we have texts that displace and decenter one another—we do not have to follow historical priority here—by dispersing and discriminating each other's parts or elements: letters, words, sentences, themes, images, characters and plot (1993b: 45).

In this article, he focuses on Isaiah read as one book (1993b: 47) and examines the relations between Isaiah and Gen. 1.1–2.4a, reading them as 'intertexts'. In an earlier article, he pursues the imagery of light in the book of Isaiah ('in good deconstructive fashion', 1991: 104). Starting with Isaiah 2.5 ('Come and let us walk in the light of the LORD') he traces the imagery of light back and forth in what he calls a 'Labyrinth' (for example, 10.17; 30.26; 60.1, 19). In this approach, the reader decides which textual threads to follow and whether or not to finally tie them all together or just leave them without resolution (1991: 107). He also pursues the images of fire and water, good light, evil darkness, water, dryness, sun and shade, and smelting. When this kind of reading is done by a scholar as skilled as Miscall, it can be interesting and evocative, but I cringe to think about the results of such reading by most laity and preachers in the churches.

K.P. Darr has written a book (1994) in which she uses some of the same methods as Miscall. However, she also works in terms of reader-response, 'a reader-oriented method' (1994: 23) built on three premises: (1) literature has rhetorical function and uses literary strategies to communicate with readers; (2) meaning emerges from the interaction of the rhetorical strategies of texts and the interpretative repertoire of readers; (3) many historical, social, linguistic, and literary factors in ancient texts are relevant for contemporary interpretation by modern readers, which means that readers of ancient texts should reconstruct culture-specific factors of the texts as best they can (1994: 24-25). Thus Darr shows great appreciation for historical-critical studies, while using current literary-critical analyses.

An interesting example of Darr's approach is her treatment of proverb-performance, focusing on Hezekiah's use of a proverb in Isa. 37.3:

> This day is a day of distress, of rebuke, and of disgrace; children have come to birth and there is no strength to bring them forth. (RSV)

Darr examines the traditional saying involving a lack of strength to give birth in the context of Hezekiah's situation in ch. 37 and then follows it into other references in Isaiah (26.17-18 and 66.1-16). The analysis of proverb-performance needs to be expanded in prophetic literature, and Darr has demonstrated its value.

In this category, I may return to John Watts's commentary since he sets forth a reading of Isaiah's Vision as a drama in twelve acts (see above). His use of drama on this scale is not persuasive; it seems much too subjective and contrived. The problematic nature of the thesis of prophetic drama is heightened by the lack of any historical evidence that dramas were staged in Israel. A proposal for some sections of Isaiah as quasi-drama, para-drama, or the like might have some probability, but drama on the scale proposed is unlikely. Of course the presence of what has been termed 'street theater' and the prophets as 'street actors' may very well be a factor in Isaiah (for example, chs. 7 and 20). Also, the rejection of Watts's thesis leaves an unanswered question both for Isaiah and for other prophetic literature: How were the prophetic pronouncements made available to the public? If drama was not used, what means of presentation were used? M. Sweeney concludes that 'the book of Isaiah as a whole demonstrates that it functions as an exhortation to reestablish and maintain the Jewish community in Jerusalem in the mid- to late fifth century BCE' and was 'directed to the post-exilic Jewish population in general' (1988: 185). Fair enough, but *how* did it function and *how* was it directed to the general Jewish population?

Conclusion

The huge output of written work on the book of Isaiah is almost overwhelming. I have been very selective and rather superficial in dealing with the literature available. If this article has sketched out some of the major lines of study, that will be enough for which to hope. I am sure that some major pieces of work have been ignored or overlooked. I have devoted my attention primarily to literary matters and neglected work in the theological interpretation of Isaiah. With these qualifying statements, I will put my conclusion in the form of questions related to what seems to me to be unfinished work in the study of the book of Isaiah. Some projects may never be finished, but they merit attention.

First, an emphasis on the book of Isaiah raises the question of the nature of the unity we seek. D. Carr observes that 'unity' can mean different things and contends that Isaiah lacks 'a single macro-structural perspective that can be found in the book as a whole' (1993: 71). He argues that there are multiple 'macro-structural conceptions' in Isaiah (1993: 77). Perhaps the best thing that Carr does is to suggest the concept of 'collection' to 'better exemplify' the 'textual unity that does not occur in Isaiah' (1993: 79). The nature and function of collections in relation to prophetic literature (and other types of biblical writings) should be followed up. The collection concept can accommodate the highly complex unity in Isaiah without having to assume a tight, precisely fitted macro-literary structure. A collection should not be regarded as simply a haphazard agglomeration of materials. Work in the wisdom literature and the Psalter has already established this point. The unity of a collection will move along redaction, thematic, rhetorical and intertextual lines. In passing, we might remember that the genre of the collection is prevalent in modern literature; it is not alien to our own literary contexts.

C. Mathews (1995a: 251, 263-65) calls attention to the difficulty of reading the book of Isaiah in a strictly linear fashion. For example, the book is generally organized along the lines of historical chronology, but, when the reader comes to chs. 13–14, the content suddenly leaves the Assyrian context of the first part of the book and oracles against Babylon appear. These fit more easily with chs. 40–55. She comments that

> The mingling of Assyrian and Babylonian material suggests that in Proto, as in Deutero- and Trito—Isaiah, history is not to be conceived of solely as the forward march of events, as the 'latter' things overtaking the 'former,' as the unfolding of ever new circumstances. Rather, what unfolds in the present, while new in terms of the historical particular, may be in important respects analogous to the past... (1995a: 251).

The events are analogous in the metahistorical involvement of Yahweh in human affairs—chronologically separate, but metahistorically analogous. As noted above, she finds a similiar situation with the oracle against Edom in ch. 34, which we would expect to find in chs. 13–23, and which is analogous to 63.1-6 in an intertextual sense. Such examples lead Mathews to ask, in her conclusion, what we mean 'when we speak of Isaiah as a prophetic book' (1995a: 265). Our attention is directed toward prophecy as a literary phenomenon and the 'production of prophetic texts', thus it 'may be instructive to consider what our hypothesized redactors thought of themselves as doing' (1995a: 265).

Second, Mathews's reflections lead naturally to the question of the extent to which Isaiah is the product of scribal prophecy. This is clearly an issue for further exploration. We need not doubt a core of material from the eighth century Isaiah of Jerusalem, but the hypothesis of an Exilic/Second Isaiah as a prophet in the traditional sense is open to question, and even more so for Third Isaiah. Has the time come to bury Exilic Isaiah? Probably not yet, but it may be well to start making funeral plans! Third Isaiah is hardly viable at all.

Related matters cluster here. The probability of a prophet-pastor among the Babylonian exiles has been diminished—though it may still be true. The question of the geographic provenance of chs. 40–55 seems open again. The whole question of the nature and function of scribal prophecy needs careful investigation: Who were the scribal prophets? By what authority did they write? For whom did they write? How were their writings disseminated and preserved? (The comments of Lau, 1994: 7-10, 316-329, are worth attention in relation to the question of authority). We may like these prophets very well when we get better acquainted with them, although we will miss Exilic Isaiah sorely.

Third, new insights into the sociology, economics, and politics of exilic and post-exilic Judean communities should be applied to the study of Isaiah. For example, the extrapolation of the implied Isaianic community (as in Conrad above) needs checking and correlation with what we know of the socio-economic nature of the post-exilic community around Jerusalem.

Fourth, there is a need to sort out, categorize, evaluate, and extend the various thematic and intertextual bands of unity in the Isaiah collection. The studies of such matters are presently scattered in the literature, and obviously they are not of equal importance, and still other elements remain to be identified. All in all, Isaiah studies should be a happy hunting ground for dissertation writers in the years ahead.

Finally, the one-prophet approach to the Book of Isaiah faces a marginalized future. The substance of the work of scholars along this line has not improved over the past century. The conservative scholars R.B. Dillard and T. Longman III have put the matter well in their introduction to the Old Testament. They reject the thesis that the book of Isaiah is the work of Isaiah of Jerusalem: a 'later author saw in Isaiah's prophecies of Exile and a remnant events that were transpiring in his own day.' They wisely argue that the complex questions of authorship are not subject to being settled by 'slogans or theological dicta'; the authorship of Isaiah should not be made 'a theological *shibboleth* (Judg. 12:6) or test for orthodoxy' (1994: 275). They add that the whole issue of authorship is 'somewhat moot: whether written by Isaiah in the eighth century or by others who applied his insights to a later time'. These are words of wisdom and other scholars should heed them.

I am grateful for the privilege of writing this article as a tribute to my colleague, John D.W. Watts, on the occasion of his seventy-fifth birthday. His work on Isaiah is continuing, and I expect to see his commentary in a revised form before too many years have passed. He has blessed me with his friendship and support for many years.

BIBLIOGRAPHY

Ackroyd, P.R.

1987 *Studies in the Religious Tradition of the Old Testament* (London: SCM Press). The articles on Isaiah are: 'An Interpretation of the Babylonian Exile: A Study of II Kings 20, Isaiah 38–39': 152-71 (orig. publ. 1974); 'Isaiah 1–12: Presentation of a Prophet': 79-104 (1978); 'The Death of Hezekiah: A Pointer to the Future?': 172-80 (1981); 'Isaiah 36-39: Structure and Function': 105-20 (1982).

Anderson, B.W.

1986 *Understanding the Old Testament* (Englewood Cliffs, NJ: Prentice-Hall, 4th edn)

1988 'The Apocalyptic Rendering of the Isaiah Tradition', in J. Neusner, et al (eds.), *The Social World of Formative Christianity and Judaism. A Tribute to Howard Clark Kee* (Philadelphia: Fortress Press): 17-38.

Barth, H.

1977 *Die Jesaja-Worte in der Josiazeit: Israel und Assur als Thema einer produktiven Neuinterpretation der Jesajaüberlieferung* (WMANT, 48; Neukirchen–Vluyn: Neukirchener Verlag).

Beuken, W.A.M.

1990 'The Main Theme of Trito-Isaiah "The Servants of Yahweh"', *JSOT* 47: 67-87.

Carr, D.

1993 'Reaching for Unity in Isaiah', *JSOT* 57: 61-80.

Childs, B.S.

1979 *Introduction to the Old Testament as Scripture* (Philadephia: Fortress Press).

Clements, R.E.

1980 *Isaiah 1–39* (NCBC: Grand Rapids: Eerdmans).

1982 'The Unity of the Book of Isaiah', *Int* 26: 117-29.

1985 'Beyond Tradition-History: Deutero-Isaianic Development of First Isaiah's Themes', *JSOT* 31: 95-113.

Clifford, R.J.

1993 'The Unity of the Book of Isaiah and Its Cosmogonic Language', *CBQ* 55: 1-17.

Conrad, E.W.

1991 *Reading Isaiah* (OBT; Minneapolis: Fortress Press).

Darr, K. P.

1994 *Isaiah's Vision and the Family of God* (Louisville: Westminster/John Knox Press).

Dillard, R.B. and T. Longman, III

1994 *An Introduction to the Old Testament* (Grand Rapids: Zondervan).

Duhm, B.

1922 *Das Buch Jesaja* (HKAT 3.1; Göttingen: Vandenhoeck & Ruprecht, 4th edn; orig. publ. 1892).

Eissfeldt, O.
1965 *The Old Testament: An Introduction: The History of the Formation of the Old Testament* (trans. P.R. Ackroyd; New York: Harper & Row).

Elliger, K.
1928 *Die Einheit des Tritojesaia* (Stuttgart: W. Kohlhammer).

Emmerson, G.I.
1992 *Isaiah 56–66* (OTG; Sheffield: Sheffield Academic Press).

Fohrer, G.
1968 *Introduction to the Old Testament* (trans. D.E. Green; Nashville: Abingdon Press).

Hanson, P.D.
1979 *The Dawn of Apocalyptic* (Philadelphia: Fortress Press).
1995 *Isaiah 40–66* (Interpretation; Louisville: John Knox Press).

Harrison, R.K.
1969 *Introduction to the Old Testament* (Grand Rapids: Eerdmans)

Hermisson, H.-J.
1989 'Einheit und Komplexitat Deuterojesajas: Probleme der Redaktionsgeschichte von Jes 40–55', in J. Vermeylen (ed.), *The Book of Isaiah* (BETL, 81; Leuven: University Press): 287-312.

Hill, A.E. and J.H. Walton
1991 *A Survey of the Old Testament* (Grand Rapids: Zondervan).

Kiesow, K.
1979 *Exodustexte in Jesajabuch: Literakritische und motivgeschichtliche Analysen* (OBO, 24; Fribourg: Universitaires Fribourg).

Kratz, R.G.
1991 *Kyros in Deuterojasaja-Buch: Redaktionsgeschichtliche Untersuchungen, Entstehung und Theologie von Jes 40–55* (Forschungen zum Alten Testament 1; Tübingen: Mohr-Siebeck).

Laato, A.
1992 *The Servant of Yahweh and Cyrus: A Reinterpretation of the Exilic Messianic Programme in Isaiah 40–55* (ConBot, 35; Stockholm: Almquist & Wiksell).

Lau, W.
1994 *Schriftgelehrte Prophetie in Jes 56–66* (BZAW, 225; Berlin: de Gruyter).

Mathews, C.R.
1995a 'Apportioning Desolation: Contexts for Interpreting Edom's Fate and Function in Isaiah', in E.H. Lovering, Jr (ed.), SBLSP, 1995 (Atlanta: Scholars Press): 250-66.
1995b *Defending Zion: Edom's Desolation and Jacob's Restoration (Isaiah 34–35) in Context* (BZAW, 236; Berlin: de Gruyter). This work was not available to me when this article was written.

Merendino, R.P.
1981 *Der Erste und der Letzte: Eine Untersuchung von Jes 40-48* (VTSup, 31; Leiden: Brill).

Mettinger, T.N.D.
1983 *A Farewell to the Servant Songs: A Critical Examination of an Exegetical Axiom* (trans. F.H. Cryer; Lund: Gleerup).

Melugin, R.F.
1976 *The Formation of Isaiah 40–55* (BZAW, 141; Berlin: de Gruyter).

Miscall, P.D.
1991 'Isaiah: The Labyrinth of Images', *Semeia* 54: 103-21.
1993a *Isaiah* (Sheffield: JSOT Press).
1993b 'Isaiah: New Heavens, New Earth, New Book', in D.N. Fewell (ed.), *Reading Between Texts* (Louisville: Westminster/John Knox): 41-56.

Motyer, J.A.
1993 *The Prophecy of Isaiah: An Introduction and Commentary* (Downers Grove, IL: InterVarsity Press).

van Oorschot, J.
1993 *Von Babel zum Zion: Eine literarkritische und redaktionsgeschichtliche Untersuchung* (Berlin: de Gruyter).

Oswalt, J.N.
1986 *The Book of Isaiah, Chapters 1–39* (NICOT; Grand Rapids: Eerdmans).

von Rad, G.
1965 *Old Testament Theology*, II (trans. D.M.G. Stalker; New York: Harper & Row).

Rendtorff, R.
1986 *The Old Testament: An Introduction* (trans. J. Bowden; Philadelphia: Fortress Press).
1991 'The Book of Isaiah: A Complex Unity, Synchronic and Diachronic Readings', in E.H. Lovering, Jr (ed.), SBLSP 1991 (Atlanta: Scholars Press): 8-20.
1993 'The Composition of the Book Isaiah', in *Canon and Theology: Overtures to an Old Testament Theology* (OBT; trans. M. Kohl; Minneapolis: Fortress Press): 145-69 (orig. publ. in *VT* 34 [1984]: 295-320).

Schmidt, W.H.
1984 *Old Testament Introduction* (trans. M.J. O'Connell; New York: Crossroad).

Seitz, C.R.
1991 *Zion's Final Destiny: The Development of the Book of Isaiah: A Reassessment of Isaiah 36–39* (Minneapolis: Fortress Press).
1992 'Isaiah, Book of (First Isaiah)' and 'Isaiah, Book of (Third Isaiah)', in D.N. Freedman, ed., *The Anchor Bible Dictionary H-J* (New York: Doubleday): 472-88, 501-507.
1993a *Isaiah 1–39* (Interpretation; Louisville: John Knox Press).
1993b 'On the Question of Divisions Internal to the Book of Isaiah', in E.H. Lovering, Jr. (ed.), SBLSP, 1993 (Atlanta: Scholars Press): 260-66.

Sekine, S.
1989 *Die tritojesajanische Sammlung (Jes 56–66) redaktionsgeschichtlich untersucht* (BZAW, 175; Berlin: de Gruyter).

Smart, J.D.
1965 *History and Theology in Second Isaiah: A Commentary on Isaiah 35, 40–66* (Philadelphia: Westminster Press).

Smith, P.A.
1995 *Rhetoric and Redaction in Trito-Isaiah: The Structure, Growth, and Authorship of Isaiah 56–66* (Leiden: Brill).

Soggin, J.A.
1980 *Introduction to the Old Testament* (trans. J. Bowden; Philadelphia: Westminster Press, rev. edn).

Steck, O.H.
1985 *Bereitete Heimkehr: Jesaja 35 als redaktionelle Brücke zwischen dem Ersten und dem Zweiten Jesaja* (SBS, 121; Stuttgart: Katholisches Bibelwerk).
1991 *Studien zu Tritojesaja* (BZAW, 203; Berlin: de Gruyter).

Sweeney, M.A.
1988 *Isaiah 1–4 and The Post-Exilic Understanding of the Isaianic Tradition* (BZAW, 171; Berlin: de Gruyter).

Vermeylen, J.
1987 'Le Motif de la creation dans le Deutero-Isaie', in P. Beachamp (ed.), *La Creation dans l'Orient Ancien* (LD, 127; Paris: Cerf): 183-240.
1989 'L'Unite de livre d'Isaie', in J. Vermeylen (ed.), *The Book of Isaiah* (BETL, 81; Leuven: University Press): 11-53.

Watts, J.D.W.
1985 *Isaiah 1–33* (WBC, 24; Waco, TX: Word Books).
1987 *Isaiah 34–66* (WBC, 25; Waco, TX: Word Books).

Weiser, A.
1961 *The Old Testament: Its Formation and Development* (trans. D.M. Barton; New York: Association Press)

Westerman, C.
1969 *Isaiah 40–66* (OTL; trans. D.M.G. Stalker; Philadelphia: Westminster Press).

Wildberger, H.
1982 *Jesaja 28–39* (BKAT X/3; Neukirchen–Vluyn: Neukirchener Verlag)

Willey, P.T.
1995 'The Servant of Yahweh and Daughter Zion: Alternating Visions of Yahweh's Community', in E.H. Lovering, Jr (ed.), SBLSP, 1995 (Atlanta: Scholars Press): 267-303.

Williamson, H.G.M.
1994 *The Book Called Isaiah: Deutero-Isaiah's Role in Composition and Redaction* (Oxford: Clarendon Press).

A Light to the Nations: A Central Theme of the Book of Isaiah

Ronald E. Clements

The book of Isaiah is a very complex structure, so much so that, even in the present, it is open to contend that modern scholarship has encountered very considerable difficulty in elucidating its message. Indeed, it remains possible to question whether there is an overall series of propositions that can properly be called 'the message of the book', or whether we must not rather settle for a simple acceptance of a whole variety of 'messages' that belong to the various prophets who have contributed to its separate parts. For more than a century, the contention that the book must be regarded as composed of at least three separate prophet 'books', or collections, has dominated scholarship. As a result it has become commonplace to treat the various sections separately in histories of Israelite prophecy—the so-called First, Second and Third Isaiah—and to look for different authors to contribute introductions and commentaries to each of them. There is then little expectation that the unity of the book will prove an issue that requires careful examination and detailed treatment. All too often, it is taken apart before the question of whether it belongs together as a unity is ever considered.

1. *Isaiah as Prophet and the Prophetic Book*

All these assumptions and procedures now stand in radical need of revision and rethinking, and far more attention needs to be paid to the canonical form and structure of the book, not simply as a literary salutation to the canonical, or 'final form' of the text, but as a theological and literary concern to understand its essential character and purpose[1]. After

1. Cf. my essay, 'The Unity of the Book of Isaiah', *Int* 36 (1982), pp. 117-29; J. Vermeylen, 'L'unité du livre d'Isaie', *The Book of Isaiah* (BETL, 81; Leuven: J.P. Peeters, 1989), pp. 11-53; C.R. Seitz, 'Isaiah 1–66. Making Sense of the

all, we know very little of how prophetic books were expected to appear to assume that the book of Isaiah is somehow extraordinarily odd, or should really be regarded as three separate books. During the past decade a considerable change of outlook has taken place, a revision of methods of critical analysis and a generally altered angle of perception in the study of the prophetic literature. Inevitably, this has had considerable impact on the study of the book of Isaiah[2]. We may claim with confidence that the hypothesis of a basic three-part division of the book, as advocated by Bernhard Duhm in his commentary of 1892,[3] is obsolete and must now be considered as simply a provisional, and recognizably inadequate, attempt to understand its origin and to interpret its significance.[4] In seeking to trace the processes which led to the formation of the book, and which can explain its present structure, such a hypothesis concedes too little to its compositional complexity and ignores too much of the undoubted internal connectedness of its various component parts.

The recent studies by C.R. Seitz,[5] Marvin Sweeney[6] and H.G.M. Williamson[7] have shown that those parts of chs. 40–66 which were at one time thought to be unrelated to the earlier section of the book must certainly be interpreted in relation to it. So far as chs. 40–55 are concerned the case is modest but sufficiently clear to be decisive. Similar changes of outlook have taken place in regard to chs. 56–66, which were left in Duhm's analysis as a rather forlorn miscellany.[8] They have subsequently been rather hesitantly ascribed either to the mysterious Deutero-Isaiah or, more probably, to his less poetically inspired disciples.

Whole', in C.R. Seitz (ed.), *Reading and Preaching the Book of Isaiah* (Philadelphia: Fortress Press, 1988), pp. 105-26; E.W. Conrad, *Reading Isaiah* (Overtures to Biblical Theology; Minneapolis: Fortress Press, 1991).

2. A full and extensive survey of these changes is to be seen in the volume by M.A. Sweeney, *Isaiah 1–39 with an Introduction to the Prophetic Literature* (FOTL; Grand Rapids : Eerdmans, 1996).

3. B. Duhm, *Das Buch Jesaja* (HAT; repr.; Tübingen: J.C.B. Mohr, 1892, 5th edn, 1968).

4. Cf. the critique by C.R. Seitz, *Zion's Final Destiny: The Development of the Book of Isaiah* (Minneapolis: Fortress Press, 1991), pp. 37-46.

5. Cf. especially the works cited above in notes 1 and 4.

6. M.A. Sweeney, *Isaiah 1–4 and the Post-Exilic Understanding of the Isaianic Tradition* (BZAW, 171; Berlin: de Gruyter, 1988) and the work cited in note 2 above.

7. H.G.M. Williamson, *The Book Called Isaiah: Deutero-Isaiah's Role in Composition and Redaction* (Oxford: Clarendon Press, 1994).

8. Duhm, *Jesaja*, pp. 7-10, 14-15, 418-19.

Now, at least, through the excellent studies of a number of scholars, most especially O.H. Steck[9] and W.A.M. Beuken,[10] the close relationship to the earlier parts of the book of these seemingly errant and orphaned eleven chapters is becoming much clearer.[11] Nor can we leave aside the importance of the studies of Rolf Rendtorff[12] in recognizing the close internal connections between the various parts of the great Isaiah collection. In a rather surprising fashion, therefore, it appears that these chapters, which at one time appeared of least importance to the book as a whole, and of only marginal interest theologically, have, nevertheless, provided some of the most important clues to understanding the whys and wherefores of its structure and formation. The reason for this is that they display with varying degrees of clarity a concern to hark back to, and to develop, themes and imagery which have appeared earlier. To a startling degree, they serve as a kind of historical and theological commentary on the earliest parts of the book which must certainly date back to the eighth century BCE.

It is a major point of significance in the two volumes of commentary on Isaiah which John Watts has published[13] that they undertake to provide a treatment of the whole book and seek to elucidate from its contents the message of the 'vision of Isaiah, the son of Amoz'.[14] Clearly, this cannot simply be a statement about authorship, relating only to those sayings and prophetic images which were declared by Isaiah of Jerusalem when the major threat to Israel from Assyria first materialized. It becomes readily apparent that there is much material in the book which must incontrovertibly be dated to a time long after the original prophet's death if it is to be adequately understood.[15]

9. O.H. Steck, 'Tritojesaja im Jesajabuch', in J. Vermeylen, ed., *The Book of Isaiah* (Leuven: Leuven University Press, 1989), pp. 11-53.

10. W.A.M. Beuken, *Jesaja deel IIIA and IIIB* (Nijkerk: Callenbach, 1989).

11. Cf. the valuable critique and review in G.I. Emmerson, *Isaiah 56–66* (OTG; Sheffield: Sheffield Academic Press, 1992).

12. R. Rendtorff, ' The Composition of the Book of Isaiah', in *Canon and Theology. Overtures to an Old Testament Theology* (trans. M. Kohl; Edinburgh: T. & T. Clark, 1994); *idem*, 'Isaiah 56:1 as Key to the Formation of the Book of Isaiah', *Canon and Theology,* pp.181-89.

13. J.D.W. Watts, *Isaiah 1–33, Isaiah 34–66* (WBC 24, 25; Waco: Word Books, 1985, 1987).

14. Watts, *Isaiah 1–33,* pp. xxiv-xxix.

15. Watts (*Isaiah 1–33,* p. xxiv) regards the literary form of the Isaianic vision as complete by approximately 435 BCE.

Nevertheless, the book is formally a unity. There is good reason why it is headed by the name of the prophet Isaiah, and it becomes evident on close examination that it seeks to maintain a kerygmatic consistency. It proclaims a coherent, connected and integrated message concerning God's purpose for Israel. It sees this purpose as directly related to Jerusalem—Zion, to the central role of the royal dynasty of David, and to the leadership that Israel is to assume among the nations. These themes recur in different ways and with different emphases, needing continual revision and development in the light of events. God's word is presented as two-edged, on one side voiced through the mouth of a prophet and on the other confirmed, modified and realized through historical events. Its vitality was necessary because the perspective of the reader was ever-changing, and its was open-ended because it pointed to a future which came under the category of 'not yet'!

Two concepts, especially, dominate the Isaianic perceptions of Israel as the prophecies come to terms with the destruction, disappointments and internal conflicts which marred the period of more than two centuries since 'the year in which king Uzziah died' (Isa. 6.1). Both disaster and deliverance befell Judah and Jerusalem during those years which witnessed the dismemberment of the Northern Kingdom but, by contrast, Judah survived under its Davidic head for more than a century longer.

Prophecy was God's means of rescuing events from the category of being meaning*less* to becoming meaning*ful*. Against such a background, it can be seen why the images of 'remnant' and 'servant' provide the book of Isaiah with fundamental themes which recur several times, and which proved capable of being developed and applied in different ways as it became necessary to comprehend both disaster and deliverance within the divine scheme of things. They show how Judah, the Davidic dynasty, and the city of Jerusalem could function and maintain hope for the nation of Israel more broadly within the context of the disasters and humiliations suffered during this period. Through judgement, pain, suffering and national break-up neither the purpose nor the reality of God were denied, but they were inevitably subjected to new limitations and qualifications.

In turn these qualifications brought to birth new insights and possibilities which did not nullify the vision of Israel's final triumph but set it in a larger, and more rounded, perspective. It should not occasion surprise for us, therefore, that the book of Isaiah provides us with two of the most durable and meaningful concepts by which the entire belief in a community of God-called people can be upheld. These are precisely those images of 'remnant'[16] and 'servant'[17] which were to become central to the New Testament's reinterpretation of Israel as an *ekklesia*—a Church.

Without such qualifying metaphors the destructive triumphalism of election without suffering or service takes over, making the notion of spiritual power into an arrogant delusion. More than once in its history the Christian Church has proved as blind and deaf to the challenge of God's calling, as the prophet Isaiah saw to be true of his contemporaries! In this light, the book of Isaiah can be claimed to represent a 'Bible in miniature', since its central themes have subsequently provided two key Christian hermeneutical guidelines for the Bible when interpreted as a canonical whole.

Surprisingly, the theme of Israel's land and of the various territorial units into which Israel was broken up during the pain-ridden centuries in which the book of Isaiah came into existence figure only marginally in its contents, contrasting sharply with the near-contemporary development of the Deuteronomic literature. All too often in the prophecies of the book of Isaiah the geographical horizons and descriptions which appear are difficult to focus with any sharpness. At times it becomes impossible to ascertain even where the prophet is himself located, leaving open, for instance, the question of whether a common geographical setting is to be presupposed for the whole of 40–55 where 'Zion' is explicitly addressed, but where a virtual imprisonment in Babylon is openly referred to. Instead, we find that geographically vague, but theologically highly charged and meaningful, designations are employed extensively. They have left us with imagery which has made it possible to transpose the Isaianic poetry into wholly new Christian environments. Accordingly such terms as 'Zion', 'the coastlands', 'the ends of the earth', and even 'the nations' figure prominently. Israel's relationship to the LORD God is seen as established through worship and total spiritual loyalty, making the language of servanthood and remnant into primary terms through which the bond between God and the nation is given expression.

16. Cf. my essay 'A Remnant Chosen by Grace (Romans 11:5)', in D.A. Hagner and M.J. Harris (eds.), *Pauline Studies: Essays in Honour of F.F. Bruce on his 70th Birthday* (Exeter: Paternoster Press, 1980), pp. 280-300.

17. Cf. W.A.M. Beuken, 'The Main Theme of Trito-Isaiah "The Servants of YHWH"', *JSOT* 47 (1990), pp. 67-87.

2. *Prophecy as Metaphor*

One of the great gains of the recent recovery of the awareness that the book of Isaiah has been fashioned to create an intricately woven tapestry of carefully arranged themes and images, is that it re-emphasizes the need to understand it as a whole. However blurred some of its pictorial images are, it has been intended to present a theological and literary unity. This is not because it all has the same author, but because it all bears witness to the same God and to a belief that a whole sequence of events reveals a divine plan and purpose. Seen in such a light, the path is open to trace the development of certain basic themes within the book through their various stages of development.

In historical perspective we are well aware that from earliest times such a method of study has been employed by scribes and scholars, pursued simply by associating different occurrences of the same, or closely related, words, frequently with little real consideration whether any connection was ever intended or can properly be construed. There are, however, a significant number of key words, images and themes to be traced in the book of Isaiah which recur in such a fashion as to indicate that they were themselves intended to serve as signposts and markers within a complex process of prophetic imagery and compositional development. It is this fact that has made them key features in the book's structure and which makes them central to what can be called the book's message.

High on a list of such themes, the idea of Israel as a 'remnant' must be placed. This undoubtedly originated with the name Shear-jashub given to the oldest and first-mentioned of the prophet's children. Similarly, the metaphor of the 'briers and thorns' which ruin the vineyard of the LORD of Hosts (Isa. 5.6) provides a cover term for the various enemies and threats which emerged within Judah's history,[18] as does the portrayal of the 'blindness and deafness' of Israel which the prophet regarded as afflicting the majority of the people.[19]

18. Cf. Isa. 7.3-25; 27.4.

19. Cf. R. Rendtorff, 'Isaiah 6 in the Framework of the Composition of the Book', in *Canon and Theology*, pp. 170-80; R.E. Clements, 'Patterns in the Prophetic Canon: Healing the Blind and the Lame', in G.M. Tucker, D.L. Peterson, R.R. Wilson (eds.), *Canon, Theology and Old Testament Interpretation: Essays in Honor of Brevard S. Childs* (Philadelphia: Fortress Press, 1988), pp. 189-200.

The number of such themes can readily be added to, and attention has already been drawn to the fact that the metaphor of 'The Servant of the LORD' provides a further example of just such a central image which proved capable of being developed and applied in a variety of ways. For more than a century, attention to the actual literary contexts in which the theme appears has been a regrettable casualty of the scholarly frustration of trying to elucidate who the 'Servant of the LORD' might have been and what actually happened to him. By separating a mere four so-called 'Servant Songs' from the rest of Isaiah 40–55, and no less frustratingly from the rest of the book of Isaiah, it is not surprising that scholars have found themselves unable to provide a solution. Throughout the book the theme is used frequently but applied in a number of diverse ways in relation to changing events. In very similar fashion, the way in which the concept of the 'remnant' is used does not have one single, all-encompassing, application. It carries both judgemental as well as saving overtones.

Besides these terms, however, attention should also be given to the manner in which other powerful metaphors are used and re-used in the prophecies, enabling them to carry much of the meaning which must, in the very nature of prophetic language, remain enigmatic. Truths and imagery by which the meaning of an event is to be apprehended must often be mysterious, and even ambiguous, in exposing to a human audience the feelings and intentions of God. So imagery of the tree with its cycles of growth and decay provides a major cluster of metaphors to show how God deals with Israel and the nations. Similarly metaphors drawn from the familial relationships of parenthood, and especially motherhood, are employed in order to engage the attention of the reader in a direct and inescapable manner. They are transparent in the directness with which they convey a sense of the emotional burden latent in fundamental human relationships and, by implication, point to the high level of passion which must be construed as shaping the divine purpose. The reader is not left searching for a non-existent dictionary of theological concepts because the prophet's imagery lies freely exposed in the everyday world of persons and things. His metaphors become part of an argument which insists that if human beings feel like this then how much more must God experience such pain and passion.

3. *A Light to the Nations*

It is against this background of recognizing the extent to which several of the basic metaphors that are to be found in Isaiah reappear in distinctive literary and historical contexts that it is valuable to reconsider one of the most popular of them. This concerns the imagery of light as a metaphor of salvation and its use in a number of key texts within the collection. All told the noun 'light' (Heb. *'or*) occurs no less than twenty-two times in Isaiah, but we should probably add to these the four occurrences (Isa. 24.15; 31.9; 47.14; 50.11) of the closely related noun for 'brightness, fire' (Heb. *'ur*). It appears that at least some of these occurrences make a deliberate play on the similarity of sound with the noun for 'light', perhaps because fire was the simplest and most immediate way of bringing light out of darkness. In any event it must be noted that in Isa. 10.17 the fact that the metaphor of 'light', implying salvation, could also convey a sense of 'fire', bringing judgement, becomes a significant feature of the Isaianic imagery. Once again, ambiguity is deliberately employed, as in the metaphor of the 'remnant', in order to show that both judgement and salvation can be comprehended within a single series of events. The actions which bring salvation to some, imply judgement for others:

> The light of Israel will become a fire,
> and his Holy One a flame;
> and it will burn and devour
> his thorns and briers in one day
> (Isa. 10.17)

A very similar contrast is to be found in Isa. 50.10-11 where those who fear God, but who walk in darkness, are assured of security and salvation. The irony of the ambiguity is skillfully expressed in vv. 10-11:

> Who among you fears the LORD
> and obeys the voice of his servant.
> who walks in darkness
> and has no light,
> yet trusts in the name of the LORD
> and relies upon his God?
> But all of you are kindlers of fire,
> lighters of firebrands.
> Walk in the flame of your fire,
> and among the brands that you have kindled!

This is what you shall have from my hand:
you shall lie down in torment.
(Isa. 50.10-11)

Our primary intention in following the most prominent of the occurrences of the imagery of 'light' through the book of Isaiah is to note two points which appear to be of primary exegetical significance. The first of these is that it certainly appears to be the case that the imagery of light, which is so familiar a feature of life as to make it a readily available, and almost obvious, metaphor of salvation, provides an important counterpart to the imagery of blindness which occupies a central place in the Isaianic theology. The second point is that the association of light with fire makes it a convenient metaphor for elucidating what it means that Israel is to become 'a light to the nations'.

The first point, that light will serve to remove Israel's blindness, becomes particularly evident in the introduction of the theme as a metaphor of salvation in Isa. 9.2 (9.1 in the Hebrew):

The people who walked in darkness
have seen a great light;
those who lived in a land of deep darkness-
on them light has shined.
(Isa. 9.2 [Heb. 9.1])

From a structural point of view, the royal messianic oracle of 9.2-7 (Heb. 9.1-6) forms a conclusion to the unit, built around the three sign-names given to the prophet's children in 7.1–8.4, which began with the account of the prophet's call in 6.1-13. In this the fundamental theme of the 'blindness and deafness' of Israel is introduced and given a powerful reinforcement in 8.22 where no less than three nouns describe the intensity of the darkness that will afflict Israel. It transpires that this is not a physical darkness but rather the spiritual darkness which accompanies Israel's blindness. It is, then, of great importance to the Isaianic understanding of how salvation will come and how new light will arise for Israel. It will take the form of a new deliverer-king.

The actual, royal, messianic oracle of 9.2-7 is probably among the most contested passages of the entire corpus of prophecy, and I have discussed it extensively elsewhere.[20] It is sufficient to reiterate my

20. R.E. Clements, 'The Immanuel Prophecy of Isa. 7:10-17 and Its Messianic Interpretation', in E. Blum, C. Macholz, E.W. Stegemann (eds.), *Die Hebräische Bibel und ihre zweifache Nachgeschichte: Festschrift R. Rendtorff 65 Geburtstag,*

conclusion that it is an accession oracle for a new king, not directly foretelling the birth of a royal heir but rather of announcing the glory that will accompany the arrival of a new heir of the Davidic house to the throne of Israel. Within the structure of the book, it is evidently intended to point to the accession of Hezekiah in succession to Ahaz, with whose policies the prophet Isaiah had violently disagreed.

Within the larger setting of the book, the significance for the use of light imagery as a metaphor of salvation is its direct link to the royal, messianic claims of the Davidic dynasty. There seems little doubt that the reference in 10.17 to 'the light of Israel' which will become a flame to devour 'thorns and briers' intends an allusion back to 9.2 (Heb. 9.1), just as the thorns and briers allude back to 5.6. The passage, however, must probably be regarded as among the very latest to have been incorporated in Isaiah 1–12 along with the other material in 10.16-27 which throughout shows every indication of being a kind of commentary on various key metaphors taken from 6.1–9.6.[21]

The Deutero-Isaianic development of the metaphor of light is taken up in 42.6-7 where the conjunction of the imagery of light, darkness and blindness, strongly suggests that the earlier occurrence of these metaphors in Isaiah 6–9 is being openly alluded to:

> I am the LORD, I have called
> you in righteousness,
> I have taken you by the hand and kept you;
> I have given you as a covenant to the people,
> a light to the nations,
> to open the eyes that are blind,
> to bring out the prisoners from the dungeon,
> from the prison those who sit in darkness.
> (Isa. 42.6-7)

The close connection between the metaphor of light as a sign of salvation and the ending of the 'darkness' of Israel's spiritual blindness is then further elaborated in 42.16:

(Neukirchen: Neukirchener Verlag, 1990), pp. 225-40. Cf. also the extensive study of the importance of this prophetic oracle within the context of Isaiah 1–35 by P.D. Wegner, *An Examination of Kingship and Messianic Expectation in Isaiah 1–35* (New York: The Edwin Mellen Press, 1992).

21. O. Kaiser, *Isaiah 1–12: A Commentary* (OTL; trans. J. Bowden; Philadelphia: Westminster, 2nd edn, 1983), pp. 221-28; J. Vermeylen, *Du prophète Isaie à l'apocaplyptique* (EBib, 1; Paris: Gabalda, 1977), p. 442.

I will lead the blind
by a road they do not know,
by paths they have not known I will guide them,
I will turn the darkness before
them into light,
the rough places into level ground,
These things I will do,
and I will not forsake them.
(Isa. 42.16)

The further extensive development of the theme of Israel's blindness and deafness in 42.18-20 points yet again to the dependence on the earlier material of chs. 6–9 for an understanding of the word and idea-associations that are present.

It should not escape our attention that 42.1-4 provides the first of the so-called Servant Songs and that vv. 5-9 are taken, either as an original part of such a servant passage, or more plausibly as an intended commentary upon it. Moreover, it also deserves attention that the phrase 'a light to the nations' has proved to be one of the most memorable, if also one of the more controversial, features of the prophetic development in chs. 40–55 of the book. What exactly is meant by such a phrase? Does it mean, as most have taken it, that the gentile nations also will share in Israel's salvation, or merely that they will see the light as a sign that the time for Israel's deliverance has come?[22] The former meaning would certainly appear to be confirmed by the elaboration of the theme of 'a light to the nations' in 49.6:

He says,
'It is too light a thing that you
should be my servant
to raise up the tribes of Jacob
and to restore the survivors of Israel:
I will give you as a light to the nations,
that my salvation may reach to
the end of the earth.'
(Isa. 49.6)

The most striking development of the metaphor of light, and in its emphases most directly connected with the earlier occurrences of 9.2

22. Cf. the review of the various possibilities in D.W. van Winkle, 'The Relationship of the Nations to Yahweh and to Israel in Isaiah xl-lv', *VT* 35 (1985), pp. 446-58; G.I. Davies, 'The Destiny of the Nations in the Book of Isaiah', in Vermeylen (ed.), *The Book of Isaiah,* pp. 93-120.

(Heb. 9.1), 42.6 and 49.6, is then to be seen in Isa. 60.1-3. It would appear that this passage quite plainly assumes that the reader is familiar with the earlier assurances that light will dawn for Israel, marking a new era of deliverance. It should be noted, however, that the use of the same metaphor in 58.8 and 10 already anticipates the usage that is found in ch. 60. The prophecy is addressed to Jerusalem and the allusion back to the royal-messianic motifs of 9.2 is strongly evident:

> Arise shine; for your light has come,
> and the glory of the LORD has
> risen upon you.
> For darkness shall cover the earth,
> and thick darkness the peoples;
> but the LORD will arise upon you,
> and his glory will appear over you.
> Nations shall come to your light,
> and kings to the brightness of
> your dawn.
> (Isa. 60.1-3)

The closeness of the reference back to the darkness covering the earth taken from 8.22 is noteworthy and the importance of the imagery of light is then given a further poetic exposition in 60.19-20. What such light implies is then interpreted in practical terms in 60.21-22.

4. *Conclusion*

My argument has primarily sought to relate closely the three key passages in which the metaphor of light as a sign of salvation occurs in Isa. 9.2 (Heb. 9.1), 42.6 and 60.1-3. Other occurrences in the book are certainly relevant and related, but it is these key passages which are most directly concerned. It has been a consequence of the conventional division of the book of Isaiah into three separate collections of prophecies, each possessing its own context and character, that the close connections between all three passages have been largely ignored, or overlooked. The result has been that the ambiguities and uncertainties regarding what it means, in an Isaianic context, for the servant-Israel to be 'a light to the nations' is far from clear. It is also worthy of note that the close links with the royal-Zion motifs are also more fully brought out when all three passages are seen in conjunction with each other.

Seen in this broader context of the book of Isaiah as a formal and structural unity, certainly, the nations are expected to participate in

Israel's salvation, not simply as onlookers and spectators, but directly as those who will enjoy its benefits. Ancient motifs, in their origin closely tied to the mythological motif of the temple mount as a divine dwelling-place and of the royal dynasty of David as bringers of truth and righteousness, are then vividly expressed in Isa. 2.2-4. Mount Zion is the location from which truth, righteousness and justice will be dispensed among all nations. Those who come there will come willingly to seek knowledge of the ways of God (Isa. 2.3). Jerusalem is to be a city of light, as the late passage 30.19-26 further affirms.

It then becomes a wholly fitting rubric in 2.5, no doubt inserted by an enthusiastic scribe, to invite Israel to walk in the light of the knowledge of God, which is its treasure:

> O house of Jacob
> come, let us walk
> in the light of the LORD!
> (Isa. 2.5)

ISAIAH 15–16

Thomas G. Smothers

Virtually every aspect of the poem about Moab in Isaiah 15–16 remains in dispute. This is true whether one is dealing with text-critical matters, with questions of literary unity, with the problem of a possible historical setting, with its redactional history, or with its function within the ensemble of oracles concerning foreign nations in Isaiah 13–23. Since space limitations preclude a full treatment of each of these concerns, this study will offer the following: (1) a translation and notes which reflect the author's understanding of the poem, (2) a detailed study of Isa. 16.1, 3-5, and (3) a reflection on how the poem functions in its context.

The author is delighted to present this study to John D.W. Watts, master teacher and esteemed colleague, from whom he has learned so much about the book of Isaiah.

Translation

15.1 Burden of Moab:
Indeed, overnight it is devastated,
Ar Moab is silenced;
indeed, overnight it is devastated,
Kir Moab is silenced.

2 Dibon has gone up to the temple,
to the *bamoth* to weep,
about Nebo and Medeba Moab wails.
On every head is baldness,
every head is shorn,

3 in its streets they gird on sackcloth,
upon its rooftops and in its squares
everyone wails,
descends in weeping.

4 Heshbon and Elealeh cry out,
as far as Yahaz their voice is heard;
therefore, the loins of Moab tremble,
its very life quivers.

5 My heart cries out for Moab,
its refugees (flee) to Zoar, [to Eglath-shelisha];
indeed, at the ascent of Luhith they go up,
indeed, on the road to Horonaim
a cry of shattering they raise.

6 Indeed, the waters of Nimrim have become desolate;
indeed, the grass has withered,
the green grass has failed,
the verdure is no more.

7 Therefore, the remainder one had made
and their stores
over the Brook of Poplars they carried.

8 Indeed, the outcry goes around the area of Moab,
to Eglaim (is) its wailing,
to Beer-elim (is) its wailing.

9 Indeed, the waters of Dibon are full of blood.
[Indeed, I will put more on Dibon:
for the fugitive of Moab a lion,
for the remnant of the land a young lion].

16.1 ['Send lamb(s) to the ruler of the land,
from Sela across the desert
to the mountain of daughter Zion.'

2 [Like a fleeing bird,
like a scattered nest,
the daughters of Moab are at the fords of the Arnon].

3 'Give a plan,
render a decision,
make your shade like night at noon-time,
hide the expelled one,
do not reveal the fugitive.

4 Let the expelled ones of Moab sojourn with you;
be a hiding place for them from the destroyer.
When the oppression has ended,
devastation is at an end,
the trampler has completely gone from the land,

5 then a throne will be established in covenant fidelity,
and one will sit upon it in truth
in the tent of David there will be a ruler,
    one seeking justice,
    one prompt in righteousness.'

6 We have heard of the pride of Moab—
    exceedingly proud—
his pride, his arrogance, his insolence,
his idle talk is false.

7 Therefore, let Moab wail,
    let everyone wail for Moab,
for the raisin-cakes of Kir-hareseth
    they moan, utterly stricken.

8 Indeed, the tendrils of Heshbon (are destroyed),
    withered the vine of Sibmah,
    the lords of nations have struck its grapes;
unto Yahaz they reached,
they spread out to the desert,
its shoots branched out,
they crossed the sea.

9 Therefore, I weep with the weeping of Yazer,
    for the vine of Sibmah,
I drench you with my tears,
    O Heshbon and Elealeh.
For upon your fruit and your harvest
    the battle-shout has fallen.

10 Joy and gladness are taken away from the fruitful field,
in the vineyards one does not sing,
    one does not raise a shout;
the wine in the presses the treader does not tread,
    the harvest-shout I have ended.

11 Therefore, my insides moan like a lyre,
    my heart for Kir-heres.

12 [And it will be:
    when he appears
    when he wearies himself,
        Moab at the *bamah*,
    (when) he enters his sanctuary to pray
        he will not be successful.]

13 [This is the word which the Lord spoke to Moab in the past.

14 But now the Lord says:
In three years, like the years of a hireling, the glory of Moab
will be despised, along with the great multitude,
and the survivor(s) will be few and feeble].

Textual Notes

15.1 Point בְּלַיִל instead of construct בְּלֵיל; cf. 16.3. Render 'at night' or 'overnight.'

2 Dibon is taken as the subject of the sentence. The *waw* is pleonastic.[1]

4 Read חַלְצֵי 'loins of' with LXX. Strangely LXX has: 'the hip of the Moabites cries out'. In any case 'loins' parallels 'its life' and makes better sense than 'soldiers'. For יריעו read ירעו 'they tremble', understanding the same root as the following verb.

5 Eglath-shelisha is metrically superfluous. Its exact location remains uncertain. Its collocation here with other sites in south-western Moab provides a general location. Eglath-shelisha may be compared with the reference to Agaltain, the 'second Eglah', in one of the deeds from the Nahal Heber in the time of Bar Kochba. Two of the contracting parties, then resident in Ein-gedi, were originally from Luhith in the district of Agaltain.[2]

9 Dimon = Dibon. Read שחל to parallel אריה (haplography with the following שלחו).[3]

16.1 Retain MT שִׁלְחוּ (impv).

3 Read הבי (from יהב) and עשׂי to agree with the following impvs.

6 בדיו may mean 'diviners,' in light of Isa. 44.25 and Jer. 50.36.

7 Read הגו for תהגו (dittography).

8 Tentatively understand שדמות as 'tendrils' rather than 'fields' or 'terraces'. In *KTU* 1.23:8-9 *šdmt* parallels *gpn* as in Deut. 32.32 and Hab. 3.17. The sense of 'tendrils' does not fit the occurrence in 2 Kgs. 23.4.[4]

10 LXX understood, or had a text which had, הָשְׁבָּת 'is ended'.

1. M. Dahood, 'The Moabite Stone and Northwest Semitic Philology', in L.T. Geraty and L.G. Herr (eds.), *The Archaeology of Jordan and Other Studies* (Berrian Springs: Andrews University, 1986), pp. 437-38.

2. Y. Yadin, 'Expedition D', *IEJ* 12 (1962), pp. 249-51.

3. For the suggestion, see J. Reider, 'Contributions to the Scriptural Text', *HUCA* 24 (1952–53), p. 87.

4. See M.H. Pope, 'Mot', in *IDBSup*, p. 607.

Isaiah 15.1-9; 16.2, 6-12

Most traditional literary analysis has concluded that at least Isa. 15.1-8, 16.6-11 comprise the poem about Moab's calamity. Rather than being a prophecy or a taunt song of Moab's future devastation, the poem describes in the most vivid language an actual catastrophe. 15.1-4 focuses on cities which lay north of the Arnon, giving the impression that an invader came from the north. In that area the lament began, centering on Dibon where the population went up to the temple and to the *bamoth* to wail.[5] The cry of calamity was heard far and wide.

15.5-8 describes the flight of refugees toward the south as they carried their belongings across the border into the territory of Edom, while the outcry resounded throughout the land.

16.8-11 resumes the theme of 15.1-8 in other terms. Whereas 15.1-8 focuses on the loss of cities, the dislocation of the populace, and the loss of water and grass, 16.8-11 describes Moab's calamity in terms of the loss of its famed viticulture. 15.1-8 and 16.8-11 thus balance and complement each other.

Whether the poem was occasioned by a natural disaster or by an invader is in dispute. Jenkins thinks that any hint of military invasion is ambiguous. In his view, the catastrophe was probably due to loss of fertility (15.6; 16.8-10). The lamentation in 15.2-3 would reflect cultic practices intended to restore fertility, whose futility is underscored in 16.12. For Jenkins, the reason for Moab's plight was its reliance on false worship.[6] On the other hand, it is more likely that the poem reflects a military invasion which resulted in the destruction of cities and the accompanying end to the land's fertility. 16.8 as read above ('the lords of nations have struck its grapes') most likely refers to the invaders and their attack on the economy of Moab.[7]

A vexing question presented by the poem relates to the author's weeping over Moab's desolation (15.5; 16.9, 11). Hayes and Irvine believe

5. This understanding of 15.2 follows the interpretation of W.B. Barrick, 'The Bamoth of Moab', *MAARAV*, 7 (1991), pp. 79-81.

6. A.K. Jenkins, 'The Development of the Isaiah Tradition in Is 13–23', in J. Vermeylen (ed.), *The Book of Isaiah* (Leuven: Leuven University Press, 1989), pp. 241-42.

7. Wildberger reads in 16.8: 'the lords of the nations were overcome by their choice grapes', on the basis of Isa. 28.1; see H. Wildberger, *Jesaja*, 2 (BKAT, 10; Neukirchen–Vluyn: Neukirchener Verlag, 1978), pp. 589, 594.

that the weeping was ironic, a taunt over Moab's troubles.[8] Kaiser regards the weeping as a stylistic device to emphasize the severity of the blow.[9] Others prefer to see in the weeping a genuine sympathy for the Moabites. Wildberger is probably correct in understanding the author's sorrow in light of the fact that the severest blows came against cities and areas north of the Arnon where Israelites had traditionally dwelled.[10]

16.8-11 describes the destruction of a basic component of Moab's economy, wine production. The spreading of the vines and their shoots in all directions may point to political realities as well as the export of its product. The shout of battle (הידד) had fallen on Moab (16.9), putting an end to its vintage hurrah (הידד) (16.10). If השבתי in 16.10 is retained, then finally it is understood that Yahweh had brought about the calamity.

15.9bcd; 16.12 are editorial additions pointing to later events. 15.9b clearly points to an additional calamity for Moab. 16.12, which recalls 15.2, seems to point to the future as well. Whether these two verses are to be read as referring to a later application of the poem as a threat to Moab is difficult to say. 16.2 seems to be an editorial comment because it breaks the flow of 16.1, 3. Some have wanted to move it up to follow 15.9, but 15.9 suggests a definitive end for Moab.[11]

Isaiah 16.13-14

16.13-14 is an addition which contrasts 'then' and 'now'. These verses have the effect of saying that no matter that Moab underwent horrific devastation in the past and still managed to exist as a nation, within a very short time Moab would be so humiliated, and the population would be so diminished, that the nation might have no future. The poem itself is called 'the word which Yahweh spoke to Moab before' (16.13), indicating that Moab's calamity was Yahweh's doing. That a report of the fulfilment of Yahweh's intention in the past could be the basis for a new fulfilment in the future seems to be the intent of 16.13-14.[12]

8. J.H. Hayes and S.A. Irvine, *Isaiah the Eighth Century Prophet: His Times and His Preaching* (Nashville: Abingdon Press, 1987), p. 242.

9. O. Kaiser, *Isaiah 13–39: A Commentary* (trans. R.A. Wilson; Philadelphia: Westminster, 1974), p. 68.

10. Wildberger, *Jesaja II*, p. 628.

11. Wildberger, *Jesaja II*, p. 600.

12. Jenkins, 'The Development of the Isaiah Tradition in Is 13-23', p. 242.

Isaiah 16.1, 3-5, 6-7

The treatment of 16.1, 3-5 is crucial for an interpretation of Isaiah 15–16 as a whole. It is just as important for deciding how the poem functions in its larger context.

The difficulties in interpreting these verses are reflected in the ancient versions. The LXX understood the verses to be a Yahweh speech rather than a quotation of the Moabites. 16.1 in the LXX reads: 'I will send as it were reptiles on the land' (כרמש for כר משל). Moab was counselled to find a shelter from grief in its flight (16.3). The fugitives of Moab would sojourn with Judah and would be a shelter for Judah from the pursuer because Judah's alliance had been taken away. 16.5 seems to serve as an assurance of the restoration of the Davidic dynasty. While at times the LXX seems to reflect a text quite different from MT, the overall result of its treatment suggests confusion in the face of a difficult text.

The Targum provides a messianic interpretation of the verses. The text is expansionistic and, therefore, its interpretation is quite clear. Like the LXX, the Targum did not understand 16.1, 3-5 as a speech of the Moabites. They (the Moabites) would offer tribute to the Messiah of Israel (16.1). Not only would the Moabites be driven from their land (16.2), but, in the time leading up to the messianic age, the Moabites would be a refuge from the distresser (16.4). Then the throne of the Messiah would be established in the city of David; he would sit on it seeking justice and doing truth (16.5).

The Peshitta, like the LXX, took the verses to be a speech of Yahweh to Judah. The translation follows the MT closely except for 16.1-2: 'I will send the son (בר for כר) of the ruler of the land from the rock city of the wilderness to the mount of the daughter of Zion. And he will be like a bird which changes its nest, so the daughters of Moab will be deserted at the fords of the Arnon.' 16.3-5 seems to be Yahweh's words to Judah, and consequently 16.5 was understood as a promise to Judah to re-establish the Davidic throne in Jerusalem.

The Vulgate treated 16.1-5 messianically. In 16.1 the prophet asked the Lord to send the Lamb, ruler of earth, from the desert of the east to Zion, apparently on the pattern of Yahweh's advance from the desert of Edom in Judg. 5.4-5. In 16.3 the Lord is implored to provide protection for those who flee, while in 16.4 Moab is commanded to provide security for the fugitives, apparently Judeans. 16.5 points to the preparation of a throne in the tabernacle of David for one who would rule justly.

In view of these disparate interpretations in ancient times, it hardly comes as a surprise that more recent interpreters have taken such contradictory approaches.

Oswalt has the opinion that 16.1-4b are words which Isaiah put in a Moabite messenger's mouth, so that a Moabite gives voice to a messianic prophecy. 16.4b-5 are then a response to the request of the Moabites for help and asylum which offers a messianic prophecy as the fulfilment of the hope of both nations. Oswalt places these verses in the context of Isa. 2.2-4, so that Moab is seen as representative of the nations which would come to the mountain of the house of the Lord to learn Torah.[13] 16.6-7 would not be a response to Moab's plea for help in 16.1-4a, but rather a larger reflection on the folly of human pride.[14]

Kaiser thinks that 16.1, 3-4a, 6 could be pre-exilic, but no certainty can be claimed.[15] Originally 16.6 was a rejection of Moab's plea for help, but 16.4b-5, which Kaiser takes to be an eschatological insert, broke that connection. Since 16.4b-5 were eschatological, they reflected a future situation in Jerusalem when the city's siege would have been over and a Davidide would be sitting on the throne.[16] As such the eschatological passage would not be a response to Moab's plea; it would be of benefit to Judah only, and only then at some future date.[17] Kaiser's treatment posits, therefore, a redaction history of several stages which effectively severs any real connection of 16.1, 3-5 to the rest of the poem. In its final form the poem would have the effect of assuring Yahweh's elect that the divine promises were still in effect and that mocking nations would be made to realize this.[18]

Wildberger rejects the idea that 16.6-7 forms any kind of response to the Moabite plea for aid in 16.1, 3-4a. It is his opinion that 16.1, 3-5 is a relatively late, eschatological insertion and that it cannot be understood or interpreted in relationship to the rest of the poem about Moab's plight. 16.4b-5 must be seen as Jerusalem's response to Moab's request.[19]

13. J.N. Oswalt, *The Book of Isaiah, Chapters 1–39* (NICOT; Grand Rapids, Eerdmans, 1986), p. 343.

14. Oswalt, *The Book of Isaiah, Chapters 1–39*, p. 345.

15. Kaiser, *Isaiah 13–39*, p. 75.

16. Kaiser, *Isaiah 13–39*, p. 72.

17. Kaiser, *Isaiah 13–39*, p. 73.

18. Kaiser, *Isaiah 13–39*, p. 75.

19. Wildberger, *Jesaja II*, p. 601.

Wildberger is of the opinion that this section does not refer to any definite historical event. He points to the indeterminate expressions 'ruler of the land' and 'daughter Zion' for support. If the passage reflected an actual pre-exilic event, one would expect Moab to appeal to the king in Jerusalem, or if to an event after the fall of Jerusalem, to the authorities in Jerusalem. He suggests, therefore, that the author had in mind Isa. 2.2-4 when he wrote 16.1, 3-5, especially the response in 16.5. 16.4b-5 then constitutes Zion's answer to Moab's request for help, and the answer takes the form of a messianic prophecy of post-exilic times which parallels Isa. 2.2-4. The inbreak of the eschatological time of salvation would result not only in help for Moab but also for Jerusalem, which Wildberger understands to be in need also.[20]

In general, then, these dispositions to treat 16.5 messianically mean that the poem about Moab's catastrophe became simply a vehicle for a later messianic prophecy which included the nations, Moab, for example, within its purview. It is unclear how this approach to the interpretation of the poem in chs. 15–16 and its purported post-exilic inset, 16.1, 3-5, contributes to discovering how the poem as a whole functions within the larger context of the oracles concerning the nations in Isaiah 13–23.

In contrast to Kaiser and Wildberger, Rudolph argued that, with the exception of 15.9, 16.2, 12, 13-14, the poem is a literary unity. 15.1-8 is a mournful poem which presupposes actual facts. 15.1-4 deals with Moab's fate in the north, 15.5-8 with her fate in the south. 16.1 formally begins something new: a summons to petition Judah for help. But the summons presupposes the content of 15.1-8; indeed, 15.7 points to Edomite territory from which the embassy was sent (16.1). In Rudolph's opinion 16.3-5 gives the wording of the petition, to which 16.6 provides the negative response. Since the negative response presupposes that the report was untrue and undependable, 16.3-5 was spoken by the Moabites. Following the negative response there remained nothing for Moab to do but to continue mourning (16.7). 16.7-11 continues the wailing over the despoiled land, focusing on the destruction of viniculture, for which Moab was famous. In this way Rudolph argued for the poem's unity.[21]

With respect further to 16.1, 3-5, Rudolph took 16.1 as a Moabite self-summons to send lambs as tribute to the ruler in Judah from Edom

20. Wildberger, *Jesaja II*, pp. 619-24.

21. W. Rudolph, 'Jesaja XV–XVI', in D.W. Thomas and W.D. McHardy (eds.), *Hebrew and Semitic Studies presented to G.R. Driver* (Oxford: Oxford University Press, 1963), pp. 138-39.

where the refugees had fled. He took this as proof that Edom was at that time under Judean sovereignty. 16.3-5 is the request for help. Moab requests counsel and refuge, non-extradition, admission as 'sojourners', and vows that, when the land is free of the enemy, she will shelter under the rulership of the Davidic kingdom, will establish a throne in (vassal-) fidelity, its occupant a ruler who will seek justice and be an expert in righteousness. But in view of the response in 16.6, which emphasizes Moab's insufferable pride, Moab's vow in 16.4b-5 is taken as unacceptable and untrustworthy.[22]

Rudolph concluded that the poem is the oldest written prophecy in the Old Testament. It reflects the pre-exilic era (16.5—David's dynasty was ruling), a time when Edom was under Judean sovereignty, a time when Judah was not threatened and could supply help to Moab, a time when Moab's area extended well to the north of the Arnon. Rudolph argued that the reign of Jeroboam 2 provided the best setting for the poem since Jeroboam's campaign resulted in the incorporation of Moabite territory into his realm and since Uzziah ruled in Edom (2 Kgs 14.22).[23]

Eichrodt also argued for the unity of the poem, with the exception of 15.9, 16.2, 12. Despite the variety of verse-forms, he thought that 15.1-8, 16.6-11 formed two parallel sections, different only in content, which described Moab's calamity.[24] Belonging to the poem, but quite different in form and meter, was the middle section, 16.1, 3-6, which Eichrodt thought was the speech of the Moabites seeking a vassal relationship with Judah. He saw the gift of the lamb as a symbol of the willingness of Moab to become tributary.[25] He saw the statement in 16.5 as Moab's commitment to institute a government in Moab under the mandate of the Judean ruler which would carry out the will of the Judean king.[26]

Eichrodt rejected attempts to interpret 16.4b-5 as a messianic prophecy because the passage thereby would be isolated from its context. If 16.4b-5 was spoken by Moabites, it would be odd to have them speaking a messianic prophecy for Judah. If 16.4b-5 was spoken by Judah to Moab as a messianic prophecy, it would postpone any help for Moab to the far-distant future. Since 16.6 provides the opposite of

22. Rudolph, 'Jesaja XV–XVI', p. 140.

23. Rudolph, 'Jesaja XV–XVI', pp. 141-42.

24. W. Eichrodt, *Der Herr der Geschichte: Jesaja 13–23 und 28–39* (Die Botschaft des alten Testaments 17, II; Stuttgart: Calwer Verlag, 1967), pp. 42-43.

25. Eichrodt, *Der Herr der Geschichte*, p. 44.

26. Eichrodt, *Der Herr der Geschichte*, pp. 44-45.

comfort, one must either strike the messianic passage as a later addition or remove 16.6 as a later addition. For Eichrodt, the best solution was to affirm the basic unity of Isaiah 15–16, with 16.1, 3-5 sharing the same contemporary scene as the rest of the poem.[27]

Noteworthy in the treatments of 16.1, 3-5 by Rudolph and Eichrodt is their mention of a Moabite request for vassal status. Neither commentator, however, provided an analysis of the language of the verses to support their contention. The following remarks are offered to fill this gap.

In 16.1 the words שלחו כר 'send lambs' recall 2 Kgs 3.4. Mesha, king of Moab, was נקד for the house of Omri, furnishing to the king of Israel one hundred thousand lambs and the wool of one hundred thousand rams as tribute. It is unlikely that the Moabites in Isa. 16.1 were simply sending a gift of lambs to Jerusalem in order to win a favorable hearing for temporary protection for their exiles. Almost certainly they were seeking vassal status that characterized Mesha's early relationship with the house of Omri. MT has שִׁלְחוּ, imperative, and that is to be retained against the Targum, which reads: 'They will bring', and against BHS which proposes to read: 'they sent'. What is presented is a decision of state. In any case, sometimes שלח is employed in the forming of a treaty, as is seen in 2 Sam. 5.11 (1 Chron. 14.1) and Judg. 3.15. Of course, other verbs are used for the paying of tribute as well: נשׂא in 2 Sam. 8.2, 8; שוב in 2 Kgs. 3.4, 17.3; עלה in 2 Kgs.17.4; and נתן in 2 Chron. 28.21. Unless it can be shown that the sending of lambs was intended as payment for the upkeep of the Moabite sojourners (16.4), it seems best to understand the sending of the lambs as a willingness to become tributary to Judah.

The request to 'give counsel' (16.3) points in the direction of forming a pact with Judah. The word עצה, usually translated 'counsel', can also mean 'plan', as it often does in Isaiah (5.19; 14.24, 26; 19.3; 25.1). It means ' a plan of action,' a 'goal,' or a 'purpose'. In the account of the Levite and his murdered concubine, עצה figures prominently in the context of the Israelite covenant. The Levite sent a message to the Israelites to take action: 'Consider concerning her, form a plan (עֻצוּ) and speak' (Judg. 19.30). When Israel assembled, the Levite repeated his request: 'Give your word and counsel here'(הבו לכם דבר ועצה) (Judg. 20.7). The Levite's request was a call for the provisions of the Israelite alliance to be met. The עצה was not advice about how to proceed; rather, it was a plan to redress a breach in the covenant. The Moabite request for Zion

27. Eichrodt, *Der Herr der Geschichte*, p. 45.

to 'give עצה' seems to have been a request for protection within the bounds of a political alliance.

The clearest passage is Isa. 30.1-5. There לעשות עצה is paralleled by לנסך מסכה, 'make an alliance' (cf. LXX συνθηκας). The rebellious children have woe pronounced on them because they made an alliance with Egypt that was not Yahweh's עצה, and in doing so they were guilty of adding covenant violation to covenant violation. The Moabites in Isa. 16.3 were not asking for advice; they were asking for the protection which a vassal could expect from an overlord.

The term פלילה is difficult and must not be pressed, but its collocation with עצה suggests a meaning of 'judgement'. On the basis of 1 Sam. 2.25, it may not be too much to suggest that פלילה may carry the sense of 'intervention'.[28] If so, the Moabites thought Judah would be powerful enough to provide the benefits of an overlord.

The symbolism of 'shade' as protection is transparent. But more importantly, the providing of shade was an appropriate way to express rulership or overlordship. This is clear in Jotham's parable of the trees in Judg. 9.8-15. In Judg. 9.15a the bramble said: 'If in אמת (truth, fidelity) you are anointing me as king over you, come and take refuge in my shade.' In Ezek. 17.22-24 there is the promise that Israel, the sprig of cedar, would reign at last. Every bird would dwell in the shade of its branches (17.23). The following verse makes it clear that it is Yahweh's overlordship, however, which is the subject: 'all the trees of the field will know that I am the Lord'. Ezekiel 31 employs the same imagery of trees and shade to express Egypt's sovereignty among the nations. Ezek. 31.6c says: 'in its shade dwelled all the great nations'. But when Egypt was humbled, all the peoples of the earth descended from its shade and left it' (31.12). In the end even those nations which departed Egypt's shade were doomed to descend to Sheol with Egypt. Finally, in Isa. 30.1-5, the futility of Israel's departure from dependence on Yahweh and trusting in an alliance with Egypt is underscored. Those who 'take refuge in the shade of Egypt' (30.2) would find that the shade of Egypt would be the source of their humiliation (30.3). From this it follows that Moab was not just seeking a respite from calamity; rather, Moab was asking for vassalage which held the promise of real protection from the destroyer.

In Isa. 16.4b Moab requests that Judah become a סתר ('hiding place') for the refugees from the destroyer. It is instructive that in Isa. 28.15, 17,

28. E.A. Speiser, 'The Stem *PLL* in Hebrew', *JBL* 82 (1963), p. 304.

סתר is the hiding place which Jerusalem's rulers sought in their treaty with death. Judah's covenant infidelity is characterized as 'in falsehood we have found a hiding place' (28.15). שקר means not only falsehood but breach of treaty. In Isa. 16.3-4 Moab was not just requesting temporary haven for displaced persons. Rather, Moab was requesting protection which a faithful vassal could expect from an overlord.

Isa. 16.4cd must be read with 16.5. After the danger from the invader was past, a throne would be set up in חסד, and a ruler would sit on it in אמת. He would seek justice and be practiced in righteousness. It is not contested that such exalted language would fit a messianic ruler. But in context Isa. 16.5 would fit even better a Moabite promise to establish a rule in Moab under the aegis of Judah (the tent of David) which would not only be exemplary but would be wholly consistent with the demands which an overlord would impose on a vassal. Nelson Glueck demonstrated that חסד and אמת expressed relationship in a covenant, while at the same time having their place in everyday personal relationships where kindness and integrity are crucial.[29] Subsequent study of international treaties from the ancient Middle East has shown even more clearly that these terms characterized relationships within a juridical sphere. M. Weinfeld has shown that חסד is the equivalent of *damiqtum* in Akkadian treaties and that אמנה, אמונה, אמת, and מישרים correspond to Akkadian *kittu*. These Hebrew terms signify either a treaty itself (Dan. 11.6) or the kinds of faithful behavior which would keep a treaty in force.[30] Thus, Moab was not only requesting the benefits of a vassal treaty with Judah but was also promising to institute a reign in Moab which would adhere to the proposed treaty with Judah in all fidelity.

In summary, the position taken here is that Rudolph and Eichrodt were essentially correct. Isaiah 15–16, including 16.1, 3-5, form a unified poem and reflect an actual historical situation. Moab was devastated, especially the area north of the Arnon, by an invader from the north (15.1-4). The flight from the assault carried Moabite refugees toward the south, eventually to Edom (15.5-8). From there an embassy was sent to Jerusalem to seek the protection of vassal-status. Despite Moab's apparent willingness to become tributary, the proposal received a negative response due to the storied pride and arrogance of Moab (16.6). Moab

29. N. Glueck, *Hesed in the Bible* (trans. A. Gottschalk; Cincinnati: The Hebrew Union College Press, 1967).

30. M. Weinfeld, 'Covenant Terminology in the Ancient Near East and its Influence on the West', *JAOS* 93 (1973), pp. 191-92.

would have to suffer its woes alone (16.7). 16.8-11 replays 15.1-8 in other terms, with the emphasis on the devastation of viticulture.

15.9bcd, 16.12, and perhaps 16.2, represent a redactional stage which threatened Yahweh's action against Moab in a new situation. 16.13-14 clearly declare that, whatever past tragedy may have been visited on Moab, a new catastrophe awaited.

There follows, then, the question of a possible or likely historical setting which would accomodate this understanding of the poem. Kaiser has provided a helpful summary of attempts to discover a setting.[31] If one assumes, with Hayes and Irvine, that the poem reflects a possible Assyrian campaign against Moab in the last half of the eighth century,[32] one is left with the fact that no extant Assyrian text mentions it. If one follows Christensen in supposing that the poem reflects the victory over the coalition of Moab, Ammon, and the Meunites under Jehoshaphat as recorded in 2 Chron. 20.1-30,[33] then one is left to ponder how a defeat of the coalition on Judean soil corresponds to any of the events described in Isaiah 15–16. A setting in the time of Jeroboam 2 remains the most likely setting for the reasons given above by Rudolph.

Isaiah 15–16 in Context

All of the nations mentioned in Isaiah 13–23, including Israel and Judah, faced Yahweh's judgement. In general terms the foreign nations were due judgement chiefly because of their pride and arrogance (13.11; 14.12-14; 23.9), while Israel and Judah could expect judgement because of their foreign worship (17.10-11) and because they spurned Yahweh (22.12-14).

But it is possible to be more precise. An over-arching theme in the book of Isaiah is the theme of Yahweh's plan (עצה). The book portrays Yahweh as the sovereign of the universe who was carrying out a plan which impacted all the nations. When the plan of Yahweh and the plans of nations intersected, the prophet declared the victory of Yahweh's plan. In 8.9-10 the nations are cautioned that, although they have planned a plan, it will be turned aside.

31. Kaiser, *Isaiah 13–39*, pp. 61-62.

32. Hayes and Irvine, *Isaiah the Eighth Century Prophet*, pp. 238-40.

33. D.L. Christensen, *Transformations of the War Oracle in Old Testament Prophecy: Studies in the Oracles Against the Nations* (Missoula: Scholars Press, 1975), p. 141.

14.26-27 emphasizes that Yahweh's plan for the whole earth cannot be annulled. Assyria, the razor of Yahweh (7.20), the rod of Yahweh's wrath against Judah (10.5), would be broken in Yahweh's land (14.24-25) because Assyria had overstepped Yahweh's intention (10.7-14). Egypt's wise counsellors are taunted because of their inability to discern Yahweh's plan against Egypt since it sought to be the major power player in international politics (19.11-17). Tyre, a small kingdom with international clout and large intentions, received the news of Yahweh's plan to defile its pride (23.8-9). Damascus and Ephraim were subjects of judgement oracles because of their attempt to intervene in the political alignments of 734 BCE (17.1-6).

Judah's counter-plan consisted, in part, of attempting to achieve military security through alliances with foreign nations. In 30.1-5 Yahweh pronounced woe on Judah for carrying out a plan, in opposition to Yahweh's plan, which involved making an alliance with Egypt, a prime example of covenant infidelity. Again, Yahweh pronounced woe on Judah for trying to hide deep their plan from Yahweh (29.15). Yahweh's plan for Judah was that Judah would exhibit repentance and rest, quietness and trust (30.15-18). Judah's plan was to stake all on alliances with foreign nations.

Although the oracles concerning the foreign nations in Isaiah 13–23 announced judgement on the nations because of their prideful attempts to obstruct the realization of Yahweh's plan, without doubt these oracles were intended primarily for a Judean audience. How better to demonstrate to Judah the futility of trusting in foreign alliances than to highlight the vulnerability and helplessness of these nations? All plans of the nations, including Judah, would come to naught against the plan of Yahweh (7.7-9; 14.29-32; 18; 28.14; 30.1-5). The sign-act of Isaiah in ch. 20 regarding the coming defeat of Egypt underlined the hopelessness of placing reliance on foreign nations.

The plan of Yahweh and the hopeless counter-plans of all the nations characterize the literary context for the poem about Moab in Isaiah 15–16. The poem serves as a reminder from history that Judah could make the right choice because they had once done so. In order to encourage Judah not to neglect this lesson from history, the editorial comment in 16.13-14 announces that Moab faced another catastrophe that would again make it an undependable ally.

The Twelve: Methods

The literary similarities between Isaiah and the Twelve raise the possibility that their compositional histories and the reading strategies which they invite may be similar as well. Such questions prompted John Watts's efforts to organize the Book of the Twelve Consultation in the Society of Biblical Literature as well as his recent research on questions regarding the unity of the Book of the Twelve Prophets.

The three essays in this section address various aspects of that 'unity'. Russell Fuller examines the earliest manuscripts of the Twelve for signs of how the tradents understood the relationship between them. James Nogalski argues that several layers of redaction have intentionally tied the Twelve together. Ehud ben Zvi takes issue with Nogalski's conclusions, arguing instead that the Twelve lack any clear signs of being intended as a single book.

THE FORM AND FORMATION OF THE BOOK OF THE TWELVE: THE EVIDENCE FROM THE JUDEAN DESERT

Russell Fuller

The Greek and Hebrew Manuscripts

This article is a report of a project in progress. The project is an attempt to integrate all of the ancient manuscript data we now possess for the text and history of the collection known as the Twelve Minor Prophets. One of the goals of the project is to present a coherent account of the redactional and compositional history of *the completed collection* based on the manuscript evidence.

The project is not concerned simply with the textual criticism of the Hebrew text of the Twelve Minor Prophets, although the amount of evidence from the Judean Desert for the text of the Twelve is enormous. Nor is it exclusively concerned with the filiation of Hebrew and Greek manuscripts of the Twelve, although both tasks are a part of the overall project. Rather this paper is part of an attempt to integrate the data we now possess for the text and history of the collection known as the Twelve Minor Prophets in order to present a coherent account of the redactional and compositional history of *the completed collection*. I should immediately qualify that statement; I wish to trace the history of the collection as far back as the limits of our manuscript evidence allow.

I will first very briefly survey the manuscript evidence available in Hebrew and Greek and discuss the overall implications of this evidence in the area of the extent of the collection and the 'shape' of the collection. By 'shape' I mean the order of material within the collection and to a lesser extent also the division of material and formatting of material within the collection.

A listing of the available manuscript evidence, as far as I know it, is given in Table I. I will merely summarize.[1] For the Minor Prophets we have what might reasonably be called an 'embarrassment of riches'.

1. The list does not include the citations from CD, the Qumran fragments which

Hebrew Manuscripts

The ancient manuscript evidence in Hebrew ranges in date from approximately the middle of the second century BCE (4QXII[a & b]) to the second half of the first century CE (Mur 88). It includes seven scrolls from cave IV at Qumran which date for the most part from the Hasmonean period (ca. 150–30 BCE) and seem to have been complete scrolls of the Minor Prophets. The textual character of the scrolls varies. Some are closely aligned with the textual tradition which later culminates in the Masoretic Text (two of seven); some are closely aligned with the Hebrew *Vorlage* of the Septuagint (two of seven); and some are what Emanuel Tov and others have referred to as nonaligned texts in terms of textual affiliation (two of seven; one is too small to ascertain its textual character).[2] The percentage of the entire collection of the Twelve which is preserved in each manuscript varies tremendously from a low of one or two verses to substantial sections of entire compositions. The number of separate 'books' partially preserved also varies greatly among the seven manuscripts from cave four. The amount of material preserved can best be seen in Table II.

From caves one, four, and five at Qumran there are commentaries (*pesharim*) on some of the individual books of the Minor Prophets, but many of these are quite fragmentary, and they are of use primarily because they present additional evidence for the text of the passages cited and of the attitude of the Qumran community regarding the composition from which the citations are taken.[3]

There are also several compositions which for convenience we may call sectarian documents, which cite passages from the Twelve, some of which are listed in Table I; these include 4QCatena[a & b] and

are not yet published but are accessible through the microfiche publication of the photographs. L. Vegas Montaner (*Biblia del Mar Muerto: Profets Menores Edicion critica segun Manuscritos Hebreos procedentes del Mar Muerto* [Madrid: Instituto 'Arias Montano', 1980]) did present the citations in a section of his work on the Minor Prophets. He collated CD (S. Zeitlin, *The Zadokite Fragments* [Cambridge: Cambridge University Press, 1952]), 1QS, 1QSb, 1QM. Timothy Lim (unpublished list provide to me by E. Tov) did not collate the citations of the XII in CD, 1QS, 1QSb, 1QM, but he did collate 8HevXIIgr and Mur 88.

2. E. Tov, *Textual Criticism of the Hebrew Bible* (Minneapolis: Fortress, 1992).

3. There are *pesharim* on Micah, Habakkuk, Zephaniah, Hosea, Nahum, Amos, and perhaps Malachi.

4QFlorilegium (plus CD; 1QS; 1QM).[4] These compositions, which are also not biblical manuscripts, nevertheless provide additional information concerning the text of the passages which are cited, as well as the way in which the community perceived the compositions cited. The *pesharim* and the sectarian compositions are of secondary importance for the topic of this paper.

The Hebrew manuscript evidence also includes the Murabba'at Minor Prophets scroll which dates to the second half of the first century CE. It has been described as virtually identical to the Masoretic Text. In the terminology of E. Tov, which he uses in his recent book on the textual criticism of the Hebrew Bible, Mur 88 is a proto-Masoretic text.[5] In

4. See the reclassification of 4QCatena[a] and 4QFlorilegium as parts of one larger composition which A. Steudel has called 4QMidrash on Eschatology. See provisionally Annette Steudel, '4QMidrEschat: <<A Midrash on Eschatology>> (4Q174 + 4Q177)' in J. Trebolle Barrera and L. Vegas Montaner (eds.), *The Madrid Qumran Congress Proceedings of the International Congress on the Dead Sea Scrolls Madrid 18–21 March, 1991* (vol. 2; Leiden: Brill, 1992), pp. 531-41.

5. Mur 88 contains a number of variations from MT.

(a) א/ע confusion four times—Mur 88 always has א for MT's ע.

(b) *qere/ketib* five times

Mur 88 = *ketib* four times (three times when *yod* is missing)

Mur 88 = *qere* one time.

(c) Interlinear corrections/additions

of a word or a phrase—seven times

of a letter to a word—three times.

In only one case (Amos 7.13 עוד) does Mur 88 agree with LXX in deleting עוד against MT.

(d) Thirteen times Mur 88 is written plene with *waw* when MT lacks *waw*.

Six times Mur 88 is written defectiva when MT is written plene.

(e) Ten times Mur 88 is written plene with *yod* when MT lacks *yod*.

One time Mur 88 is written defectiva when MT is plene. Note that three times when Mur 88 lacks *yod* it agrees with the *ketib*.

As Milik states, it is unclear whether or not the interlinear corrections/variants were made in comparison to the archetype of Mur 88 or against another manuscript. What is also unclear on the basis of the microfiche, is whether the 'corrections' were made in the same hand or in another hand. It appears to me that the 'corrections' were made in another hand. It also seems clear that (1) the corrector's manuscript always agreed with MT (actually proto-MT); (2) the corrector felt free to add individual letters (esp. *waw* and *yod*) as well as words and phrases but did not correct the orthography of Mur 88 (fuller than MT) to agree with his source. He sometimes 'corrected' the spelling when it was not morphologically significant, but usually it was.

comparison to the sometimes strong variation from the Masoretic Text among the seven Minor Prophets scrolls from cave four at Qumran, Mur 88 shows relatively little variation from MT (only one time in agreement with LXX against the Masoretic Text). The largest differences in comparison to MT are omissions where the omitted word or phrase was added interlinearly. These additions or 'corrections' occur seven times and always correct the text of Mur 88 to agree with the reading of the consonantal text of MT. This correction of the text of Mur 88 may be indicative of the process of standardization of the consonantal text.

There is a gap of nearly eight hundred years between Mur 88 and the next manuscript of the Twelve, the Cairo Codex. The Cairo Codex is a Masoretic manuscript of the Ben Asher family.[6] It includes vowels, accents, and Masora. The Aleppo Codex is only slightly younger (925 CE).

Greek Manuscripts

The Greek manuscript evidence is much less extensive but very important for our understanding of the history of the Greek translation of the Twelve as well as the relationship between the Greek and the Hebrew textual traditions. There are two manuscripts which predate Origen's Hexapla (finished ca. 240–245 CE): (1) the manuscript of the twelve discovered in the Nahal Hever (R) and (2) the Washington papyrus. 8HevXIIgr (R)[7] was identified by Barthelemy, the original editor, with

Regarding the classification of Mur 88 as proto-Masoretic, I can compare it to the texts from cave four and classify it in comparison to those (that is compare the degree of variation from MT). 4QXII[a] is a non-aligned manuscript. The statistics are: 4QXII[a] = LXX≠MT seven times; 4QXII[a] = MT≠LXX four times; 4QXII[a] is independent eleven times. 4QXII[c] = LXX≠MT seven times (three times in errors); 4QXII[c] = MT≠LXX four times (one time in an error); 4QXII[c] is relatively close to the Vorlage of LXX. 4QXII[e] = LXX≠MT six times (four times in errors); 4QXII[e] = MT≠LXX four times (one time in an error); 4QXII[e] is very close to the Vorlage of LXX.

6. Tov, *Textual Criticism*, p. 47.

7. See now the editio princeps of E. Tov, *The Greek Minor Prophets Scroll from Nahal Hever (8HevXIIgr)* (DJD, 8; Oxford: Oxford University Press, 1990) and the preliminary publication of D. Barthélemy, *Les devanciers d'Aquila* (VTSup, 10; Leiden: Brill, 1963). 8HevXIIgr (R) is dated to the latter part of the Hellenistic period or the early Roman period; ca. 100–50 BCE (according to P. Parsons in Tov, *Greek Minor Prophets Scroll*, pp. 25-26). Note that the order of 'books' in this Greek MS is the same as the MT. This manuscript is identified with Kaige/Theodotion by Barthelemy. Tov groups R, in terms of agreements, with Sym, Aq, Th, Quinta, Washington, and the text of the Minor Prophets cited by Justin Martyr. O'Connell, following Barth, states that Aq used R as the basis for his recension of LXX ca. 130 CE.

Kaige/Theodotion. As Barthelemy and Tov have shown, R is a *recension* of the LXX, that is, a conscious revision of the LXX to agree with a Hebrew text which was not quite identical with the consonantal text of MT, but differed from it in only small ways.[8] As Tov noted in his recent edition, R agrees especially with Symmachus, Aquila, the so-called 'Theodotion', the so-called Quinta, as well as with W and the biblical text cited by Justin (ca. 130 CE).

The existence of R shows that a Greek speaking Jewish community of the first half of the first century BCE (ca. 100–50 BCE) felt a need to bring the older Greek translation (LXX) into conformity with a Hebrew text of the Twelve. It is evident that for that particular community, a Hebrew text was superior to or perhaps more authoritative than an older(?) Greek translation.[9] Although R was found in Palestine, the provenance of this manuscript or that of its Hebrew *Vorlage* is not known.

There is a gap of approximately three centuries between R and the next oldest Greek manuscript of the Twelve. The Washington papyrus comes from the mid to late third century CE and is important in that it is also pre-Hexaplaric.[10] From the fourth century CE we have the Codex Vaticanus and the Codex Sinaiticus. From the fifth century CE the Codex Alexandrinus, and from the sixth century CE the Codex Marchalianus. (These codices may exhibit some degree of influence from the revised Septuagint text of Origen.)

Symmachus (end of 2nd century CE, during the reign of Commodus 180–192) may have used R and Aq(?). Did Origen (184–254) have access to R for his Hexapla (finished ca. 240–245)? Both Origen and Eusebius mention that Origen consulted (and used?) a sixth Greek version of Psalms which came from a cave near Jericho (Eusebius, *EH* 6.16.1).

What was available to second century Theodotion and third century Lucian (d. 312) remains to be seen or established.

8. E. Tov, *Greek Minor Prophets Scroll*, pp. 145-53.

9. D. Barthélemy; E. Tov. We do not know the age or the provenance of the Hebrew text which served as the basis for this revision of the LXX. It is curious that those who produced this revision of the LXX anticipated not just the activity of Origen almost three centuries later, but that they may also share his assumption that the LXX needed to be revised, not the Hebrew text. Origen clearly thought that the Hebrew text had not changed; did these people share that assumption as well? Cf. F.M. Cross, 'Problems of Method In the Textual Criticism of the Hebrew Bible', in W.D. O'Flaherty (ed.), *The Critical Study of Sacred Texts* (Berkeley: Graduate Theological Union, 1979), p. 31.

10. J. Ziegler, *Septuaginta*. XIII. *Duodecim prophetae* (Göttingen: Vandenhoeck & Ruprecht, 1967; 3rd. rev. edn, 1984), p. 33.

In both the Hebrew tradition and the Greek tradition, there exist chronological gaps. In the Hebrew tradition, we have no manuscript evidence between Mur 88, approximately 100 CE until the Cairo Codex (896 CE), nearly eight hundred years (even if we include here the medieval copies of CD which contain thirty-eight citations of the Twelve). The gap in manuscript evidence for the Greek textual tradition is smaller, running from approximately 50 BCE, the Nahal Hever manuscript, to the third century CE, the Washington papyrus, a gap of only perhaps three hundred and fifty years.

Some Implications of the Evidence

1. *The Extent and Order of Compositions in the Collection*

a. *Hebrew.* At about 150 BCE, the oldest manuscript evidence seems to confirm that the collection of the Twelve is complete (4QXII[a & b]). This we knew indirectly from Ben Sirah/Sirach 49.10 (ca. 190 BCE) dating to approximately forty years earlier than these manuscripts. The 'books' attested from the Minor Prophets Scrolls from cave four at Qumran, as distinct from *pesharim* and other compositions, include all of the Twelve, although none of the scrolls which originally contained the entire collection preserves fragments of more than nine of the books (XII[g]) and usually fewer than that. The following table lists the transitions between 'books' which are preserved or reconstructed (rec.) in the Hebrew and Greek manuscripts.

MS	*Material Preserved*	*Transition(s)*
XII[a]	Zech., Mal., Jonah	Mal.–Jonah (?)
XII[b]	Zeph., Haggai	Zeph.–Hag.
XII[c]	Hos., Joel, Amos, Zeph., Mal.(?)	Joel–Amos(?)
XII[d]	Hos.	
XII[e]	Haggai, Zeph.	
XII[f]	Jonah	
XII[g]	Hos., Amos, Obad., Jon., Mic., Nah., Hab., Zeph., Zech.	Amos–Obad.
Mur 88	Joel, Amos, Obad., Jon., Mic., Nah., Hab., Zeph., Hag., Zech.	Jon.–Mic. (col. 2) Mic.–Nah. (col. 16) Hab.–Zeph. (col. 19) Zeph.–Hag. (col. 21) Hag.–Zech. (col. 23)

MS	*Material preserved*	*Transition(s)*
8HevXIIgr	Jon., Mic., Nah., Hab., Zeph., Zech.	Jon.–Mic. (rec./col. 4)[11] Nah.–Hab. (rec./col. 16) Hab.–Zeph. (rec./col. 20) Hag.–Zech. (rec./col. 28)

Codex Vaticanus (4th CE)	*MT*
1. Hosea	1. Hosea
2. Amos	2. Joel
3. Micah	3. Amos
4. Joel	4. Obadiah
5. Obadiah	5. Jonah
6. Jonah	6. Micah
7. Nahum	7. Nahum
8. Habakkuk	8. Habakkuk
9. Zephaniah	9. Zephaniah
10. Haggai	10. Haggai
11. Zechariah	11. Zechariah
12. Malachi	12. Malachi[12]

In the cave four scrolls two certain transitions between 'books' are preserved; Zephaniah–Haggai in XII[b] (ca. 150 BCE) and Amos–Obadiah in XII[g] (ca. 50–25 BCE). In addition, XII[a] (ca. 150 BCE) may preserve the unique transition/order Malachi–Jonah. Finally, XII[c] (ca. 75 BCE) may preserve the transition Joel–Amos. The text is quite damaged, so it is impossible to be certain. Aside from the uncertain order attested in XII[a], the order of the 'books' in these Hebrew Minor Prophets scrolls from the first and second centuries BCE seems to conform to the order which later became standard in the Masoretic tradition.

Variation between the order of the twelve in the Greek textual tradition versus the Hebrew textual tradition exists only in the first six books and then only in positions two through six. The order attested in XII[g] (Amos–Obadiah) and perhaps also in XII[c] (Joel–Amos) supports the antiquity (beginning of the first century BCE) of this order of the first six 'books' of the Twelve which later becomes standard in the Masoretic tradition. Likewise the order in 'books' seven through twelve (Nahum–Malachi) is confirmed by the order attested in 4QXII[b] Zephaniah–Haggai (ca. 150 BCE).

11. The transition reconstructed in col. 4 is based on a physical join.

12. LXX[LC] seem to agree with MT in the order of the books·

Additional evidence for the order of the books as they are later found in the Masoretic tradition surprisingly comes from the early Greek manuscript from the Nahal Hever, 8HevXIIgr (R) ca. 100 BCE–50 BCE. Although the first four 'books' of the Twelve are missing (as is Malachi), Jonah and Micah apparently came in positions five and six as they do in the Masoretic tradition. The Nahal Hever scroll, uniquely among Greek manuscripts of the Twelve, follows what was apparently already the (dominant?) Hebrew order. Given the possible evidence of 4QXII^{c} (Joel–Amos) ca. 75 BCE and the evidence of R (Jonah–Micah) ca. 100–50 BCE, it is clear that the order of the first six 'books' of the Twelve which later became standard in the Masoretic tradition is at least as ancient as the end of the second century BCE to the beginning of the first century BCE.

b. *Greek.* The Nahal Hever scroll of the Twelve which provides this evidence for the antiquity of the Hebrew order of the 'books' in the collection is also the oldest manuscript in Greek of the Twelve. R does not provide evidence for the Greek order of the 'books' of the Twelve at this time unless we assume that it, that is the Greek order, was identical to the Hebrew order. The earliest manuscript evidence for the Greek order of the first six 'books' of the Twelve (Hosea, Amos, Micah, Joel, Obadiah, Jonah, which is attested also in Codex Vaticanus) is found in the Washington Papyrus of the mid to late third century CE. That order is also attested in most of the other Greek manuscripts.[13]

2. *Paragraphing/Division of Material within the Collection*

J. Oesch has prepared the groundwork for our discussion in his thorough study of Mur 88 and 8HevXIIgr(R).[14] It seems to be the case that the division of the Hebrew text into sense units in Mur 88 agrees closely with the division of the text in Masoretic manuscripts, especially the Cairo Codex (90% for Petuchot; 70% for Setumot) and also the Aleppo Codex (75%). In Mur 88 the scribe also consistently marked the division between compositions (or books) by leaving three lines uninscribed if the

13. An exception is Codex Basiliano-Venetus (N+V) which shows the order: Hosea, Amos, Joel, Obadiah, Jonah, Micah. The dominant order is also possibly found in the Old Latin manuscripts as well, in other words, La^{s} (9th century CE) and La^{c} (5th century CE).

14. *Petucha und Setuma* (Freiburg: Universitätsverlag; Göttingen: Vandenhoeck & Ruprecht, 1979), pp. 284-89, esp. pp. 288-89.

transition occurred on the same column but leaving five lines blank at the top of a column if the preceding book ended at the end of a column. The smaller divisions in the midst of a book (running text) are marked in different ways.[15] The agreement with the system of division and placement of division of later Masoretic manuscripts is very strong and clearly supports the classification of Mur 88 as a proto-Masoretic text.

Oesch also investigated 8HevXIIgr (R) and concluded that it too stood close to Masoretic manuscripts in its system of division. A more precise description of that system is now available following the publication of the *editio princeps* by Tov, who states that R distinguishes between open and closed sections as does the Masoretic Text.[16] (Open: remainder of line blank after last word; Closed: a given number of spaces left blank between sections.) According to the data he presents, R agrees in open divisions with codex L in six out of six occurrences. R agrees with codex L in closed sections one time definitely, four times reconstructed, and a closed section in R agrees with an open section in codex L five times (three definite/two reconstructed). Indeed the scribes of R also indicated verse divisions and made frequent use of the *paragraphos* sign.

4QXII$^{a\text{-}g}$: First it is important to realize that all seven of these manuscripts are quite fragmentary, much more so than either Mur 88 or 8HevXIIgr. This means that our conclusions must remain tentative. In addition, it is not apparent that any of these seven manuscripts make a distinction between open and closed sections as is the case in codex L.

Beginning with the oldest manuscripts, 4QXII^{a} and 4QXII^{b}, both dating to approximately 150 BCE, 4QXII^{a} agrees with codex L one time in a closed section (Mal. 2.16) and two times has blank spaces where codex L does not. (One time codex L has nothing, one time codex L has a closed section several verses earlier.) 4QXII^{b} does not show any divisions in sections of Zephaniah and Haggai which are preserved where codex L has three or four closed sections. 4QXII^{b} does preserve the transition between books on the same column, and this scribe left one line completely blank and began the first line of Haggai at the

15. Oesch, *Petucha und Setuma*, pp. 285-86: (1) Empty line: when the preceding line is more than half full. Very frequent (32 times). (2) Free line end: usually more than half the line (10 times). The following section begins at the beginning of the next line. (3) The Blank Line: (eight times) Usually 6–9 letter spaces in length, the preceding line is 'more or less filled'. (4) The Large Space: (five times) It is usually 6–9 letter spaces in length, which Oesch compares to MT's *setumot*.

16. *Greek Minor Prophets Scroll*, p. 10, table 12.

beginning of the next line, in contrast to the practice attested in Mur 88.

4QXII^{c} dates from approximately 75 BCE, and so it is roughly contemporary with 8HevXIIgr (R). It agrees two times with codex L in closed sections, four times it has divisions of part of a line where codex L has no division, and four times it leaves lines blank in the middle of books where codex L has no division. 4QXII^{e} (ca. 75–50 BCE) agrees with codex L one time in a closed section and has a division where codex L has no division one time. 4QXII^{f}, from approximately 50 BCE, shows no divisions in material where codex L also shows no divisions. Finally 4QXII^{g}, from approximately 50–25 BCE, agrees with codex L one time in an open section, five times in closed sections, and has divisions which do not correspond to divisions in codex L six times. In addition, 4QXII^{g} leaves one line blank between books where the transition occurs in the midst of a column in agreement with the practice attested in 4QXII^{b}.

It appears, from this brief survey of the early manuscripts, that there were a variety of systems in use between the middle of the second century BCE until the middle of the first century CE for indicating sense units in Hebrew manuscripts of the Twelve. Mur 88, the youngest manuscript, is clearly very close to the system which comes to be standard in later Masoretic manuscripts. In contrast, the Hebrew manuscripts from the earlier period may be said to show marked disagreement from this later system. It may be said that while in the passages preserved these manuscripts preserve divisions which do not appear in codex L, codex L generally has far more divisions than do these seven Hebrew manuscripts. Both 8HevXIIgr and Mur 88 are far closer to codex L and other Masoretic manuscripts than are 4QXII^{a-g}. This variation from the system of division into sense units later found in Masoretic manuscripts may be taken to indicate that the system in use in the Masoretic tradition, although in existence (that is, 8HevXIIgr) at an early date was perhaps only one of many 'systems'. It was certainly not standardized until after the time of Mur 88, perhaps in conjunction with the standardization of the consonantal text.

Summary

(1) Hebrew and Greek manuscript evidence for the Minor Prophets exists dating from the second century BCE to the end of the first century CE.
(2) This evidence includes seven Hebrew manuscripts from Qumran, Cave 4, all of which predate the turn of the era.

(3) The manuscript evidence allows us to trace variations in the Hebrew and Greek texts of the Minor Prophets as well as the order of the material in the collection and the division into sense units.
(4) The order of the compositions or books, with one exception, conforms to the order later found in the Masoretic tradition. The one exception, 4QXII^{a} (ca. 150 BCE) may preserve the unusual order Malachi–Jonah.[17]
(5) The manuscript evidence seems to indicate that: (a) The system of division of material used in the Masoretic tradition is closely paralleled as early as the first half of the first century BCE (R). (b) The Hebrew manuscripts from Qumran show variation from the system used in the Masoretic tradition. Although the evidence is fragmentary, in general, fewer divisions are indicated. (c) Mur 88 from the second half of the first century CE conforms closely to the Masoretic system. This may indicate standardization of the consonantal text and its 'shape'.

Reflections: On 'Canon' And the Status of the Twelve at Qumran

Summary of Observations

1. The fact that in cave four seven scrolls of the Twelve were found indicates a great deal of interest in this material on the part of the community.

2. Commentaries on several books of the Twelve also indicate both a clear interest as well as the status of this material. It is considered the word of Yahweh revealed to his servants the prophets.

3. Citations of several of the books of the twelve in sectarian documents, especially the Damascus Document, further strengthen this impression.

4. Based especially on point three, it is incontrovertible that the community at Qumran considered the Twelve, certainly a collection of reasonably great age, to be the word of Yahweh revealed to the prophets.

17. See the recent book by B.A. Jones, *The Formation of the Book of the Twelve: A Study in Text and Canon* (Atlanta, GA: Scholars Press, 1995). Unfortunately I received this work too late to fully incorporate Jones's research into this paper. He argues that this unusual order attested only in 4QXII^{a} (Malachi-Jonah) reflects the 'original' or earliest placement of the Book of Jonah in the collection of the Twelve Minor Prophets and is important evidence in the ongoing discussion of the development of this collection of material and its canonization. Jones is the first scholar to attempt to incorporate manuscript discoveries from the Judean wilderness in a discussion of redactional issues.

They also worked with the conscious assumption that the words of the prophets contained the secrets of Yahweh's plan for the end of days and that they had received the proper interpretive 'key' to understand these words through their 'Teacher of Righteousness' and later interpreters within the community.

5. Canon, however, is a term which does not have an equivalent at Qumran. It was first used much later in Christian circles. Nor do we find the Pharisaic/Rabbinic concept of holy books 'defiling the hands'. What we do find, as mentioned previously, is an awareness that this collection of compositions, which we call the Book of the Twelve, contains the revealed word of Yahweh. This particular attitude toward these writings may be as close as the Qumran community came to later views within Judaism and Christianity which also regarded this material as sacred.

At Qumran we can definitely say that the community viewed the Book of the Twelve as did other Jews and later Christians, but there is a difference. By the end of the first century CE, probably before the revolt of Bar Kokhba, the form and shape of the text of the Hebrew Bible seems to have been standardized so that the entire Jewish community used a text which was identical in terms of its content as well as its text. The text could not be changed. At Qumran also it seems that the text of the Prophets was not changed in the course of interpretation. However, this does not seem to have been the case with the text of the Torah of Moses, as is clearly shown both by the Temple Scroll and by the soon-to-appear Pentateuchal Paraphrases which have been edited by S. White and E. Tov. The Torah could be expanded and rewritten. And it is not simply a matter of adding commentary to the text: in the Temple Scroll new material is added and the speaker is not Moses but God speaking in the first person. This attitude toward the Torah, which is exemplified by the Temple Scroll and the Pentateuchal Paraphrases, stands in contrast both to many carefully prepared manuscripts of pentateuchal books as well as to texts of the prophets where this free attitude does not seem to be found. However, there is an additional factor which must be emphasized: this community used variant forms of the same texts alongside each other. The most obvious example is the Book of Jeremiah where Hebrew manuscripts corresponding to the shorter text of the Septuagint were found as well as texts corresponding to the longer form of Jeremiah found in Masoretic manuscripts. Both forms of the text were apparently used, at least that is the logical assumption since both were found in the community's collection. What does this have to do with the question of canonicity? Simply that in dealing with the Biblical material from Qumran we are in a stage before the standardization of the text. This standard text is part of the idea of 'canon' in Christianity and in Judaism. It was evidently not part of the concept of what constituted a sacred text at Qumran. In addition, if citation of a composition as an authority is indicative of canonical status, and several scholars have suggested that this is the case, then at Qumran there was a larger collection of writings which had authoritative status than we find later in Judaism and Christianity, as shown by CD and 1QS, to take only two examples.

The concepts contained in the expressions 'canon' and 'canonical' have equivalents at Qumran, but these concepts also differ strongly from those which were held later in Judaism and Christianity.

Table I

A Listing of the Manuscript Evidence in Hebrew and Greek in Relative Chronological Order

A. Hebrew	**B. Greek**
1. 4QXII^{a} & 4QXII^{b} (4Q76-77) both ca. 150 BCE	
2. 4QXII^{c} (4Q78) ca. 75 BCE	
3. 4QXII^{e} (4Q80) ca. 75–50 BCE	1. 8HevXIIgr (=kaige/Theodotion) ca. 50 BCE
4. 4QXII^{f} (4Q81) ca. 50 BCE	
5. 4QXII^{g} (4Q82) ca. 50–25 BCE	
(6. *Pesharim*, etc. of various dates)	
(a. 1QpMic [1Q14])	
(b. 1QpHab)	
(c. 1QpZeph [1Q15])	
(d. 4QCatena^{a} [4Q177] ancient Herodian)	
(e. 4QCatena^{b} [4Q182] ancient Herodian)	
(f. 4QpHos^{a} [4Q166] Herodian)	
(g. 4QpHos^{b} [4Q167] Herodian)	
(h. 4QpMic [4Q168] Herodian)	
(i. 4QpNah [4Q169] Hasmonean-Herodian)	
(j. 4QpZeph [4Q170] ancient Herodian)	
(k. 4QpIsa^{c} [?])	
(l. 4QFlor [4Q174] ancient Herodian)	
(m. 5QAmos [5Q4])	
(n. 5QpMal. [5Q10])	
7. Mur 88 ca. 50–100 CE	

A. Hebrew	B. Greek
	2. Washington Papyrus 3rd century CE
	3. Codex Vaticanus 4th century CE
	4. Codex Sinaiticus 4th century CE
	5. Codex Alexandrinus 5th century CE
	6. Codex Marchalianus 6th century CE
	7. Codex Venetus 8th century CE
8. Cairo Codex of the Prophets 896 CE	
9. Aleppo Codex 925 CE	

Table II

Passages Preserved in Hebrew and Greek Minor Prophets Manuscripts

4QXII[a]:

Mal. 2.10-14
2.15–3.4
3.5-14
3.15-24

Jon. 1.1-8
1.9–2.1
2.7
3.2

4QXII[b]:

Zeph. 1.1-2
2.13-15
3.19-20

Hag. 1.1-2
2.2b-4

4QXII[c]:

Hos. 2.13-15
3.2-4
4.1–5.1
13.4-8
13.15–14.6

Joel 1.10–2.1
2.8-10
2.10-23
4.6-21

Amos 2.11–3.7
3.8–4.2
6.13–7.16
Zeph. 2.15–3.2
Mal. 3.6-7?

4QXII[d]:

Hos. 1.6-9
2.1-5

4QXII[e]:

Hag. 2.20-21
Zech. 1.4-6
1.9-10, 13-14

Zech. 2.10-14
3.4–4.4
5.8–6.5

Zech. 8.3-4
8.6-7
12.7-12

4QXII^{f}:

Jon. 1.6-8
1.10-16

4QXII^{g}:

Hos. 2.1-2
2.5
2.15-17
2.18-19(?)
4.1
4.13-14
6.3
7.13-16
7.16–8.1
9.9-13
9.14
10.3b-8a
10.8c-9
10.10-14
11.3-5
11.8-11
13.6-8(?)
14.4(?)

Amos 1.3-5
1.11-13
4.5-9
5.11-18
6.1–7.6(?)
7.7-12
7.16–8.3
8.11c-13a
8.14b
9.14–

Obad. 5
9-11
14-15

Jon. 1.1-5
1.5-?
2.3–3.3
4.5-11

Mic. 1.7
1.12-14

Mic. 2.3-4
3.12–4.1
5.6-7
7.2-3

Nah. 1.7-9
2.10-11
3.17

Zeph. 3.3-5

Zech. 10.12–11.2

Mur 88:

Joel 2.20, 26-27
3.1-5

Amos 1.5-15
2.1
6.1(?)
7.3-17
8.3-7, 11-14
9.1-15

Obad. 1-21

Jon. 1.1-16
2.1-11
3.1-10
4.1-11

Mic. 1.1-16
2.1-13
3.1-12
4.1-14
5.1, 5-14
6.1-7, 11-16
7.1-20

Nah. 1.1-14
2.1-14
3.1-19

Hab. 1.3-13, 15
2.2-3, 5-11,
18-20
3.1-19

Zeph. 1.1, 1-18
2.1-15
3.1-6, 8-20

Hag. 1.1, 12-15
2.1-8, 10,
12-23

Zech. 1.1-4

8HevXIIgr:

Jon.	1.14-16	**Nah.**	1.13-14	**Zech.**	1.1-4, 12-14
	2.1-7		2.5-10, 13-14		2.2-4, 7-9,
	3.2-5, 7-10		3.3, 6-17		11-12, 16-17*
	4.1-2, 5	**Hab.**	1.5-11, 14-17		3.1-2, 4-7
Mic.	1.1-8		2.1-8a, 13-20		8.19-21, 23
	2.7-8		3.9-15		9.1-5
	3.5-6	**Zeph.**	1.1-6a, 13-18		
	4.3-10		2.9-10		
	5.1-6(7)		3.6-7		

* LXX 1.19-21; 2.3-5, 7-8, 12-13.

INTERTEXTUALITY AND THE TWELVE

James D. Nogalski

Ancient traditions irrefutably establish that the writings of the twelve prophets were copied onto a single scroll and counted as a single book from at least 200 BCE.[1] Naturally, one presumes that someone intended these twelve writings to be read together. Unfortunately, the conventions for reading this entity called the Twelve were not transmitted with the writings themselves. In order to speak meaningfully of 'unity' with respect to the Book of the Twelve, one must first establish that the texts of the Twelve relate to one another. Second, one must begin to evaluate what the intertextual relationships offer as clues for reading the Twelve as a 'united' piece of literature.

The term 'intertextuality', particularly in English language discussions, can mean many things. Here, 'intertextuality' means the interrelationship between two or more texts which *evidence suggests* (1) was deliberately established by ancient authors/editors or (2) was presupposed by those authors/editors.[2] Such delimitation intentionally avoids the question

1. For more thorough treatments of the ancient traditions reflecting the Twelve as a corpus, see J.D. Nogalski, *Literary Precursors to the Book of the Twelve* (BZAW, 217; Berlin: de Gruyter, 1993), pp. 2-3, and especially B.A. Jones, *The Formation of the Book of the Twelve* (Atlanta: Scholars Press, 1995), pp. 1-13, and R.E. Fuller, 'The Form and Formation of the Book of the Twelve: The Evidence from the Judean Desert' in this volume.

2. For a thorough discussion and illustration of the variety of approaches dealing with intertextuality and related topics, see D.N. Fewell, *Reading Between Texts: Intertextuality and the Hebrew Bible* (Literary Currents in Biblical Interpretation; Louisville: Westminster/John Knox, 1992), especially pp. 11-39. The primary distinction between definitions of intertextuality is the source of the intertextuality. One end of a rather long spectrum can be represented by Derrida, Kristeva, Barthes, and others, whose understanding of intertextuality orients itself more toward a 'modern reader'. At the other end of the spectrum, those like Fishbane opt for an approach tied more concretely to Old Testament texts and the deliberate use of earlier traditions.

of readings which are oriented toward the modern reader. Such reader-oriented intertextual studies are avoided not because they have nothing to offer but because this study reflects my own ongoing attempt to try to understand the foundational stimuli behind the compilation of the Book of the Twelve. To do so, one must *attempt* to recapture the intentions of those responsible for the development of the Book of the Twelve. Of course, any attempt to rediscover the development enters the realm of the hypothetical and contains its own risks. Safeguards should be established to avoid idiosyncratic re-creations which do not exhibit some reasonable likelihood of having actually occurred.

However, even by limiting intertextuality to intentional and/or cognizant interrelationships, not every instance of intertextuality contributes equally to the question of understanding the conventions of reading the Book of the Twelve. For this reason, this investigation will focus on two aspects simultaneously: (1) illustrations of types of intertextuality in the Book of the Twelve which suggest some implications for reading the Twelve, and (2) reflections about a methodology of working with intertextuality. For reasons of ongoing research, I have chosen to illustrate these types of intertextuality using Joel as the primary, though not exclusive, focal text.

Recognition of types of intertextuality adds significantly to one's ability to reconstruct reading strategies intended by those who developed the Book of the Twelve; however, it complicates one's understanding of the unity of the Book of the Twelve considerably. The Book of the Twelve exhibits at least five different types of intertextuality: quotations, allusions, catchwords, motifs, and framing devices. Some of these devices overlap with one another, and in a very real sense some are more objective than others. Nevertheless, each type of intertextuality offers an evaluatable perspective for the reading of the Twelve as a corpus.

1. *Quotations*

The use of a pre-existing *phrase, sentence, or paragraph* which is taken from another source constitutes a quotation.[3] Several factors complicate the recognition of quotations. First, Old Testament writers rarely footnote

3. In practical terms, one should not label the use of a single word as a quotation. Instead, one should more accurately treat the use of a single word as an allusion or a catchword, both of which will be discussed below.

the source of their quotations.[4] Second, modern exegetes often work with a narrow focus on a book or a passage within a book and thus do not evaluate the possibility that one text quotes another. Recognition of quotations often depends upon painstaking concordance work or the use of secondary literature. Third, quotations may come from sources no longer at our disposal.[5] Finally, a quotation may not be easily recognized because the words are not identical, a fact which requires further explanation.

An author may 'quote' another text inexactly. An author may work from memory and simply record a slightly different version of the text, or an author may also deliberately alter the quotation to fit the context or to make a different point. One should attempt to make a decision regarding these alternatives since the presupposition of an intentional change or an oversight can directly impact how one interprets the function of the quotation. A few examples will illuminate the use of quotations of various lengths in the Book of the Twelve.

Obadiah 1-5 extensively quotes Jer. 49.14-16 and 49.9, but the texts are not precise duplicates. The imprecise nature of the quotation naturally creates questions: Which is the source text and which is the receiving text, or is there is an unknown source text from which both Obadiah and Jeremiah 49 draw?[6] A perspective on the Book of the Twelve as a literary work sheds considerable light on these questions. Previously, I have documented in detail how the differences in the parallel texts allow some relatively specific conclusions.[7] Space does not permit replication of those details, but the conclusions can be summarized. The vast majority of the differences between Obad. 1-5 and Jer. 49.9, 14-16 can be plausibly explained as adaptations to the context of the Book of the Twelve. Obad. 1-5 shows a remarkable tendency to imitate the structural

4. See M. Fishbane, *Biblical Interpretation in Ancient Israel* (Oxford: Clarendon Press, 1985), pp. 530-43.

5. For this reason, one must necessarily limit the study of quotations to those whose source can be documented with some degree of certainty.

6. Compare discussions in the following: H.-W. Wolff, *Obadiah and Jonah: A Commentary* (trans. M. Kohl; Minneapolis: Augsburg, 1986), pp. 38-40; J. Wehrle, *Prophetie und Textanalyse der Komposition Obadja 1–21. Interpretiert auf der Basis textlinguistischer und semiotischer Konzeptionen* (Arbeiten zu Text und Sprache im Alten Testament, 28; St. Ottilien: EOS, 1987), pp. 12-15; D. Stuart, *Hosea–Jonah* (WBC, 31; Waco: Word Books, 1987), pp. 414-16.

7. See J.D. Nogalski, *Redactional Processes in the Book of the Twelve* (BZAW, 218; Berlin: de Gruyter, 1993), pp. 61-68.

components of Amos 9.1-15 by modifying the quotation from Jeremiah. However, the similarities do not end with the quotation of Jer. 49.9, 14-16 since virtually the entire book of Obadiah exhibits the same structural elements as Amos 9.[8] How does one explain these structural similarities?

The first step toward explaining the similarities requires one to eliminate the possibility that the similarities are unintentional. In this case, the evidence that the quotation from Jer. 49.9, 14-16 was adapted offers significant evidence that the changes were made deliberately.

Given the deliberate changes, one must ask: why would someone go to the trouble of structuring Obadiah similarly to Amos 9, and, just as importantly, why would these two writings appear sequentially in the Book of the Twelve? Again, thorough investigation of these questions is not the purpose of this discussion, but one can make a strong case that the compiler of the anti-Edom sayings of Obadiah wanted to communicate the conviction that the same fate which befell the Northern Kingdom would befall Judah's 'brother' to the south. Context (Amos 9.2b and Obad. 4b; cf. also Amos 9.12; Obad. 18) supports this suggestion in addition to the structural arguments. The implications of this intertextual relationship for understanding Obadiah are not insignificant. Obadiah studies often treat this booklet as just another foreign prophecy. It is not. Edom receives special treatment because it should have been an ally.

The length of the Obadiah quotation is unusual. Direct citations typically appear as considerably smaller units. For example, scholars have long recognized Joel 4.16 as a quotation of Amos 1.2, and there is no reason to doubt this consensus. Rarely, however, do scholars ask why Joel 4.16 cites Amos 1.2. Several possibilities could explain the citation. For methodological reasons, one should always attempt to eliminate (1) accidental occurrence. In this instance, significant rationale all but preclude this possibility.[9] Given the great probability that Joel 4.16 quotes Amos (and not the other way around), one should consider two

8. Nogalski, *Redactional Processes*, pp. 61-74 (esp. pp. 71-72).

9. For several reasons, one can reject the notion that the phrase in Joel merely reflects a common saying rather than a quotation. First, the saying is not that common. Second, the quotation is rather precise. Third, literary observations indicate a significant probability that the compiler of Joel 4 combined several short preexisting pieces by quotations and allusions to other parts of Joel and the Twelve (see S. Bergler, *Joel als Schriftinterpret* [Beiträge zur Erforschung des Alten Testaments und des antiken Judentums, 16; Frankfurt: Peter Lang, 1988]). Fourth, Joel 4.16 is not the only quotation of Amos in the context (cf. Joel 4.18 and Amos 9.13)

additional possibilities.[10] (2) Joel quotes Amos but the citation functions apart from the literary horizon of the Twelve. (3) Joel deliberately anticipates Amos as part of the Book of the Twelve.

Making a decision between the second and third possible explanations requires a broader perspective than just the immediate context. To summarize: the compositional technique for Joel indicates a tendency to unite preexisting text units by quotations and allusions.[11] These intertextual linking devices manifest two primary literary foci—the book of Joel and the Book of the Twelve. One must draw careful distinctions, however, between Joel's use of other writings (especially in the Twelve) and citations/allusions to Joel in other parts of the Twelve.[12] Joel demonstrates considerable awareness of the adjacent writings (Hosea and Amos), and, to a lesser degree, an awareness of other writings as well.[13] This tendency suggests that Joel's direct quotation of Amos 1.2 likely intends some type of linking function for the Book of the Twelve.

Two avenues present themselves when considering the rationale for Joel's citation of Amos 1.2. These possibilities need not be mutually exclusive and both must be evaluated. First, authorial intention may derive from the content of the actual quotation, or second, as with the Obadiah text above, the significant clue may be gleaned from the divergence in the quotation. For the first possibility, the quotation manifests a significant theological concept: 'Yahweh roars from Zion, and from Jerusalem he utters his voice.' The Jerusalem orientation of this pronouncement marks a substantive theological perspective: Jerusalem is

10. Virtual consensus about the respective dates of the two texts eliminates the possibility that Amos quotes Joel. Scholars almost universally date Joel 4 later than Amos 9.11-15. See full discussion in Wolff, *Joel and Amos* (Hermeneia; Philadelphia: Fortress Press, 1977), p. 81; L.C. Allen, *The Books of Joel, Obadiah, Jonah and Micah* (NICOT; Grand Rapids: Eerdmans, 1976), p. 120.

11. See Bergler, *Joel*, especially pp. 153-80, 295-326, 338-39.

12. In the case of the former, see discussions below regarding catchwords and allusions to Joel inserted into other literary contexts which refer back to Joel, especially with regard to the locust imagery designating the conquering nations motif and the motif of agricultural bounty to refer to the restoration of Israel's relationship to Yahweh.

13. This awareness is not limited to the Twelve. Joel apparently draws from the Pentateuch (Bergler, *Joel*, pp. 247-94), other prophetic writings (E. Bosshard, 'Beobachtungen zum Zwölfprophetenbuch', *BN* 40 [1987], pp. 30-62, esp. 31-32, 37-42), and from the Twelve (for example, Joel 2.2 cites Zeph. 1.15).

the place from which Yahweh acts. Joel 4.16 could thus be strengthening the Jerusalem orientation of the Twelve, particularly since the books on either side of Joel (Hosea and Amos) focus on the fate of the Northern kingdom. Joel 1–4 focuses on Jerusalem, but 'anticipating' Amos by quoting one of the less numerous Jerusalem texts in Amos encourages the reader of the Twelve not to forget to read Amos in light of Joel. One would then expect to find other touchstones between the two writings which would assist this process (for example, compare the eschatological judgement against the nations in Joel 4 with Amos 1–2; or the locust imagery of Joel 1 with Amos 4.9).

For the second possibility, it is necessary to evaluate how Joel modifies the quotation. Here one enters a less objective realm. Nevertheless, a few remarks provide a starting point for interpreting the quotation.

Amos 1.2	*Joel 4.16*
ויאמר יהוה מציון ישאג ומירושלם יתן קולו ואבלו נאות הרעים ויבש ראש הכרמל	ויהוה מציון ישאג ומירושלם יתן קולו ורעשו שמים וארץ ויהוה מחסה לעמו ומעוז לבני ישראל:

The first line of the verse contains virtually an exact quotation.[14] However, the next lines of Joel 4.16 depart significantly from Amos 1.2. The second line of Amos 1.2 depicts the results of Yahweh's roar of judgement as the withering of the top of Carmel, a reference to the Northern Kingdom. By contrast, the second line of Joel 4.16 broadens the effect to include the trembling of 'heaven and earth' rather than the Northern Kingdom. In addition, the third line introduces a very different outcome. 'Yahweh will be a refuge for his people, and a stronghold for the sons of Israel.'

Joel's adaptation thus broadens Amos 1.2 into a universal theophanic portrayal of judgement, the purpose of which is to encourage Yahweh's people. This adaptation fits well with the overall purpose of Joel 4, which describes a universal judgement scene where Yahweh acts on behalf of Jerusalem and Judah (cf. Joel 4.1, 9-17, 20); however, it also subtly reinterprets Amos in the process, if one is reading the Twelve in canonical succession. Because Joel precedes Amos, the sensitive reader of the Twelve will filter Amos 1.2 through Joel 4.16. In so doing, lines two and

14. Amos 1.2 structures the text as a statement from Amos (the "he" in ויאמר refers back to Amos in 1.1), while Joel's quotation receives no special introduction. Nevertheless, Joel does modify the text by adding the *waw* before Yahweh.

three of Joel 4.16 acquire more significance because they illustrate larger thematic developments which Joel introduces and which continue to 'play out' in the Twelve. Specifically, the themes of universal eschatological (apocalyptic?) judgement of the nations (line two) and Yahweh as refuge for his people (line three) recur relatively frequently in the Twelve.[15] Given Joel's tendency for thoughtful intertextual nuances, it seems quite plausible to suggest that Joel deliberately frames the oracles against the nations in Amos 1–2 as part of Yahweh's ongoing actions on behalf of his people. Simultaneously, the explanation of the identity of Yahweh's people for whom Yahweh will be a refuge develops rather more subtly across the Twelve.[16]

2. *Allusions*

Without doubt, defining a term as diversely used as allusion creates more difficulty, and involves more subjectivity, than defining a quotation.[17] Those difficulties aside, most commentators recognize the use of

15. While space does not permit full exploration, note that the Twelve treats the theme of universal judgement in various ways. Some of these variations derive from the particular prophetic book (for example, the Day of Yahweh in Zephaniah) while others may be part of motifs deliberately implanted by a redactor working with more than one writing. Note, for example, that the root רעשׁ occurs ten times in the Twelve (Joel 2.10; 4.16; Amos 1.1; 9.1; Nah. 1.5; 3.2; Hag. 2.6, 7, 21; Zech. 14.5), either in the context of Yahweh's judgement or the earthquake in the time of Uzziah (Amos 1.1; Zech. 14.5).

16. The identity of Yahweh's people shifts as one reads the Twelve. One can detect a decided tendency to broaden the understanding beyond a political orientation. The Northern Kingdom is destroyed for its lack of faithful response to Yahweh (Hosea/Amos), leaving only a remnant. Judah experiences a similar judgement (Zephaniah). In the Twelve, Yahweh's people periodically face significant points which call for a decision (for example, Hos. 14; Joel 1–2; Hag. 1.2-4; Zech. 1.2-6), and which increasingly imply an awareness that only some inside (Mic. 4.6-7; Zeph. 3.18-20; Zech. 8.3-12) and outside (Zech. 8.21-23) Judah will be delivered. By the end of the Twelve, Malachi leaves the reader with the impression that the people in Judah still have not understood the message that Yahweh requires faithful obedience (cf. Mal. 1.6-9), so that Yahweh will distinguish between the righteous and the wicked (Mal. 3.16-18)—a remnant based upon one's attitude toward Yahweh, not one's political pedigree.

17. Allusions deserve treatment separately, but in many respects the general term is used for several techniques of referring to another text, particularly catchwords and motifs.

allusions as a significant compositional technique.[18] An allusion consists of one or more words whose appearance intends to elicit the reader's recollection of another text (or texts) *for a specific purpose*. In practice, various types of allusions appear with some frequency in exegetical treatments, but exegetes should approach each of these with care to evaluate the likelihood of intentionality and/or cognizance by the author/redactor. In some respects, allusions are more readily discussed by techniques (catchword, motif, etc.), but all of these techniques share some common aspects which can apply to all types of allusions.

When working with allusions, caution dictates that one perform several subjectivity cross-checks. First, one must carefully distinguish between allusions and formulas. Formulas, especially introductory and concluding formulas, play an essential role in understanding a text, but unless they appear in conjunction with other criteria, they may or may not constitute an allusion.[19]

Second, what evidence suggests that the suspected words/ideas do not simply represent random recurrence? Addressing this question necessitates careful evaluation of at least five factors: word frequency, word pairings, motif development, literary homogeneity, and specific text combinations. The *frequency* of the word(s) involved in the alleged allusion affects the degree to which one can expect to convince others that an allusion is present. For example, arguing that the verb בוא alludes to another text is not a strong argument because that verb is simply too common in too many texts to make a convincing argument. Evidence of

18. For example, note the following discussions about recognizing dependence upon other texts and/or traditions: H. Utzschneider, *Künder oder Schreiber: Eine These zum Problem der »Schriftprophetie« auf Grund von Maleachi 1,6-2,9* (Beitrage zur Erforschung des Alten Testaments und des Antiken Judentums, 19; Frankfurt: Peter Lang, 1989), esp. pp. 17-22, 42-44; Fishbane, *Biblical Interpretation*, pp. 283-91; O.H. Steck, *Bereitete Heimkehr: Jesaja 35 als redaktionelle Brücke zwischen dem Ersten und dem Zweiten Jesaja* (Stuttgart: Verlag Katholisches Bibelwerk, 1985), especially pp.13-29; H. Donner, '"Forscht in der Schrift Jahwes und lest!": Ein Beitrag zum Verständnis der israelitischen Prophetie', *ZTK* 87 (1990), pp. 285-98, especially p. 288; T. Willi, *Die Chronik als Auslegung: Untersuchungen zur literarischen Gestaltung der historischen Überlieferung Israels* (Göttingen: Vandenhoeck & Ruprecht, 1972).

19. For example, the formulas ביום ההוא and נאם יהוה by themselves do not constitute allusions, but in Amos 9.11-15, these formulas appear as part of a series of structural imitations of Amos 8, thus implying a deliberate attempt to call that text to mind. See detailed treatment in Nogalski, *Literary Precursors*, pp. 117-18.

typically recurring *word pairings* also decreases the likelihood of a deliberate allusion if no other criteria exist. For example, the presence of the antonyms 'light' and 'darkness' in two texts does not offer very strong evidence that one text alludes to another. By contrast, one cannot simply assume that an author could not allude to another text(s) using only uncommon words, and thus one should, even in the case of common words or word pairs, evaluate the extent to which other criteria might be present. For example, if one finds that a common word pair appears regularly in a specific writing, and actually helps to develop a *continuing motif* (see discussion of motifs below), then the likelihood that the word pair alludes to another text(s) increases substantially, even though the burden of proof will still fall to the one arguing for the presence of an allusion.[20] One should evaluate the text's *literary homogeneity*. Does literary critical analysis indicate significant reasons for suggesting the word is part of a unit which was edited for the book (for example, a literary introduction, conclusion, or a redactional gloss)? Finally, concordance studies could indicate that several words (common and/or uncommon) recur in two *specific texts* so that one suspects that the two texts were somehow related in the mind of the writer.[21]

Within the Twelve, one can illustrate allusions whose literary horizon focuses on another part of the same writing (internal allusions) and allusions which anticipate or reach back to another text (external allusions). Illustrating internal allusions is not difficult. For example, Wolff has presented a strong case that the end of the book of Joel (4.18-20) specifically alludes to texts in the first two chapters (using catchwords and themes).[22] This allusion deliberately reverses the situation of need

20. See for example, P.D. Miscall, 'Isaiah: New Heavens, New Earth, New Book', in *Reading Between Texts*, p. 49. Miscall argues that the significance of 'light' in Isaiah 1–66 (used in a variety of meanings) and Gen. 1.1–2.4a provides a touchstone between the two texts. Note that Miscall does not attempt to argue for deliberate allusions between these two texts, opting instead to explore a 'poetic reading' without arguing for 'a particular historical priority' (p. 47). However, if one wishes to bring allusions into the discussion of the development of a corpus, one cannot avoid the question of priority.

21. For example, see Utzschneider, *Künder oder Schreiber*, pp. 50-53, who argues that Mal. 1.8b-11 alludes to Genesis 32–33, as well as other intertextual relationships. See also Nogalski, *Literary Precursors*, pp. 155-58, for the argument that Mic. 7.8-20 alludes to Isaiah 9–12 and that this intertextuality supplies some of the missing logic necessary to follow Mic. 7.8-20.

22. Wolff, *Joel and Amos*, p. 83.

in Joel 1–2, creating a potent promise of abundance.[23]

External allusions are more complicated but equally important for discovering meaningful reading strategies and for speculating about the formative development of the Book of the Twelve. As with internal allusions, external allusions employ catchwords, motifs, and aggregate associations as the primary techniques to 'reference' another text(s). Two recurring allusions to Joel, locust imagery and the motif of agricultural bounty, are mentioned here as illustrations. These will be explored more fully below in the respective sections related to catchwords and motifs. The Twelve periodically alludes to locusts as invading armies. These locust allusions constitute one hallmark of what I have elsewhere labeled the Joel-related layer. They appear at significant junctures in the Twelve, and often appear to have been inserted into existing units.[24] Similarly, allusions to coming agricultural bounty, or the lack thereof, recur with regularity in the Twelve using language which one readily recognizes from Joel.[25] One can document these allusions and speculate about their role in the literary intentions of the Twelve, but they also illustrate that the term allusion actually encompasses several techniques, some of the most significant of which now require discussion.[26]

23. Hence the עסיס (juice) which is cut off (1.5) will drip from the mountains (4.20), and the אפיקים which are dried up (1.20) will flow with water (4.18).

24. The locusts first appear in Joel 1.4, where the reader learns of their associations with invading armies (Joel 1.7). Catchwords continue this association for the reader of the Twelve. Amos 4.9 contains several words 'reminiscent' of Joel. Amos 4.9 likely predated Joel, and may even have influenced Joel's compilation. Nahum 3.16b contains an inserted redactional gloss (Nogalski, *Redactional Processes*, pp. 125-26) which, using catchwords, associates Assyria as one of the series of locusts mentioned in Joel 1.4, who will now pass from the scene. Hab. 1.9 alludes to the locust-like characteristics of Babylon, drawing upon the motif without using specific catchwords. Mal. 3.11 also draws upon the locust motif in a manner recalling Joel 1–2 (Nogalski, *Redactional Processes*, pp. 204-206).

25. Following the decimation of the land mentioned in Joel, the Twelve keeps the promise of agricultural bounty alive by quotations (Amos 9.13 cites Joel 4.18, see Nogalski, *Literary Precursors*, pp. 117-19), redactional glosses (Hag. 2.19aß; Zech. 8.12, see Nogalski, *Literary Precursors*, pp. 228-29, 263-65), and thematic development (Obad. 5, see Nogalski, *Redactional Processes*, pp. 66-67).

26. The allusions to locusts and to agricultural bounty illustrate the variety of techniques utilized to allude to texts, but by no means should one presume these two elements constitute the only allusions which transcend the writings of the Twelve. For example, note the essay in this volume by M. Odell, 'The Prophets and the End

3. *Catchwords*

Old Testament studies have long recognized catchwords as a device utilized by those who 'arranged' various transmission units, especially when collecting wisdom sayings, legal sayings, psalms, and prophetic logia. Catchwords played a significant role in the arrangement of developing collections during both oral and written stages of transmission. More recently, however, the discipline has recognized that, in some texts, catchwords also play a significant role in a text's internal logic.[27] Thus, catchwords function as a type of allusion by using/reusing significant words to refer to another text(s). Intertextual work in the Twelve must recognize that catchwords play a significant role in the literary logic of the Twelve as both an ordering principle and a logical principle in light of significant evidence that catchwords recur consistently across neighboring writings and that many of these catchwords have been deliberately (redactionally) implanted into existing texts to highlight these connections. In addition, catchwords also reach across non-adjacent writings in the Twelve, thereby serving as potential guides to any reading strategy.[28]

As with allusions, key questions must be resolved, as far as possible, regarding the likelihood that the catchwords were intentionally created for the sophisticated reader of these texts (see subjectivity cross-checks under allusions). Having established the plausibility and/or likelihood that someone deliberately created these links, one then turns to the most significant (and perhaps the most difficult) question: WHY? The answer to this question will vary from text to text but requires careful evaluation. A specific, though certainly not isolated, example will serve to

of Hosea', which traces the view of the prophet as it develops from Hosea. The Twelve also offers several perspectives on the Day of Yahweh which must be evaluated for their relationship to one another, as well as for their potential for understanding the development of the Twelve.

27. See Nogalski, 'The Redactional Shaping of Nahum 1 for the Book of the Twelve', in P.R. Davies and D.J.A. Clines (eds.), *Among the Prophets: Language, Image and Structure in the Prophetic Writings* (JSOTSup, 144; Sheffield: JSOT Press, 1993), pp. 195-96. Note also Steck, *Bereitete Heimkehr*, pp. 13-37; Utzschneider, *Künder oder Schreiber*, pp. 42-44.

28. See Nogalski, *Literary Precursors,* p. 20-57, for translations highlighting the 'catchword phenomenon' in the Twelve. The remainder of *Literary Precursors* and *Redactional Processes* then evaluate evidence of redactional implantation in those texts.

highlight catchwords used in juxtaposition and in the explication of paradigmatic intentions.

Examination of the catchwords which appear in the 'seams' (that is, the concluding and opening passages) of the writings of the Twelve reveals a notable tendency. These words often appear in contexts which offer contrasting messages. Take the Hosea–Joel connection as an example, where 'inhabitants' (Hos. 14.8; Joel 1.2), 'vine' (Hos. 14.8; Joel 1.7, 12), 'wine' (Hos. 14.8; Joel 1.5), and 'grain' (Hos. 14.8; Joel 1.10) offer specific catchword connections which deliberately strengthen the 'agricultural' ties between the two passages.[29] However, the words do not convey the same message. Hos. 14.8 functions within the *positive* promise of *future* agricultural bounty. By contrast, Joel 1.2-20 paints a *negative* picture of *current* agricultural disaster. One must broaden the investigation at this point to understand this juxtaposition more fully. First, many of the catchword connections utilize a similar technique—juxtaposing a promise of weal with a situation of suffering.[30] Second, these catchwords appear as part of a larger pattern in the Twelve of catchword associations to Joel 1–2. Third, the catchwords related to Joel 1–2 often appear to be redactionally inserted.[31] Fourth, one can detect significant literary development of the motif associated with these catchwords. This final statement requires further illustration.

In Hos. 2.10-15, the reader of the Twelve first learns that these agricultural images (with others that appear in Joel 1) serve as a significant point of tension between Yahweh and his bride. As a result of this tension Yahweh will punish her by the removal of these elements (2.14), in the hope of getting her to recognize that these elements are gifts which come from Yahweh. The end of Hosea contains the promise of the future restoration of these elements (but the text still implies their loss

29. Because the words involved are relatively common, one should initially be cautious regarding intentionality. Note, however, that all of these words appear in one verse in Hosea. Careful literary analysis reveals a strong likelihood that three of these words (inhabitants, grain, vine) entered Hos. 14.8 as a 'redactional gloss', presumably by editorial hands working on the Twelve. See Nogalski, *Literary Precursors*, pp. 67-68.

30. See my discussions of the Zephaniah/Haggai connection (*Literary Precursors*, pp. 206-207, 212-15), and the Zechariah 8/Malachi connection (*Redactional Processes*, pp. 199-200) in particular.

31. See my literary analyses of Nah. 1.2-10; Hab. 3.17; Hag. 2.19; and Zech. 8.12 (*Redactional Processes*, pp. 115-17, 176-79; *Literary Precursors*, pp. 228-29, 262-67).

before their restoration). Joel 1–2 depicts the devastation of the locust/ enemy as the loss of these agricultural elements but further explicates how Yahweh will restore agricultural bounty (2.18-19) if the people repent (2.12-17). From this point, the agricultural elements come back into play at significant junctures (Hab. 3.17; Hag. 2.17, 19; Zech. 8.12; Mal. 3.10-11). One can make a strong case that these texts know the Joel passage and that each of these texts are redactionally related to one another (either as part of compositional material or redactional glosses oriented toward the Book of the Twelve). Finally, one can document a consistent, developed point of view operating in the logic uniting these texts.

Briefly summarized, Hab. 3.17 anticipates the coming Babylonian invasion, but specifically anticipates Judah's destruction through references to the agricultural images from Joel 1–2.

> [17]Though the fig tree will not blossom, nor fruit be on the vines, the produce of the olive will fail, and the fields will not produce food, the flock will be cut off from the fold, and there will be no cattle in the stalls, [18]yet I will rejoice in Yahweh, I will exult in the god of my salvation.

Inserted into a typical affirmation of confidence in Yahweh (Hab. 3.16, 18-19),[32] this allusion to Joel in the context of the coming Babylonian invasion emphasizes the certainty of the coming destruction (as proleptically stated in Joel), but reminds the sophisticated reader that this (literarily imminent) action should be seen as part of Yahweh's activity. The righteous need not fear (cf. Mal. 3.17). By contrast, the context of Haggai (and the historical framework of the Twelve as a whole) presumes that the reader of Hag. 2.19 knows that the generation which returned from exile stands at an important crossroad. This 'generation' must decide whether to obey Yahweh or to act as earlier generations had done by breaking covenant with Yahweh (cf. also Zech. 1.2-6). When work on the temple begins, Haggai's message asks the people to take note of their fate after the foundation of the temple has been laid to see whether Yahweh remains true to his promise. Again, agricultural catchwords from Joel 1–2 come back into play in a phrase which is literarily suspect:[33] 'Is the seed yet in the storehouse? *(or the vine, the fig*

32. See Nogalski, *Redactional Processes*, pp. 176-79.

33. See Nogalski, *Literary Precursors*, p. 228-29. If studies of מגורה are correct, the hyperbole of placing a vine, a fig-tree, or a pomegranate into underground storage makes more sense as a literary reference back to Joel than a literal statement.

tree, the pomegranate?), or the olive tree not producing? From this day I will bless you.' Zechariah 8.12 validates this challenge by affirming Yahweh's faithful dealing with that generation in a speech set two years later (Zech. 7.1). After calling upon the people to recall the days before the laying of the foundation (note the connection back to the context of Hag. 2.19), Zech. 8.11-12 asks the *current* generation to consider their own situation since that point.[34]

> [11]But now I am not like the previous days to the remnant of this people, says Yahweh Sebaoth. [12]For a seed (there) is peace. The vine gives its fruit, and the land gives its produce, and the heavens give dew, and I have caused the remnant of this people to inherit all these things.

Within this passage, Yahweh asserts that he has kept his part of the bargain to the generation which began building the temple, but following the thread of these catchwords through the Twelve reveals that in Malachi Yahweh's people return to the cultic abuses of the earlier generations by offering less than their best to Yahweh (1.6-14) which prompts Yahweh to send a messenger to prepare for the day of his coming. Again, Yahweh's speeches in Mal. 3.6-12 reference the language of Joel. Consider Mal. 3.7 in light of Joel 2.12-14 and Amos 4.6-11: 'From the days of your fathers you have turned aside from my statutes and have not kept them. *Return to me and I will return to you*, says Yahweh Sebaoth.' Note how Mal. 3.10-11 reflects the language of Joel in a new challenge similar to Hag. 2.19:

> [10]Bring the full tithes into the *storehouse*, that there may be food in my house; and put me to the test in this, says Yahweh Sebaoth, to see whether I will not open the windows of heaven for you and pour down for you until there is no sufficiency. [11]And I will rebuke the *devourer* for you, so that it will not destroy the fruits of your soil. And the *vine of the field* will not stop producing for you.

Even though most commentators have not previously interpreted this text in light of Joel 1–2, it is significant how many times the devourer in 3.11 has been treated as a locust.[35]

34. For the temporal significance of the phrase 'but now' as a reference to the current generation, see Nogalski, *Literary Precursors*, pp. 262-65.

35. For example, see W. Rudolph, *Haggai–Sacharja 1-8/9-14-Maleachi* (KAT, 13.4; Neukirchen–Vluyn: Neukirchener, 1976), pp. 284-85; P.A. Verhoef, *The Books of Haggai and Malachi* (NICOT; Grand Rapids: Eerdmans, 1987), pp. 308-309; P.L. Redditt, *Haggai, Zechariah, Malachi* (NCBC; Grand Rapids: Eerdmans, 1995), p. 180.

When the catchwords are recognized, one can see how these passages work together to develop an agricultural motif based on allusions back to Joel 1–2. Common words may certainly occur naturally between two writings. If one speaks of catchwords, however, one should make an effort to determine the extent that one can speak of recurring words as intentionally created vehicles of meaning across the writings of the Twelve. The examples of catchwords could be multiplied, but space does not permit a more complete listing. Instead, it will be beneficial to use the agricultural motif as a springboard into a discussion of motifs as an intertextual device in the Twelve.

4. *Themes and Motifs*

Literary works naturally develop themes and motifs as devices used for 'telling the story', or conveying meaning. The ability to recognize, analyze, and assimilate these devices will necessarily depend upon the level of sophistication of both author and reader. Thematic development in the Twelve requires one to presume a sophisticated author and reader, a presumption which constitutes a fairly recent development in Old Testament studies. In addition, similar types of literature will naturally share certain themes and motifs, and this similarity drastically complicates any attempt to trace the intentionality of themes and motifs within the Twelve. For example, judgement is a constitutive motif of prophetic literature, so judgement alone offers little help as an intertextual theme in the Twelve, if one wishes to consider the question of intentionality. Conversely, however, one cannot ignore the motif of judgement if one hopes to address the question of intentional literary development within the Twelve.

To say that Hosea, Joel, and Amos pronounce judgement on Israel is a true statement but offers little help regarding the purpose of the formation of the Twelve as a corpus. However, analyzing and comparing the type of judgement, the presuppositions, the metaphors, and the recipients of that judgement may lead one to isolate specific line(s) of thought more concretely. For example, the locust metaphor in Joel provides the unifying imagery for the instrument of judgement in Joel 1–2. Locust imagery unites diverse material presupposing threats from locusts, drought, and enemy attack.[36] Later in the Twelve, several passages (Amos 4.9;

36. See Bergler, *Joel*, pp. 45-68. For example, cf. Joel 1.7 (locust as nation-enemy) with the effects of a drought in Joel 1.17-20.

Nah. 3.16b, 17; Hab. 1.9; Mal. 3.10) use locust metaphors to refer to divinely-initiated threats to Yahweh's people. Notably, Nah. 3.16b, 17 and Hab. 1.9 associate the locust metaphors with nations which invade the land, a connection which has explicit connections to Joel 1–2. Both texts exhibit other tendencies which orient them to the Book of the Twelve, not just to the literary horizon of the particular writing in which they appear.[37] Amos 4.9 plays a key role in Hag. 2.17 where the context exhibits other Joel-related vocabulary that appears to be deliberately inserted.[38] Finally, the context of Mal. 3.10-11 also appears to be one which deliberately references Joel.[39] Thus, all of these passages have plausible links to the same editorial movement which spans several writings of the Twelve. Not only can each of these texts be explained as part of the development of the Book of the Twelve, but they point to a consistent hermeneutic which interprets the locusts of Joel as the political superpowers (Assyria, Babylon, Persia) who 'devour' the land.

Simultaneously, these images are interwoven with the promise of agricultural bounty which threads its way through the writings of the Twelve. As noted in the discussion of catchwords, the promise of agricultural bounty reappears at significant points using the language of Joel. Thus, both the locust and agricultural bounty motifs recur throughout the Twelve by catchwords and allusions to the language of Joel. The locust motif represents the 'continuing threat' to the 'agricultural bounty' which Yahweh promises if the people repent. Joel 1.4 speaks of a series of locust plagues, each devouring the left-overs from the previous plague. Joel 1.7 associates the 'locusts' with an enemy attack. Joel 2.1-11 depicts the threat of that locust/army in more detail. Following an invitation to repentance (Joel 2.12-17), Joel 2.18-25 promises the removal of the enemy from the North (2.20), restoration of agricultural bounty (2.19, 22-24), and a reversal of the effects of all the predicted locust plagues (2.25).

These motifs continue to develop and to intertwine as one progresses

37. Nah. 3.16b, 17 represents two 'redactional glosses' explicitly connoting Assyria as one of the invading locusts mentioned in Joel (see Nogalski, *Redactional Processes*, pp. 124-27). Hab. 1.9 appears in the Babylonian commentary which imitates Nah. 3.1-19 (see Nogalski, *Redactional Processes*, pp. 140-42, 146-50).

38. Note note 25, which demonstrates how Hag. 2.19 restates the promise of Joel while drawing upon the agricultural bounty motif. Note also the discussion of Amos 4.9 below.

39. See note 24 above.

through the writings of the Twelve. In Amos 4.9, Yahweh laments that the Northern Kingdom refused to heed warnings (drought, locusts), and refused to repent. This refusal effectively discontinues Yahweh's attempts to lure Israel back to him (Hos. 2.14). Nah. 3.16-17 portrays the destruction of one 'locust' by another which in turn becomes an even larger threat to Judah (Hab. 1.5-17).[40] By the end of Habakkuk the destruction of Jerusalem is anticipated in terms of the threat to the agricultural bounty (note 3.17).[41] Following the return of the exiles, the book of Haggai (note also Zech. 1.2-6) documents the repentance of the people and their leaders which results in the rebuilding of the temple. At that point, the promise of agricultural bounty reappears (Hag. 2.17, 19) using language from Amos 4.9 and Joel 1–2. Zechariah 8.12 confirms that Yahweh has begun answering the promise of bounty. However, the optimism of Zechariah 7–8 is short-lived. Malachi presumes the people have reverted to the practices which led to the locust attacks in the first place. They no longer recognize Yahweh's faithful actions. As a result, the devourer remains a threat to agricultural bounty (Mal. 3.10-11).

This thematic development does not simply illustrate a modern reading of the Twelve. Several of these texts have likely been inserted into their respective contexts as redactional glosses. The book of Joel contains several of the major themes and/or motifs which recur in the Twelve (in addition to agricultural bounty and locusts, note especially the day of Yahweh). The threads of the motif recur in significant and appropriate locations within the Twelve. Thus, one can and should pay careful attention to the question of thematic development as a means for analyzing possible motives for the editing of the Twelve as a single (albeit composite) literary work.

5. *Framing Devices*

Having illustrated quotations, allusions, catchwords, and themes, one should also note the occurrence of framing devices as significant vehicles for developing meaning in the Twelve. Framing devices constitute a

40. For arguments delineating Hab. 1.2-17 as a deliberate intensification of the Babylonian threat in comparison to Assyria, see Nogalski, *Redactional Processes*, pp. 146-50. Note especially the reference to the face of the (locust) horde moving forward in Hab. 1.9.

41. Zephaniah, the next writing, moves from the destruction of Jerusalem and Judah (chs. 1–2) to the anticipated return. See Nogalski, *Literary Precursors*, pp. 198-200.

somewhat broader category than the previously discussed types of intertextuality. The questions raised by these devices require more complex treatment than can be accomplished here, but for the sake of completeness they must at least be mentioned briefly. Within the Twelve, at least five types of framing devices can be illustrated: superscriptions, genre similarities, structural parallels, juxtaposition of catchwords, and canonical allusions. Questions of intentionality become significantly more difficult to ascertain when evaluating the texts, but these devices demand evaluation.

Superscriptions play a key role in the macrostructure of the Twelve.[42] Six superscriptions provide the chronological framework to the Twelve and represent the largest group which influences the reading of the Twelve. The superscriptions of Hosea, Amos, Micah, Zephaniah, Haggai, and Zechariah all contain chronological indicators, and, very significantly, *all six* appear in a literarily constructed chronological order.

The chronological presentation of the first four superscriptions derives from the patterned combination of the kings and the kingdoms mentioned in the superscriptions.

Hos. 1.1	Amos 1.1	Mic. 1.1	Zeph. 1.1
Uzziah (Judah)	Uzziah (Judah)		
Jotham (Judah)		Jotham (Judah)	
Ahaz (Judah)		Ahaz (Judah)	
Hezekiah (Judah)		Hezekiah (Judah)	(Hezekiah)
Jeroboam (Israel)	Jeroboam (Israel)		↑
			Josiah (Judah)

This pattern encompasses the eighth and seventh centuries. It focuses upon the kings of Judah, but both Hosea and Amos also list Jeroboam, probably due to the fact that the messages of these writings relate

42. For a more thorough analysis of the varieties of superscriptions, see J.D.W. Watts, 'Superscriptions and Incipits in the Book of the Twelve' (a paper given to the Formation of the Book of the Twelve Consultation during the 1994 SBL Meeting).

primarily to Yahweh's dealings with the Northern Kingdom. Mic. 1.2-7 already presumes the destruction of Samaria, and even though the Northern Kingdom still existed during the reigns of Jotham, Ahaz, and part of the reign of Hezekiah, Mic. 1.1 does not mention the kings of the Northern Kingdom. Zeph. 1.1 places the prophet's ministry in the reign of Josiah and traces the prophet's ancestry back to Hezekiah, thus linking the two most significant Judean kings (outside of David and Solomon) in the Deuteronomistic History.

In a separate grouping, Haggai and Zechariah also contain an interrelated chronological presentation. Haggai and Zechariah contain multiple chronological references.[43] These references are stylized but manifest a radically different linguistic pattern from the first group of four. Within each book, these dated speeches appear in chronological order. The last three dated references in Haggai post-date the first dated reference in Zech. 1.1, with the result that the time periods of those two prophets overlap.

Literary analysis suggests neither chronological schema is accidental nor simply the result of completed writings being placed next to one another.[44] However, both sets of chronologies appear to have been created prior to incorporation of the respective writings into the Twelve. Nevertheless, when these six writings were incorporated into the larger corpus, they were kept in chronological order.[45] As a result, one may state with relative confidence that the chronological order of these six writings constitutes an intentionally created framework which casts a historical perspective on the collection of the Twelve.

A second notable group of related superscriptions creates a threefold division at the conclusion of the Book of the Twelve. Zechariah 9.1; 12.1; and Mal. 1.1 introduce groups of texts with the phrase 'the burden (or oracle) of the word of Yahweh', which appears only in these three places within the entire Old Testament. As with the chronologies, this pattern appears to have been created deliberately.[46] These

43. Hag. 1.1; 1.15; 2.1; 2.10; 2.18; 2.20; Zech. 1.1; 1.7; 7.1.

44. Likely, these superscriptions grew in two stages, as indicated by the redactional shaping of the Deuteronomistic superscriptions (Hos. 1.1; Amos 1.1; Mic. 1.1; Zeph. 1.1) and the superscriptions of Haggai and Zechariah which are also very similar to one another. See Nogalski, *Literary Precursors*, pp. 84-87.

45. Note that the LXX rearranges the order of the first six but still keeps the dated superscriptions in their proper order.

46. See Nogalski, *Redactional Processes*, p. 217.

superscriptions link blocks of material which focus on the fate of Ephraim and Judah (Zech. 9–11); Judah and Jerusalem (Zech. 12–14); and the post-exilic community (cf. Mal. 3.16-18).

A third category of superscriptions is more difficult to evaluate. Most of those writings which do not contain chronological superscriptions demonstrate an affinity to their contexts or to neighboring superscriptions. The superscription in Joel 1.1 mirrors the word of Yahweh superscriptions of Hosea (1.1), but without the chronological indicators. Obadiah's superscription labels the booklet as 'the vision of Obadiah', which appropriately follows the visions of Amos. Nah. 1.1 and Hab. 1.1 both make reference to the burden/oracle. Malachi 1.1, in addition to the phrase 'burden of the word of Yahweh', contains reference to the message coming 'by the hand' of Malachi, which appears elsewhere only in Haggai within the Twelve. It is difficult to draw any firm conclusions from this phenomenon, but these similarities do at least add to the impression of deliberately created linkages noted elsewhere within the texts.

Genre repetition provides a second framing device which can be illustrated in the Twelve. In at least two instances, one can note distinctive recurrences of genres which, if not intentionally created for the larger corpora, certainly serve an appropriate literary function within the respective writings. The first example of genre repetition appears with the occurrence of the 'vision' of Obadiah which follows the five visions of Amos. The fact that Obadiah patterns itself after Amos 9 strengthens the impression that this reference to the vision of Obadiah is intentionally created at the point Obadiah was composed for its place next to Amos.[47]

In the Twelve, portrayals of theophanies of judgement begin or end four successive works.[48] Micah begins with a portrayal of a theophany which threatens Judah with the same fate as Samaria. Nahum begins with a semi-acrostic theophany of universal judgement (1.2-9) which introduces the book's major theme of the destruction of Assyria. Habakkuk concludes with a theophany announcing the future destruction of the enemy, which in the context of the book implies Babylon. Zephaniah begins with a theophanic portrayal of judgement on Jerusalem.

47. See Nogalski, *Redactional Processes*, pp. 61-68, especially p. 64.

48. See discussions concerning the origin and development of Old Testament theophanic portrayals by J. Jeremias, 'Theophany in the OT', *IDBSup*, pp. 896-98, and *Theophanie: Geschichte einer alttestamentlichen Gattung* (Neukirchen: Neukirchener Verlag, 1965).

All four theophanies contain at least hints of universal judgement while also pointing to judgement upon specific entities.[49] In previous discussions, I have suggested that Nahum and Habakkuk were expanded considerably for their place in the Twelve by the addition of these theophanic poems. It seems likely that the shorter theophanic material in Micah existed prior to the Joel-related layer, while portions of the universal theophanic portrayal in Nah. 1.2-8; Hab. 3.1-20; and Zeph. 1.2-3 all show strong linguistic and paradigmatic connections to Joel.[50]

Structural parallels constitute the third category of framing devices. Occasionally, adjacent passages in the seams of the Twelve exhibit significant parallels in the text markers and themes within the passages. Two examples (Amos 9/Obadiah; Nahum 3/Habakkuk 1) will illustrate this device. In both cases, the concluding chapters of Amos and Nahum have a similar structure to the previous chapters of those books.[51] It is not illogical, then, that the structural parallels of the context are continued in the editorial work of the following book. First, as noted above, Obadiah manifests most of the same structuring devices as Amos 9. These devices likely intend to equate (hence the parallel) Edom's fate with the fate of the Northern Kingdom.[52] The presence of an extended quotation in Obad. 1-5 provides a cross-reference which increases the likelihood that this structural imitation was accomplished deliberately.

Second, Hab. 1.5-17 utilizes catchwords and word plays to point back to Nah. 3.1-8, but the connections also demonstrate a tendency to heighten the threat of Babylon in comparison to the threat which Assyria had posed previously. For example, Nineveh is attacked by horsemen (3.3), while Babylon attacks with horsemen (Hab. 1.8); Nineveh will go into captivity (Nah. 3.10) while Babylon collects captives (Hab. 1.9). Nineveh becomes a mockery whose fortifications are ready to be destroyed (Nah. 3.12, 14), while Babylon laughs at the fortifications of rulers (Hab. 1.10). Nineveh's shepherds and king are defeated (Nah. 3.18) while Babylon mocks rulers and kings (Hab. 1.10).

49. Note that the universal elements of Mic. 1.2a and Zeph. 1.2-3 come prior to the specific judgements. Nah. 1.2-8 and Hab. 3.1-20 convey much more universal imagery, although the context of the two books imply Assyria and Babylon are the primary targets of Yahweh's judgements.

50. Nogalski, *Literary Precursors*, p. 198-200.

51. For Amos 9 as the structural parallel to Amos 8, see Nogalski, *Literary Precursors*, pp. 117-18. For the manner in which the structure of Nahum 3 parallels Nahum 2, see Nogalski, *Redactional Processes*, p. 123.

52. See above.

In evaluating the possibility of intentionality in this example, the Babylonian commentary material in Habakkuk expands a previously existing wisdom piece about the prosperity of the wicked, making it plausible (but admittedly less objectively so) that Habakkuk was edited to create this parallel.[53] Thus, the literary transition from Nahum to Habakkuk implies that Judah endures the threat of Assyria only to hear that it will fall to the Babylonians.

The juxtaposition of catchwords represents the fourth framing device which needs to be brought into a discussion of intertextuality in the Twelve. Frequently, the catchwords which appear between two writings heighten the tension between a promise to Yahweh's people and the reality of the current situation. The Hosea–Joel connection illustrated this tendency in the discussion above. In addition, the end of Zephaniah relates Yahweh's promise to the people that he will gather the people 'in that time' (3.18-19), while Hag. 1.2 confronts 'this people' who says 'the time' has not yet come. Haggai ends with a promise to overthrow the nations with their chariots, horses, and riders while Zechariah's first night vision (1.6-17) portrays the nations at rest while the horses and riders of Yahweh patrol the earth. Zechariah 8.9-23 manifests more than twenty words and phrases in common with the beginning of Malachi.[54] In most cases, the word or phrase in Zechariah is used positively while the counterpart in Malachi appears as part of the prophet's confrontation of the people's lack of obedience to Yahweh.

Canonical allusions constitute a fifth type of framing device which deserves attention. This device serves an important function in at least one series of texts: Zech. 13.9; 14.1-21; Mal. 3.22-24. Zechariah 13.9 reads: 'And I will bring the third part through the fire, refine them as silver is refined, and test them as gold is tested. They will call on my name, and I will answer them; I will say, They are my people. And they will say, the LORD is my God.' The first half of this verse clearly alludes to Mal. 3.3 while the second half draws from Hos. 2.25 (Eng: 2.23). The second text of this series combines a series of allusions to Isaiah 2 and 66.[55] Finally, it has frequently been noted that Mal. 3.22 alludes to Josh. 1.2, 7. The canonical implications of these three series of allusions and partial quotations may be graphically illustrated:

53. Nogalski, *Redactional Processes*, pp. 138-44.

54. See Nogalski, *Literary Processes*, pp. 53-55.

55. See Nogalski, *Redactional Processes*, pp. 242-44.

Beginning of Former Prophets	Beginning & end of 1st book of Latter Prophets	Beginning & end of the Twelve (last book of the Latter Prophets)	Alluding Texts		
		Hos. 2.25 & Mal. 3.3	Zech. 13.9		
	Isa. 2 & 66			Zech. 14	
Josh. 1.2, 7					Mal. 3.22

The canonical allusions move outwardly across the entire prophetic canon. Could this framing device be accidental? It is possible since the allusions are of different types, but the number of persons working independently who have noted these allusions argues strongly for the intentionality of the individual allusions. The meaningful order of the series certainly raises one's suspicions that the three passages belong to the same editorial movement.

Evaluating framing devices in the Twelve admittedly requires much more work before making definitive statements on the intentionality of all these devices. Still, the presence of these categories raises questions which deserve treatment about the possibility that editors intended readers to note them when reading the Twelve.

This paper has illustrated several intertextual devices which can help to develop reading strategies for the Book of the Twelve. Many of these devices can be attributed with some confidence to ancient editorial work on more than one writing within the Book of the Twelve. Others provide intriguing insights but raise more questions than can be answered in this paper. The presence of such a wide variety of techniques begs for more study.

TWELVE PROPHETIC BOOKS OR 'THE TWELVE': A FEW PRELIMINARY CONSIDERATIONS*

Ehud ben Zvi

1. *Introduction*

1.1 *Presentation of the Issue*

A renewed interest in the issue of the Book of the Twelve (to be distinguished from the twelve prophetic books of which it is composed), its unity and redaction history has appeared in the last several years.[1] The

* I wish to express my appreciation to my colleague James Nogalski for his questioning of commonly accepted premises and for his role in promoting a historical-critical discussion of the 'Twelve Prophetic Books or "The Twelve"'. The fact that I happen to disagree with him on many significant issues—as the reader of this article will easily notice—does not have any bearing at all in this regard.

1. See, for instance, D.A. Schneider, *The Unity of the Book of the Twelve* (PhD diss.; Yale University, 1979), E. Bosshard, 'Beobachtungen zum Zwölfprophetenbuch', *BN* 40 (1987), pp. 30-62; P.R. House, *The Unity of the Twelve* (JSOTSup, 97; Sheffield: Almond Press, 1990); J.D. Nogalski, *The Literary Precursors of the Book of the Twelve* (BZAW, 217; Berlin: de Gruyter, 1993); *idem*, *Redactional Processes in the Book of the Twelve* (BZAW, 218; Berlin: de Gruyter, 1993); B.A. Jones, *The Formation of the Book of the Twelve: A Study in Text and Canon* (SBLDS, 149; Atlanta: Scholars Press, 1995). A similar emphasis is found in the earlier work of R.E. Wolfe, 'The Editing of the Book of the Twelve', *ZAW* 53 (1935), pp. 90-129. For a survey and critical evaluation of the history of scholarship in regards to either the unity or the formation of the Book of the Twelve, see esp. Jones, *Formation*, pp. 13-40.

The mentioned trend seems to be associated with—but certainly not fully dependent on—recent tendencies towards canonical criticism/s. Besides some titles that already point to this association (e.g., Jones, *Formation*), one may observe, for instance, the absence of studies on the unity of Joshua–Judges despite the presence of data suggesting that such a volume existed at one time, or at least within a certain group. See A. Rofé, 'The End of the Book of Joshua according to the Septuagint', *Henoch* 4 (1982), pp. 17-36; cf. E. Tov, *Textual Criticism of the Hebrew Bible* (Minneapolis: Fortress, 1992), pp. 330-32. Of course, no 'canonical' version of the

result of this trend has been a gamut of new suggestions, proposals and heuristic questions. The present paper advances several preliminary considerations whose purpose is to contribute to the evaluation of a major historical-critical claim that seems to be evolving within this general trend. This claim may be formulated as follows:

> From some point either in the late monarchic or early postmonarchic period, a direct precursor of the Book of the Twelve was considered a single literary, theological/ideological work. Moreover, this work *as a whole* not only underwent several redactions but significant portions of it were written from the outset within a perspective informed by the perceived literary unity of the (ongoing) Book of the Twelve.[2] In other words, the educated Judahite or Yehudite cadres who wrote the prophetic books (and most of the rest of biblical literature) considered the Book of the Twelve and its direct forerunner/s a unified work and *not* a collection or anthology of separate books.

1.2 *Significance of the Issue for Historical-Critical Studies*

If this claim is indeed accepted, then a substantial shift in the historical-critical study of prophetic literature will follow because much of the present research is focused on a literary corpus that is conceptualized as including (at least) fifteen[3] essentially separate, prophetic books, each one with its distinctive compositional and/or redactional history and its particular messages.

Two simple examples, each pointing to a different set of critical questions, may suffice to illustrate the manifold implications of the aforementioned claim. If the Book of Jonah is understood as an integral part of a unified Book of the Twelve in its MT order, then one would tend to stress two of its likely messages:

(a) The possibility and value of repentance, a theme that will set this book as a 'counterpiece to Nahum', though significantly, Nahum follows Jonah and not vice versa.

Hebrew Bible includes a Joshua–Judges volume.

2. For a detailed argument in favor of such a claim, one may consult Nogalski, *Literary Precursors* , and *idem, Redactional Processes.*

3. That is, Isaiah, Jeremiah, Ezekiel and the twelve books included in the Twelve. Of course, even the most cursory survey of modern historical-critical research shows that the number fifteen is a minimal number, for much research has focused on, for instance, Deutero and Trito-Isaiah and Zechariah 1–8 as separate, independent units.

(b) The impossibility of escaping divine punishment, a theme that will associate this book with those preceding it, especially Obadiah and Amos, and which emphasizes the issue of obedience to the divine.[4]

Yet, this approach to Jonah de-emphasizes what seems to be the most significant point conveyed by the book, namely that prophecy is not about prophesying the future but about influencing the recipients of the prophetic message.[5] In fact Jonah, if (re)read on its own, is more of a theological (or ideological) comment and a possible interpretative key for the (re)reading[6] of other prophetic books—including Isaiah, Jeremiah and Ezekiel—than a prophetic book in itself.[7] If so, much depends on the literary context within which the Book of Jonah is to be interpreted from a historical-critical perspective that focuses on the audiences for which the book was written and on their (re)readings of Jonah.[8] Significantly, the case of Jonah is only one example of a more general trend. If a researcher adopts a strategy of interpretation based on a

4. Cf. Nogalski, *Redactional Processes*, pp. 270-73.

5. The narrative character of Jonah already alerts the intended audience that this is not a 'typical' prophetic book. In addition, the fact that the book does not conclude in ch. 3 but continues in ch. 4 clearly disallows a reading that centers mainly on the issue of repentance. In addition, if Jonah is read as a separate unit, it is difficult to see obedience, and the related issue of punishment for lack of it, as the main issue of the book. Not only is no one severely punished in Jonah—only the *qiqayon* plant is destroyed in this book—but also Jon. 4.11 seems to explicitly contradict this interpretative approach. But, again, if the Book of Jonah is read as an integral part of a unified Book of the Twelve, then these issues may be approached differently.

6. Prophetic books were not composed to be read once and then be discarded or forgotten but were written to be read again and again, to be studied and reflected upon by a community or communities of readers (cf. Hos. 14.10). Hence, the term reading here stands, in fact, for rereading. I discussed these issues in E. ben Zvi, *A Historical-Critical Study of the Book of Obadiah* (BZAW, 242; Berlin: de Gruyter, 1996), pp. 3-6 *et passim*.

7. It is worth noting that a somewhat comparable conclusion led Jones to propose that the original position of the Book of Jonah within the Twelve was after Malachi (cf. 4QXII[a]). See Jones, *Formation*, pp. 129-69.

8. It seems that a similar situation evolves, for instance, regarding possible readings of the MT Tanakh and the Protestant or Catholic Old Testament as unified works, rather than as a collection of individual books. If the collection approach is taken, neither the other entries in the collection nor ordering of the books provide main interpretative keys, but if the unified approach is taken, then the opposite is true, and to say the least, a book concluding with Chronicles is not the same book as one concluding with Malachi.

reading of the 'Book of the Twelve' as a coherent, unified, literary text, then it is likely that she or he will find or emphasize meanings and properties in the text that are different from those brought to the forefront by those who study each book as a separate unit. To illustrate, P.R. House maintains that (a) Obadiah 'elaborates on the sin of hating one's neighbor, which breaks the most fundamental of God's laws (cf. Lev. 19.18);'[9] and (b) 'in Jonah the "heathen" characters are certainly sinful, since the sailors in 1.6 recognize the validity of a number of gods...'.[10] Moreover, when advancing a proposal concerning the comic plot of the twelve, House maintains that (c) 'the fortunes of Israel and the rest of the creation begin to plunge downward in Hosea and Joel, fall even further in Amos-Micah... [and] begin to inch upwards towards the end of Zephaniah...'[11] None of these three positions is likely to have developed if House's strategy of analysis would have been to study each prophetic book separately. If Obadiah is read as a complete literary unit in itself, one is—at the very least—less likely to characterize that text as an elaboration on 'you shall love your neighbor as yourself'. In Jonah the sailors are not characterized in a negative light, nor are they condemned for praying to their own gods.[12] If one reads Hosea, Joel, Amos and Micah as separate books, one is likely to reach the conclusion that each of these books is written so as to convey the image that the fortunes of Israel will not only 'inch upwards' but ascend to the highest level imagined within the discourse of the period (see Hos. 14.6-10; Joel 4.17-21; Amos 9.11-15; Mic. 7.18-20). Of course, it is because of these conclusions of the prophetic books that a long tradition of interpretation (attested already in Ben Sira) understood each of these books, in the main, as a message of hope and salvation. House clearly recognizes these concluding markers of hope in each of these texts,[13] but he allows them only a minor role in his analysis, for he is more interested in the plot of the Book of the Twelve rather than in the plot of the individual books.

A somewhat different set of critical implications of the claim mentioned in section 1.1 can be illustrated by the following example.

9. See House, *Unity*, p. 118.

10. See House, *Unity*, p. 213.

11. See House, *Unity*, p. 123.

12. See, for instance, A. Rofé, *The Prophetical Stories* (Jerusalem: Magnes Press, 1988), p. 161.

13. See House, *Unity*, p. 55.

J.D. Nogalski claims that: 'These imitations [those of Amos 9.1-15 in Obadiah] serve two functions: First, they provide a judgement against Edom which both parallels and heightens the judgement against Israel in Amos 9.1-10. Second, they introduce the motif of a Jerusalem-centered repossession of the Davidic monarchy.'[14] Even if for the sake of the argument one were to accept that there were such imitations—a position against which I have written at length elsewhere[15]—the issue is whether these presumed imitations may have served the mentioned function. Significantly, as long as Obadiah is read (or was read by its intended audience) as an integral part of a unified Book of the Twelve and as a section closely attached to Amos, Nogalski's claims might stand. But, if Obadiah is read (or was read) on its own, in other words, as a separate book, then it is noteworthy that there is no reference there to judgement against the House of Jacob/Israel in Obadiah, nor any reference to the Davidic monarchy at all. To the contrary, Obadiah mentions judgement against Edom and 'the nations', clearly excluding the House of Israel—that Israel is not like the Cushites (cf. Amos 9.7) or any of 'the nations' is a central issue in Obadiah.[16] Moreover, the kingship of the LORD is presented in Obadiah in such a way as to evoke an association with what was understood to be 'Israel' in the time of the Judges. Furthermore, if Obadiah is read on its own, the lack of mention of the restoration of the Davidic dynasty and the emphasis on the kingship of the LORD clearly identifies Obadiah with Zephaniah and the redactional processes shaping the Book of Psalms. All of them can be understood as expressions of one stream of theological (or ideological) thought that stands in tension with that reflected in, for instance, Amos 9.11.

With so much being at stake, an open debate on the validity of the aforementioned claim is more than warranted. The issue, of course, cannot be resolved by a single paper, nor may it be fully approached by any discussion that does not take into consideration the full extent of the evidence provided by the prophetic literature and by a serious study of the socio-historical context in which this literature was written, read, (re)read, edited, and transmitted from generation to generation. Yet, it is my hope that the following preliminary considerations may contribute to this necessary debate. Some of these considerations are expressed in the form of clear propositions so as to sharpen the discussion.

14. Nogalski, *Redactional Processes*, p. 73.
15. See ben Zvi, *Obadiah*, *passim*.
16. See ben Zvi, *Obadiah*, *passim*.

2. *Dealing with the Question: Introductory Considerations*

2.1 *Preliminary Considerations*

A few preliminary considerations are in order:

(a) The Book of the Twelve either in the masoretic or the Septuagint or in any other order, can be read as a unit if one chooses such a reading strategy. But from this obvious observation it does not follow that the ancient Yehudite or Judahite cadres of writers and (re)readers responsible for the prophetic literature present in the Hebrew Bible actually followed this strategy. It certainly does not follow from this observation that the twelve prophetic books were intentionally written or edited so as to convey a sense of close unity among them that set them apart as a unit from the other prophetic books, that is, Isaiah, Jeremiah, and Ezekiel.

(b) The issue of whether later Jewish or Christian communities whose horizon of thought was strongly influenced by the (traditional) concepts of Miqra' or Old Testament read the Book of the Twelve as a single unified work or as a collection of twelve essentially independent pieces or followed a reading strategy somewhat in between the two mentioned options is not particularly relevant to the evaluation of the aforementioned claim because it deals with much later societies and theological discourses.

(c) The earliest evidence that strongly suggests the writing of the Twelve in one scroll is from about 150 BCE.[17] Even if, for the sake of the argument, one were to grant that Sir. 49.10 suggests this arrangement,[18] the fact remains that this evidence seems significantly later than

17. That is 4QXII[a-b]. Significantly, 4QXII[a] seems to suggest a sequence Malachi–Jonah. See R. Fuller, 'The Form and Formation of the Book of the Twelve', in this volume; cf. Jones, *Formation*, pp. 53-54, 129-69. A date ca. 150 BCE is certainly later than that of the composition of the prophetic books (in other words Isaiah–Ezekiel + Hosea–Malachi) and most likely later than any major redaction of these books.

18. From Sir. 49.10, it does not necessary follow that the twelve prophetic books were written in a single scroll. Sirach 49.10 indicates that the twelve prophets were among the great men of the past, along with Job (Sir. 49.9), Ezekiel (Sir. 49.8) and Zerubbabel (Sir. 49.11) and others. Sir. 49.10 points also to a clear and most significant interpretative approach to these twelve prophets, namely, mainly as those who comforted Israel. This approach is likely to be grounded in the conclusions of the twelve prophetic books. See above. From the fact that Sir. 48.10 quotes Mal. 3.23-24, it does not follow that 'Ben Sira knew the collection of the Twelve in

the date of composition (and, at least, most of the redaction) of the prophetic books. For the reasons mentioned above, this evidence is not necessarily helpful for the study of composition, redaction, and above all, for reconstructing the way in which these prophetic books were read and (re)read within the communities within which and for which they were written.

(d) Even if, for the sake of the argument, one were to grant that the twelve prophetic books or their precursors were produced in the form of a single scroll since the Achaemenid period or even earlier, from the writing of books in one scroll, it does not follow that they *had* to be (re)read as a unified literary unit, in other words, as a work in which several prophetic books are integrated far beyond what may be expected from a collection or anthology of separate, independent works that share only a certain type of discourse among themselves and that belong to a common repertoire. In other words, one scroll does not necessarily mean one single, literary unit that was (or must have been) (re)read as such.

First, collections of works did exist in antiquity and in ancient Israel, as the book of Proverbs along with its underlying collections clearly shows.[19] Secondly, there is also ample evidence—although from later times—that clearly falsifies the idea that one scroll must mean one reading strategy, namely that of reading the scroll as a unified literary unit.[20] To illustrate, the *pesharim* from Qumran provide an obvious example of ancient communities who were aware of the fact that the twelve prophetic books were written in one scroll but yet considered them separate works.[21] Later on, rabbinic texts and the masoretic tradition—both of

essentially its completed form' (Jones, *Formation*, p. 8), unless one assumes beforehand that Ben Sira could not have had access to the separate books. On this issue see also consideration (h) below.

19. See also the Book of Psalms and the Egyptian collections of love songs (see, for instance, Papyrus Harris 500; Papyrus Chester Beatty I).

20. Significantly, the fact that some books were written in different scrolls does not disallow the possibility that they were (re)read as belonging to a collection of related texts, see the Dtr. history which seems to be a collection of different, but interrelated books, and cf. the Pentateuch, or even the so-called 'primary history' (that is, Genesis–2 Kings). In other words, one cannot reconstruct ancient strategies of reading only or even mainly on the basis of the criteria of one scroll versus many scrolls. (Cf. all the discussions about which books can be included in one scroll in rabbinic literature, for example, *Soferim* 3.)

21. See esp. 1QpHab. and 4QpNah; M.H. Horgan, *Pesharim: Qumranic*

which were clearly aware of the twelve being written in one scroll—indicate an understanding of the Book of the Twelve as a collection of books rather than as a unified book.[22] One may also notice that

Interpretations of Biblical Books (CBQMS, 8; Washington, DC: The Catholic Biblical Association of America, 1979). In fact, Pesher Habakkuk seems to suggest an exegetical approach that focuses on textually marked units, even if they are below the level of the 'book', and needless to say of the scroll, for it contains no reference to the 'Prayer of Habakkuk' (that is, Hab. 3). Jones's assertion that 'the unity of the Book of the Twelve is taken for granted in the Qumran literature', in spite of his admission that there is no specific reference in this literature to the existence of the Twelve as a unified collection, is strongly coloured by his assumptions concerning the Twelve, and an implied assumption that 'one scroll' must mean 'one book'. See Jones, *Formation*, pp. 9-10.

22. The text in *b. B. Bat.* 13b is often mentioned as an argument supporting the idea that the twelve prophetic books were considered to be a single (literary) unit in talmudic times (for example, Jones, *Formation*, p. 3). This text reads:

בין חומש לחומש של תורה ארבעה שיטין
וכן בין כל נביא לנביא ובנביא של שנים עשר ג׳ שיטין

(i.e., 'between one of the five books of the Torah and another book of the Torah, four lines [should be left blank], and similarly, between one Prophet [i.e., one book included among 'the Prophets'] and another Prophet [i.e., four lines are to be left blank], but concerning one Prophet [i.e., a prophetic book] of the Twelve [and another] three lines [should be left blank]')

In fact, the thrust of the text here points to the opposite claim, in other words, to a strong marking of each book as a separate book, rather than a chapter within a unified work. Against the background of a traditional writing of the Twelve in one scroll, it is noticeable that the text claims that the separation between two subsequent books included in this collection should be almost the same as that prescribed for completely independent books (also cf. *Soferim* 2.4). It is obvious that the text in *b. B. Bat.* 13b maintains that these prophetic books should not be considered as chapters within a unified book, nor even as integral members of a collection to be understood as a whole (for example, Proverbs, Psalms). Perhaps even more revealing of the perspective of the text is the fact that the same term נביא is used for both the books included in the Twelve and those that are not. Moreover, if one would still doubt that this is the case, the (related) text in *b. B. Bat.* 14b unequivocally decides the issue because the claim there is that the logic governing the arrangement of the (prophetic) texts demands that Hosea should be written separately and positioned before Isaiah. Of course, it was well known that at the time of the composition of *b. B. Bat.* 14b (and centuries before) such was not the case, so an explanation (or, better rationalization) of the traditional and socially accepted sequence of prophetic books follows. In any case, the fact that there is no argument at all that Hosea should have been written separately clearly implies that it was considered a given that the

there are instances in which more than one independent work is found in one scroll.[23]

book was an 'independent' work by the communities of readers of Hosea within which *b. B. Bat.* 14b and similar texts were written. One may also mention, in this regard, that *Num. R.* 18.17 (121) sets the Book of Jonah apart from the other eleven prophetic books 'in other words, eleven from the twelve except Jonah which stands by itself'). It is true that the classification of biblical books advanced in this source serves the purpose of the midrash and its need to reach the target number of fifty. Yet the exclusion of Jonah is clearly consonant with, and also probably implies, a reading of the Twelve as a collection of separate works, rather than as a unified book. Significantly, the Book of Jonah is read as a whole and as a separate literary unit in the Yom Kippur liturgy. It has been suggested that for that reason, it was once written in a single scroll for liturgical purposes, like Esther. Incidentally, Jones's discussion about the different places of Jonah within the Book of the Twelve also implies a reading of Jonah as a separate book (*Formation*, pp. 128-69).

A different avenue to assess the approach in 'rabbinic' Judaism to the unity of the Book of the Twelve is to check if the references in their literature to the different prophetic figures seem to be influenced by their order of appearance in the Book of the Twelve, and whether inclusion, or lack of, in the Book of the Twelve is a significant exegetical category for biblical prophetic figures, in other words, to study, for instance, whether Amos tends to be associated more with Obadiah and Joel than with Isaiah. Such a study is beyond the limits of this paper, but if impressions are suggestive, rabbinic literature does not seem to bear a preferential approach to, for instance, Joel–Amos–Obadiah.

The fact that the Masoretic tradition includes a note about the number of verses of each one of the twelve prophetic books also suggests that the Masoretes and those following their approach considered the twelve prophetic books as independent as possible within the limits of a tradition that associated them in a collection. In any case, their approach is not consistent with a reading of the Book of the Twelve as a unified book. Their approach in relation to the Book of the Twelve can (and perhaps should) be contrasted with that towards Ezra–Nehemiah and books which are clearly a collection of works such as Proverbs, Psalms, Lamentations. (Of course, there is a Masoretic note concerning the total number of verses in the Book of the Twelve, but there are similar Masoretic notes concerning literary units higher than a single book [or scroll], such as those concerning 'the Prophets' [including Former and Latter Prophets], and the Miqra' as a whole. Yet it is also worth noticing that whereas there are Masoretic notes concerning the 'middle verse' of the books of Isaiah, Jeremiah and Ezekiel [namely Isa. 33.21; Jer. 28.11; Ezek. 26.1], there is no correspondent note concerning the middle verse of each prophetic book, but there is one about Mic. 3.12 as the middle verse of the Book of the Twelve.)

23. For example, 1QS, 1QS[a] and 1QS[b] are all in one single scroll, though other copies of the Manual of Discipline include neither the 'The Rule of the Congregation' nor 'The Rule of Blessings'. One may also mention that 4Q448 includes both Ps. 154

(e) The fact that there seems not to be a completely fixed order for the twelve prophetic books strongly undermines the hypothesis that the communally accepted, main strategy of reading and learning the scroll of the Twelve was grounded on a sequential reading of the twelve prophetic books as a unified, single literary and theological work,[24] for if the sequential order of the books was determinant of their socially accepted meaning, one would have expected a fixed order.[25]

The claim that this strategy of reading was eventually discarded, so that, for instance, by the time of the LXX it was forgotten, runs the risk of multiplying hypotheses without necessity. From a different but related perspective, Nogalski observes that the translators responsible for the LXX and the Vulgate were for the most part not aware or not concerned with the immense majority of his proposed *Stichwort* connections between sequential books. Significantly, these connections are, according to Nogalski, a major literary feature that directly results from a

and a prayer for the welfare of King Jonathan. In addition, see the revealing discussion in *Soferim* 3.

24. Four different sequences of books in addition to the Masoretic order seem to be supported, in one way or another, by the evidence: (a) the Septuagintal order which is also supported by 4 Ezra 1.39-40, namely Hosea, Amos, Micah, Joel, Obadiah, Jonah, Nahum, Habakkuk, Zephaniah, Haggai, Zechariah, Malachi; (b) one suggested by the *Martyrdom and Ascension of Isaiah* 4.22, namely Amos, Hosea, Micah, Joel, Nahum, Jonah, Obadiah, Habakkuk, Haggai, Zephaniah, Zechariah, and Malachi; (c) one suggested by *The Lives of the Prophets*, namely, Hosea, Micah, Amos, Joel, Obadiah, Jonah, Nahum, Habakkuk, Zephaniah, Haggai, Zechariah and Malachi—the list actually begins with Isaiah, Jeremiah, Ezekiel and Daniel—and (d) one suggested by 4QXII[a] in which there is a possible sequence Malachi–Jonah. Cf. J.M. Sasson, *Jonah* (AB, 24B; New York: Doubleday, 1990), pp. 13-15; Fuller, 'Form and Formation'; and Jones, *Formation*, passim, and esp. concerning (b) and (c), pp. 11-12. Given that the order in *The Lives of the Prophets* follows the LXX in fifteen out of sixteen prophetic characters and their associated books, it is doubtful that it represents a 'random listing of individual names'. Cf. Jones, *Formation*, pp. 11-12.

25. The contemporaneous fluidity in the order (and to some extent even the composition) of the last two books in the Book of Psalms (that is, Pss. 90–150 in the MT) is worth noticing. (Incidentally, one may observe that in the Twelve, the differences between Masoretic and Septuagintal order concern only books 2–6 [that is, the first books]; books 7–12 are in identical order.) Needless to say, if the sequential order of the books is not a determinant factor in the reading community, then one can reconstruct at best a general shift in the atmosphere and the claims of the individual books included in the collection, but one certainly cannot claim that the reading of the collection at that time involved a 'plot' evolving from book to book.

conscious redactional pattern whose purpose was to link these prophetic books to one another as one single composition.

In other words, the logic of Nogalski's argument requires a historical reconstruction involving three levels: (a) first there was a particular, fixed order which was determinant for the communally accepted reading of the text and for its composition and redaction; (b) later on there was a tendency away from this order and likely from this type of reading strategy (see the translation of the Twelve in the LXX around the third century BCE); and (c) about 100–50 BCE there was a renewed tendency towards standardization and towards the original (=MT) order,[26] which may or may not have involved a return to the first reading strategy. Needless to say, this three-stage reconstruction is required only by the hypothesis that there was an original, fixed order that was determinant for the reading (and writing or editing) of the book, which is in turn a hypothesis required by the proposal that the Book of the Twelve, or its precursor, was composed as a unified work.[27]

(f) The mere presence of allusions, clearly 'parallel' texts (or quotations) and thematic similarities among the twelve prophetic books does not carry much weight as an argument in favor of the aforementioned claim. This is so because:

(i) One can find probable allusions, some 'parallel' texts and thematic similarities among the twelve prophetic books included in

26. See 8HevXIIgr; cf. Fuller, 'Form and Formation'. Schneider also claimed that the LXX order of the Twelve depends on and is secondary to an original order which is identical to that of the MT. This claim is based on his reconstruction of the redactional history of the Twelve and its precursors, and mainly on the existence and lasting influence of a pre-exilic, independent book that included only Hosea, Amos and Micah. See Schneider, *Unity*, pp. 224-26; cf. pp. 18-43. Jones advances a (very) different reconstruction of the original order of the Twelve and of its subsequent changes. According to him, (a) 4QXII[a] reflects the original sequence of the first Book of the Twelve; (b) this sequence is identical to that in LXX except that Jonah occupies the last slot—4QXII[a] contains only portions of Malachi and Jonah, the likely related 4QXII[b], of Zephaniah and Haggai (including Zeph. 3.20 and Zeph. 1.1)— (c) the next stage in the ordering of the books is represented by the LXX; and (d) the sequence represented by the MT points to an even later stage. See, Jones, *Formation*, esp. pp. 221-42.

27. An alternative and simpler explanation is that the collection was first ordered in a less than authoritative, somewhat flexible order, which later on become fixed. Such an explanation is also more consonant with the development of the Psalter and likely also with that of the Book of Proverbs.

the Book of the Twelve but also among many of these prophetic books and the three prophetic books that are not included in the Book of the Twelve, namely, Isaiah, Jeremiah and Ezekiel.[28] Only if one can show that the density of quotations, allusions, thematic links and the like is substantially higher within the books included in the Book of the Twelve—or within a series of subsequent books within it—than with 'outside' texts can one consider these features as supporting the claim that these cadres wrote, copied, transmitted and continuously (re)read four separate prophetic books (that is, separate units within a common ideological/ theological discourse) and not fifteen.

(ii) Quotations, allusions, thematic links and the like can be found also between some of these twelve books and non-prophetic texts in the Hebrew Bible. Especially in light of the widespread presence of 'parallelism', of probable allusions and of thematic macrothemes in biblical literature,[29] it is highly questionable if these literary features *per se* must be explained in terms of 'unified readings'. Unless additional considerations are taken into account, it seems reasonable to assume that these features may only prove the presence of shared elements of ideological/ theological and literary discourse across a wide range of texts and types of texts which originated within cadres who lived under more or less similar circumstances. The presence of these shared elements is, in fact, only to be expected given the limited size of the cadres of writers and readers within which and

28. Of course, one may claim that to some extent all the prophetic books were understood in the light of others, but if the borders of the literary referent are widened to include not only the twelve books included in the Book of the Twelve but also Isaiah, Jeremiah and Ezekiel (or their forerunners), then the claim cannot be one of literary unity but of common literary repertoire or sub-repertoire based on a common type of discourse/genre, namely, prophetic book.

29. Such as the role of Zion/Jerusalem in the divine economy, the kingship of Yahweh—and more generally the patronship of Yahweh, the day of Yahweh, the fall of the monarchy and of Jerusalem/Zion as a justified, divine punishment. See ben Zvi, *Obadiah*, *passim*; *idem*, 'Inclusion in and Exclusion from Israel as Conveyed by the Use of the Term "Israel" in Postmonarchic Biblical Texts' in S.W. Holloway and L.K. Handy (eds.), *The Pitcher Is Broken: Memorial Essays for Gösta W. Ahlström* (JSOTSup, 190; Sheffield: JSOT Press, 1995), pp. 95-149; *idem*, 'Understanding the Message of the Tripartite Prophetic Books', *ResQ* 35 (1993), pp. 93-100.

for which most of (Hebrew) biblical literature was written, the inner flow of information within these cadres, and the fact that they most likely shared at least the essentials of their theological/ideological discourse, and needless to say, their literary language(/s). One should also take into account the presence of likely limitations on the size of the repertoire of written texts that these relatively small cadres were supposed to copy, study, (re)read, compose, edit and the like.

(iii) To evaluate the claim that the books included in the Book of the Twelve were written (and rewritten) by these cadres so as to lead to (re)reading of the Book of the Twelve as a unit, one must examine both the presence of inner allusions, 'parallel' texts, shared stylistic devices, common themes and also the discontinuities of style, perspective, and even ideology/theology among the same text. Both types of features may function as textually inscribed markers influencing the (re)reading and understanding of the text.

(g) *The most significant and unequivocal internal evidence, namely that of the titles (or incipits) of the prophetic books, sets them on the same level with Isaiah or Jeremiah or Ezekiel, namely as separate prophetic books*. Most significantly, there is no heading, nor incipit, nor introduction that may serve to orient the readers about the nature of the Book of the Twelve. In this regard, the Book of the Twelve is not only unlike other prophetic books but also unlike clear heterogeneous collections of works such as Proverbs and Psalms. To be plausible, the proposal that those who wrote or edited the books that were eventually included in the Twelve wished to communicate to their readers that these books should be read as a unit must be able to explain why these writers provided none of the accepted discursive markers for introducing a prophetic book or even for introducing a collection of books. Moreover, it has to do so without multiplying ad hoc hypotheses, and without falling into circular thinking (see [h] and especially section 3, below).

(h) It is perhaps worthwhile to conclude these preliminary observations with an explicit statement regarding the obvious: in no case can one allow a historical-critical study aimed at evaluating the claim mentioned in 1.1 to derive any of its conclusions on the implicit or explicit assumption that the Book of the Twelve, or its precursor, was read or edited as whole, for if it were the case, then the entire argument will be circular.[30]

2.2 The Way to Go: Two Main and Alternative Approaches

This being so, and especially since the points made above indicate what cannot count as evidence to evaluate the aforementioned claim, the remainder of the discussion should focus on how the proposed evaluative endeavor can be carried out.

It seems that two approaches are potentially helpful in this regard. Significantly, they come from opposite perspectives. The first approach focuses on the writing side, that is, on the authors, and especially the redactors of the prophetic books. In practice, it has tended to search for potential markers of a conscious editing of the Book of the Twelve as a unified unit. But, of course, these markers—if found—should be evaluated along with potential markers of a conscious editing of each prophetic book as a separate work. It goes without saying that only an analysis of the complete spectrum of the potential markers may lead to the most likely reconstruction of the compositional and redactional processes involved in the creation of this literature.

30. To illustrate, from an observation that the double divine name appears in Amos 9.8a and Obad. 1, it does not necessarily follow that a forerunner of the Book of Amos which did not include Amos 9.8b-15 and the Book of Obadiah underwent a similar redactional process (cf. P. Weimar, 'Obadja. Eine redaktionskritische Analyze', *BN* 27 [1985], p. 45, and esp. n. 31) nor that each of these books informed the (re)reading of the other more than any other prophetic, or, for the sake of the case, biblical book. In fact, the expression כה אמר אדני ה׳ ל-X (see Obad. 1) occurs elsewhere in the Hebrew Bible only in Ezekiel (Ezek. 6.3; 7.2; 12.19; 16.3; 26.15; 36.4; 37.5), and the double divine name occurs mostly in Ezekiel (213 out of 280 times). Moreover, it occurs also in other prophetic texts, including the beginning of Micah—which is the book following Amos in the LXX order— immediately after the superscription (Mic. 1.2; the double divine name does not occur in the titles of the prophetic books, for example, Hos. 1.1; Joel 1.1; Mic. 1.1; Zeph. 1.1) and see, for instance, Jer. 1.6 and Zeph. 1.7. For a full discussion of this issue see my *Obadiah*. The relation between the presence of the double divine name in Amos 9.8a and Obad. 1 is potentially meaningful only within a framework of analysis that assumes a close relationship between the books of Amos and Obadiah.

Another example, it is self-evident that when Jones writes, 'if the reasoning of Tov concerning the significance of sequence changes [between the MT and the LXX of Jeremiah] for literary criticism is applied to the Book of the Twelve, then...' (*Formation*, p. 53), he *assumes* already that the Book of the Twelve belongs to the same (literary) category as the Book of Jeremiah.

The second approach focuses on the recipient rather than on the production end of this corpus of prophetic literature. The shift to recipient is grounded on the speculative character of reconstructions of the writers' intention and on the fact that the mentioned cadres had access to the written text (rather than the actual intentions of the writer), so even their own reconstruction of the writer's intention (actually of that of the implied author) is an act based on their reading of the written text. This approach will search for textually inscribed markers that can reasonably be assumed to have led the intended audience and the historical cadres mentioned above to prefer certain reading strategies over others.

3. *Addressing the Question by means of the 'Writer/Redactor' or 'Production' Centered Approach*

3.1 *The Catchword Phenomenon. Illustrations from a Test Case: The Book of Obadiah*

Given 'basic consideration' (g), it seems that catchwords linking together subsequent books are perhaps the potentially most helpful feature that may indicate conscious editorial processes. It has usually been accepted that one among several possible principles for ordering consecutive texts either in a collection or a unified literary work involved catchwords. For instance, Cassuto pointed to cases such as Joel 4.16 and Amos 1.2, 9.12, Obad. 19, Hab. 2.20, and Zeph. 1.6 to mention some of his examples from prophetic literature; others reached somewhat similar conclusions in regards to Psalms.[31] Significantly, neither Cassuto nor

31. See, U. Cassuto, 'The Sequence and Arrangement of the Biblical Sections', *Biblical and Oriental Studies*, I (Jerusalem: Magnes Press, 1973), pp. 1-6 (the paper was originally read in 1947). As for Psalms, see, for instance, D.M. Howard Jr, 'Editorial Activity in the Psalter: A State-of-the-Field Survey', in J.C. McCann (ed.), *The Shape and Shaping of the Psalter* (JSOTSup, 159; Sheffield: JSOT Press, 1993), pp. 52-70.

Cassuto pointed to this phenomenon not only in the prophetic books but in Canticles and in legal texts as well. Also cf. F. Polak, הסיפור במקרא (Biblical Encyclopaedia Library, 11; Jerusalem: Mosad Bialik, 1994), pp. 91-92 and the bibliography mentioned there. As it is well known, catchwords were one of the criteria influencing the arrangement and sequence of texts in Rabbinic literature. Moreover, word associations play a most substantial role in works in which intertextuality is a main feature, such as the midrash. For one example, see *Num. R.* 16.24; for a discussion on intertextuality and Midrash see, for instance, D. Boyarin, *Intertextuality and the Reading of Midrash* (Bloomington: Indiana University Press, 1990).

those researchers working on Psalms have considered this system of catchwords the only or even the main principle for arranging the material; other principles were also at work and were probably more significant.

In any case, the presence of isolated instances of catchwords within sequential prophetic books does not imply anything beyond that they may have had a limited role in the arrangement of the books. Of course, a reappraisal of the entire issue is due if instead of isolated instances one faces a comprehensive system of catchwords. Such an argument has been advanced in a detailed way by Nogalski who claims that 'throughout the Book of the Twelve, the end of one writing contains significant words which reappear in the opening sections of the next writing'.[32]

Yet it seems that Nogalski's expectations concerning the Twelve shaped his observations and the significance he attached to them, rather than being the other way around. To illustrate, Nogalski points to five catchwords between Obad. 15-21 and Mic. 1.1-7. These words are: הר, יעקב, אש, שמרון and שדה.[33] Of course, the five occur in both texts, but these are five fairly common words. Moreover, the similarities end at the level of the single word detached from its linguistic context. In fact the term שדה שמרון which encompasses two of these words occurs only in Obad. 19 in the entire Hebrew Bible. Furthermore, these words do not necessarily convey similar associative (or even affective) connotations. In any case, it is worth stressing that these words rather than others were selected *from the outset* because they occur in both texts. To illustrate, given that שדה אפרים and שדה שמרון occur one by the other in a 'parallel' structure in Obad. 19, there is no reason to select (or, conversely, unmark) one of the two terms—and then separate the two nouns that constitute the term—except that if one selected שדה אפרים rather than שדה שמרון the resulting set of five independent words would have a set of catchwords binding together Obad. 15-21 and Psalm 78, rather than Mic. 1.1-7 and Obad. 15-21. In other words, Nogalski's observation is not a property of the text by itself but results from the significance he attaches *from the outset* to the sequence Obadiah–Micah,

32. Nogalski, *Literary Precursors*, p. 20. He points to Jon. 4.1 and Zech. 14.1 as exceptions. To a large extent, Schneider, *Unity*, may be seen as a precursor of Nogalski's position in this regard. For a comparison of Schneider's work with that of Nogalski, see Jones, *Formation*, pp. 37-38.

33. Nogalski, *Literary Precursors*, pp. 31-33.

which is the sequence that results if one takes the Book of Jonah away from the Book of the Twelve on the grounds that it was a late addition.

Moreover, catchwords are not reliable indicators. It is worth stressing that had a scholar followed this approach and, by any grounds, claimed that Amos rather than Micah followed Obadiah, such a scholar would have observed that four key words in just the last two verses of Obadiah, namely ציון, ירושלם, גלות and ישראל, occur also in Amos 1.1-9. Such a scholar most likely would have added to these repeated words the mention of Edom in one text and of Esau in the other, pointing both, at least at some level, to the same referent. We can even imagine the kind of rhetorical question that such a scholar could have raised would be something like: 'is it likely to be an accident that four key words and a key reference appear all together in such a brief text as Obad. 20–21 and in Amos 1.1-9, but nowhere else in the entire Hebrew Bible?'

To be sure, this set of repeated words does not indicate that Amos was read in sequence after Obadiah and certainly not that a unified literary unit consisting of Obadiah–Amos in that order existed at any time in history. In fact, one may find some shared terms, though less significant than those in Obadiah–Amos, between Jer. 52.31-34 and Ezek. 1.1-2.[34] But the striking differences between Ezekiel 1 and the end of Jer. 52.31-34 are so significant, and so overpower the few common words, that it is hard to even consider that ancient readers or writers would have seen these two sections, and needless to say the entire books of Jeremiah and Ezekiel, as a unified literary work that had to be read and understood as such.

Finally, there is the question of proper emphasis: the stress on a few, not necessarily key, shared words in the discussions mentioned above relegates to a position of secondary significance the *clear particularity* of the endings of many of the prophetic books. To remain with Obadiah as a test case, there is no ending similar to that in Obad. 21 in any prophetic book. Yet, it is worth noting that Obadiah is not an 'odd' book in this regard, for highly particular endings are present in other prophetic books (for instance, Isa. 66.24; Ezek. 48.35; Hos. 14.10; Jon. 4.11; Mal. 4.24 [or Mal. 4.22-24]). Moreover, if one wishes to think in terms of catchwords, one may observe that that there is no verse in the

34. See the common reference to Jehoiachin, the word מלך, and words related to dates (שנה and חודש). These 'commonalities' are certainly stronger than those among Obad. 19 and Mic. 1.6, and see the discussion in section 3.3.

entire Hebrew Bible—not to say the prophetic books—that shows a set of *keywords* that is similar to that in Obad. 21.[35] This being so, if catchwords are due to a cognizant editorial activity whose goal was to bind neighboring books, what message do these highly particular endings convey?

The rationale for emphasizing, on the one hand, a few shared words within relatively flexible, construed endings as evidence for an intentionally-created, literary unity of the Twelve, while on the other hand de-emphasizing the obvious particularism of a clearly concluding verse seems to be grounded on an initial, deep-rooted conception of the unity of the Twelve rather than on any feature of the text itself.

3.2 *Evaluation of the Significance of the Catchword Phenomenon*

In sum, there are catchwords in the Hebrew Bible. It is also possible that along with other considerations, a trend towards catchwords may have influenced the ordering of the prophetic books within the Twelve.

It is also true that one may find a few words that appear towards the end of a prophetic book included in the Twelve and around the beginning of the next prophetic according to the sequence found either in the masoretic Book of the Twelve or in a reconstructed forerunner of this book. The main issue, however, is what the significance of this observed phenomenon is in historical terms. The discussion above strongly suggests that, rather than proving the unity of the Twelve, these observations and especially any interpretation of them that points to a unified understanding of the Twelve are based on a pre-ordinate conception of the unity of the Twelve. As such, these considerations fall under the category of 'proving what was already assumed', that is circular thinking.

3.3 *Further Considerations and Illustrations Regarding the 'Writer/Redactor' or 'Production' Centered Approach to this Question*

To avoid the problem of circular thinking, independent evidence must be brought to bear on the case for the unity of the Twelve. Within the realm of historical-critical studies much of the additional evidence comes from redactional approaches. Both Wolfe and Nogalski have advanced

35. To illustrate, הר עשׂו occurs only in Obadiah; מושיע and מלוכה appear together in Obad. 21 but nowhere else even within the frame of an entire chapter in the prophetic books; there is no verse except Obad. 21 in which the words ה׳, ציון and עשׂו appear together, in fact, there is not even a chapter in the Hebrew Bible in which this does occur, except Obad. 1.

comprehensive proposals whose aim is to reconstruct the redactional processes that led to the formation of the Book of the Twelve; others have discussed specific sections of the books included in the Twelve but their work has implications for the study of the mentioned process (for example, Bosshard, and many of the papers given at the SBL consultation about the Formation of the Book of the Twelve).

It is true that if one can demonstrate, independently of any pre-conception about the unified character of the Book of the Twelve, that the redactional processes influencing many of the books included in the Twelve indeed show an awareness of the 'ongoing' Book of the Twelve as a literary unit then independent support for the claim mentioned in 1.1 will be found. How can such an awareness be demonstrated? I would suggest that this can be done if one can prove that there are a significant number of instances in which units in one book are intentionally edited on the basis of other units found in a book that either is adjacent to the first one or was adjacent to it in a forerunner of the Book of the Twelve (as opposed to books not found in the Twelve). A similar claim may be advanced if one can prove that the mentioned sets of catchwords are due to a cognizant editorial activity whose goal was to bind neighboring books.[36]

It goes without saying that a full and complete discussion requires a separate study of each specific proposal, and then an analysis of the entire issue in the light of the conclusions reached in each particular case. Such a discussion cannot be carried out in this paper. Yet, it is possible within the limitations of a single article to use a particular example as a test-case.

Turning again to Obadiah, as the test-case, one must mention that Nogalski in his comprehensive study claims the following: (a) 'a substantial number of changes in Obadiah are classified best as structural alterations on the basis of Amos 9.1ff';[37] (b) the restructuring begins in Obad. 1 with the superscription of the book (the vision of Obadiah);[38] and (c) 'Obad. 19 comments upon the judgement against Samaria in Mic. 1.6...'[39]

36. Nogalski makes these precise claims. See Nogalski, *Literary Precursors* and *idem*, *Redactional Processes*, *passim*.

37. Nogalski, *Redactional Processes*, p. 64.

38. Nogalski, *Redactional Processes*, p. 64.

39. Nogalski, *Redactional Processes*, pp. 83-84, the quotation from p. 84.

In all fairness to Nogalski, one must also mention that he explicitly maintains that 'were the use of חזון the only touchstone with Amos 9.1ff, this option [that 'someone deliberately selected חזון as a superscriptive element as part of an attempt to correlate Amos 9.1ff and Obadiah'] would seem less likely, but given other structural parallels between the sections, this option must be open'.[40] Hence, claim (b) stands on the strength of claim (a). Nogalski states that 'the most concrete example of the connection to Amos appears in Obad. 4 with the phrase "from there I will bring you down"'.[41] The main argument advanced in favor of the proposal points (a) to the presence of אוֹרִידְךָ in Obad. 4 and אוֹרִידֵם in Amos 9.2 and (b) to 'several alterations made in the surrounding text in Obadiah'.[42] Concerning (a), Nogalski's claim is that 'the rarity of the verb form makes it highly unlikely that the two would "accidentally" appear so close to one another'.[43] It goes without saying that the expression 'so close to one another' reveals that the analysis is governed by a pre-existing assumption about the lack of independence of the Book of Obadiah and about the literary unity of Amos–Obadiah. This being the case, the result of the analysis cannot be counted as independent evidence pointing to the literary unity of Amos–Obadiah, nor to that of an ongoing Book of the Twelve (see above).

But one may also wonder about the assumption that use of אוֹרִידְךָ in Obad. 4 is to be explained in terms of the use of אוֹרִידֵם in Amos 9.2 rather than in terms of its immediate context. It is not only that אוֹרִידְךָ occurs also in Jer. 49.16 (in other words, in a text that partially parallels that of Obad. 4), but, given that the immediately preceding verse describes Edom hubristically asking 'who may bring me down?' (מִי יוֹרִדֵנִי; see v. 3), is it not 'natural' that the text will continue with a direct or indirect report about the LORD saying 'I will bring you down' (אוֹרִידְךָ)? Why should one assume that the writer responsible for אוֹרִידְךָ in Obad. 4 had to resort to the written text of Amos 9.2 rather than rely on his (or less likely her) basic competence in his (or her) own language?[44]

40. Nogalski, *Redactional Processes*, p. 64.

41. Nogalski, *Redactional Processes*, p. 64.

42. Nogalski, *Redactional Processes*, p. 65.

43. Nogalski, *Redactional Processes*, p. 65.

44. Moreover, even if, for the sake of the argument, one were to agree that מִי יוֹרִדֵנִי in v. 3 is a late addition to the Book of Obadiah, the text in v. 4 still requires a verb announcing that Edom will be brought down or the like. This being the case, the use of ירד in the *hiphil* here (rather than, for instance a form of קבץ) is easily explainable because of the negative connotations—from the perspective of the one

This question leads to the issue of the model of writing that researchers assume in their studies. In this regard, one may mention, that as a rule, it seems more reasonable, and more consonant with the basic principle that one should not multiply hypotheses without necessity, to prefer as the *default* model of writing one based on people activating potential patterns in their language in a way that is (a) consistent with the text being written and (b) comprehensible to their actual or intended audience with which they share a common language, rather than a model based on 'read and copy' from other sources. This is especially so when dealing with the use of very common words such as those associated with ירד in the *hiphil*.[45]

As for the intended and actual audience of the Book of Obadiah (the latter consisting of the highly educated members of the group within which and for which the Book of Obadiah was written), one may safely assume that their competent Hebrew included an awareness of the root ירד in the *hiphil*, and, accordingly, they would not find אוֹרִידְךָ either strange or in need of an 'intertextual' explanation through Amos 9.2, and the more so, since there are no similarities at the level of the wording between Amos 9.2 and Obad. 4 except מִשָּׁם אוֹרִידְךָ.[46] In sum, the intertextual explanation neither results in nor addresses any exegetical need within the Book of Obadiah as it stands[47] but is fully dependent and derives its impetus on a preconception about the Amos–Obadiah nexus.

Needless to say, one may counter-claim by advancing the argument that although such a situation holds true in regards to the final form of the Book of Obadiah, this is not the case regarding a literary precursor of the present Book of Obadiah. In fact, Nogalski's argument in regards

who is brought down—of ירד in the *hiphil* (for example, 2 Sam. 22.48; Isa. 10.13; Ps. 56.8). These connotations are certainly activated in Obad. 4 (and Jer. 49.16). I discuss these issues in ben Zvi, *Obadiah*.

45. There are more than sixty instances of ירד in the *hiphil* in the Hebrew Bible. The first person form was activated in Obad. 4 because the discourse developed there required it, and the same holds true concerning the choice of the *yqṭl* form.

46. The presence of מִשָּׁם in the first position in the clause, that is before the *yqṭl* form, serves the purpose of emphasizing the reversal, cf. Deut 30.4; Neh 1.9, and see ben Zvi, *Obadiah*.

47. For a full analysis of v. 4 see ben Zvi, *Obadiah*. Of course, one may propose redactional stages that reflect such a need. But the question is how strong the arguments in favor of these reconstructed texts are if the Amos–Obadiah nexus is not accepted from the outset. See below.

to Obad. 4 (and Obad. 19, see below) is partially based on his detailed reconstruction of the redactional history of the text. Of course, a proposal that rests on a hypothetical textual reconstruction carries an additional burden of proof, that is, that it does not multiply hypotheses without necessity. Moreover, the likelihood of such a proposal is in the most optimal circumstances only as good as the textual reconstruction on which it rests. This being the case, it is worth noting that whereas one can safely assume that redactional processes took place in prophetic books, it seems doubtful that any degree of certainty can be associated with precise textual reconstructions of the individual redactional stages of a particular book.[48] Moreover, these difficulties are even compounded if, rather than dealing with known books, one focuses from the outset on literary units whose very existence is hypothetical, such as a precursor of the Book of the Twelve that contained only Hosea, Amos, Micah and Zephaniah.[49] Furthermore, and focusing on the test case, one may observe the tentative, and even controversial, character of some of the assumptions used by Nogalski to establish the precise textual history of Obad. 4, such as those relating to the textual relationship between Obad. 1-9 and Jer. 49.7ff.,[50] and those relating to the issue of criteria to discern between the compositional level of the Book of Obadiah—to be

48. As I wrote in a footnote in chapter 1 of my *Obadiah*:

> One has to strictly distinguish between the likelihood that a text underwent redactional development or that it relies on pre-compositional sources and the likelihood of any particular textual reconstruction of the posited written works. We all recognize that Chronicles follows Samuel and Kings (or closely related texts), but none of us could have reconstructed Samuel and Kings out of the Book of Chronicles. This is so, because it is impossible to reconstruct from the final text what was omitted from the sources—unless the sources are present somewhere, and because ancient authors and editors worked in a 'logical', but certainly not consistent, nor always predictable manner. Needless to say, the more sophisticated these authors/redactors were, and the more they tended to communicate or express more than one perspective on a single issue, or the more that they tended to present a vision that results out of a set of contrasting perspectives, and the more ambiguous they were, then the more hopeless, from a critical point of view, this work of reconstruction becomes' (p. 7).

49. Nogalski points to a corpus consisting of these four books; Schneider prefers to develop the idea of a 700 BCE Hosea–Amos–Micah collection. See Schneider, *Unity*, pp. 35-43. Incidentally, Schneider sees many similarities between Isaiah and Zephaniah (pp. 45-48).

50. See Nogalski, *Redactional Processes*, pp. 61-68, and his bibliographic references to alternative approaches. I discussed elsewhere these issues at length and reached a conclusion significantly different from that advanced by Nogalski. See ben Zvi, *Obadiah*, *passim*.

distinguished from any of its possible sources—and later additions to the already existent text of the Book of Obadiah.[51]

As for the third claim in the test case, namely, that 'Obad. 19 comments upon the judgement against Samaria in Mic. 1.6',[52] this claim is based on redactional hypotheses and to some extent on (a) the significance given by Nogalski to the occurrence of the word שׂדה in Mic. 1.6 and Obad. 19 and (b) the reference to שׁמרון in both texts. The issue of resting proposals on possible but speculative reconstructions of texts has been addressed above. As for שׁמרון, neither text requires the other in order to be understood by their ancient audiences. Moreover, one may observe that the reference to שׁמרון does not play the same role in Obad. 19 and Mic. 1.6. Furthermore, שׁמרון is characterized in different ways in both texts, and, in addition, it is likely that different (historical) referents were alluded to by the 'code-word' שׁמרון in each text.[53] Finally, the texts are dissimilar in content, style and language. These considerations seriously undermine the strength of any proposal that Obad. 19 was written as a comment on the judgement of Samaria in Mic. 1.6. Nogalski brings in support of his proposal the presence of the word שׂדה in both Mic. 1.6 and Obad. 19. But, whereas in Mic. 1.6 שׂדה appears in the expression עי השׂדה, it occurs in שׂדה שׁמרון in Obad. 19. Again, this is a case of a selection made at the level of the single word, with disregard to the contextual meaning it carries, and which is based on a preconception of the relation between Micah and Obadiah. It is also worth stressing that all the words in Obad. 19 appear elsewhere, and so does the only clear word-pair (for example, שׁמרון־אפרים; see Isa. 9.8; Hos. 7.1). There is no intrinsic reason for the choice of the word שׂדה here over and against any other word in the text.[54] The selection of

51. For instance, did the original text of the Book of Obadiah—again to be distinguished from any possible source—lack ואם־בין כוכבים? Can this issue be convincingly settled by stating that 'it not only interrupts the syntax, it also exaggerates the metaphor...'? See Nogalski, *Redactional Processes*, pp. 65-66, and cf. ben Zvi, *Obadiah*, chapter 3.

52. Nogalski, *Redactional Processes*, pp. 83-84, the quotation from p. 84.

53. On the northern tribes of Israel in Obadiah, see ben Zvi, *Obadiah*, chapters 8 and 9.

54. Nogalski points out that the word שׂדה occasionally bears a meaning akin to 'territory', and that this may be the case in Obad. 19. In fact, שׂדה may also mean 'highland' or 'mountain'. But if this is the case, and if one assumes that the writer wished to effectively communicate a message to the readership of the book, one has to imagine that the writer responsible for Obad. 19 wished to lead the readers of this

the repetition of שׂדה as 'significant' evidence is based on Nogalski's hypothesis rather than vice versa.[55]

A final consideration: prophetic books are texts written to be read and understood; they serve a communicative purpose. If the writer responsible for Obad. 19 wished to communicate to the readers of the book that Obad. 19 should be understood as a comment on the judgement of Samaria in Mic. 1.6, it is reasonable to assume that the mentioned repetition of שׂדה, amid the sea of differences between the two texts, is not an efficient way of doing so, to say the least.[56] Hence, one must assume that this writer was either unable to introduce a clear marker so as to lead the readers of the book to an interpretation consonant with his intentions or was intentionally misleading the intended audience. The first approach is extremely unlikely given the literary sophistication of the trained cadres of writers and readers responsible for the prophetic literature. The second approach leads to an ad hoc hypothesis for which there is no support.

text to an understanding of Obad. 19 as a comment on the judgement on Samaria in Mic. 1.6 by introducing, and *only* by introducing the word שׂדה carrying the meaning of 'highland' or 'mountain' or 'territory' in Obad. 19, even if in Mic. 1.6 שׂדה means 'field'. Is this a likely image? See also below.

55. This observation is strongly supported by the fact that the kind of 'catchword' evidence advanced to support the link between Obadiah and Micah, or even 'superior evidence', may be 'found' in artificial sequences of prophetic books. The case of Obad. 20-21 and Amos 1.1-9—which has been discussed before—is an obvious and perhaps even extreme example because of the density of 'sharing' given that these are two very short pericopes, and esp. so Obad. 20-21. Yet other instances come to mind. As it is well known, according to *b. B. Bat.* 14b, the order of the three larger prophetic books is Jeremiah, Ezekiel and Isaiah. Someone who assumes that (a) this sequence is original, (b) Ezekiel 40–48 is a later addition—a relatively common position—and (c) 'catchwords' such as those between Obad. 19 and Mic. 1.6 point to a conscious redactional attempt to bind the two book together, is likely to 'observe' a play between אדמתכם in Isa. 1.7 and אדמתם in Ezek. 39.26, 28. The same person may point to the occurrences of verbs from יתר in the *hiphil* (see Ezek. 39.28 and Isa. 1.9) and even note that this is the only instance of יתר in the *hiphil* in the entire Book of Isaiah. Perhaps, such a person would also like to mention that a few common nouns appear in both texts, such as גוי, ארץ, ישראל. And yet there is a great difference between Ezek. 39.25-29 and Isa. 1.1, 2-9. In sum, these examples show that this type of consideration cannot be considered as convincing evidence pointing to redactional intentions. In fact, they are most likely a result of a pre-conception held by the scholar proposing them.

56. It is worth noting that those responsible for the ancient versions 'missed' this marker.

3.4 *Some Inherent, Unavoidable Weaknesses of the 'Writer/Redactor' or 'Production' Centered Approach*

To conclude the present discussion of the writer's approach, it seems worthwhile to explicitly mention three inherent, unavoidable weaknesses of this approach:

(a) It relies on precise and *cumulative* textual reconstructions of redactional stages, *each* of which is far from secure.

(b) It reconstructs the intention of the actual not the implied writer on the basis of literary analysis.

(c) It recovers authorial intentions on the basis of proposed common words taken from different literary contexts, rather on the internal discursive markers and contexts of each text.

3.5 *Conclusion: The Need for an Alternative Approach*

The present discussion has clearly shown the limitations of the first approach. It has also raised an important issue (esp. at the conclusion of 3.3), namely that of textually inscribed, communicative markers whose purpose is to provide the intended audience with interpretative keys for their reading of the text. These markers may provide a better way of approaching our task, namely the evaluation of the claim mentioned in 1.1. This issue is at the center of the next section in this article.

4. *Addressing the Question by means of the 'Audience' or 'Reception' Centered Approach*

4.1 *General Introduction and Assumptions*

Prophetic books are written works composed and produced to be read and (re)read. The meanings evolving out of the interaction between the ancient readers for which the book was written and the text being read are not only partially shaped by the socio-cultural—in an inclusive, general sense—circumstances of these educated cadres but also partially shapes these circumstances, including their theological/ideological horizons. Thus, this approach does not focus on the author, editor, or redactor of the text but on the reception of the text by the communities for which and within which it was written, in other words, on how the text was likely read by these communities consisting of the educated cadres who were able to write and to read and reread the type of literature represented by the prophetic books, and, eventually, on how this literature contributed to the shaping of their discourse.

The first basic assumption of this approach is that, although the intended readers implied in the text are obviously not identical with the actual readers and learners of these written texts, the former provide a significant approximation to the main features of the latter.[57] This assumption is reasonable because had this not been the case, one can hardly imagine acceptance of the book within the repertoire of the community of actual readers and learners of these books.

The second basic assumption is that the intended readers were more likely to follow textually inscribed markers suggesting a scheme about what the book was about, and about strategies of reading and rereading, rather than to decide that the text was written so as to mislead them, and accordingly, to ignore these discursive and literary markers.

If this is true, then these markers provide at least a potential way to evaluate the claim mentioned in section 1.1. The heuristic questions are, therefore: (a) which textually inscribed markers could have led the audience to choose their reading strategy? and then (b) whether the books included in the Twelve are written so as to clearly convey to their intended audience that they read them as a unified, sequential unit, or not?

4.2 *Illustration and Implications of this Approach: The Book of Obadiah as a Test Case*

A full historical-critical study of the Book of Obadiah or even any of its subunits is obviously beyond the scope of this paper,[58] but still, it seems possible to point to the presence in this text of clear, textually inscribed markers that it is most reasonable to assume likely contributed to the intended audience's preference of a particular reading strategy (in this case, as a separate book) over its alternatives.

The significant role of introductions as interpretative keys for the developing of, at the very least, the first mental scheme about what a book is about is widely recognized. Introductions not only help the (first) audience to create a provisional scheme of what the following text is about—and accordingly suggests to the readers or learners of this text a set of questions and issues to be dealt with—but also evoke the memory of the read material among the (re)readers of the book, an important function if the prophetic books were written to be (re)read.

57. Cf. D. Kraemer, 'The Intended Reader As a Key to Interpreting the Bavli', *Prooftexts* 13 (1993), pp. 125-40.

58. For my contribution in this respect, see ben Zvi, *Obadiah*.

The title of the Book of Obadiah provides already the first, textually inscribed, and most significant interpretative key for the (re)readers of this book. This title communicates to the audience that (i) the book should be understood as חזון, and accordingly, that the authority and legitimacy of its message are grounded on the divine, and (ii) this specific חזון is associated with a particular personage, Obadiah, and should be read accordingly. The title certainly does not ask its readership to read the ensuing book in terms of any other book nor as a comment on another prophetic book. In fact, it is most reasonable to assume that the title asks its audience to read the book in its own terms—significantly, there is no title to the Book of the Twelve.[59]

One may also easily notice that all the literary units in the Book of Obadiah are cross-referenced to other units in the book, and they show some form of the 'terrace pattern' linking them to the preceding and the following unit—if the case is applicable. One example will suffice for the present purposes. The reader of vv. 19-21 cannot help but notice the similarities between וְיָרְשׁוּ at v. 19 and at the beginning of v. 17b. Significantly, this verbal form is not only dominant, but the only one present in vv. 19-20. The expression הַר עֵשָׂו is selected in vv. 19 and 21, but also in vv. 8 and 9. It is worth noting that this expression occurs in the Book of Obadiah but nowhere else in the Hebrew Bible. The reader may also notice the reference to הַר צִיּוֹן in v. 21 and in v. 16, and the (at least) phonetic resemblance between חֵל in v. 20 and חֵיל in vv. 11 and 13. In addition, it is obvious that vv. 19-20 take up the issues and, to some extent, the wording and imagery evolving out of the preceding unit in Obadiah.[60] Significantly, there is nothing remotely similar between Obad. 19-21 and the following text in the Twelve, Jon. 1, or, for the sake of the case, between Obad. 19-21[61] and Mic. 1,[62] or any other text in the Hebrew Bible—on the particularizing endings of many prophetic books see above, section 3.1. If the intended audience of the

59. See ben Zvi, *Obadiah*, chapter 2.

60. For a full discussion, see ben Zvi, *Obadiah*, chapter 9.

61. Whether Obad. 19-21 was an integral part of the Book of Obadiah from the outset or was added later by an editor, the fact is that it is integrated by dense sets of cross-references to the preceding unit and to other units in the Book of Obadiah, just as other units in the book are bound to one another in this book (see ben Zvi, *Obadiah*, *passim*).

62. Cf. section 3.3.

book followed these textually inscribed markers, it must have read the Book of Obadiah as a unit by itself.

4.3 *From the Test Case to a General Evaluation*

It is beyond the scope of this paper to study each prophetic book in detail and then to assess whether its internal discursive and stylistic markers seem to ask their readers to understand them as separate units or (mainly, or above all) as an integral part of a larger unit, 'the Book of the Twelve'. In any case, it seems, at the level of preliminary observations, that if the general issue of the 'Twelve Prophetic Books' as opposed to 'The Twelve' is to be addressed from this perspective, then the illustrations from Obadiah along with several of the considerations mentioned above seem to delineate a reasonable path for the investigation. This path seems to lead to significant, though preliminary, conclusions.

First, the issue of titles and incipits[63] has been briefly mentioned in point (g) of the 'preliminary considerations' (section 2.1) and then in the preceding example. Titles and incipits (for the latter, see, for instance, Jon. 1.1) help the readership of the prophetic books to think of them as separate, self-standing works.

It is true that some of these titles are actually subtitles (for example, Isa. 2.1, 13.1; Jer. 45.1; Hab. 3.1) within a book, but no prophetic book contains subtitles that directly associate the ensuing text with someone other than the main prophetic character referred to by the main title,[64] unlike the case in Proverbs (cf., for instance, Prov. 1.1 and 31.1). If the association of the text to multiple personages contributes to the characterization of a work as a collection of separate literary units (for example, Psalms, Proverbs), the association of the entire text of a book with one character seems to convey a sense of unity within the single prophetic book. This feature stands irrespective of any likely compositional or redactional history of the book. Within the world created in the Book of Isaiah, there is no character 'Deutero-Isaiah,' nor 'Trito-Isaiah.'

63. The significant role of introductions as interpretative keys for developing at the very least the first mental scheme about what the book is about is widely recognized. Within the realm of biblical studies see, for instance, P.D. Miller, 'The Beginning of the Psalter', in *The Shape and Shaping of the Psalter*, pp. 83-92. I discuss this issue at relative length in my *Obadiah*, chapter 2.

64. That is there are no multiple 'Xs' in formulas such as X-חזון, X-דברי, or X-דבר ה׳ היה אל and the like in a single prophetic book.

In fact, it is the (literary) claim of the book that all the material included there is to be associated with a personage identified as Isaiah, the son of Amoz. The present discussion strongly suggests that the socially-accepted conventions for a 'prophetic book' at the time of the composition and redaction of these books could not have allowed the presentation of a character such as 'Deutero-Isaiah' nor a title such as 'the vision of Deutero-Isaiah' in Isa. 40.1 or anywhere in the Book of Isaiah. Such a title could have been written only if Isa. 40.1 had been the beginning of a separate, independent prophetic book.[65]

Secondly, the conclusions (in other words, the final words) of prophetic books tend also to be highly particular (see above).

Thirdly, a preliminary overview of prophetic books seems to show an overwhelming tendency to contain one or more systems of cross-references and idioms that are common within the book but rare in the other books. Beyond the observations made in regards to Obadiah, obvious illustrations of this tendency are בן־אדם and the system of cross-references associated with כבוד ה' in Ezekiel, and קדוש ישראל, as well as the network of references to Zion, in Isaiah. In fact, my previous studies in Obadiah and Zephaniah pointed out that each book shows an Obadianic or Zephanic flavour that is noticeable even when the writers of these books relied on written sources, for this flavour shaped and integrated the relevant text into an integral unit, be it the Book of Obadiah or the Book of Zephaniah.[66]

It is possible and even likely that the presence of distinctive language also serves the purpose of characterizing and 'individualizing' the persona of the prophet to whom the book is attributed.[67] These particularizing tendencies are the more significant once one recognizes that it is

65. It is worth stressing that in most prophetic books not only the beginning of the book signals to the readers its separate status, but also the endings show clear particularizing tendencies. See above. That the ending of a book carries an important communicative message to its readership is widely accepted. In relation to biblical books see, for instance, Miller, 'Beginning'.

66. See ben Zvi, *Obadiah*, chapter 5 and bibliography mentioned there. In regards to Zeph. 3.3-4 (and its 'parallel' text in Ezek. 22.25-29) see ben Zvi, *A Historical Critical Study of the Book of Zephaniah* (BZAW, 198; Berlin: de Gruyter, 1991), pp. 190-206.

67. For a study on the characters in the Book of Job and their characterization by means of their reported language, see M. Cheney, *Dust, Wind and Agony: Character, Speech and Genre in Job* (ConBOT, 36; Lund: Almqvist & Wiksell International, 1994), *passim*.

extremely unlikely that those social groups who were responsible for the postmonarchic literary activity that led to a particular prophetic book as we know it, did not at least read and (re)read and likely redacted other prophetic books. The size of the postmonarchic cadres of educated writers and sophisticated readers within which these books were written, and their probable geographical concentration, are not conducive to an extreme fragmentation in which each splinter group develops a particular sociolect and a particular theological approach that comes to the surface in one single book. Moreover, it is not only hard to imagine 'Obadianic', 'Zephanic', 'Jeremianic', 'Isaianic' groups (or 'disciples groups') each using its own characteristic expressions, each redacting one single book, and, perhaps, each considering one single book as the divine teaching for the community, but also there is absolutely no evidence for such a proposal. Needless to say, one may also rightly wonder about the literary repertoire of these hypothetical 'Isaianic', 'Zephanic', and the like groups of highly educated writers and readers. If so, it is more reasonable to assume that in a wide sociological and historical sense the same groups developed the prophetic literature.

In sum, these preliminary observations strongly suggest that the aforementioned cadres of postmonarchic writers and readers aimed at shaping each prophetic book and, perhaps above all, each prophetic personage in a distinctive way, in spite of macrothemes like those mentioned in 2.1-2.[68] At least, their work seems to reflect such a tendency.[69]

5. *Conclusions and Questions for Further Thought*

Preliminary considerations can lead only to preliminary conclusions. The general trend of the results is, however, significant. None of the arguments supporting the validity of the claim mentioned in 1.1 withstood scrutiny. Moreover, clear, textually inscribed pieces of evidence seem to invalidate such a claim.

68. I discussed some of these issues in ben Zvi, *Obadiah*, chapter 11.

69. The only alternative is to assume that they were sloppy or misleading writers. Neither of the two alternatives seems likely. See above. The fact that prophets are not described as citing each other in prophetic books (cf. Schneider, *Unity*, pp. 195-97) is clearly consonant with the mentioned tendency, and it may well reflect it. The contrast with later literature where citations of earlier sources abound is obvious (see, for instance, Mt. 1.23). On Jer. 26.18, see Schneider, *Unity*, p. 195.

Whereas these preliminary considerations consistently lead to the rejection of the mentioned claim, they also open possibilities for the 'unity of the Twelve', even if it is a unity of a different nature. Rather than assuming a unified book that is read and redacted as such, it is perhaps better to focus on the common repertoire of a relatively small social group consisting of educated writers and readers within which and for which prophetic—and other 'biblical'—books were written, at the very least in their present form. Such a focus is likely to uncover a (largely) shared discourse, a common linguistic heritage, implied 'intertextuality',[70] and shared literary/ideological tendencies.[71]

70. The reference is to instances in which the background of the intended audience of a particular text includes an awareness of ideas, images, and the like expressed in another text within the repertoire of the community of readers and writers. For instance, I recently claimed elsewhere that some sections in Chronicles that are not paralleled in Kings strongly suggest an intended audience that is well aware of the narrative in Kings. See ben Zvi, 'The Chronicler as a Historian: Building Texts', in M.P. Graham, K. Hoglund, and S. McKenzie (eds.), *Chronicles and the History of Ancient Israel* (R. Dillard Memorial Book; JSOTSup; Sheffield: JSOT Press, forthcoming).

71. If an 'audience' rather than 'redactor' centered approach is to be followed—as this study suggests—then it is likely that many of these relations will be construed according to a 'net' instead of an 'arrow' metaphor. The net metaphor reflects the claim that it is reasonable to assume that—in most cases—the reading of a text within the educated cadres of the Achaemenid period was set within a context that included the other 'related' texts they were aware of. The 'arrow' metaphor, which is more characteristic of the 'author/redactor' centered approach, reflects a claim about an unequivocal relation between a proposed 'prototext' and a 'metatext', the latter being a conscious allusion, comment or rework of the former which is read as such. (Scholars advocating a 'author/redactor' centered approach will likely focus on 'arrow' metaphors because their main interest is on the presumed manner in which the author or redactor worked when writing the text; see above.) These two approaches are also likely to differ on the evaluation of the significance of the observed intertextual relations. The 'author/redactor' approach may tend to emphasize their role even if they seem to play a minor role in the book itself (in other words, a detail here and there) because they presumably shed light on the intention of the author/redactor (for example, Nogalski); the 'audience' approach will evaluate them according to their centrality in their own text. That is, for instance, even if, for the sake of the argument, one were to agree that the word שׂדה in Obad. 19 served as an intertextual marker pointing to Mic. 1.6 and was recognized as such by the intended audience of Obadiah, this second approach will de-emphasize the significance of the marker because of the less than central role that one is to assign to the word (or half-word in this context) שׂדה within the literary frame of the Book of

One of the most significant preliminary conclusions of this paper is that the literary and theological/ideological features shared by all the prophetic books seem to include strong textually-inscribed requests to the readership of these books to understand each prophetic personage and each prophetic book as distinct from the others.

Taking into account that in this discourse the divine revelations and the divine knowledge associated with the (accepted) prophetic figures could be approached only by means of reading, (re)reading, and meditating upon the prophetic books held dear by the community/ies reading (and writing and redacting) them, then a clear conclusion seems to emerge: a manifold, theological/ideological discourse was developed in these communities of educated readers and writers by means of a series of readings of particular books informing one another. If this is so, it follows that the discourse/s of these cadres of writers and readers can be reconstructed only through the plurality of points of view—one informing the other—expressed in their repertoire.[72]

Obadiah. Perhaps even more important, the repertoire of intertextual markers observed by scholars following an 'audience' approach is likely to be significantly smaller than the one advocated by those following an 'author/redactor' approach because the former will tend not to incorporate possible intertextual markers that are not clearly conveyed as such to the intended audience. See, for instance, the example of אוֹרִידְךָ in Obad. 4 and אוֹרִידֵם in Amos 9.2 which has been discussed in section 3.3.

72. It goes without saying that this plurality existed within certain theological/ideological limits. It is worth noting that manifold approaches also characterize individual prophetic books. See ben Zvi, *Obadiah*, *passim*, but esp. chapter 11.

THE TWELVE: INTERPRETATIONS

John Watts's work on the Twelve Prophets has more often focused on specific passages and books than on the whole, yet it has usually drawn attention to the impact of the larger context on a text's meaning. The eight essays in this section bring that same concern to a variety of passages in the Twelve.

Margaret Odell and Jörg Jeremias deal with the beginnings of the collection in Hosea and Amos, drawing attention to how these books shape the meaning of 'prophet' in surprising ways. The similar trio of Nahum, Habakkuk and Zephaniah are analyzed from the perspectives of the history of interpretation, thematic analysis, and genre by Duane Christensen, Paul House, and James Watts respectively. Kenneth Craig, Paul Redditt and Donald Berry address the concluding books of Haggai, Zechariah and Malachi, looking for literary shaping which influences the meaning of the Twelve as a whole.

THE PROPHETS AND THE END OF HOSEA

Margaret S. Odell

The book of Hosea is a masterpiece of editing: it begins with a tragic story of two marriages gone awry, and it ends with voices of longing, reconciliation, and hope. The core of the book contains oracles that are no less vivid but whose interpretation remains overshadowed by this story of the lost loves of Hosea and Yahweh. The effect of this editing is so profound that no critical discussion of the structure of the book can afford to omit these chapters.

However, in this essay, I wish to shift the focus and explore the *end* of the book and ask whether the sayings concerning the prophets are related to it. This topic needs some justification. For one thing, there are not many references to the prophets. One occurs as an aside in an oracle concerning a priest (Hos. 4.5); and five others treat the prophets only briefly (6.4-5; 9.7, 8; 12.11, 14). It would thus appear unlikely that these sayings play any major role in the final editing of the book. Indeed, scholars who have investigated the book's structure have not highlighted them.[1]

On the other hand, one would think that a proper interpretation of these sayings would be fundamental to the whole question of the book's formation. With the possible exception of Hos. 4.5, these sayings describe how God uses the prophets; and so one might reasonably ask whether they contribute to an understanding of Hosea's message as it

1. M.J. Buss, *The Prophetic Word of Hosea. A Morphological Study* (BZAW, 111; Berlin: A. Töpelmann, 1969), esp. pp. 28-33; E.M. Good, 'The Composition of Hosea', *SEÅ* 31 (1966), pp. 21-63; I. Willi-Plein, *Vorformen der Schriftexegese innerhalb des Alten Testaments. Untersuchungen zum literarischen Werden der auf Amos, Hosea und Micha zurückgehenden Bücher im hebraïschen Zwölfprophetenbuch* (BZAW, 123; Berlin: de Gruyter, 1971); and B. Peckham, *History and Prophecy: The Development of Late Judean Literary Traditions* (ABRL; New York: Doubleday, 1993), pp. 183-206.

achieves its final canonical form. Do they generate certain expectations about the message of Hosea and, by extension, of the rest of the Book of the Twelve?

It is the current consensus that these sayings do define Hosea's message, along with that of the other prophets of Northern Israel. Accordingly, they are mined for biographical information about Hosea, and they are generally read as statements depicting the prophets as those who preserve and present the word of God to a corrupt society in which all other means of divine-human intermediation have gone awry.[2] This reading of the prophetic passages takes us well on the way to perceiving the Book of the Twelve as a Deuteronomistic collection of the words of Yahweh's servants the prophets.

But is this an accurate reading of the prophetic passages in Hosea? Recently, several critics have questioned the tendency to equate the classical prophets with the references to the *n^ebî'îm*, particularly in the early prophetic writings. Auld, for example, has pointed out that the term *nābî'* carried largely negative connotations until after the Babylonian exile. He has therefore suggested that it is more appropriate to view the authors of the prophetic books as 'poets' who came to be identified as 'prophets' only during the postexilic period.[3] Vawter has also raised the question whether it is appropriate to think of the authors of the prophetic writings as *n^ebî'îm*.[4] Finally, Carroll draws attention to the strange formal contradiction between the condemnation of the *n^ebî'îm*, on the one hand, and the high value placed on the canonical prophets, on the other, and he resists the scholarly tendency to resolve this tension by means of the distinction between true and false prophecy.[5]

2. For the basis of this consensus, see H.-W. Wolff, 'Hoseas geistige Heimat', *TLZ* 81 (1956), pp. 83-94. Nearly every commentary and general reference work on the prophets since then is dependent on Wolff's interpretation of the prophetic passages.

3. A.G. Auld, 'Prophets through the Looking Glass: Between Writings and Moses', *JSOT* 27 (1983), pp. 3-23, esp. p. 20.

4. B. Vawter, 'Were the Prophets *nābî's*?', *Bib* 66 (1985), pp. 206-19.

5. R.P. Carroll, 'Night Without Vision: Micah and the Prophets', in F. García Martínez, A. Hilhorst, C.J. Labuschagne (eds.), *The Scriptures and the Scrolls* (Festschrift A.S. van der Woude; VTSup, 49; Leiden: Brill, 1992), pp. 74-84. See also Carroll's 'Poets not Prophets: A Response to "Prophets through the Looking-Glass"', *JSOT* 27 (1983), pp. 25-31.

Whether or not one agrees fully with these scholars,[6] one notes that they have raised important questions concerning the understanding of the relationship between the early phenomenon of prophecy and the final form of the prophetic books. It is this relationship which I wish to explore: What did Hosea have to say about the prophets, and did these sayings contribute to the shaping of the book? These two questions provide the outline for what follows. I will answer each question and then return to larger theoretical issues at the end of the essay, where I will also ask whether these findings have any bearing on our interpretation of the Book of the Twelve.

Hosea's Message Concerning the Prophets

Although it is common to assume that Hosea regarded the prophets as Yahweh's valid messengers over against an impure cult, there are good reasons to doubt this characterization. I have argued the case more fully elsewhere, so I will simply outline the key points here.[7]

First, Hosea identifies the prophets' social location as the cult: they are not, as it is commonly assumed, socially marginalized intermediaries preserving the traditions of Yahwism. Rather, they are fully bound up in the institutions which Hosea condemns (Hos. 4.5; 9.8; 12.12). If Hosea does not condemn them outright, nevertheless, he harbors a deep ambivalence toward them. On the one hand, he declares that they, like their sacrifices, are worthless (12.12);[8] and, he says that they will stumble (4.5). On the other hand, Hosea also clearly suggests that Yahweh is using them in some way to execute a plan (6.4-5; 12.11). The exegetical task is not to resolve these apparently contradictory presentations of the

6. For criticisms of Auld's position, see H.G.M. Williamson, 'A Response to A.G. Auld', *JSOT* 27 (1983), esp. pp. 33-35; and T.W. Overholt, 'Prophecy in History: The Social Reality of Intermediation', *JSOT* 48 (1990), pp. 3-29.

7. 'Who Were the Prophets in Hosea?', *HBT* 18 (1996), pp. 78-95.

8. Although commentators tend to treat 12.12 as a characterization of popular worship, the third-person plural pronouns most likely have as their antecedent the noun *nᵉbîʾîm* in the last line of v. 11; the sacrifices described in v. 12 are, therefore, those of the prophets (for syntactical parallels supporting this reading, see Hos. 5.10; 7.16; 8.8, 11; 9.10, 17; 13.3). Hosea 12.12 continues the disclosure of Yahweh concerning the prophets in v. 11: God has allowed their sacrifices to fail, and this, in turn, has led to Israel's destruction (for prophetic sacrifices, see Num. 23.2-4, 13-14, 28-30; 1 Kgs 18.23).

prophets so much as to see how these two dimensions of prophetic work might be held together.

A typical interpretation of these passages would suggest that the prophetic message is clear. So, for example, in Hos. 6.5, Yahweh uses the prophets to announce judgement:

> It is for this reason that I have hewn by the prophets;
> I have slain you[9] by the words of my mouth
> And my judgement[10] goes forth like light.

Since the verse employs affix verb forms, it is often assumed that it refers to the long line of Northern Israelite prophets who have spoken to Israel in the past.[11] This is, of course, a loaded comparison since it imports the Deuteronomistic portrayal of these figures into the discussion. It is then assumed that the message of Hosea's prophets, like that of the Deuteronomistic prophets, intelligibly points to the work of Yahweh in human affairs[12] and is to result in restoration and renewal.[13]

This interpretation of Hosea's prophets in light of the northern prophets depicted in the Deuteronomistic history can be criticized on a number of points. For one thing, the conclusion that these prophecies are to result in a favorable outcome rests more on the description of the 'prophet like Moses' in Deut. 18.15-22 than it does on the actual narrative accounts in Kings.[14] For another, there is the matter of what Hos. 6.5 actually says. The verse does not describe *how* the prophetic

9. Emending *hāragtîm* to read *hāragtîkâ*.

10. Following LXX.

11. W. Rudolph, *Hosea* (KAT, 13.1; Gütersloh: Gerd Mohn, 1966), p. 139; J.L. Mays, *Hosea* (OTL; Philadelphia: Westminster, 1969), p. 97; G.I. Davies, *Hosea* (NCB; Grand Rapids: Eerdmans, 1992), p. 167.

12. J. Jeremias, *Der Prophet Hosea* (ATD, 24.1; Göttingen: Vandenhoeck & Ruprecht, 1983), p. 87; E.M. Good, 'Hosea 5:8-6:6: An Alternative to Alt', *JBL* 85 (1966), p. 281.

13. Rudolph, p. 139; Wolff, *Hosea* (trans. G. Stansell; Hermeneia; Philadelphia: Fortress, 1974), p. 120. The basis of this generally optimistic reading of the verse is the reference to light, which is considered to have salvific connotations. However, Davies has pointed out that parallels in the psalms suggest another meaning: 'the phrase "as the light" probably refers here to the public recognition of Yahweh's right' (p. 169). The line, 'and my judgement shall go forth as the light', therefore, refers to the assertion of Yahweh's right over against the claims of Israel for deliverance.

14. For a study of the complexity of the prophetic tradition in DtrH, see E. ben Zvi, 'Prophets and Prophecy in the Compositional and Redactional Notes in I–II Kings', *ZAW* 105 (1993), pp. 331-51.

message will bring death; and despite the use of the terms 'words' and 'my mouth', it does not say that death will come through a clearly articulated sentence of judgement. Indeed, other passages would seem to suggest that the full meaning of prophetic activity is disclosed only after the work of judgement is complete. In 9.7-9, for example, the people realize, only on the appointed day of judgement, that the prophets have misled them. It is only at that time that they cry out, 'the prophet is a fool, the man of the spirit is mad'. Such a declaration would suggest that they have been given no clue what is to befall them.[15]

In Hos. 9.7-9, Hosea reveals what has been a hidden dimension of the prophetic activity: Yahweh had been using the prophets to intensify the guilt of Israel. The allusion to the days of Gibeah in 9.9 suggests that the situation is analogous to that of the battle between the Israelites and the men of Gibeah, when inquiries of God had led to greater and greater bloodshed (Judg. 20.18-28). In 9.8, Hosea suggests that the prophets are the means whereby Israel's guilt is intensified:

> Ephraim lies[16] in wait against[17] my God[18]
> a prophet[19] is a trap spread out against all his ways;
> hostility is in the house of his God.

The verse describes Ephraim's approach to God not as a patient inquiry for divine assistance but rather as an effort to ensnare divine power for

15. Although 9.7-9 is often taken as an indication of the controversy between Hosea and the people, the text is far too ambiguous to support such a reading (see Vawter, 'Were the Prophets *nābî's*?', p. 212; J. Blenkinsopp, *A History of Prophecy in Israel* [Philadelphia: Westminster, 1983], pp. 98-100, 130 n. 49). It is more likely that this unit reflects Hosea's distrust of the prophetic spirit (cf. S. Mowinckel, '"The Spirit" and the "Word" in the Pre-Exilic Reforming Prophets', *JBL* 53 [1934], p. 204 n. 21).

16. The term *ṣōpeh* should be read as a participle; for comparable use of participles elsewhere in Hosea, see Hos. 4.17; 5.11; 10.1; 12.1, 2; 13.12.

17. For the adversative connotation of the preposition *'im*, see Gen. 26.29; Ps. 94.16; also Hos. 4.1; 12.3. Since other more neutral prepositions acquire an adversative connotation when used with the verb *ṣph* (*l*, Ps. 37.32; *b*, Ps. 66.7), there is no reason to doubt that *'im* does not function similarly in Hos. 9.8.

18. The term 'My God' here should probably be understood as an allusion to the personal god; cf. 9.17.

19. Following the versification of MT and LXX. Much of the difficulty in interpreting 9.8 has arisen from the attempt to read *n^{a}bî'* as part of the first line. That tendency, however, necessitates rather extreme emendations to the text. For a review and discussion of proposed readings, see R. Dobbie, 'The Text of Hosea IX 8', *VT* 5 (1955), pp. 199-203.

his own purposes. The prophet is Yahweh's countermeasure, a trap for catching Ephraim at his own game. The suggestion is that prophets not only do not save, but also that they make Israel's situation much worse.

A similarly shocking disclosure is found in Hos. 12.10-14, where Yahweh reveals that he has been using the prophets to send Israel back to Egypt. Where Israel has counted on its prophets to deliver them (14a), Yahweh now guards himself against their pleas (14b)[20] and makes their sacrifices futile (12). All of this is presented as a message in which the full import of prophetic activity is only now being revealed.

These prophets hardly appear as messengers who announce a sentence of judgement according to clearly articulated principles. Rather, Hosea's understanding of the prophets more clearly resembles two other well known prophetic passages which depict the prophetic task as one which plays off human delusion. One of these, 1 Kings 22, is often treated in discussion of true and false prophecy, and the other, Isaiah 6, is rarely brought into such discussions but provides an interesting eighth-century parallel to Hosea's prophets. When these three passages are brought together, there is an entirely different picture of the prophetic task than that suggested by the comparison with the Deuteronomistic prophets.

In 1 Kings 22, a lying spirit volunteers to confuse the message of Ahab's prophets so that Ahab will be killed in battle. Yahweh agrees to the ruse, thus allowing the spirit to cloak the divine plan so that Ahab can neither discern nor subvert it. Although we tend to treat the prophets of Ahab as false, it may be better to see them as unwitting instruments whose message of salvation allowed Yahweh to accomplish his work. Indeed, the narrative is less concerned with truth and falsehood than it is with efficacy. The prophets speak a message of divine promise which results in disaster; and yet, it is affirmed that this message comes from Yahweh and accomplishes Yahweh's will. Other elements in the story suggest that human willfulness plays a role in the plot as much as the lying spirit of the prophets: even when Micaiah lets Ahab in on

20. Although commentators ordinarily interpret the *niphal ûbᵉnābî' nišmār* of 12.14 as a passive construction describing a prophet's care for Israel ('and by a prophet he was guarded'), the more usual sense of *niphal šmr* is reflexive. The implied subject is Yahweh, as suggested by the contrasting parallelism of 14a ('but he—Yahweh—guards himself against a prophet').

God's plan, Ahab does not seek God's mercy but rather pursues his own aims and gets himself killed.[21]

The phenomenon that the narrative seeks to explore seems, then, to be rather more multidimensional than is suggested by the category of 'true and false' prophecy. If 1 Kings 22 is about true and false prophecy, it is also about true and false kings. I would therefore suggest that we would do well to think about the interaction between lying spirits and false kings. The narrative may be more concerned with the human capacity for self delusion. As an explanation of this phenomenon, the narrative suggests that divine and human strategies mirror one another. If Ahab attempts to deceive God by going into battle disguised, then Yahweh also disguises his plan in the words of the prophets.

That the human capacity for self delusion is at the heart of these conceptions of prophecy is suggested by a second prophetic passage, the commission of Isaiah (Isa. 6.9-13). Isaiah is told that his message is to have the effect of inducing a dullness that will allow Yahweh to complete his work. It does not occur to us to ask whether Isaiah's message is false or true. Nevertheless, it is the case that it functions analogously to the message of the lying prophets in 1 Kings 22—to be sure, not so much through deception as through confusion. Nevertheless, this confusion allows the Holy One of Israel to complete his plan. One notes, furthermore, that in Isaiah, the effect of stupefaction can be extended indefinitely and is capable of becoming a principle of history. The prophet responds to the commission with the lament, 'How long, O Lord?' The answer allows for endless expansion into the future. The redactors of the book have taken advantage of this schema so that Isaiah's message encompasses the full range of Jerusalem's misfortunes—and self-deceptions—down to its destruction in 586.

When we return to Hosea's sayings concerning the prophets, we see a similar pattern: the prophets, while bringing judgement, have not brought a clear indictment. Hosea suggests, in fact, that the nation is stunned by the prophets' failure. Rather than effectively mediating between the divine and human realms, the prophets have only increased the hostility between Yahweh and the people. Because Hosea ties this failure to Israel's attempts to deceive and entrap God, Hosea's message resembles the narrative of 1 Kings 22, in which a divine deception matches a corresponding human one. Yet, because Hosea also emphasizes Yahweh's use of the prophets to complete the work of judgement, his

21. I am grateful to my first year students at St Olaf College for this insight.

message resembles the commission of Isaiah. Yahweh's plan is effective because it remains hidden: as unwitting agents of Yahweh's destruction, the prophets are incapable of averting disaster. Hosea alone discerns the nature of their work and discloses it as yet a further dimension of the divine judgement.

The Prophetic Sayings and the End of Hosea

What impact, if any, would this understanding of the prophets have on the structuring of the book? For this part of the essay, I want to focus on the intertextual associations among Hos. 5.15–6.6, ch. 12, and 14.2-3, the concluding oracle of Hosea. These associations are interesting both for what they say and do not say about the role of the prophets in the eventual restoration of the people.

Each of these units revolves around the question of Israel's return to God. That in itself is an important point, since, although the term *šûb* appears relatively often in Hosea, the meaning of repentance is relatively infrequent.[22] In each of the above-mentioned passages, the term *šûb* is used with the connotation of repentance. However, in each of the two passages where prophetic activity is described, Israelite efforts to return fail. It is only in 14.2, where prophets do not appear, that a real possibility for repentance is offered.

In 5.15–6.6, the disclosure concerning the prophets marks God's refusal to accept Israel's repentance. The reason for Yahweh's refusal is given in 5.15, which declares that Yahweh will remain in hiding *until* Israel has fully borne its guilt. The crux of the verse is the ambiguous verb *'šm*, which can mean either to incur guilt or to bear the consequences of guilt.[23] The ensuing verses, which depict Israel's plea and Yahweh's rejection of that plea, suggest that Yahweh's condition for

22. For repentance: 3.5; 5.4; 6.1; 7.10; 11.5; 14.8. The remaining instances are: 2.9, 11; 5.15; 6.11; 7.16; 8.13; 9.3; 11.5, 9; 14.5.

23. For the notion of incurring guilt, see Hos. 13.1; for the notion of bearing the consequences of guilt, see Hos. 10.2; 14.1. It is interesting to note that other uses are as ambiguous. For example, Hos. 4.15 is often translated, 'If Israel should stray, let not Judah become guilty', and it is assumed that Judah is being exhorted here not to follow in the way of Israel. Another possible meaning could be that Judah, understood as the victim of Israel's actions, should not bear the consequences of Israel's straying. D. Kellerman suggests that all five instances of the verb in Hosea have the connotation '"to act wrongly, to become guilty", and thus "to make oneself culpable"' ('*'āshām*', *TDOT* 1, pp. 435-36).

reconciliation has not yet been met. In this context, the saying concerning the prophets in 6.5 implies that the prophets are one means whereby Yahweh forces Israel to bear this guilt. Yahweh will use the prophets to kill, and not to heal, as the people had hoped. If the verb *'šm* has the meaning of incurring guilt, then the prophets are not only the means whereby punishment is inflicted, then they are also the means whereby punishment continues to be deserved (cf. 9.7-9).

In ch. 12, God again rejects any attempt at reconciliation, this time charging Ephraim with lies and deceit. As in 5.15–6.6, the disclosure concerning the prophets in 12.11-12 illustrates God's rejection of the people: he does not use the prophets to heal or deliver but instead condemns their efforts as worthless.

By contrast, Hos. 14.2-3 offers a real possibility of reconciliation. The difference is that now the people are exhorted to appeal directly to God, not through the intermediation of the prophets. That is the import of v. 3, where the people are encouraged to take words instead, presumably, of sacrifices, which have failed so utterly in the past (5.6; 12.12). In this light it is interesting to note the unusual apposition in the last line of v. 3, where the people declare that they will offer as bulls their lips (*ûnešallᵉmâ pārîm śᵉpātênû*).[24] Where most translations understandably follow the LXX reading and emend *pᵃrîm* to *pᵉrî* (fruit) so that the line says that they offer the 'fruit of their lips,'[25] this emendation obscures an interesting contrast between Yahweh's estimation of the prophets' sacrifices in 12.12 and what is now required as an acceptable sign of Israel's devotion. Words now replace sacrifices; they are acceptable because they represent a direct appeal to Yahweh. Furthermore, if these words are vows, as Andersen and Freedman suggest, they are also truthful, no longer the lies that Yahweh has had to endure (cf. 12.1).[26]

One can conclude, then, that the prophetic passages contribute to the end of Hosea by illustrating how not to approach God. The institution of prophecy has utterly failed; accordingly, the summons to return in 14.2 instructs Israel in the only proper way to come to God—directly, not through the mediation of the prophets.

24. Cf. Exod. 24.5; see B. Waltke and M. O'Connor, *An Introduction to Biblical Hebrew Syntax* (Winona Lake, IN: Eisenbrauns, 1990), 12.3bc.

25. Wolff, *Hosea*, p. 231; Jeremias, *Hosea*, p. 168.

26. F.I. Andersen and D.N. Freedman, *Hosea: A New Translation with Introduction and Commentary* (AB, 24; Garden City, NY: Doubleday, 1980), p. 645.

Does this understanding of the prophets play any further role in the shaping of the book of Hosea? At the beginning of this essay, I had mentioned the importance of chs. 1–3 to the interpretation of the rest of Hosea. It would seem reasonable to ask, then, whether this view of the prophets has had any impact on the structuring of these introductory chapters. There may be a reverberation of Hosea's understanding of prophets in two features of chs. 1–3: in the depiction of the beginning of Israel's downfall and in the portrayal of the regeneration of Israel. First, the name of Hosea's child Jezreel alludes, if obliquely, to the kinds of political disasters one can blame on the prophets. Where the narrator in 2 Kings sees Jehu's revolt as the fulfillment of a divine word spoken by a *nābî*, Hosea views it as the beginning of the end of Israel's covenant with Yahweh. Hosea does not directly indict the prophets for the event at Jezreel; nevertheless, his attitude toward the event is consistent with his understanding of what the prophets unleash on Israel. That is, the prophets can intensify Israel's guilt, but they cannot absolve it. In the case of Jehu's revolt, a prophet could initiate the punishment of the House of Omri for its sins but only by creating what in Hosea's view was a more dangerous and volatile situation—and what would lead ultimately to Israel's complete destruction.

If prophets can only make matters worse, then they certainly cannot assist in Israel's regeneration. Rather, Israel must seek Yahweh directly. For that to happen, Israel must live without all the customary forms of political and cultic order:

> For the Israelites will live for many days, without king or prince, without sacrifice or pillar, without ephod or teraphim. (Hos. 3.4)

As the verse suggests by its inclusion of the ephod and teraphim, the people are prohibited even from employing customary means of seeking God's will.[27] Here again, prophets are not directly mentioned; however, if it is indeed the case that Hosea located the prophets in the Israelite cult, then it seems likely that the ephod and teraphim allude to their institutional role.

Concluding Observations

If the sayings concerning the prophets perform only a negative role in the book of Hosea, what are the implications for understanding Hosea as

27. Cf. Wolff, *Hosea*, p. 62.

a collection of prophecy? The first, and most obvious one, is that we would do well to re-evaluate our designation of Hosea as a prophet. He did not think of himself as one: like Amos, he most likely would have rejected the title *nābî* (Amos 7.14);[28] and like Micah, he would have seen a clear contrast between his words and theirs (Mic. 3.5-8).[29] The words collected under his name should, therefore, also be considered something other than prophecy.[30] However, I agree with Carroll that at this stage of the game we can do little more than say that Hosea is not a prophet.

A second implication is that this assessment of the prophets should be differentiated from that of DtrH. DtrH establishes the truthfulness of prophecy by illustrating its fulfillment. Hosea, on the other hand, is less concerned with truth than with efficacy and the assertion of the divine will. Genre conventions may contribute to this divergence. It is well known, for example, that the Deuteronomistic criterion for determining whether a prophecy is true or false lacks any practical applicability since it is worthless precisely at the moment when one needs to test the reliability of a prophetic message. But for a historiographical work it functions perfectly well, and the historians can demonstrate the truth of the prophets by depicting historical events as a fulfillment of their prophecies. In a work like Hosea, on the other hand, the literary concern is quite different: to recreate the moment of hearing and decision by presenting words which by their nature cannot be fully understood. The depiction of prophets as ambiguous figures underscores that fact.

A third implication is that Hosea may establish a hermeneutical principle for evaluating the prophets in the rest of the Book of the Twelve. The prophetic message (as opposed to the message of the Book of the Twelve) is not simply ambiguous, it is dangerous. On this point the Book of the Twelve may consciously set itself in opposition to DtrH. As an example, I would point to the respective treatments of Jonah in DtrH

28. Cf. H.-W. Wolff, *Joel and Amos: A Commentary on the Books of the Prophets Joel and Amos* (trans. W. Janzen, S.D. McBride, and C.A. Muenchow; Hermeneia; Philadelphia: Fortress Press, 1977), p. 313. For a recent review of the critical issues in interpreting Amos 7.14, see S.M. Paul, *Amos: A Commentary on the Book of Amos* (Hermeneia; Minneapolis: Fortress Press, 1991), pp. 243-47.

29. Cf. Carroll, 'Night Without Vision', p. 77.

30. So Carroll: 'The insistent and unrelenting opposition to prophets in these books is, in my opinion, better explained in terms of non-prophets versus prophets than in terms of the more conventionally favoured prophet versus prophet approach' ('Night Without Vision', p. 82).

and the Book of the Twelve.[31] In the Deuteronomistic corpus, Jonah appears as one of the 'true' prophets whose word of salvation is fulfilled during the reign of Jeroboam II (2 Kgs 14.25-27). In the book of Jonah, on the other hand, Jonah is a particularly unsavory character. Fleeing Yahweh's presence, he becomes an agent of death and chaos. He sleeps while all around him struggle to save themselves. Once he is awakened, he does not call on his God as the captain asks but leaves it to the sailors to divine 'on whose account' they are in distress (1.7). When the sailors ask him, 'What is your occupation?' he does not quite say.

As a polemic against prophets, the narrative presents Jonah as self-serving, profoundly uninterested in carrying out the will of God, and, in the end, more concerned with his own welfare than with that of God's creatures. Because Jonah's character does not change after he has been delivered from the fish, his prayer in 2.3-10 has a whiff of hypocrisy about it.[32]

In some respects, the book of Jonah echoes themes in Hosea. First, since Nineveh's preservation means Israel's eventual destruction,[33] the tale ironically underscores the inevitability of disaster at the hands of the prophets. Like Elisha, whose anointing of Hazael as king of Damascus would set in motion the events that would lead to the destruction of Israel, so also does Jonah preserve the city of Nineveh for God's future purpose of judging Israel.[34] Second, the story draws attention to the great contrast between Jonah's petulance and God's mercy. If Jonah has

31. For discussions of the purpose of Jonah, see R.E. Clements, 'The Purpose of the Book of Jonah', *Congress Volume, Edinburgh 1974* (VTSup, 28; Leiden: Brill, 1975), pp. 16-28; and, more recently, J.M. Sasson, *Jonah: A New Translation with Introduction, Commentary, and Interpretation* (AB, 24B; New York: Doubleday, 1990), esp. pp. 24-26.

32. Compare J. Nogalski, *Redactional Processes in the Book of the Twelve* (BZAW, 218; Berlin: de Gruyter, 1993), pp. 265-69. Nogalski argues that in the prayer of 2.3-10, Jonah becomes a symbol of Israel (p. 266). Especially interesting in this context is Nogalski's treatment of the intertextual connections between Jonah's prayer and Hos. 5.15–6.6 (pp. 268-69). I would call attention as well to the association between Jonah's (that is, Israel's) sacrifice of thanksgiving of 2.10 and the acceptable sacrifice of words of Hos. 14.2-3.

If Nogalski is correct, the current shape of the story of Jonah sets up a tension between real prophets, or perhaps we should say Deuteronomistic ones, and an idealized community of Israel. Israel succeeds in doing what the prophets were unable to do.

33. Sasson, *Jonah*, p. 344.

34. Sasson, *Jonah*, p. 344.

been roped unwillingly into the divine plan of judgement against Israel, he also has nothing to do with the evolution of God's plan in response to Nineveh's repentance. This comes rather from God's direct, unmediated response to the citizens of Nineveh.

What Hosea, and the Book of the Twelve suggests, is that there is something greater than Jonah—and all the prophets. Although the prophets are irrevocably associated with judgement, Hosea affirms that something greater survives apart from their sad legacy—and that is God's insistence on bringing mercy and not curse.

The Interrelationship between Amos and Hosea

Jörg Jeremias

The books of Amos and Hosea have much in common. This fact is not surprising but is to be expected since both prophets spoke at nearly the same time and since both spoke in the northern kingdom which would soon come to an end. Naturally, they shared common convictions, and they condemned similar guilt and crime, and of course the younger one, Hosea, knew the older one.

Common traits of this kind should be differentiated sharply from the cases of literary dependence with which this paper is concerned. Let me state the basic result in advance. I can understand these literary connections on different levels only if the pupils of Amos and the pupils of Hosea who handed down the message of the prophets wanted to teach the readers that they could not grasp the central ideas of these prophets by reading their books in complete isolation from one another. By contrast, the readers of the written words of the prophets were supposed to notice the similarity of Amos's and Hosea's message from God. The pupils were not interested in stressing the differences between the two prophets. The literary structure of both prophetic books—from the initial level—shows that these books were meant as associated entities and should not be read as isolated pericopes. The literary connections between these books show that they should be read in relation to each other.

I stress this fact because historical-critical scholarship pursues just the opposite intention. This intention is directed toward the singular and incomparable traits of the message of each prophet, such as when it differentiates between different layers of tradition. Though historical-critical scholarship for me is an indispensable tool in opening the riches of biblical texts, I want to stress the fact that its interest—to gain the historical dimension of the texts by understanding the way they grew—has nothing to do with the interest of the biblical traditionists who wanted to state the relation between different prophets and different texts by showing their common elements.

I want to show that these traditionists are on their way to discovering something like a common prophetic theology, not by denying that each prophet lived in singular historical circumstances, but by denying that this fact is decisive for their message.

I

Amos and Hosea share many subjects, such as the condemnation of Israel's pilgrimages to Bethel and Gilgal, the proclamation of the insurmountable harshness of divine punishment (Amos 8.2: 'the end has come to my people Israel'; Hos. 1.9: 'Not my people'). However, the differences between their words are much more impressive, as historical-critical insight has shown. I recall just a few examples:

Both prophets proclaim God's punishment of Israel to be very close, but they give quite different reasons for it.

1) Social accusations make up the center of Amos's message, as even a superficial reader of his words knows. However, this subject plays a minor role in the book of Hosea, where it is only intimated occasionally (cf. the summary in Hos. 7.1 after 6.7-9 and 12.8).

2) In the book of Amos, criticism of the lack of justice would come next in importance. Justice as a gift of God should be the only means to regulate opposing claims from different occupations, but it is no longer effective because the prevalence of bribery in Israel cares only for the interest of the rich. Again, this subject is very rare in the book of Hosea. When it does occur, Hosea charges that the violation of justice takes place at cultic places (Hos. 5.1).

3) Amos and Hosea pursue different purposes in their criticism of the cult, an interest which is important for both of them. For Hosea the multiplication of cult places, altars, and priests proves that Israel's worship has become Canaanized by centering around sacrifice and its effects. By increasing sacrifices, Israel fails to care for the 'knowledge of God', i.e., God's history with his people and his will for everyday life. For Amos, God judges Israel's cult because it deludes Israel into feeling secure, thus preventing the recognition of guilt. A true cult would awaken the desire for justice.

4) Nowhere else does Hosea become as emotional in his judgement as when condemning the bull image of Bethel (8.5-6; 10.5-6; 12.2). Amos does not even mention the bull when describing pilgrimages to Bethel.

5) The last chapters of the book of Hosea are full of historical reminiscences. This prophet is convinced that Israel loses God when she 'forgets' him by forgetting his history with her. Amos very seldom mentions history, and when doing so (2.9; 9.7), he does so broadly.

I could continue enumerating differences between the historical Amos and the historical Hosea. These differences likely show what it meant to grow up in the northern kingdom as opposed to a little village of Judah at the border of the desert. Amos has much in common with Isaiah, the Jerusalemite, Hosea only little. Hosea strongly influences Jeremiah and the deuteronomistic movement, while Amos exhibits only slight influence on them.

However, this picture of two very different prophets by no means reveals the picture which earlier generations of Bible readers gained prior to historical-critical scholarship. Earlier generations noticed many common traits between these two prophets. Historical-critical scholarship at its peak[1] was interested in showing that the standardization of the message of the prophets was the work of generations which post-dated the prophets themselves.

When did this standardization start? It is easy to grasp this development during the exile. At that point, the classical prophets, who had previously been rejected by the majority, became recognized as 'true' prophets. It was the so-called deuteronomistic theology which created common superscriptions for prophetic books and unified the message of the prophets by reworking it.[2] Yet, the basic conviction of this paper is that the process of standardization started much earlier, soon after the destruction of Samaria in 722 BCE. I restrict myself to observations on the books of Hosea and Amos.

II

I touch the book of Hosea only briefly because our subject is less fruitful for that book than for the book of Amos. For many decades it has been noted that the book of Hosea contains some verses which, when taken separately, sound as if they could be taken from the book of Amos. A

1. Cf., for example, B. Duhm, *Israels Propheten* (Tübingen: Mohr [Siebeck], 1916).

2. Cf. especially W.H. Schmidt, 'Die deuteronomistische Redaktion des Amosbuches', *ZAW* 77 (1965), pp. 168-93.

very clear example is Hos. 4.15. I cite the context using the translation of the commentary of J.L. Mays:[3]

> 11 Harlotry and wine and must take away the mind!
> 12 My people consults his piece of wood,
> and his staff interprets for him.
> For a spirit of harlotry has brought confusion,
> and they have gone a-whoring away from their God.
> 13 On the mountain tops they sacrifice
> and on the hills they burn offerings,
> under oak and poplar
> and terebinth because its shade is pleasant.
> Therefore your daughters play the harlot
> and your sons' wives commit adultery.
> 14 I will not punish your daughters for playing the harlot,
> or your sons' wives for committing adultery;
> for they themselves go apart with harlots
> and sacrifice with sacred prostitutes.
> A people that does not understand shall be ruined.
> 15 Though you, O Israel, play the harlot,
> let Judah not incur such guilt.
> Do not enter Gilgal.
> Do not go up to Beth-awen.
> Do not swear 'As Yahweh lives...'

In ch. 4, Hosea describes the worship on the cultic heights in more detailed terms than anywhere else. After having attacked the increase of cult places and priests in order to increase sacrifices and create well-being (vv. 7-8), he laments the consumption of alcohol (v. 11), rhabdomancy (in other words, the consultation of pieces of wood) even though Israel possesses prophets (v. 12), and finally sexual rites which are to create fertility (vv. 13-14). Only here at the peak of his accusation does the text briefly use the form of direct address. But, at the end, it takes up the form of complaint about 'my people' from the beginning (vv. 11-12; v. 14b says only 'a people') thus rounding and completing the unit.

Then v. 15 follows, evidently using the language of Amos. The address is now directed to Judah. The first two imperatives are citations of Amos 4.4 adding a negation (and thus giving up the irony of Amos). The last one may be an oblique reference to Amos 8.14 (where the

3. *Hosea: A Commentary* (OTL; Philadelphia: Westminster Press, 1969), pp. 72, 76.

Israelites swear: 'As the way of Beersheba lives').[4] What is the idea behind these citations of verses of the book of Amos? Apparently, Judean readers of the book of Hosea were to be prevented from reading it 'historically'. As far as we know the increase of cultic heights with rhabdomancy and sexual rites was not a problem for Judah. On the other hand, v. 15 presupposes pilgrimages from Judah to Bethel and Gilgal, the old and venerated places of the Jacob tradition and of Israel's immigration into Palestine, both less than 20 km away from Jerusalem. Pilgrimages to Beersheba are even more likely since it was part of Judah. From Hosea 4, we learn that the actualization of the words of Hosea for Judean readers was more difficult when a speech addressed situations which were specific to the northern kingdom. Actualization of prophetic words for later readers generally tends to touch basic and general topics (here, the dangers of false worship) because they could be translated into contexts of a different kind. The intention of verses like Hos. 4.15 was to actualize the prophetic words for people living later than the prophet and living under new circumstances.

A second example of a verse in the book of Hosea using Amos's language is Hos. 8.14.[5] Hosea 8 is a very artistic chapter in which the prophet's criticism of his society is intensified step by step. For that reason, the pupils of Hosea gather accusations from earlier chapters and put them side by side. Criticism of the state (v. 4: 'They themselves made kings, but I had nothing to do with it') is combined with criticism of the state cult (v. 5 speaks of the rejection of 'your bull, O Samaria'), criticism of foreign affairs (vv. 8-9 calls it harlotry), and, as a climax, with criticism of worship:

11 When Ephraim multiplied altars to atone for sin,
they became for him altars for sinning.
12 Though I write for him a multitude of my instructions,
they are considered as an alien thing.
13 Sacrifice they love, so they sacrifice;
flesh (they love), so they eat;
but Yahweh does not accept them.
Now he will remember their iniquity
and punish their sin.
They shall return to Egypt.

4. The connection between the root *šb'* 'to swear' and Beersheba is explicitly evident from Genesis 26 and is presupposed.

5. A third example which I skip is Hos. 11.10.

No further intensification of Hosea's accusations is possible. Verses 11-13, with their criticism of the cult, lead into the center of Israel's relation with God. For Hosea, this represents a completely misleading attempt to get close to God. The consequence is the hardest punishment imaginable: God ends the relationship by extinguishing his history with Israel. Israel is to return to Egypt, where this history started when God saved her from slavery.

When everything has been said there is a final verse coming *post festum*:

> 14 Israel forgot his maker
> and built palaces.
> Judah multiplied
> fortified cities.
> I will send fire on his cities
> and it will devour her strongholds.[6]

The style of v. 14, using narrative, is very different from that of vv. 1-13. Again, the verse addresses Judah, and again, we encounter citations from the book of Amos, in this case stemming from the stereotyped framework of the announcement of punishment against foreign nations (Amos 1.4). Again, the problem behind this evident addition seems to be that Judah might feel exempted from accusations specific to the northern kingdom (the murders of kings, the bull of Bethel, the worship on the heights). Again, a typical subject of Amos, the luxury inside the palaces of the capital and the feeling of security, is cited to prevent Judean readers from escaping the accusations of Hosea. In the case of Hos. 8.14 the progress of time becomes discernible. Hosea proclaimed Israel's return to Egypt prior to the destruction of Samaria; Hos. 8.14 proclaims the end of all luxury in Judah's palaces after the destruction of Samaria.

To summarize, the verses in the book of Hosea recalling the language of Amos are redactional. These 'Amos-like' verses presuppose fixed compositions in Hosea to which they are added. They presuppose that at least parts of the book of Hosea are already fixed in written form. They prevent Judean readers from taking the content 'historically', without feeling touched themselves. The additions show that the later inhabitants of Judah felt more acquainted with Amos who stemmed from Judah, though he proclaimed in the northern kingdom, than with Hosea who

6. Translations by Mays, *Hosea*, p. 114.

was born in the north. The additions must have been made in the century between 720 and 620 BCE. The fall of Samaria is presupposed, but the polemics against palaces in 8.14 shows that Jerusalem has not yet been taken, and the warning not to go to Bethel (4.15) proves that Bethel had not yet been destroyed by Josiah.

III

The result of my investigation is very different for the book of Amos. The influence of the book of Hosea can be observed in nearly every chapter. By no means is the influence restricted to actualizing additions and to redactional layers. At least part of it belongs to the oldest literary layer of the book. Of course, the oral words of Amos cannot show an influence of this kind since Amos was the older prophet. On the other hand, I am deeply convinced that there was never a book of Amos without a clearly discernible effect from Hoseanic texts. This observation, if correct, would be of importance in many respects. It would imply that some time must have passed before the oral words of Amos were written down. Even more, it would imply that the book of Hosea (in its oldest form) is older than the book of Amos (in its oldest form) though Hosea is the younger prophet. But let me state the facts first.

I want to start with one of the most impressive examples taken from the report of visions: Amos 7.9. In order to be clear, I have to go into detail for a while.

As is nearly universally recognized in critical scholarship, the report of visions originally formed a separate collection comprising at least the first four visions (Amos 7.1-8; 8.1-2) and probably the fifth (9.1-4). For my purpose I can leave the fifth aside. The reason for reckoning with a separate collection is the fact that the first four visions are grouped in pairs. These pairs are so clearly related to each other that no doubt exists that they were intended to be read together, while in the present arrangement the second pair (7.7-8; 8.1-2) is separated by 7.9-17.

The reason for the separation becomes clear when the two pairs of visions are compared with each other. The first two visions have Amos viewing an unnamed subject who is none other than God himself creating terrible events which Israel will not survive. In the first vision, it is the plague of locusts which devours Israel's harvest when it is needed most, before the dry period of the summer. In the second vision, it is a cosmic drought which results from a fire devouring the subterranean waters which create the fountains. In both cases, the prophet utters a sudden, urgent prayer which is very similar. In the first vision, it is 'Lord Yahweh, forgive!', in the second, more desperately: 'Lord Yahweh, desist!' In both cases the prophet gives the same reason for his prayer: 'How shall Jacob survive? For he is small!' The prophet is pleading for the pity of God for his chosen people ('Jacob'). Both times the prophet reaches his goal (though the text does not speak of God's forgiveness). The reaction of Yahweh is identical again ('Yahweh repented concerning this')[7] and leads to identical consequences ('It shall not take place, said Yahweh'; in the second vision: 'Neither shall this take place...'). Quite evidently, the parallel structure of both visions shows the readers that they have to relate them to each other. Together the visions teach Israel that she survives, in spite of her guilt, only because she possesses prophets who intercede for her and prevent Yahweh from practicing the judgement he has in mind.

Yet, the second pair of visions shows that there is a limit to God's patience. Again, both visions are structured in a parallel manner but very differently from the first pair. In both cases, Amos is shown a picture, a metal (probably tin) in the first case, a basket of fruit in the second, and he is called to name it (both times: 'What do you see, Amos?'). When he does so, the disaster takes place which is represented by the picture. Both times a play on words is used. Amos, without knowing it, is calling forth the disaster. The reason given is identical both times: 'I cannot spare them further'; in other words, as in the earlier two visions. Of course, the intercession of the prophet has to end here.

There cannot be any doubt that the two pairs of visions are to be read in connection with each other. Together they show how Amos was led by God. In the first two visions, Amos was able to elicit the pity of God by the power of his prayer and to move God to 'repentance' in favor of Israel. In the second pair of visions he has to learn that God's patience with guilty Israel is not unlimited. Now there is no longer room for prayer. The prophet may no longer prevent God from practicing disaster. He has to join the side of God's justice in calling for disaster.

The legitimizing character of the four visions read together is very clear. They prove that it was not Amos's decision to call for disaster.

7. Repentance does not mean the recognition that Yahweh's punishment was unjustified. Rather it means changing God's plan in favor of Israel. Cf. J. Jeremias, *Die Reue Gottes* (Biblische Studien, 65; Neukirchen: Neukirchener, 1975), pp. 40-48.

Amos struggled against God's punishment as long as he could. Then he was taught that God 'cannot spare them further'.

When did that change in God's will take place? Apparently, the famous narrative of the encounter between the priest Amaziah and the prophet Amos (Amos 7.10-17) wants to answer this question, thereby interrupting the second pair of visions. The visions read by themselves neither named the guilt of Israel which was presupposed (cf. Amos's intercession: 'Lord Yahweh, forgive!') nor did they tell why God's willingness 'to repent' came to an end. If the visions were written down to serve as a legitimation for the proclamation of Amos, quite clearly this message itself gave the answer to both questions. Amos named the guilt of Israel and Amos proclaimed that this guilt was too heavy for God to let the prophet play the intercessor.

Yet, later readers of the visions wanted to know exactly where the limitation of God's patience begins. For them, the narrative of the encounter between priest and prophet, between the faithful servant of the king and the faithful servant of Yahweh, answers the question. In short, God's patience ends where the state represented by the priest tries to decide when and where God may speak through his prophet. Amos cannot decide what he has to say in the name of God, and he cannot decide where to do so. The priest Amaziah, in the name of the king, does not prevent Amos from speaking his message, but from speaking the message of God. It is not the guilt of Israel itself that brings God's patience to an end, but the state ends God's patience by preventing the prophet from speaking. The prophet was God's last way to save Israel by showing her guilt. Israel is lost when her prophet is silenced.

The narrative of the encounter between priest and prophet, however, is not linked immediately to the third vision which ends with God's desperate utterance: 'I cannot spare them further'. There is a verse (7.9) bridging the gap between vision and narrative.

> The high places of Isaac shall be destroyed;
> the sanctuaries of Israel shall be devastated;
> and I will rise against the house of Jeroboam with the sword.[8]

This verse, though poetic in structure, shares its vocabulary not with the visions, but with the narrative. Apparently, it serves as an introduction to the narrative.

8. Translation by Mays, *Amos: A Commentary* (OTL; Philadelphia: Westminster Press, 1969), p. 131.

1) It speaks of 'sanctuaries' to be devastated—Amos 7.13 calls Bethel the 'sanctuary of the king'.
2) It speaks of the 'sword' which will meet the king's house—Amos 7.11 cites Amos's threat that Jeroboam will die by the 'sword'.
3) It speaks of the high places of 'Isaac'—Amos 7.16 cites the priest forbidding Amos to preach to the 'house of Isaac'.[9]

But though the bridging verse evidently is oriented to the narrative, its language differs remarkably. It generalizes the facts of the narrative.

1) Where the narrative speaks of the 'sanctuary of the king'in the singular, Amos 7.9 uses the plural 'sanctuaries'.
2) Where the narrative speaks of the sword killing Jeroboam, in Amos 7.9, the sword in Yahweh's hand reaches 'the house of Jeroboam'.
3) Where the narrative speaks of Isaac in terms of the state ('house of Isaac'), Amos 7.9 aims at the cultic 'high places of Isaac'.

Apparently, Amos 7.9 serves as a hermeneutical key to the exegesis of the narrative. The reader should not understand the narrative as being valid only for a singular situation in the life of Amos but as the starting point for a disastrous development. By describing this development Amos 7.9 shows that it wants to point out the consequences of the third vision.

A second observation is even more important. Though the language of Amos 7.9 is taken mostly from the narrative, the subjects of the verse are not typical of the book of Amos; they are typical of the book of Hosea. Amos never touches the 'high places' elsewhere, while Hosea very often does, for the most part without using the vocabulary 'high places' (Hos. 10.8) or 'sanctuaries'. From chs. 2 and 4 onwards, the cult of the high places is a dominant theme of Hosea's message. But this subject is not the only indicator of Hoseanic influence on Amos 7.9. There is also the combination of guilt in worship and guilt by the state, which is especially characteristic of the message of Hosea from ch. 1 through ch. 14. Amos 7.9 thus sounds like a precise condensation of Hosea's general message. Amos, on the other hand, does not mention the king outside the narrative cited above.

9. It should be noted that 'Isaac' a) does not occur elsewhere in pre-exilic prophecy and b) is written both times unusually with *ś*.

Is Amos 7.9 then a later addition? As stated above, the report of visions, because of their evident structure in pairs, very likely once formed a separate collection which probably originated with the prophet himself. But as such it was never part of the book of Amos. Recent studies of the narrative concerning priest and prophet have shown that this narrative consciously takes up the language of the third vision at various points.[10] Whether the narrative once existed separately or not, it has been fashioned to fit its context. The same is true for Amos 7.9, as we saw. One can learn from Amos 8.3-14 what additions look like, with its abundance of redactional formulas. The book of Amos very probably never existed without 7.10-17, and 7.10-17 very probably never existed without its hermeneutical key in 7.9. This verse urges the reader not to perceive Amos as an isolated prophet but to relate his message to the message of Hosea. They are to be seen as two messengers with one common message.

Amos 7.9 stands at a very central position in the structure of the book. It stands at the point where God's pity on Jacob ends. With the cessation of God's pity, the possibility that the prophet could intercede ends. The visions themselves do not state the point at which this occurs. Amos 7.10-17 explains the reason by relating the experiences of Amos, and Amos 7.9 states beforehand that these experiences concern Israel's guilt in the realm of worship and the actions of the state, about which Hosea spoke. Only Amos *and* Hosea together teach where God's patience with his people comes to an end.

IV

A second example of Hoseanic influence on the words of Amos, Amos 3.2, again appears at a central position which I shall treat more briefly. The middle part of the book of Amos consists of a collection of words of Yahweh to Israel through his prophet Amos (chs. 3–6). Its first part is a smaller collection of words directed against the inhabitants of the capital Samaria (Amos 3.9–4.3). Yet, a more principal introduction takes the lead. It consists of three parts: 1) a superscription in prose announcing God's word (3.1); 2) a short confirmation of this word (v. 2); and 3) a chain of questions combining reason and result (vv. 3-8). This chain

10. The most careful paper in this respect is that of H. Utzschneider, 'Die Amazjaerzählung (Amos 7,10-17) zwischen Literatur und Historie', *BN* 41 (1988), pp. 76-101.

leads to its goal in v. 8, where the obligation of the prophet to speak God's word is stated. A primary goal is reached in v. 6, where Yahweh is called the cause of disaster in a town. The legitimizing function of the questions is evident. Amos did not choose to speak God's word, even less did he choose to speak God's word of disaster. The word of Yahweh which the superscription proclaims (v. 1) according to vv. 3-8 is a word of disaster forced upon Amos.

Between the superscription and the legitimizing questions stands v. 2. From its position, it becomes quite clear that this verse is more than just a simple word of Amos. It is a contraction of the words that follow, a programmatic condensation.

> You alone have I known from all the families of the earth;
> therefore, I will punish you for all your iniquities.

Yet, remarkably enough, v. 2 uses vocabulary which is quite unusual for Amos's words.

1) The verb 'to know' with God as its subject never appears again in the book of Amos. The only other verse treating the subject of election does so in a very different way (Amos 9.7).
2) The verb *pqd* for punishment occurs only in 3.14 which is dependent on 3.2.
3) Amos quite often speaks of Israel's guilt. Yet he never uses *'āwôn* otherwise, but usually *paeša'*, sometimes *ḥaṭṭā't*.

If the language used in Amos 3.2 is unfamiliar to Amos, it is very familiar to Hosea.

1) God's 'knowing' Israel is used in a word play of Hos. 13.5 (MT).[11]
2) The verb *pqd* is met in very different chapters: Hos. 1.4; 2.15; 4.9,14; 8.13; 9.9; 12.3. Few verbs can be as typical for Hosea's message as this one.
3) More or less the same is true for *'āwôn*, which is used in Hos. 4.8; 5.5; 7.1; 8.13; 9.7, 9; 12.9; 13.12; 14.2, 3.

Apparently, the pupils of Amos who were handing down his message wanted it to be related to the message of Hosea from the very beginning. For that purpose, they formulated a programmatic motto for

11. Moreover, the subject of election is very typical for Hosea's message; cf., for example, Hos. 1.9; 2.16-17; 9.10; 10.11; 11.1.

Amos's message in a central hermeneutical position which is full of hints of Hosea's words. In the case of Amos 3.2, there can be no doubt whatsoever that this verse is no addition to the text. Taking it from its context would leave a torso without meaning. Quite the contrary, Amos 3.2 for the traditionists is the key to understanding Amos. And this key is formulated using phrases and vocabulary of the book of Hosea.[12] To understand God's word through his prophet Amos, one should read the book of Hosea as well.

V

Let me briefly mention three other examples without trying to be complete and without going into all the reasons:

1) Amos 2.6-8 is the introduction to the peak of Amos's words against the nations. It states how Israel is more guilty than all the other nations. While the nations are cruel to their enemies, in Israel, neighbor is cruel to neighbor. Only in the last strophe against Israel are the 'three and four crimes' enumerated which the stereotyped framework to all strophes announces. Yet, while the first three crimes in vv. 6-7 touch the social realm,[13] Amos 2.8 stresses the cultic places, where they occur.

> They spread out (upon) pledged garments beside every altar;
> they drink wine from those who were fined in the house of their God.

For many decades, it has been observed that the stress on cultic places sounds Hoseanic.[14] The oppression of the poor is no longer the only subject of the accusation as in the previous verses. Now the context of worship has become the central focus. The increase of cultic places and of priests mentioned so often by Hosea (Hos. 4.7-8; 8.11-13; 10.1-2) is presupposed here even though Amos never cares about them elsewhere. 'In the house of their God' in the context of divine speech probably intends Bethel, an attack again characteristic of Hosea (Hos. 8.5-6;

12. This leaves the phrase 'all the families of the earth'. Is it dependent on Gen. 12.3 (cf. 28.14)? Otherwise it could be seen originating from language in the book of Jeremiah; cf. Jer. 1.15; 2.4; 25.9 as well as Ezek. 20.32.

13. Except v. 7bβ which uses the language of Ezekiel and of the holiness code. Verse 7bβ) seems to be an addition in the fashion of v. 8 discussed below.

14. Cf. the letter of A. Alt to K. Galling (*ZDPV* 67 [1945], pp. 37-38) and more recently the commentaries of H.-W. Wolff and of J.A. Soggin as well as J.L. Sicre, *'Con los pobres de la tierra': la justicia social en los profetas de Israel* (Madrid: Ediciones Cristianidad, 1984), p. 110.

10.5-6; 13.2) and not Amos. For these reasons, H.W. Wolff proposed that 2.8aβ and 2.8bβ should be taken as secondary, and he was followed by Soggin. Yet, there is no sign of literary expansion. It is much more likely that this reference to a Hoseanic subject and to Hoseanic language was made consciously by the pupils of Amos themselves. Only Hosea and Amos together can tell the full story of the special weight given to the guilt of God's people.

2) Amos's sharp word against Israel's worship in Amos 5.21-24 rejects this worship in the name of God when there is no justice. It concludes with a question that introduces a very different argument (Amos 5.25):

> Was it sacrifices and offerings you brought to me in the wilderness (forty years), O house of Israel?

This didactic question very probably does not want to teach that Israel knew nothing of sacrifices before entering Palestine. Rather, it wants to confront the present habit of sacrificing huge amounts of animals and fruit with Israel's ideal communion with God during the time of her wandering through the wilderness.[15] It is not the automatism of sacrificing that brings Israel close to God (cf. Hos. 8.11-13 above) but a return to the ideal beginnings of true communion with God during the time of the wilderness. Without doubt, this is a Hoseanic subject (cf. Hos. 9.10; 2.16-17) being consciously added to a typical message of Amos in the preceding verses.

3) My last example is taken from Amos 6. Following Amos's accusation regarding the way the wealthy are celebrating in the capital, Samaria (vv. 1-7), there follows a terrible oath of Yahweh (Amos 6.8):

> Lord Yahweh has sworn on his own person (a saying of Yahweh, God of hosts),
> 'I abhor the pride of Jacob;
> I hate his strongholds;
> I will deliver up the city with its inhabitants'.

The polemics against Samaria's 'strongholds', the very places of the celebration, are typical for Amos (such as when taking up the theme of Amos 3.9-11). However, for the first time the text creates an abstract conception for the guilt of the capital: 'the pride of Jacob'. This conception is exceptional in the book of Amos.[16] On the other hand, it is quite

15. The '40 years' typical of priestly and Dtr. theology is probably a later addition.
16. The word-play with the term in Amos 8.7 is clearly dependent on 6.8;

familiar to readers of the book of Hosea (cf. Hos. 5.5; 7.10; 12.8-9; 13.6). It denotes Israel's feeling of security leaving no room for God's punishment. Again, the entirety of the guilt of Samaria for the traditionists can be told only when relating the message of Amos to the message of Hosea.

VI

Let me draw some conclusions from my observations:

1) Historically speaking, Amos and Hosea were two very different prophets using different subjects to convince Israel of her guilt. This observation is rather surprising since both prophets proclaimed in the northern kingdom and both were nearly contemporary. Apparently, these differences, at least to a certain degree, are due to the fact that Amos grew up in the south, Hosea in the north.

2) The pupils of Amos and Hosea, however, in handing down the prophet's message consciously related it to the message of the other prophet. This merging already occurred in pre-exilic times. They wanted to prevent their readers from isolating the message of one prophet. They were interested in those traits of the message of their masters which were common to both. The curiosity of the modern historian about the specific and singular elements in one prophet was quite alien to the traditionists. They did not want the words of either Hosea or Amos to be read with historical interest for a distant past but with a current interest in their words as a help for present problems. They were asking about the one message of God by two messengers (but without creating something like Tatian's harmony of the gospels).

3) Yet, the process of reading the words of one prophet in relation to the other did not start in the circles of pupils of both prophets at the same time. In the case of the book of Hosea, it began only when this book already existed. The relationships to the words of Amos can be isolated easily by literary means. Since Judah is addressed in these words, it becomes evident that Samaria must have already been destroyed some time previously. It is the period when the young prophet Jeremiah becomes influenced by the message of Hosea. The

cf. J. Jeremias, 'Jakob im Amosbuch', in M. Görg (ed.), *Die Väter Israels: Festschrift J. Scharbert* (Stuttgart: Katholisches Bibelwerk, 1989), pp. 139-54; cf., more recently, J. Jeremias, *Hosea and Amos* (Forschungen zum Alten Testament, 13; Tübingen: Mohr [Paul Siebeck], 1996), pp. 257-71.

additions to the book of Hosea, influenced by the thinking of Amos, want to prevent readers from understanding Hosea's accusations as something alien. In other words, they want to prevent them from reading his book with the attitude of a spectator. In the case of the book of Amos, the very composition of the book was already initiated under the strong influence of the book of Hosea. At least two of the words with Hoseanic flavor are put in central hermeneutical positions and serve as a kind of key to the book of Amos as a whole. From these observations, it appears that the book of Amos is younger than the book of Hosea, speaking in both cases of the original form. Hosea's words seem to have been written down very early by the fugitives fleeing to the south after the fall of Samaria. The destruction of Samaria had proved their truth very early, too. If this imagination is correct, then the fact that the collection of the twelve prophets starts with Hosea (and not with Amos) would be quite natural.

4) The theological intention to relate the message of the two prophets to each other only started at the beginning of the 7th century. The final stage of this development is the Book of the Twelve. This book is full of cross connections, partially early, partially late. These cross connections prove that the twelve parts of the Book of the Twelve were not conceived as twelve different messages of God but as one message through the mouth of twelve witnesses. O.H. Steck has tried to show recently that the development went further and the final redaction of the Book of the Twelve was oriented to the final redaction of the book of Isaiah.[17] Be that as it may, the cross connections between the twelve are evidence enough to prove that our modern quest for a theology of the prophets (not only of one prophet) is basically as old as the handing down of the message of the prophets. To find the one word of God behind the many words of his messengers remains a central task of theology ever since.

17. O.H. Steck, *Der Abschluß der Prophetie im AT. Ein Versuch zur Frage der Vorgeschichte des Kanons* (Biblisch-theologische Studien, 17; Neukirchen: Neukirchener Verlag, 1991).

THE BOOK OF NAHUM: A HISTORY OF INTERPRETATION

Duane L. Christensen

This paper, which traces in broad outline the history of interpretation of the book of Nahum from the biblical period to the present, is intended as a contribution to the study of this text in honor of an esteemed colleague and personal friend, John D.W. Watts. It provides perspective for understanding and evaluating his current interest in the larger structural coherence of the Book of the Twelve, the Minor Prophets taken as a whole, and the function of the book of Nahum within this structure.

Interpretation of the book of Nahum through the centuries has focused on the need to trust God in the presence of tyranny. Yahweh remains a dependable refuge for the people of Israel in the face of national injustice, whether at the hands of Assyria, Babylon, or Rome. Even the most powerful oppressor will ultimately be overthrown.

In its present canonical form, the book of Nahum is closely related to the books of Jonah and Habakkuk. The books of Nahum and Jonah are the only two books in the Hebrew Bible which end in a question and both are closely connected structurally with what follows: Jonah with Micah, and Nahum with Habakkuk. Moreover, both Nahum and Jonah have the city of Nineveh as their subject, with Nahum addressing the destruction of that city and Jonah its salvation. The book of Nahum is best read as a complement to the book of Jonah. The books of Jonah and Nahum may be read as midrashic reflection on the so-called 'attribute formula' in Exod. 34.6-7, with Jonah focusing on God's compassion and Nahum on God's wrath. Jonah presents God as 'compassionate, gracious...abounding in steadfast love' (Exod. 34.6-7a), whereas Nahum presents God as the 'one who punishes sons and grandsons to the third and fourth generation for the iniquity of their fathers' (Exod. 34.7b). In short, Nahum focuses on the 'dark side' of God, while Jonah portrays God's mercy and compassion toward the same wicked city of Nineveh. Both aspects are essential for an understanding of the divine nature.

The opening verses of the book of Nahum witness to the phenomenon of what Nahum Sarna has called 'Inner Biblical Exegesis'.[1] Original terms of compassion from the so-called 'attribute formula' in Exod. 34.6-7 are here transformed into terms of war: 'who maintains kindness (*noser*)' becomes 'who rages (*noter*) against his enemies' (cf. Lev. 19.18); 'assuages anger' becomes 'long of anger'; and 'great in kindness' becomes 'mighty in power'.[2] In short, the history of interpretation so far as the book of Nahum is concerned begins with the book itself, which is a reinterpretation of a central text from the Torah in a moment of need so far as Israel's national security was concerned. Though Yahweh is merciful and slow to anger, this time his patience toward those who flaunt him has run out.

The Qumran pesher 4QpNah (4Q169) read the text of Nahum as a prediction of impending disaster on the community's opponents, in which the hostile foes of old are identified with contemporary powers.[3] One Greek tradition of Tobit 14.4 (Sinaiticus), which has its fictional setting in ancient Nineveh, cited the prediction of the fall of Nineveh by Nahum (elsewhere Jonah) that the writer saw fulfilled at the hands of Nebuchadnezzar and Ahasuerus (both names used anachronistically). This understanding of Nahum as distant, prophetic prediction subsequently fulfilled appears also in Josephus (*Ant.* 9.239.42). The Aramaic Targum of Nahum emphasizes God's goodness to Israel while looking to the ultimate destruction of the nations who have ravaged the people of Israel and their temple. Nahum is here presented as later than Jonah, which reflects the Hebrew ordering of the individual books within the Book of the Twelve (the so-called Minor Prophets).

The book of Nahum is quoted only once in the New Testament (Rom. 10.15; cf. Isa. 52.7). Among the Church Fathers the book is cited infrequently: Tertullian (twice), Clement of Alexandria (once), Origen (four times), Eusebius (eight times), Epiphanius (five times), Cyril (twice),[4] Hippolytus Romanus (twice), Melito of Sardis (once), and John

1. See M. Fishbane, *Biblical Interpretation in Ancient Israel* (Oxford: Oxford University Press, 1985), pp. vii-viii.

2. M. Fishbane, 'Torah and Tradition', in D.A. Knight (ed.), *Tradition and Theology in the Old Testament* (Philadelphia: Fortress Press, 1977), pp. 280-81.

3. M.P. Horgan, *Pesharim: Qumran Interpretations of Biblical Books* (CBQMS, 8; Washington, DC: Catholic Biblical Association, 1979), pp. 158-59.

4. See P.E. Pusey (ed.), *Cyrilli Archiepiscopi Alexandrini in XII Prophetas* (Brussels: Culture et civilisation, 1965).

Chrysostrom (twice). Two traditions of interpretation appear in the several patristic commentaries within Christian circles: the 'allegorical' exemplified by Theodore of Mopsuestia,[5] and the 'literal' reading of Jerome,[6] who also presents a spiritual interpretation in which the book speaks of the certain destruction of those who oppose God and reject the safety of the church.[7]

The book of Nahum received relatively little attention within early Jewish interpretation, with eight references in the Babylonian Talmud and thirty-one in Midrash Rabbah.[8] The interpretation of the medieval exegetes Rashi (d. 1105), Ibn Ezra (d. 1164), and David Kimchi (d. 1235) focused on the judgement of God on Israel's national enemies.[9]

Like the main stream of Jewish exegesis before him, Martin Luther's 'Lectures on Nahum' (1525) assume a historical approach.[10] Nahum is taken as a contemporary of Isaiah who spoke in light of the suffering Judah was to experience under Sennacherib, of the preservation of a righteous remnant, and of the coming destruction of Nineveh. Thus Nahum, true to his name, brought 'comfort' to God's people in time of need. Few interpreters have expressed the essential message of Nahum more clearly than Luther when he wrote: 'The book teaches us to trust God and to believe, especially when we despair of all human help, human powers, and counsel, that the Lord stands by those who are His, shields His own against all attacks of the enemy, be they ever so powerful.'[11] Though Calvin's commentary is more detailed, it also is theological in orientation and largely grammatical and historical in focus.[12]

5. See H.N. Sprenger, *Theodori Mopsuesteni Commentarius in XII Prophetas* (Wiesbaden: Harrassowitz, 1977).

6. S. Hieronymi, *Commentarii in Prophetas Minores* (Corpus Christianorum; Turnholti: Brepols, 1970).

7. J.N.D. Kelly, *Jerome* (New York: Harper & Row, 1975), pp. 163-66.

8. J. Mann, *The Bible as Read and Preached in the Old Synagogue* (New York: Ktav, 1966).

9. See B.J. Bamberger, 'The Changing Image of the Prophet in Jewish Thought', in H. Orlinsky (ed.), *Interpreting the Prophetic Tradition* (Cincinnati: Hebrew Union College, 1969).

10. M. Luther, *Lectures on the Minor Prophets* (trans. D.J. Dinda; Luther's Works, 18; St. Louis: Concordia, 1975).

11. W.A. Maier, *The Book of Nahum: A Commentary* (St. Louis, MO: Concordia Publishing House, 1959), p. 86.

12. J. Calvin, *Commentaries on the Twelve Minor Prophets* (vol. 4; trans. J. Owen; Grand Rapids: Baker, 1950), pp. 183-312.

The book of Nahum was singled out by Bishop Robert Lowth for its aesthetic brilliance.[13] With the subsequent development of historical criticism in the nineteenth century, attention shifted to the question of the precise historical and geographical origin of the book as the key to its interpretation. Supposed reference to the invasion of Sennacherib and linguistic ties to Isaiah led some to posit a date late in the reign of Hezekiah. But the discovery that Thebes fell to Assyria in 663 BCE (cf. Nah. 3.8-10) led to a lowering of the date of composition, with most critical scholars arguing for a setting close to the actual fall of Nineveh in 612 BCE.

The discovery of what appeared to be an acrostic poem in 1.3-7 by a German pastor, G. Frohnmeyer (ca. 1860),[14] attracted wide attention within the scholarly community, particularly when H. Gunkel (1893) argued that this 'broken acrostic' was added to the book by a post-exilic editor of Nahum's oracles.[15] Like so many other texts in the Hebrew Bible, Nahum was regarded as composite.

Though many interpreters continued to read the book as testimony to God's just rule in history, others noted the apparently non-religious character of the poetry in chs. 2–3 and the prophet's failure to address the sins of Judah. Some scholars began to judge Nahum as a nationalistic prophet, perhaps even representative of the very 'false prophets' condemned by Jeremiah. Such views have retained their influence in some circles to the present time.

In 1907 Paul Haupt argued that the book was not prophecy at all but the festival liturgy composed for the celebration of the Day of Nikanor on the 13th of Adar, 161 BCE.[16] Though the Maccabean date was subsequently rejected, the idea that the book was a festival liturgy had profound influence in academic circles. In 1926 Paul Humbert argued that the book was a prophetic liturgy used at the New Year festival in Jerusalem in 612 BCE to celebrate the fall of Nineveh.[17] In 1946 A. Haldar argued that the book of Nahum was the work of cultic prophets who used the language of ritual combat in the New Year

13. R. Lowth, *De sacra poesi Hebraeorum* (1763), p. 281.

14. See F. Delitzsch, *Biblischer Commentar über die Psalmen* (Leipzig: Dorffling und Franke, 1867), p. 107.

15. H. Gunkel, 'Nahum 1', *ZAW* 11 (1893), pp. 223-44.

16. P. Haupt, 'The Book of Nahum', *JBL* 26 (1907), pp. 1-53.

17. P. Humbert, 'Essai d'analyse de Nahoum 1,2–2,3', *ZAW* 44 (1926), pp. 266-80.

festival as a curse on Israel's political enemies, the Assyrians.[18]

Subsequent studies placed the book within the sphere of international politics in premonarchic Israel, as reflected in the larger tradition of oracles against foreign nations in the prophetic literature. One of the more attractive hypotheses along these lines was made in 1975 by John Watts who suggested that the book of Nahum, along with Habakkuk and Obadiah, was a liturgical expression of foreign prophecies which was part of the 'Day of Yahweh' section of the Royal Zion Festival in ancient Jerusalem.[19] More recently (1981), J.H. Eaton has shown that no simple distinction exists between what some have called 'cultic' and others 'prophecy' in ancient Israel.[20] A year later, Coggins suggested that Nahum is to be read in conjunction with the foreign nation oracles of Isaiah 13–23 in particular.[21] The first heading *massa' Nineweh* (1.1a) may well be an invitation to associate the book with this Isaianic collection.

The contributions of John Watts and others, who were already raising a new set of questions about the literary structure and the meaning of the book of Nahum within the canonical process in ancient Israel, were not recognized by Sweeney in his form critical study of Nahum (1992). He concluded that 'the historical setting of the final form of this text must be placed in conjunction with the fall of Nineveh in 612 BCE rather than interpreting the book as a product of Persian period redaction, which organizes and presents Nahum's oracles according to a post-exilic eschatological scenario.'[22] Though a date close to the actual fall of Nineveh in 612 BCE is often assumed, and argued with force by Sweeney, an earlier date remains possible, so far as the historical occasion which produced the original text is concerned.[23] If the revolt of Manasseh is not to be dismissed as a figment of the imagination of the

18. A. Haldar, *Studies in the Book of Nahum* (Uppsala: Lundequist, 1946).

19. J.D.W. Watts, *The Books of Joel, Obadiah, Jonah, Nahum, Habakkuk and Zephaniah* (CBC; Cambridge: Cambridge University Press, 1975), p. 5.

20. J.H. Eaton, *Vision in Worship: The Relation of Prophecy and Liturgy in the Old Testament* (London: SPCK, 1981).

21. R.J. Coggins, 'An alternative prophetic tradition?', in R.J. Coggins (ed.), *Israel's Prophetic Tradition: Essays in Honour of Peter R. Ackroyd* (Cambridge: Cambridge University Press, 1982), pp. 77-94.

22. M. Sweeney, 'Concerning the Structure and Generic Character of the Book of Nahum', *ZAW* 104 (1992), p. 376.

23. See my discussion in the following: 'The Acrostic of Nahum Reconsidered', *ZAW* 87 (1975), pp. 28-29; and 'Nahum, the Book of', *Harper's Bible Dictionary* (San Francisco: Harper & Row, 1985), p. 681.

author of Chronicles, the situation as it existed in Judah ca. 652–648 BCE fits the occasion rather well. The basis for such a revolt on Manasseh's part would have been the conviction that Assyria's days were numbered. The book of Nahum presents precisely that message and may have been used to persuade the Judean king to take part in such a revolt—the assurance that Assyria's fall was certain, in fact that it was ordained by God the Divine Warrior. The book would then have taken on deeper meaning as part of the theological basis for the subsequent resurgence of Judean independence under king Josiah, especially after the death of Asshurbanipal in ca. 630 BCE. The final destruction of Nineveh in 612 would have been the ultimate fulfillment of this prophecy and would thus explain its inclusion in the canon.

An original acrostic hymn in Nahum 1, which is based on at least the first half of the Hebrew alphabet, has apparently been adapted to a new purpose by the author of the book,[24] perhaps to form a cipher (code) from the sequence of letters and/or other opening elements, as A.S. van der Woude has suggested.[25] The original acrostic presents the two sides of God's character: he is slow to anger, but he will vent his wrath against those who defy him. The appearance of the Divine Warrior is presented in mythic imagery, with the cosmos returning to chaos in the day of God's wrath. The cipher in 1.2-8, which continues in 1.9-10, together with 2.10, the structural center of the book, summarizes the content of the book as a whole:[26]

> I am the exalted Yahweh, and (I am) in the presence of sin;
> in a flood (I am) about to bring a full end—completely.
> What will you devise against Yahweh?
> A full end he himself will make;
> distress will not come a second time.
> For (you will be) like dry entangled thorns;
> and (though you are) like soddened drunkards,
> consumed (you will be) like dry stubble—completely.
> Desolation and dissipation and destruction, and hearts faint and knees give way—

24. See my articles, 'The Acrostic of Nahum Once Again: A Prosodic Analysis of Nahum 1,1-10', *ZAW* 99 (1987), pp. 409-15; and 'The Book of Nahum: The Question of Authorship within the Canonical Process', *JETS* 31 (1988), pp. 51-58.

25. A.S. van der Woude, 'The Book of Nahum: A Letter Written in Exile', (OTS, 20; Leiden: Brill, 1977), pp. 108-26.

26. In addition to the articles in notes 22 and 23, see my commentary on Nahum in *Harper's Bible Commentary* (San Francisco: Harper & Row, 1988), pp. 736-38.

and anguish is in all loins and all their faces; they are gathered as
boughs for burning.

In the taunt song (Nah. 2–3), sometimes described as an ode on the fall of Nineveh, the language is graphic, depicting in vivid form scenes of horror and vengeful rejoicing because Assyria is finally experiencing the atrocities she inflicted on others.

In its poetic form, the book of Nahum has no superior within the prophetic literature of the Old Testament. The vivid and rapid succession of images gives it a peculiar power. It delineates the swift and unerring execution of God's fury against his merciless foes and those of his people. At the same time, it also points rather sharply to God as the sure refuge and security for those who obey and trust him. Careful analysis of the poetry in the book reveals an elegant literary structure. The best way to explain the remarkable structural symmetry observed is to posit musical influence. The Hebrew text of Nahum bears the mark of original musical composition and performance within an ancient Israelite liturgical setting.[27] It is likely that Nahum was a central prophet functioning within the Temple cult in Jerusalem. The book belongs among the oracles against foreign nations and as such was probably motivated by political aims. In its present canonical form it is closely related to the book of Habakkuk. In fact the two books may be outlined as a single literary unit as follows:

A	Hymn of theophany	Nahum 1
B	Taunt song against Nineveh	Nahum 2–3
X	The problem of theodicy	Habakkuk 1
B′	Taunt song against the 'wicked one'	Habakkuk 2
A′	Hymn of theophany	Habakkuk 3

Clearly, John Watts was on the cutting edge of scholarship twenty years ago so far as the interpretation of the book of Nahum is concerned. The book is to be interpreted with Coggins in relation to the broader oral and literary traditions of Old Testament prophecy.[28] Moreover, as Brevard Childs has argued, the 'final form' of the book of Nahum bears witness to God's ultimate triumph over all his foes. Traditional critical assessments miss the authoritative hermeneutical role of

27. See my article, 'The Book of Nahum as a Liturgical Composition: A Prosodic Analysis', *JETS* 32 (1989), pp. 159-69.

28. Coggins, 'An alternative prophetic tradition?', pp. 79-85.

this 'canonical' shaping.[29] But of greater importance is that the book be interpreted within its present literary context as part of the structural center of the Book of the Twelve, which is arranged in three groups of four books as follows:

A Hosea, Joel and Amos + Obadiah
B Jonah + Micah
B′ Nahum + Habakkuk
A′ Zephaniah + Haggai, Zechariah and Malachi

So far as the canonical process is concerned, this larger structure emerged in the exilic and/or the Persian period, where it continued to function 'according to a post-exilic eschatological scenario', the recent comments of Marvin Sweeney notwithstanding.[30]

29. B.S. Childs, *Introduction to the Old Testament as Scripture* (Philadelphia: Fortress, 1979), pp. 44-46.

30. Sweeney, 'Concerning the Structure', p. 376.

DRAMATIC COHERENCE IN NAHUM, HABAKKUK, AND ZEPHANIAH

Paul R. House

The final form of the Book of the Twelve exhibits several types of literary coherence that link its various parts.[1] Included among these unifying factors are such key elements as genre, characterization, theme, and plot movement.[2] Though it is important to examine how each of these details impacts the whole corpus, it is also appropriate to analyze how they operate in discrete segments of the Twelve. The three consecutive seventh-century prophets Nahum, Habakkuk, and Zephaniah comprise such a unit. Not only are they from the same era,[3] they also

1. This paper focuses on literary unity in the Masoretic text of Nahum, Habakkuk, and Zephaniah. It, therefore, does not deal with redactional matters such as those analyzed in J.D. Nogalski's *Literary Precursors to the Book of the Twelve* (BZAW, 217; Berlin: de Gruyter, 1993) and *Redactional Processes in the Book of the Twelve* (BZAW, 218; Berlin: de Gruyter, 1993) or historical issues like those covered in B.A. Jones, *The Formation of the Book of the Twelve: A Study in Text and Canon* (SBLDS, 149; Atlanta: Scholars Press, 1995) or canonical matters such as those examined in A.Y. Lee, *The Canonical Unity of the Scroll of the Minor Prophets* (Dissertation: Baylor University, 1985). Still, there are places at which these works aid this article, as will become evident below.

2. For an extended analysis of these and other unifying literary details in the Twelve, consult P.R. House, *The Unity of the Twelve* (JSOTSup, 97; Sheffield: Almond Press, 1990). If I were to write this book again, the most fundamental change I would make is to change the title to *Literary Unity in the Twelve* to reflect the fact that literary unity is but one type of coherence the books exhibit. The book's epilogue (pp. 243-45) reflects this belief, but its title does not.

3. This conclusion is far from a universally-held belief among scholars, of course. Solid disagreements exist. Still, the reasoning for this position in J.J.M. Roberts, *Nahum, Habakkuk, and Zephaniah* (OTL; Philadelphia: Westminster Press, 1991); and J.M.P. Smith, W.H. Ward, and J.A. Bewer, *A Critical and Exegetical Commentary on Micah, Zephaniah, Nahum, Habakkuk, Obadiah, and Joel* (ICC; New York: Scribner's, 1911) is cogent and plausible and is assumed in this article.

share a strong thematic interest in impending or fulfilled judgement. They are approximately the same length and have been placed together in every major canonical ordering of the minor prophets.[4] Each book also utilizes alternating speakers who take on definite roles and thereby create verbal movement and major themes.[5] Clearly, then, these books are particularly appropriate for exploring possible types of unity within the Twelve in general and for noting how dramatic literary principles may link adjoining books in particular.

This article attempts to develop these ideas in three ways. First, criteria for dividing speeches in the prophecies will be determined based on the books themselves. Second, descriptions of the books' speakers will be developed to determine the function of those speakers in the prophecies. Third, an analysis of the thematic movement produced by the speeches will show how speakers proclaim a singular, though not monolithic message. Each book's own emphases are not neglected, but the article's goal is to build bridges between the books as a step toward suggesting their specific role in the Twelve.

Types of Speeches in the Books

The easiest way to begin to separate God's speeches from those of the prophets is to distinguish between first-person statements made by God and comments by the prophets that speak of God in the third-person.[6] In other words, it is necessary to know when God speaks and when someone else speaks about God. Sometimes this simple methodology is

4. The LXX orders the first six prophecies differently than the Masoretic Text, but it orders the final six books in the same way as the Hebrew Bible.

5. Scholars who do not dwell on the role of shifting speakers in the books note the phenomena. For example, Roberts, *Nahum, Habakkuk, and Zephaniah*, pp. 73, 176-77; Nogalski, *Redactional Processes*, pp. 111, 118; Smith, Ward, and Bewer, *Habakkuk*, pp. 3-6.

6. This basic methodology is followed in P.R. House, *Zephaniah: A Prophetic Drama* (JSOTSup, 69; Sheffield: Almond Press, 1988). A more detailed system applied to more complex literature is found in J. D.W. Watts, *Isaiah 1–33* (WBC, 24; Waco: Word Books, 1985) and *Isaiah 34–66* (WBC, 25; Waco: Word Books, 1987). A.R. Diamond examines Jeremiah's confessions as dialogue between the prophet and Yahweh in *The Confessions of Jeremiah in Context: Scenes of Prophetic Drama* (JSOTSup, 45; Sheffield: Sheffield Academic Press, 1987). All these works divide speeches by third-person references to Yahweh, by verbal markers such as 'says Yahweh', by narrative statements, and, when necessary, by other contextual data.

not sufficient to determine who speaks, though, so other contextual clues must be utilized.[7] These more difficult cases are made less so by categorizing the known speeches into specific categories. Then comparisons between texts can be made that may help determine a passage's speaker. Stated simply, in Nahum, Habakkuk, and Zephaniah there are three types of material that either introduce the book's literature or mark where God speaks. There are also six types of speeches made by God and the prophets. A brief examination of these types demonstrates how all three prophecies use a dramatic format.

Titles, quotation statements, and explanatory transitions all act as speech markers in the books. Each prophecy begins with a title in its initial verse. Nahum and Habakkuk are designated as 'oracles' or 'burdens', while Zephaniah is termed a 'word of Yahweh'. Though it is beyond the scope of this article to pursue the exact distinctions between these two terms, John Watts has suggested ways in which superscriptions may provide unifying keys in the Twelve.[8] Hab. 3.1 is a title for the psalm that follows in 3.2-19, and it marks the chapter as the prophet's speech. Quotation statements always denote where God talks. These phrases include, 'Thus says the Lord' (Nah. 1.12), 'Says the Lord of hosts' (Nah. 2.13; 3.5; Zeph. 2.9), 'Says the Lord' (Zeph. 1.2, 3, 10; 3.8), and 'Says the Lord' (Zeph. 3.20).[9] Two explanatory transitions that designate the succeeding words as Yahweh's appear, one in Nah. 1.14 ('Yahweh has commanded concerning you'), and the other in Hab. 2.2 ('And Yahweh answered me and said').

Each speech marker fits the book's context, as will be examined later. For example, the 'Lord of hosts' references in Nahum and Zephaniah match God's wrathful purposes in those prophecies. The 'Says Yahweh' occurrences in Zephaniah fit the text's emphasis on Zephaniah's messenger role. The explanatory transitions facilitate Nahum's emphasis on

7. Roberts makes this point in a critique of *Zephaniah: A Prophetic Drama* in his work, *Nahum, Habakkuk, and Zephaniah.* He correctly states that distinguishing between first and third-person speech does not always determine speakers, so his criticism on that point is appropriate. He overstates his case, however, when he says this distinction 'seldom provides reliable criteria for distinguishing between the voice of God and the voice of the prophet, much less for analyzing a composition's structure' (p. 161).

8. J.D.W. Watts, 'Superscriptions and Incipits in the Book of the Twelve', Paper presented to the Consultation on the Book of the Twelve, SBL, 1994.

9. The first phrase is כה אמר יהוה, the second is נאם יהוה זבאות, the third is נאם־יהוה, and the fourth is אמר יהוה.

God's royal status and Habakkuk's dialogic, question-and-answer format, respectively. It is also true that Nahum and Zephaniah are particularly similar in their usage of the phrases, while Habakkuk's unique format sets it apart. Still, the separation of speakers occurs for specific reasons in all three prophecies.

The types of speeches in Nahum, Habakkuk, and Zephaniah can be divided into six kinds. The first type of speech makes third-person references to God in a prophetic speech about a third-person plural or third-person singular audience. Such speeches are indirect in that they state what God will do to or for someone who is not addressed in the speech. For example, Nah. 1.2-8 describes God's nature as it relates to his enemies, but the enemies are not addressed directly. Similarly, Zeph. 1.7 describes how the Lord will punish 'guests' at the judgement feast, while Zeph. 1.14-16 comments on God's punishment of cities. Neither the 'guests' nor the cities are spoken to at this point in the prophecy. Zeph. 1.18, 2.10-11, and 2.13–3.5 operate in much the same manner. This type of speech allows prophets to inform interested audiences about what God will do in the future to specified parties.

The counterpart to this initial type of speech occurs when Yahweh speaks in first-person about a third-person plural or third-person singular audience. Like the first kind, these speeches are indirect in that God speaks to an audience about a different group. Only Zephaniah uses this format (cf. Zeph. 1.2-6; 1.8-13; 1.17a; 2.8-9; 3.6-13).[10] Obviously, then, both Yahweh and the prophet have many of the same sort of speeches in that book.

10. Of these speeches, Zeph. 1.17 is the hardest to divide from the prophet's comments. The verse begins with Yahweh speaking in first-person, 'I will bring distress on mankind, and they will walk like the blind'. The next half-verse says, 'Because they have sinned against Yahweh, their blood will be poured out like dust and their flesh like dung'. Obviously, 1.17b switches to third-person address, which means the verse must either be divided into two parts or that Yahweh speaks of himself in third person. Roberts points out this difficulty in *Nahum, Habakkuk, and Zephaniah*, p. 184, and again states that such verses show that changes in speakers cannot be determined by first and third-person references to Yahweh, nor used when making source-critical observations. Without passing judgement on his comments on source criticism, it is incorrect to argue from the few problem passages that the designation of speakers cannot be done with accuracy. *Zephaniah: A Prophetic Drama* inexcusably passes over the division of this verse. I now believe that 1.17a closes the book's second scene and 1.17b begins the prophet's soliloquy in 1.17b–2.7. Cf. *Zephaniah: A Prophetic Drama*, pp. 118-26.

A third form of speech includes a third-person reference to God in a prophetic speech directed to a second-person singular or plural audience. Now the speech is direct; it is aimed 'to you'. Nahum 1.9-11; 2.1-12; 3.1-4;[11] and 3.8-19 address Nineveh in this manner. Habakkuk 2.20 is a difficult text to type,[12] but it does use this format and adds an emphasis on a third-person singular culprit ('woe to you' and 'woe to him'). In Zephaniah, the prophet adopts this format to denounce cities and to encourage Jerusalem of a brighter future (cf. Zeph. 2.1-7; 3.14-17). Obviously, if the Habakkuk passage may be included in this category, then all three prophecies use this form of speech. Each book has the prophet address those who need the divine message of judgement or renewal, or both, so they are the audience's link to God's will.

The fourth type is a first-person address by God to a second-person singular or plural audience. Such speeches intensify the pressure on hearers. Surely, if direct prophetic statements apply specifically to an audience, then a message from God does so as well. God chastises Nineveh in Nah. 1.14; 2.13; and 3.5-7 but pledges freedom to Israel in Nah. 1.12-13. The Lord also promises Ethiopia judgement in Zeph. 2.12 and offers hope to Jerusalem in Zeph. 3.18-20. Both prophecies use this category to condemn and comfort. The heightening effect inherent in having God speak make these direct addresses prominent thematic markers in both books.

The final two kinds of speeches are unique to Habakkuk. In this prophecy Habakkuk questions God directly in 1.2-4 and 1.12–2.1, then praises the Lord in 3.2-19. As could be expected, God responds to the prophet's questions in 1.5-11 and 2.2-11. In Nahum and Zephaniah, the Lord and the prophets never dialogue with one another in this fashion. Rather, they act as co-revealers of what God wills for Israel and the nations. Still the format of alternating speeches endures, so the unity created by the dramatic sequencing remains. Habakkuk's speeches

11. The speaker in 3.1-4 must be determined contextually. Both 2.13 and 3.5 mark points where Yahweh speaks. Since no designation appears in 3.1 and the content of 3.1-4 approximates that of other prophet speeches, this pericope is treated as coming from the prophet.

12. The difficulty is that, unlike other speeches, Hab. 2.12-20 moves into third-person address of Yahweh without a verbal marker. Dividing the speakers after 2.11 means the Lord begins to pronounce 'woe' on the wicked, then the prophet completes the series of 'woes' in 2.12-20.

unfold differently than those in the other books, yet the artistic principles are similar.

Even this cursory glance at the material reveals a significant likeness in the genre of the three books. Each prophecy presents its message through alternating speakers whose identities can be determined contextually. Each prophecy uses verbal markers to highlight specific speeches. Each book adopts similar patterns for how and why God and the prophets speak. These conclusions will become even more apparent as the books' characters and thematic movements are analyzed.

Characterization in the Books

'Characterization' is the way in which a literary work presents its personae. Characterization includes the depiction of a character's various personal facets. Aristotle argued that effective characters must have purpose, propriety, reality, and consistency.[13]

E.V. Roberts concurs and claims that well-conceived characters have their 'drives, aims, ideals, morals, and conscience' revealed by skillful authors.[14] Such traits emerge in dramatic literature chiefly through what characters say or do to others and by how other characters respond in kind to them. An analysis along these lines of the speeches outlined above reveals in a general way the personalities of the books' major characters, Yahweh and the prophets, as well as the traits of their two main minor composite characters, Israel and the gentile nations.

God's nature in these books is summarized in Nahum's initial statements (1.2-8). In an indirect speech, the prophet explains that the Lord's patience (1.3), goodness (1.7), and protectiveness (1.7) means that God must punish the guilty (1.2-3), rule the earth effectively, express wrath appropriately, and generally pursue doggedly wicked nations like Assyria (1.6-8). Zephaniah's usage of this type of speech matches Nahum's, for Zeph. 1.7, 14-16, 17b-18; 2.10-11; and 2.13–3.5 all depict an outraged God who will judge wicked persons, cities, and nations who are arrogant and rebellious. Thus, this type of speech highlights Yahweh's righteous indignation, divine sovereignty, and resulting determination to punish the wicked.

13. Aristotle, *Poetics*, in B.F. Dukore (ed.), *Dramatic Theory and Criticism: Greeks to Grotowski* (trans. S.H. Butcher; New York: Holt, Rinehart and Winston, 1974), p. 44.

14. E.V. Roberts, *Writing Themes about Literature* (Englewood Cliffs, NJ: Prentice-Hall, 3rd edn, 1973), p. 44.

Having set the stage by informing readers about the Lord's anger and plans to unleash judgement, prophets then move to warn specific groups that *they* are *the objects* of divine wrath. Nahum 1.9-11; 2.1-12; 3.1-4; and 3.8-9 inform Nineveh directly that the earth's sovereign ruler has dispatched an attacker to destroy them because of their oppressive, shameful ways. Those who devise evil against the Lord will soon meet a divine judge. Conversely, Yahweh will restore Israel (Nah. 2.2). Habakkuk uses similar imagery to depict impending woe on the violent, disgraceful, idolatrous Babylon (Hab. 2.12-20). Once again, the Lord is sovereign ruler and cosmic judge. God is in 'his holy temple', so all earth must 'be silent before him' (2.20). Zephaniah 2.1-7 echoes these sentiments, while Zeph. 3.14-17 uses this speech type to announce renewal for Jerusalem. In this last speech, God becomes a giver of hope to the remnant of faithful Israelites, a depiction that resonates with Nahum's initial comments (Nah. 1.2-8). Thus, Yahweh's characterization grows towards greater depth and definition in these speeches. God's full activity moves beyond righteous anger and well-placed threatening to include specific reasons to judge or renew. All that Nah. 1.2-8 claims is validated by what the prophets tell the more-detached audience and by what they tell the very objects of Yahweh's displeasure. Clearly, the books' usage of these two types of speeches allows these categories to complement one another in their depiction of Yahweh. The fact that all three prophecies use this speech type in similar ways suggests a unified approach to the artful composition of characterization.

God's own statements to these same two audiences confirm the prophet's comments about his intentions. In Nah. 1.12-13, 14; 2.13; and 3.5-7, Yahweh's threats 'to you' follow directly after the prophet's 'to you' warnings. God will fulfill the prophet's dire predictions about Assyria and hopeful comments about Judah's future. Yahweh has seen Israel's affliction. God knows what has happened to the elect nation and will soon stop injustice, oppression, and cruelty. In Zephaniah, the Lord takes the lead in denouncing the wicked (cf. 1.2-6, 8-13, 17; 2.8-9; 3.6-13), then is joined by the prophet, who completes the message. In other words, the order and function of who delivers these speeches is reversed in Nahum and Zephaniah, yet the portrait of God as the one who sees, assesses, punishes, rewards, and renews remains the same.

Habakkuk's unique brand of interaction between the Lord and the prophet adds a personal dimension to Yahweh's characterization. In Nahum and Zephaniah the Lord speaks and reveals *alongside* a partner character who accepts God's viewpoint unreservedly. Habakkuk charts a different course by having the prophet ask God to explain why the evil prosper in Israel or elsewhere (1.2-4; 1.12–2.1). His faith seeks understanding in a manner that denies neither his own prophetic calling nor Yahweh's total sovereignty in human affairs. Indeed, he affirms Yahweh's authority by assuming God has the ability to do something about his concerns. When Yahweh responds by promising to judge the wicked and instill faith in the faithful (1.5-11; 2.2-11), it is the interpersonal relationship between deity and prophet that creates the scene. Habakkuk is not God's equal, but God is Habakkuk's dialogue partner, even his intimate friend. Clearly, to the faithful Yahweh is a close, personal, and communicative companion. To the wicked, however, Yahweh appears as enemy, and a universally sovereign one at that.

Obviously, certain aspects of the prophets' characterization have emerged. Amos's comment that 'surely the Lord does nothing unless he reveals his plans to his servant the prophets (Amos 3.7) applies to the prophets' portrayal in Nahum, Habakkuk, and Zephaniah. Indeed, as they report what God will do in Nahum and Zephaniah they prove themselves to have intimate, detailed knowledge of God's current attitude and future acts. They are, then, God's close associates, persons who are privileged to sit in Yahweh's inner circle. Certainly Habakkuk's dialogue with God hardly diminishes this aspect of the prophets' characterization. Rather, this exchange between two intimately-related persons magnifies their importance to the revelatory process. God answers the prophet more as a valued colleague than as a nuisance.

Scholars have long noted that prophets serve as God's messengers. The clearest evidence for this description lies in the many times the prophets 'simply' report God's words ('says the Lord'), state that God is about to speak (for example, Nah. 1.14; Hab. 2.2), or divulge God's plans accurately (for example, Nah. 1.9-11; Hab. 2.12-20; Zeph. 2.1-7).

Beyond this messenger designation, however, is the book's tendency to regard the prophets as revelational partners, co-revealers of the divine word. That is, the prophets speak an original word that God later affirms and expands further. For example, Nah. 1.2-8 and 1.9-11 are addressed by God in Nah. 1.12-13 and 1.14, while Habakkuk's probing questions are dealt with and taken to further logical conclusions in Yahweh's answers. In Zephaniah, the prophet responds in 1.7 and 1.14-16 to what God declares in 1.2-6 and 1.8-13, and the list could be extended. The juxtaposition of who fills out whose message does not eliminate the fact that these prophets are more than, or at least other than, messengers. They are God's friends, and by explaining the Lord's will to Israel they also prove the people's friends.[15]

Two composite characters deserve mention because it is their behavior that moves Yahweh and the prophets to speak in the first place. First, God's covenant people (Israel and Judah) are depicted as a split group of rebellious sinners and faithful remnant believers. Repeatedly condemned in the first six books of the Twelve, a gradual shift in the nature and destiny of the chosen people occurs in Nahum, Habakkuk, and Zephaniah. In Nahum, the chosen people are victims of Assyrian oppression who will be blessed in the future (1.12-13; 1.15). For now they can rejoice in Assyria's well-earned and highly-celebrated demise (3.19). In Habakkuk, though, the nation will be destroyed, thereby forcing righteous persons like Habakkuk to suffer alongside the wicked. Therefore, God must start over with a new group of people for the faith which Habakkuk embodies in 3.2-19 to become common. This new group receives some definition in Zephaniah, where, after denunciations of Judah's sinfulness appear in the initial speeches, a more positive note is sounded in 2.3, 7, and 9. There the prophet urges the 'humble of the land' to seek God, escape Yahweh's wrath, and thereby eventually inherit Philistia, Moab, and Ammon. By 3.8-13 the remnant of God's people are portrayed as cleansed, meek, obedient, righteous, and bold. A clearer contrast between the unrighteous in chapter one and the purified remnant of chapter three could hardly be imagined.

Second, gentile nations also play a significant role in all three books. Nahum considers Assyria the ultimate villain, a nation wholly committed to evil, and, therefore, fully deserving of divine censure. Habakkuk learns that Babylon is God's instrument for punishing Judah's wickedness, then discovers that the instrument will be devastated for its own injustices and atrocities (Hab. 2.5-11). Zephaniah concurs with this

15. A. Berlin states, 'The Prophet conveys the words of God but he also interjects his own thoughts and reactions. While the prophet fully identifies with God's message, he may step in and out of his role as God's mouthpiece. This actually strengthens the effect, because the prophet's own words confirm the words that he speaks in God's name' (*Zephaniah* [AB, 25A; New York: Doubleday, 1994], pp. 12-13). For other discussions of the prophet's role as co-revealer, consult J.A. Thompson, 'The "Response" in Biblical and non-Biblical Literature with Particular reference to the Hebrew Prophets', in E.W. Conrad and E.G. Newing (eds.), *Perspectives on Language and Text* (Winona Lake, IN: Eisenbrauns, 1987), pp. 255-68; and House, *The Unity of the Twelve*, pp. 185-203.

negative assessment of Judah's neighbors in 2.1-15 but includes gentiles in the purified remnant described in 3.8-9.[16] Thus, the characterizations of Israel and the nations follow a similar trajectory from sin to remnant standing. Israel's development transpires more gradually than their counterparts, yet the parallel remains clear. God and Zephaniah agree in 3.6-20 that neither covenant nor non-covenant peoples are hopelessly bound for destruction. Judgment creates the remnant as distinctly as it removes the rebellious.

Character development occurs from Nahum to Zephaniah. In Nahum, God and prophet alike stand against Assyria, Judah's enemy. Next, in Habakkuk, both Yahweh and the prophet state that Israel and Babylon both merit punishment. Rather than announcing judgement side-by-side as in Nahum, though, the two main characters dialogue about the future, after which Habakkuk sings a psalm of trust to the Lord. Faith has been rewarded in Habakkuk's case, and revelatory openness has been honored in Yahweh's. Finally, both Yahweh and the prophet resolve their dissatisfaction with sinful Israelites and gentiles by allowing judgement to forge a faithful remnant composed of both groups. Thus, God and the prophets begin with denunciation in Nahum, move to a shared understanding of the future in Habakkuk, and close with a vision of renewal in Zephaniah. God appears, then, as regal, merciful, kind, just, wrathful, and forgiving. The prophets are heralds, messengers, revelatory partners, and friends. All the while, the nations and Israel do not speak but are rather spoken about by the major characters.

Plot/Movement in the Books

Scholars have defined 'plot' in a variety of ways. Some consider it a structuring device, others a framework for presenting ideologies, some a causally-related pattern of events, and some a means of ordering readers' emotions. Though the issue could be, and deserves to be, debated at great length, this brief paper defines plot as the combination of causes, effects, events, actions, and attitudes that lead characters towards the solution of a major problem already announced in Hosea-Micah. Though, of course, the books are speech-oriented, it is still evident that the dialogue moves the problem towards resolution. To some scholars 'plot' is not a satisfactory way of describing what occurs in

16. Cf. Berlin, *Zephaniah*, p. 133.

prophetic books, but it is difficult to suggest a suitable alternative that communicates prophecy's movement.

Simply stated, Hosea–Micah introduces a world-wide sin problem that derives from long-term, pervasive rejection of Yahweh's person and covenant. Israel has committed idolatry and a host of other transgressions. Joel, Amos, and Obadiah indict other nations as well. Judgment is introduced as the antidote to this plague, especially in Joel, Amos, Jonah, and Obadiah, but it is not until Nahum, Habakkuk, and Zephaniah unfold that the threatened punishment impacts the wicked more directly. Likewise, a bright future for Israel is anticipated in Hos. 14.1-9, Joel 3.18-21, Amos 9.11-15, Obad. 15-21, and Mic. 7.14-20, and Jonah even indicates that gentiles may receive Yahweh's forgiveness, but this future moves closer to fruition in Nahum, Habakkuk, and Zephaniah. Thus, these three books present in concentrated form how God's judgement will remove the wicked from the scene, leave the faithful to their well-earned reward, and thereby vindicate Yahweh and the prophets' denunciations and predictions of future glory.

Nahum begins to solve the problems related to eradicating sin in three ways. First, the prophet stresses God's righteousness in 1.2-8, which removes potential accusations of divine arbitrariness or viciousness. Second, the prophet lists Nineveh as the object of the righteous God's wrath and says that the wicked city will be consumed in 1.9-11. Third, Yahweh confirms the prophet's statements in 1.12-13 and 1.14, adding that Judah will be released from Assyrian tyranny, a conviction the prophet seconds (1.15).

Swiftly, inexorably, Nahum concludes the Lord's judgement on Assyria. Descriptions of invading armies and of Nineveh's total devastation consume the speeches in Nahum 2–3. At the same time, Jacob's descendants are promised freedom (1.12-13), even majesty (2.2). Despite Nineveh's power, she has fallen, while the weak now rejoice in the oppressor's downfall. One chief source of sin has been removed, but has the universal problem of iniquity announced in Hosea-Micah and reflected in Nahum truly been resolved?

Habakkuk's opening question implies that it has not. Wicked persons exist yet in Judah and beyond (cf. 1.2-4). God's response indicates that sin remains a problem but that Babylon will soon be used to punish Judah's unrepentant sinners (1.5-11). Not yet satisfied, Habakkuk wonders what, if anything, can check Babylon's unbridled power (1.12–2.1). This time Yahweh says that Babylon will also be destroyed and that persons who are upright must live by simple faith (2.2-11; cf. 2.4). Habakkuk adds appropriate 'woes' to the violent and to idolaters (2.12-20), then closes the prophecy with a psalm of faith that pledges service no matter what the future holds (3.1-19). Clearly, the scope of judgement has widened. Still, smaller nations listed as wicked in the first six prophecies have so far escaped without mention, other than as implied victims of Assyria's wrath. Also, Habakkuk seems to negate Nahum's optimistic comments about Judah. At the end of Habakkuk, the prophet, representing all faithful persons, looks for the deliverance only faith can expect to come.

Zephaniah moves much closer to solving these plot dilemmas. God threatens world-wide, creation-repealing punishment in 1.2-6.[17] The dreaded 'day of the Lord' is announced by the prophet (1.7), and succeeding alternating speeches in 1.8-13, 14-16, 17, and 18 spell out the horrors of this 'day'. More specifically, Judah, Philistia, Moab, Ethiopia, and Assyria will be consumed (2.1–3.5). God's ultimate goal, however, is to create a multi-national remnant that includes faithful Israelites (3.6-13). Then Jerusalem may rejoice (3.14-17 and 3.18-20).

Here the plot reaches a resolution discussed more completely, yet no more definitively, in Haggai, Zechariah, and Malachi.[18] All wicked persons of any nationality will be annihilated and a remnant of believers of all nationalities will emerge and prevail. Certainly this solution is severe, yet it is thorough in its effectiveness. Every character is impacted. God's purity, the prophet's revelatory mission, Israel's faith odyssey, and the gentiles' need of cleansing reach fruition. Justice and grace have prevailed over oppression and fear. Nahum's confidence, Habakkuk's faith, and Zephaniah's clarity of purpose have all been vindicated.

Conclusion

Several literary elements bond this segment of the Book of the Twelve. Through the use of indirect speech, the Lord and the prophets inform audiences privileged to share their 'secrets' about what Yahweh plans to do regarding sinful behavior in Israel and in other countries. Readers

17. Cf. J.D.W. Watts, *The Books of Joel, Obadiah, Jonah, Nahum, Habakkuk, and Zephaniah* (CBC; London: Cambridge University Press, 1975), p. 106; and M. DeRoche, 'Zephaniah I 2-3 "The Sweeping of Creation"', *VT* 30 (1980), pp. 104-109.

18. Cf. House, *The Unity of the Twelve*, pp. 151-62.

thereby learn important details about the nature of God, the prophets, Israel, and the gentile nations. To supplement and enhance this information, the Lord and the prophets also use direct speech to warn sinners and to encourage the faithful. Habakkuk even divulges dialogue between the Lord and Habakkuk to confirm what is said in different ways in Nahum and Zephaniah.

These cohering items originate in the way the prophecies choose to develop alternating speeches generated by God in the prophets. Speeches, then, interspersed with prose markers, have created the linguistic structures called Nahum, Habakkuk, and Zephaniah. Certainly these prophecies arose in specific historical contexts, and it is important to know how those contexts impacted the books' composition. The Book of the Twelve was shaped into a unit and accepted as a canonical whole. This process also deserves careful analysis and consideration. Yet it is also desirable to examine the text as it exists in its final form. In this final form, prophecy uses many literary devices, one of which is the sort of alternating speakers found in Nahum, Habakkuk, and Zephaniah.

This paper argues that dramatic coherence exists in a specific group of three books in the Twelve. Some commentators have questioned calling prophetic speeches drama on historical grounds. For example, Berlin observes, 'It is questionable, however, if we can speak of drama in ancient Israel, there being no evidence that this genre was known'.[19] Of course, John Watts argues that drama-like elements existed in ancient cultures, including Israel's.[20] Also, Aeschylus was winning prizes in Greece for two-character drama as early as 484 BCE,[21] so before Malachi's time, dramatic productions occurred in that nation, which is, incidentally, mentioned in Joel 3.6, a fact that says events in Greece were not totally irrelevant to the Twelve's writers, though one that in no way indicates Israelites produced plays. Thus, scholars can and do disagree over the possibility that drama or dramatic principles may have influenced the writers of scripture. What remains is the text. It is true that drama may not have been produced in Israel like it was in Greece, but speakers shift, complementing one another in prophecy. Dramatic dialogue unfolds.

19. Berlin, *Zephaniah*, p. 12.

20. Watts, *Isaiah 1–33*, pp. xlv-l.

21. Cf. H.J. Rose, *A Handbook of Greek Literature* (London: Methuen, 4th edn, 1950), pp. 147-48.

Since what remains is the text, scholars will determine how to speak of textual phenomena. Thus, even if one cannot confirm dramatic productions in Israel, one must still speak understandably about the text. So terms like 'dramatic prophecy'[22] and 'dramatic coherence' in prophecy may simply be used to describe how one sort of prophecy presents its message. It is legitimate to ask for clarification and refinement of such literary concepts applied to scripture. What is odd is to eliminate using terminology like 'drama' or 'dramatic' when biblical critics freely speak of 'editors', 'redactors', 'narrative fiction', 'legends', 'myths', 'poetry', and a host of other terms they deem necessary. In this same vein, one can appropriately speak of dramatic coherence in Nahum, Habakkuk, and Zephaniah. What remains is the text, and dramatic coherence is one way, though not the only way, that the text of the Twelve unites its diverse parts.

22. This term is preferable to prophetic drama because prophecy is its own biblical genre. Dramatic principles help create prophecy in some prophetic books.

PSALMODY IN PROPHECY: HABAKKUK 3 IN CONTEXT

James W. Watts

The psalm in Habakkuk 3 resembles songs in Exodus 15, Deuteronomy 32 and 33, Judges 5 and 2 Samuel 22 in its archaic linguistic formations and vocabulary stock, victory hymn form, and appearance outside of the Psalter.[1] Unlike these hymns set within prose narratives, however, Habakkuk 3 appears within a book of prophetic poetry structured in a liturgical and dramatic fashion. Habakkuk, therefore, offers an ideal case for the comparative study of prophetic and narrative composition through the use of the same literary device. The results of such a comparison reveal a sophisticated text which mixes inherited generic conventions to create novel effects. I am delighted to dedicate this essay to my father, John D.W. Watts, whose early work included the form-critical description of inset hymnody in Amos.[2]

1. As has frequently been noted, for example, by G.H.A. von Ewald, *Commentary on the Prophets of the Old Testament* (trans. J.F. Smith; vol. 3; London: Williams and Norgate, 1878), p. 43; B. Duhm, *Das Buch Habakuk: Text, Übersetzung und Erklärung* (Tübingen: Mohr [Siebeck], 1906), p. 7; J.M.P. Smith, W.H. Ward, and J.A. Bewer, *A Critical and Exegetical Commentary on Micah, Zephaniah, Nahum, Habakkuk, Obadiah and Joel* (ICC; New York: Scribner's, 1911), p. 6; W.F. Albright, 'The Psalm of Habakkuk', in H.H. Rowley (ed.), *Studies in Old Testament Prophecy* (Edinburgh: T. & T. Clark, 1950), pp. 8-10; T. Hiebert, *God of My Victory: The Ancient Hymn in Habakkuk 3* (HSM, 38; Atlanta: Scholars Press, 1986), pp. 119-21; J.J.M. Roberts, *Nahum, Habakkuk, and Zephaniah: A Commentary* (Louisville: Westminster/John Knox, 1991), p. 149. For histories of the book's interpretation, see P. Jöcken, *Das Buch Habakuk: Darstellung der Geschichte seiner kritischen Erforschung mit einer eigenen Beurteilung* (Köln-Bonn: Peter Hanstein, 1977), and E. Otto, 'Die Theologie des buches Habakuk', *VT* 35 (1985), pp. 274-95.

2. *Vision and Prophecy in Amos* (Leiden: Brill, 1958), pp. 51-67; reprinted in *idem*, *Vision and Prophecy: Expanded Anniversary Edition* (Macon: Mercer University Press, 1996).

The appearance of psalms within non-hymnic contexts always raises issues both of literary role and of compositional history. The following study assumes the validity of both synchronic and diachronic methods of analysis and their mutual importance for the understanding of ancient literature. Only through detailed interpretation of the text as it stands can the conventions and innovations of the work be described. Only through careful description of a text's development can the place of those conventions and innovations in the history of literature be ascertained. I will, therefore, give attention to both approaches in turn.

Literary Role

Commentators have long noted the liturgical or dramatic form of the book of Habakkuk.[3] In the first two chapters, poetic genres of various kinds alternate in a question-response format. The relationship of Habakkuk's psalm to what precedes it remains, however, a matter of debate.

The language of psalmody is not restricted to the final hymn. Two laments in ch. 1 (vv. 2-4, 12-17) present the book's theme: Yahweh's inexplicable passivity in the face of Chaldean depravations. Yet, unlike these earlier hymnic passages in Habakkuk, ch. 3 explicitly marks itself as a hymn in several ways. First, an invocation of God's presence in the Temple and a call to worship establish the liturgical context (2.20).[4] Second, a superscription (3.1), identical in form to those of the Psalter, labels what follows as a תפלה 'prayer' (cf. Pss. 17.1; 86.1; 90.1; 142.1) of Habakkuk the prophet and, together with a colophon (3.19), describes the composition in the technical jargon of hymnody.[5] Third, liturgical

3. So already Ewald: 'It is... a simple scenic and declamatory piece (a drama), divided into three parts' (*Commentary on the Prophets*, p. 31). Cf. E. Sellin, *Das Zwölfprophetenbuch: Zweite Hälfte Nahum—Maleachi* (KAT, 12; Leipzig: Scholl, 2nd-3rd edn, 1930), pp. 381-82. P. Humbert argued that the book played a real liturgical role (*Problèmes du livre d'Habacuc* [Neuchatel: Secrétariat de l'université, 1944], pp. 290, 296; so also J.H. Eaton, 'The Origin and Meaning of Habakkuk 3', *ZAW* 76 [1964], pp. 160-63; J.D.W. Watts, *The Books of Joel, Obadiah, Jonah, Nahum, Habakkuk, and Zephaniah* [CBC; Cambridge: Cambridge University Press, 1975], pp. 5-7, 144).

4. Humbert argued that in three of its six occurances (here, Zeph. 1.7; Zech. 2.17), the formula הס מפני יהוה 'keep silence before Yahweh' appears immediately prior to a theophany (*Problèmes*, p. 28).

5. שגינות (3.1), appearing elsewhere only in the singular in the superscription of

markers (the little understood סלה *selah* in vv. 3, 9, and 13) interrupt the poem itself. Fourth, the archaic language and contents of the hymn identify it with a corpus of other ancient Israelite psalms, most of which appear outside the Psalter (for example, Judg. 5; Deut. 33; Exod. 15; cf. Ps. 77.16-20).

Taken together, these features of Habakkuk 3 distinguish the psalm from its literary context in a conspicuous manner.[6] They also invite comparison with similar phenomena in the narrative books of the Hebrew Bible. Narratively inset poems are often marked explicitly in both the poetry and the surrounding prose.[7] The markers alert readers to the shift in genre (from narrative to hymnody) and in mode (from prose to poetry). The narrative effects of such shifts include thematic emphasis through emotional commentary, liturgical and musical actualization of the story through audience involvement, and deepened characterizations of the singers or speakers of the poems.[8] Inset poetry expands the representational scope of prose narrative while preserving the distinctiveness of the poetic mode.

In many respects, Habakkuk 3 fits well within this corpus, but two features of the psalm distinguish it sharply from narratively inset poems. First, it contains a far greater number and variety of liturgical and musical markers, more like some hymns in the Psalter than any within

Psalm 7, has been explained variously as 'stringed music' (so LXX; see Eaton, 'Origin and Meaning', p. 146), as a 'wandering' style or meter (so P.C. Craigie, *Psalms 1–50* [WBC, 19; Waco, TX: Word Books, 1983], p. 97, on the basis of other ancient versions), or as 'psalm of lamentation' (so S. Mowinckel, *The Psalms in Israel's Worship* [trans. D.R. Ap-Thomas; Oxford: Blackwell, 1962], II, p. 209, and Watts, *Joel, Obadiah, Jonah, Nahum, Habakkuk, and Zephaniah*, p. 144). The colophon's (3.19) vocabulary, למנצח 'for the choir master' and בנגינותי 'with string music', is clearer and more standard, occurring in Psalter superscriptions fifty-five and six times respectively.

6. As interpreters have noted: 'With respect to its musical notations Habakkuk 3 again appears more distinct from its canonical setting than a part of it' (Hiebert, *God of My Victory*, p. 134); 'The new title... suggests to us an emphasis upon the fact that a particular form is deliberately being employed at this stage in the work' (M.E.W. Thompson, 'Prayer, Oracle and Theophany: the Book of Habakkuk', *TynBul* 44 [1993], p. 51).

7. See James W. Watts, '"This Song": Conspicuous Poetry in Hebrew Prose', in J.C. de Moor and W.G.E. Watson (eds.), *Verse in Ancient Near Eastern Prose* (AOAT, 42; Neukirchen–Vluyn: Neukirchener Verlag, 1993), pp. 345-48.

8. James W. Watts, *Psalm and Story: Inset Hymns in Hebrew Narrative* (JSOTSup, 139; Sheffield: JSOT, 1992).

narrative.[9] In fact, Habakkuk's psalm even exceeds that standard by using a colophon, unparalleled in the Psalms, for the otherwise familiar ascription, 'for the choir master with stringed music' (3.19).[10] Second, Habakkuk's psalm appears not in narrative but in a poetic and prophetic context. These two factors make the chapter unique. Hymnic forms and language appear throughout prophetic poetry, but only here are they explicitly marked by genre labels and liturgical instructions. Explicitly marked hymns appear frequently in Hebrew narratives, but only here in a poetic context. Liturgical instructions and genre labels introduce many psalms, but only here are they used so extensively on a psalm integrated into a larger literary context. Habakkuk 3 thus employs conventions of literary prophecy, hymnic anthology, and narrative prose simultaneously.

These unique features have generated many theories about the chapter's composition (see below), but less often has their literary effect been evaluated. Clearly, the writer(s) seems intent on calling the liturgical nature of the poem to the reader's attention. The poetic context, with its mix of genres, makes it necessary to mark such distinctions clearly. Whereas psalms set within prose narrative stand out because of their poetic mode and require relatively few explicit markers of genre, hymns in poetic books merge easily with the context and require sophisticated analysis to be distinguished. If a writer wishes the hymnic genre to be clearly recognized, relatively greater effort is required to mark it than in prose. So the unique features of Habakkuk's psalm serve at the very least to mark explicitly an inset hymn within a poetic context.

Why was reader's recognition of the hymnic genre of Habakkuk 3 so important to its writer(s)? Answers to this question must be sought in the psalm's position within the structure of the book and in its impact on the characterization of 'Habakkuk the prophet'.

Conventions of Context

Comparisons of narratively inset hymns reveals two conventional patterns which may have informed the usage in Habakkuk 3. Victory hymns appear at the end of several stories (for example, Exod. 14–15;

9. 'It is remarkable that in all of the Hebrew literature which has been preserved these notations never appear, except in this case, outside the Psalter' (Hiebert, *God of My Victory*, p. 134).

10. The Psalms invariably set such information in superscriptions. Colophons only mark divisions of the Psalter with blessings (41.14; 72.18-19; 89.53; 106.48) and (once) comments on the contents (72.20).

Judg. 4–5; Jdt. 16) but do not affect their plots. Instead, they enrich the accounts with added details, emotional reactions, and lively depictions of the divine warrior. Individual thanksgivings, on the other hand, often appear at points in stories where deliverance is promised but not yet realized (Isa. 38.9-20; Jon. 2; Dan. 2.20-23; LXX's additions to Dan. 3). By voicing thanksgivings at this point in the plot, the speakers show their trust in God.

The book of Habakkuk reveals familiarity with both narrative conventions, but it adapts them to a prophetic and poetic mode of writing. Like victory hymns in stories, Habakkuk's psalm, which incorporates a victory hymn in 3.3-15, appears at the end of the book. The psalm has little explicit effect on the argument of chs. 1–2, but it refocuses thematic attention on Yahweh as warrior and savior of Israel.[11] Whereas the earlier chapters are preoccupied with the destructive violence by and of the Chaldeans (1.5-11, 15-17; 2.5-17), the hymn celebrates the salvific violence of God in images which make the preceding descriptions pale by comparison. Thus the Habakkuk psalm, like its counterparts in narrative, uses the traditional language and form of victory hymns to establish a theocentric climax.

Like narratively inset thanksgivings, Habakkuk 3 expresses trust in a divine deliverance still to come. The hymn's theophany is a vision (2.2-3) not yet realized, as its conclusion makes clear (3.16-19). The effect is to characterize Habakkuk, the psalm's speaker (3.1), as a faithful and orthodox Yahwist, despite the complaints expressed earlier in the book (1.2-4, 12-17).

The book's use of inset hymnody, however, differs from the narrative conventions as well. Habakkuk 3 employs simultaneously both a climactic victory hymn and an expression of trust prior to deliverance, a combination never found in Hebrew narrative.[12] Neither does the book reflect the actual events of deliverance as stories surrounding psalms always do, either prior to victory hymns or after thanksgivings. Habakkuk replaces narrative closure with prophetic anticipation, with the result that the tension between oppressive reality (chs. 1–2) and

11. As with narratively inset hymns, the lack of explicit connections between the Habakkuk psalm and the preceding chapters has generated considerable debate as to the psalm's originality in this setting. See *Compositional History* below.

12. The latter half of the Song of the Sea (Exod. 15.12-18) celebrates victories not yet achieved in the narrative, but the psalm's perspective remains after-the-fact, rather than anticipatory.

salvific hope (3.2-15) remains taut to the end (cf. 3.16-17 with 3.18-19).

The suspense is sustained by one other change to the narrative conventions of inset psalmody: Habakkuk 3 uses the language and forms of laments to frame the victory hymn, rather than those of the thanksgivings found uniformly in narratives.[13] Most of the lament's traditional elements appear within a few verses (address and petition in v. 2, assurance, vow of praise, and expression of trust in vv. 16-19). The complaint itself is missing, probably because it is already voiced in 1.2-4, 12-17.[14] Laments express the anxiety of indeterminacy, rather than the closure exhibited by thanksgivings and narrative. Thus the use of lament elements, as well as the combination and modification of the structural settings of inset thanksgivings and victory hymns, adapts narrative conventions for the context of prophetic expectations in the book of Habakkuk.

Habakkuk's psalm may also function within the wider context of the Book of the Twelve in a manner analogous to some narratively inset hymns. The book of Nahum begins with a psalm, marked as such by its (partial) acrostic structure. Since Habakkuk follows Nahum in the canonical sequence of the Twelve, the psalms form a bracket around the two books. Both books use the variety of poetic genres characteristic of 'prophetic liturgies' and address the religious problems posed by invading foreign empires (Assyria in Nahum, Babylon in Habakkuk). In both books, the psalms serve to refocus attention on God.[15] In Samuel,

13. Unlike the large number of laments in the Psalter, none appear in narrative contexts of the Hebrew Bible, though secular dirges appear twice (2 Sam. 1.17-27; 3.33-34).

14. On the form-criticism of the psalm, see Humbert (*Problèmes*, pp. 24-26), K. Elliger (*Das Buch der zwölf kleinen Propheten*. II. *Die Propheten Nahum, Habakuk, Zephanja, Haggai, Sacharja, Maleachi* [ATD, 25; Göttingen: Vandenhoeck & Ruprecht, 1950], pp. 48, 51), B. Margulis ('The Psalm of Habakkuk: A Reconstruction and Interpretation', *ZAW* 82 [1970], p. 437), W.H. Bellinger, Jr (*Psalmody and Prophecy* [JSOTSup, 27; Sheffield: JSOT, 1984], pp. 84-85, who noted the adaptation of lament forms to prophetic patterns), Peckham ('Vision', p. 619), and M.A. Sweeney ('Structure, Genre, and Intent in the Book of Habakkuk', *VT* 41 [1991], pp. 78-79).

15. B. Childs commented that, in both Nahum and Habakkuk, 'older material was assigned a new role by a final redactional stamp which fashioned earlier parts into a literary unity. However, in Nahum the psalm introduced the book, in Habakkuk it concluded it... In Nahum the reader begins with the theocentric perspective of the hymn and secondarily derives the meaning of human events from the divine purpose. In Habakkuk the order is reversed. The reader begins with the

psalms (1 Sam. 2.1-10; 2 Sam. 22) bracket the bulk of the stories and emphasize God's support for Israel and its king. Thus in prose and poetic contexts, hymnic brackets can establish similar themes.

The conclusion that Habakkuk 3 has used and modified narrative conventions of inset hymnody does not exclude the possible influence of other literary conventions as well. D.E. Gowan pointed out that arguments over theodicy conclude with theophanies in Job and some lament psalms, as well as Habakkuk.[16] Other interpreters have argued that the lament form shapes the structure of much or all of the book.[17] Nothing in the present analysis disputes the presence of these patterns in the book of Habakkuk. However, the book not only employs the forms of liturgical hymnody in its structure, it also uses the conventions of narratively inset hymnody and modifies them to suit its prophetic message. The heavy liturgical markers in ch. 3 ensure that it will be recognized as a psalm in distinction from its context and will evoke the expectations associated with inset psalms in stories. Thus the description of the psalm's role in the book of Habakkuk requires not just form-critical analysis of the book's structure but an awareness of the genre conventions governing Hebrew inset hymnody as well.

Characterization

The victory hymn (3.3-15) focuses on characterizing Yahweh as the divine warrior. In the context of Habakkuk, this fierce depiction parallels the description of the Chaldeans in ch. 1. The vocabulary of the two passages differs considerably, but the themes echo each other. Thus, whereas the Chaldeans march throughout the earth (1.6), heavens and earth all reflect Yahweh's glory (3.3); whereas the Babylonians destroy nations and fortresses using earthen ramps (1.10), Yahweh shakes the

problems of human history and only subsequently are they resolved in the light of a divine oracle' *(Introduction to the Old Testament as Scripture* [Philadelphia: Fortress, 1979], p. 454); see also J. Nogalski (*Redactional Processes in the Book of the Twelve* [BZAW, 218; Berlin: de Gruyter, 1993], p. 181). On prophetic liturgies, see Sellin (*Das Zwölfprophetenbuch*, pp. 381-82) and John D.W. Watts (*Joel, Obadiah, Jonah, Nahum, Habakkuk, and Zephaniah*, pp. 1-7).

16. *The Triumph of Faith in Habakkuk* (Atlanta: John Knox, 1976), p. 70; 'God's Answer to Job: How is it an Answer?' *HBT* 8.2 (1986), p. 94.

17. G. Fohrer, 'Das "Gebet des Propheten Habakkuk" (Hab 3,1-16)', in A. Caquot, S. Légasse, M. Tardieu (eds.), *Mélanges bibliques et orientaux en l'honneur de M. Mathias Delcor* (Neukirchen–Vluyn: Neukirchener Verlag, 1985), pp. 160-61; Peckham, 'Vision', pp. 617-36.

earth and mountains on which the nations live (3.6, 9); whereas the Chaldeans' horses compare favorably to predators of land and air (1.8), Yahweh's horses also trample the sea (3.8, 15); mythologically, whereas the Babylonians compare with Death in their voraciousness (2.5), the psalm claims that Yahweh defeats Sea (3.8) which is associated in myth with Death in failed opposition to King of the gods.[18] Thus the effect of paralleling the descriptions of chs. 1–2 with that of the psalm is to undermine the enemy's ferocious reputation by comparison with Yahweh's greater war-making powers.

Speeches indirectly characterize their speakers.[19] In Habakkuk 3, the explicit attribution of the psalm to 'Habakkuk the prophet' (v. 1) links the chapter to the preceding oracles introduced by a similar superscription (1.1), and the first person statements of 3.2 and 16 place it within the autobiographical framework established by the laments of ch. 1 and especially the vision report in 2.1-3.[20] The psalm provides a completely orthodox and traditional response to the painful questions raised in earlier chapters, and thus it casts Habakkuk as a faithful Yahwist, despite his doubts. But, as with Hannah (1 Sam. 2.1-10), David (2 Sam. 22), Hezekiah (Isa. 38.9-20), and Jonah (Jon. 2), Habakkuk's voicing of a psalm does not paint a unique portrait of the prophet. Instead, it makes his experience paradigmatic for all the faithful who wait for Yahweh's deliverance. Psalmody depicts internal mental processes to a greater degree than any other genre of Hebrew literature, with the goal of expressing universal religious experiences in the context of worship. When literary contexts and/or superscriptions credit psalms to individuals, the resulting characterization describes not a unique individual but rather a universal experience which is available to all.[21]

Habakkuk's psalm deviates from the pattern of narratively inset hymns, however, by setting a victory hymn within the framework of a lament, rather than using the conventional individual thanksgiving. Both formal components of Habakkuk 3 emphasize the prophetic nature of

18. So the Ugaritic Baal cycle. See Albright, 'The Psalm of Habakkuk', pp. 8-9; Margulis, 'The Psalm of Habakkuk', p. 437.

19. See the comments on prophetic characterization by E. ben Zvi, 'Twelve Prophetic Books or "The Twelve"', and by P.R. House, 'Dramatic Coherence', in this volume.

20. W. Rudolph, *Micha-Nahum-Habakuk-Zephanja* (KAT, 13.3; Gütersloh: Gerd Mohn, 1975), p. 240; Fohrer, 'Das "Gebet"', pp. 162-63.

21. Watts, *Psalm and Story*, pp. 130-31, 191-92.

Habakkuk's experience: the lament form continues the prophet's initial complaint and the theophanic contents of the victory hymn portray the prophet's visionary experience. Using the introspective perspective of psalmody, the hymn comes as close as any Hebrew text to portraying the interior experience of prophetic vision. Yet because of that same hymnic perspective, the prophetic experience is equated with the experience of communal worship in the Temple. The psalm identifies liturgical worship and prophetic vision as one and the same thing.[22] Thus the result of the psalm's characterization of Habakkuk is not to set apart the prophet's vision from ordinary experience but rather to make it available to all who participate in the Temple liturgy.

Compositional History

The originality of Habakkuk's psalm in its literary context has been challenged by many interpreters—another distinction which it shares with inset hymns in narratives. In addition to arguments based on the themes and structures of the book as a whole, several specific features of Habakkuk 3 have stimulated questions regarding its compositional history.

Most commentators have assumed that the superscription, colophon, and other liturgical markings derive from the psalm's use in worship. Because the superscription refers to Habakkuk, these markers have usually been regarded as secondarily added to the psalm when it was adapted from the book of Habakkuk for liturgical use,[23] though other interpreters took them as evidence of the psalm's presence in a liturgical collection prior to its incorporation into Habakkuk.[24] These

22. Other prophetic texts reflect the same equation between the experiences of worship and prophecy. Temple worship shapes the images of prophetic visions in Isaiah 6, Ezek. 1.8-10, and the most personal and introspective passages in Jeremiah are cast in the language and form of laments (Jer. 11.18–12.6; 15.10-21; 17.14-18; 18.18-23; 20.7-18). Thus Hebrew prophetic literature, like narrative, often turns to psalmody to express interior experience.

23. E.g. Duhm, *Das Buch Habakuk*, p. 70; Sellin, *Das Zwölfprophetenbuch*, p. 406; Elliger, *Zwölf kleinen Propheten*, pp. 48, 51; Eaton, 'Origin and Meaning', p. 167; Otto, 'Theologie', pp. 283, 295; Roberts, *Nahum, Habakkuk, and Zephaniah*, p. 148.

24. B.S. Childs, 'Psalm Titles and Midrashic Exegesis', *JSS* 16 (1971), pp. 141-42; Hiebert, *God of My Victory*, pp. 141; Nogalski, *Redactional*

common-sense suggestions receive, however, only limited support from psalms whose presence in liturgical collections, as well as in non-hymnic contexts, is attested in the Hebrew Bible. David's Thanksgiving was excerpted from 2 Samuel 22 to become Psalm 18 with only the addition of למנצח לעבד יהוה 'to the choir master, of the servant of Yahweh' to the beginning of its superscription. Portions of Psalms 96, 105, and 106 were taken from the Psalter to create the Levitical medley in 1 Chron. 16.8-36, but whereas in the Psalter these texts are entirely devoid of liturgical or musical notations, the context in Chronicles makes explicit its performance by singers (15.16, 19, 27), specifically the Asaphites (16.5, 7), and the congregation's liturgical response (16.36b). Furthermore, like other inset hymns, Habakkuk's psalm itself appears apart from its context in the LXX's 'Odes' appended to the Psalter for liturgical use, but without the liturgical markers of its superscription and colophon in Habbakkuk 3.[25]

The comparative evidence for Habakkuk 3's liturgical markers originating from its use in worship is, therefore, mixed. Later liturgical use of David's Thanksgiving is reflected in its Psalter superscription but not in 2 Samuel 22, while later narrative use in 1 Chronicles 16 of several psalms actually emphasizes the liturgical context to a greater degree than does the Psalter. Habakkuk's psalm remains unique among inset hymns (and, in the case of the colophon, among the Psalms) for the technical nature of its markers, but this is much less true of the version excerpted for the LXX 'Odes'. Some arguments have been advanced for the liturgical markers as original to at least one stage in the composition of the book of Habakkuk itself.[26] The above observations on the effect of explicitly marking Habbakkuk 3 as a hymn support such claims, though for different reasons. The heavy and exceptional use of technical terms in and around the psalm reflects a self-conscious evocation of liturgical worship for literary effect within the book of Habakkuk.

The psalm's absence from the commentary on Habakkuk (1QpHab) found among the Dead Sea Scrolls has also been taken as evidence for

Processes, pp. 159, 180. For earlier interpreters holding this position, see Hiebert's summary, *God of My Victory*, pp. 134, 180 n. 16.

25. All that remains of them are the first two words of the superscription, 'a prayer of Habakkuk', and the three occurrences of סלה *selah*, translated as usual in the LXX by διάφαλμα.

26. So Peckham, 'Vision', p. 621; Sweeney, 'Structure', p. 65.

its secondary character.[27] Other manuscripts of nearly the same age (Mur 88; 8HevXIIgr) contain the psalm, however, so its absence from the commentary does not provide decisive evidence regarding the book's history of composition.[28]

Other arguments against the originality of the psalm within Habakkuk arise from redaction criticism of the book as a whole. In such reconstructions, the various parts of the psalm are often assigned to different redactional layers along with other parts of the book. Recent proposals include Otto's five-stage development in which a pre-existing psalm (3.3-15) was adapted by the post-exilic addition of vv. 2 and 16 to fit into the book, and the liturgical markers were added even later.[29] Hiebert suggested that Habakkuk 3 was an archaic hymn which was inserted as part of an apocalyptic reinterpretation of the book.[30] On the other hand, Peckham argued that portions of the chapter (vv. 2-12, 15-19a) were part of an original lament which was subsequently expanded by commentary on the topic of theodicy.[31]

Part of the rationale for finding redactional development in Habakkuk 3 derives from the hymn's unusual form. Form-critical analysis usually produces a (victory) hymn set within a lament—an odd combination which interpreters struggle to explain.[32] The above literary analysis has argued that the mixed form of this hymn is a creative adaptation for a prophetic context of the conventions governing narratively inset victory hymns and thanksgivings. Like psalms in stories, Habakkuk's psalm provides an emotional climax, refocuses attention on God, and characterizes its speaker as faithful, while, unlike them, it preserves the tension between harsh experience and prophetic expectations to the end. The book, thereby, builds on the expectations aroused by recognition of

27. A. Dupont-Sommer, *Observations zur le commentaire d'Habacuc découvert près de la mer morte* (Dépôt: Librairie Adrien-maisonneuve, 1950), p. 4; W.H. Brownlee, *The Text of Habakkuk in the Ancient Commentary from Qumran* (SBLMS, 11; Philadelphia: SBL, 1959), pp. 93-95.

28. Rudolph, *Micha-Nahum-Habakuk-Zephanja*, p. 240 n. 2; Roberts, *Nahum, Habakkuk, and Zephaniah*, p. 148. On the manuscript evidence, see R. Fuller, 'The Form and Formation of the Book of the Twelve', in this volume.

29. Otto, 'Theologie', p. 282.

30. Hiebert, *God of My Victory*, pp. 136-49.

31. Peckham, 'Vision', pp. 619-21.

32. Humbert, *Problèmes*, pp. 24-26; Elliger, *Zwölf kleinen Propheten*, pp. 48-51; Margulis, 'The Psalm of Habakkuk', p. 411; Bellinger, *Psalmody and Prophecy*, pp. 84-85.

narrative conventions while remaining true to its prophetic message. The psalm's mixed form, therefore, does not, by itself, point to the book's compositional history but rather illustrates the writer's creative adaptation of Hebrew literary conventions.[33]

Archaic features of the hymn's vocabulary, poetic style, and themes provide another reason for positing the hymn's original independence from its context. Albright considered the hymn a composite of pieces ranging from Israel's earliest history to the sixth century BCE and brought together in an archaizing fashion.[34] Hiebert viewed the chapter as a whole as an archaic hymn, subsequently modified to fit into the book.[35] Most other interpreters noted that, in the present form of the psalm, the archaic features seem to be limited to 3.3-15 and, therefore, suggested that an old victory hymn has been surrounded by lament forms (vv. 2, 16-19) and incorporated into the book.[36] The latter opinion accords with the above observations on the literary effect of combining lament and victory song conventions. It also emphasizes Habakkuk 3's similarity to some other inset poems which are archaic victory hymns subsequently incorporated into a wider context (Exod. 15; Judg. 5; 1 Sam. 2).

The thematic unity of Habakkuk (with the exception of ch. 3's liturgical markers) has been defended by many commentators, though most think that the author incorporated older materials.[37] The issue of divine justice provides thematic unity, and a question-answer format makes

33. The mix of various genres and forms throughout the book led Thompson to observe that the author 'had something of a *penchant* for eclecticism' ('Prayer, Oracle and Theophany', p. 47).

34. Albright, 'The Psalm of Habakkuk', pp. 8-10.

35. Hiebert, *God of My Victory*, pp. 136-49; so also Nogalski, *Redactional Processes*, p. 180, except that he regards vv. 16b-17 as a redactional link to the earlier chapters.

36. Margulis, 'The Psalm of Habakkuk', p. 438; Childs, *Introduction*, p. 451; Otto, 'Theologie', p. 282; Fohrer, 'Das "Gebet"', p. 162; Roberts, *Nahum, Habakkuk, and Zephaniah*, pp. 84, 148.

37. Duhm, *Das Buch Habakuk*, pp. 1-2, 70; Sellin, *Das Zwölfprophetenbuch*, pp. 381, 405; H.H. Walker and N.W. Lund, 'The Literary Structure of the Book of Habakkuk', *JBL* 53 (1934), pp. 355-70; Humbert, *Problèmes*, pp. 28-29, 290, 296; Elliger, *Zwölf kleinen Propheten*, p. 23; Eaton, 'Origin and Meaning', p. 167; Rudolph, *Micha-Nahum-Habakuk-Zephanja*, p. 240; Childs, *Introduction*, p. 451; Fohrer, 'Das "Gebet"', pp. 162-63; Sweeney, 'Structure', pp. 80-81; Thompson, 'Prayer, Oracle and Theophany', p. 44; Roberts, *Nahum, Habakkuk, and Zephaniah*, p. 81.

sense of the diverse genres set side-by-side. Despite its hymnic form, the last chapter picks up (in 3.2, 16) the autobiographical references from 1.2 and 2.1, thereby preserving the prophetic perspective of the book to the end. To such structural and thematic observations can be added the book's adaptation of the conventions governing inset hymnody as a further argument for the book's unity. Therefore, the most plausible reconstruction of the book's history suggests that a single writer composed the work by incorporating older materials (most notably 3.3-15) into an exploration of Yahweh's power in the face of military disaster.

Implications

Comparative analysis of Habakkuk with stories incorporating psalms has shown that the book employs and modifies narrative conventions of inset hymnody. To be effective, genre conventions must be recognized, so Habakkuk 3 provides an extraordinary number of liturgical markings. The result is that the book identifies Habakkuk's vision with the experience of Temple worship and points to this traditional hymnody as holding the answer to the political crisis facing Yahweh's people. Unlike inset hymns which maximize narrative closure, however, Habakkuk's psalm projects only a potential resolution. The use of lament forms which anticipate a future deliverance preserves the book's prophetic tension between human reality and divine possibility.

This conclusion has implications for the debate over Habakkuk's relationship to Temple worship. The use of hymnic forms and a question-answer structure led many interpreters to suggest that the book was a script for liturgical worship, and that Habakkuk was, therefore, a cult prophet.[38] Others have argued that the prophetic shaping of liturgical material removed the book and its author from the sphere of public worship.[39] The latter position receives support from the observation that Habakkuk 3 uses lament forms to create a unique adaptation of a victory hymn for prophetic purposes. However, the recognition of Habakkuk's use and modification of narrative conventions of inset

38. Humbert, *Problèmes*, pp. 28-29; Eaton, 'Origin and Meaning', pp. 166-67; John Watts, *Joel, Obadiah, Jonah, Nahum, Habakkuk, and Zephaniah*, p. 144; Fohrer, 'Das "Gebet"', pp. 160-61.

39. Childs, *Introduction*, p. 452; Rudolph, *Micha-Nahum-Habaku-Zephanja*, p. 241; Bellinger, *Psalmody and Prophecy*, pp. 86, 92; Hiebert, *God of My Victory*, pp. 132-44.

hymnody casts the whole debate in a different light. The book now appears as a sophisticated montage of not only liturgical forms but also literary conventions, one which depends on their recognition by hearers and readers for its effect. And that effect identifies prophetic vision with the experience of communal worship. It may also, through its use of traditional hymnody, provide the opportunity to actualize that experience.

In other words, I am arguing that Habakkuk's use of hymnic and liturgical elements does not arise from a life setting in worship, as if the book was a transcript of an oral worship service. It derives rather from a literary setting in which the conventions governing inset hymnody were recognized by readers and writers alike. By employing the convention of narratively inset victory hymns, Habakkuk 3 also raises the possibility of the reader(s) singing the song. Since ancient readers customarily read aloud, usually to an audience, the inclusion of an old and clearly marked hymn in a text might evoke audience participation. So Habakkuk 3's literary effect might well move towards liturgical actualization, not just suggesting the identification of prophetic vision with corporate worship, but realizing it through the experience of reading the book publicly.[40]

Chapter 3 modifies the convention of inset thanksgivings by using lament forms to frame the victory hymn, thus maintaining the perspective of prophetic expectation throughout the book. Habakkuk does not just announce that prophecy and worship convey the same experience; public readings of the book actualize that experience for hearers and readers who join in the final hymn. The prophet's experience of Yahweh's power (3.2-15) and of waiting in the midst of crisis for that power to be unleashed (3.16-19) can become the people's own through public readings and responses cued by the liturgical markers around the hymn.

Comparison of Habakkuk's psalm with other inset hymns reveals a writer and intended readers familiar with the literary conventions of Hebrew narrative, hymnody, and prophecy, and capable of appreciating the effects of their mixture in novel ways. Hebrew authors appropriated the words of prophecy, liturgy, story, and song to create richly evocative compositions. Mingling different genres did not blur their distinctiveness but rather played on reader recognition of both the

40. On literary actualization by hymns in Hebrew and other ancient narrative traditions, see Watts, *Psalm and Story*, pp. 60-61, 176, 187-89, 192, 212; *idem*, 'Song and the Ancient Reader', *PRS* 22 (1995), pp. 139-40.

conventional forms and their new application. Arguments over such an author's prophetic or cultic identity underestimate the sophistication and integration of Israel's literary culture.

INTERROGATIVES IN HAGGAI–ZECHARIAH: A LITERARY THREAD?

Kenneth M. Craig, Jr

When I wrote my dissertation under Professor Watts's supervision, he encouraged me to explore the rhetorical impact of the final question in Jonah. 'What is significant about a book ending with a question?' I remember him asking. His urging me to probe the rhetorical implications of a question in the Bible stimulated my thoughts on Jonah[1] and beyond,[2] and I return to this issue on a topic that has been one of his favorites, the unity of the Twelve.

Introduction

Coherence is a vast topic, especially as it relates to twelve books. The topic has been approached in at least three ways: unity of a single book within the Twelve that has often been fragmented in scholarly circles,[3] unity of a few books among the Twelve,[4] or unity of all twelve

1. K.M. Craig, Jr, *A Poetics of Jonah: Art in the Service of Ideology* (Columbia, SC: University of South Carolina Press, 1993), pp. 8, 17-18, 29-30, 60-70, 141-42, 157-58.

2. K.M. Craig, Jr, 'Rhetorical Aspects of Questions Answered with Silence in 1 Samuel 14.37 and 28.6', *CBQ* 56 (1994), pp. 221-39; 'The Character(ization) of God in 2 Samuel 7.1-17', *Semeia* 63 (1993), pp. 159-76; 'Asking for Rhetoric: Invoking and Fielding Questions in Eden', a paper presented in the 'Reading, Rhetoric, and Hebrew Bible Section' at the national SBL meeting in Chicago, Illinois on November 21, 1994; 'Yahweh, Cain, and their Rhetorical Interchange', a paper presented in the 'Hebrew Scriptures/Old Testament Section' at the regional SBL meeting in Gainesville, Florida on March 11, 1995.

3. Craig, *Poetics*.

4. R.W. Pierce, 'Literary Connectors and a Haggai/Zechariah/Malachi Corpus', *JETS* 27 (1984), pp. 277-89 and *idem*, 'A Thematic Development of the Haggai/Zechariah/Malachi Corpus', *JETS* 27 (1984), pp. 401-11.

prophetic books.[5] In this study I propose to support, indirectly, the unity of the Twelve thesis while looking at the unity question and two of the twelve books, Haggai and Zechariah.

The Hebrew Bible is, of course, one big book, but it does not require us to read it sequentially—from Genesis to Malachi (or Chronicles)—in quite the way the novel genre does. Indeed, its translators have different ideas on how to arrange the books, and there is no universal agreement on what to put in and what to leave out. A question we confront implicitly each time we read is where to begin and where to end. Scenes, chapters, but perhaps most often, the books themselves serve as boundaries. I will argue that literary textual clues suggest that there is no reason to imagine a reading boundary between Haggai and Zechariah, as I address these questions: Does the frequent invocation of interrogatives in these two books suggest literary affinity? Do these interrogatives reflect a distinct rhetorical pattern, and is there a typological scheme to the questions invoked along the text continuum from Hag. 1.4 to Zech. 8.6? I will comment on the interrogatives while analyzing their literary function. Because the biblical authors had the option of telling the story straight—what happens, to whom, for what reason, and so forth—the invocation of a question represents a special literary phenomenon. And these two books are loaded with interrogatives.

The books of Haggai and Zechariah can be linked on historical grounds. Both prophets find themselves confronting unfamiliar circumstances at the time of Darius I's reign, and together they give prophetic authority in support of the reestablished province of Yehud (Judah). They are concerned with reestablishing institutions during a period of restoration, and the same set of characters appears in the books: the high priest Joshua, the governor Zerubbabel, the priests, and the citizenry (or representatives). But despite obvious similarities in context and content, not to mention shifting currents in biblical studies, discussions about so-called 'primary' and 'secondary' (or 'original' and 'additional') material continue.[6] Apart from the obvious overlap in context, are there textual

5. P.R. House, *The Unity of the Twelve* (JSOTSup, 77; Sheffield: Sheffield Academic Press, 1990), and D.A. Schneider, *The Unity of the Book of the Twelve* (PhD dissertation, Yale University, 1979).

6. P.L. Redditt, 'Zerubbabel, Joshua, and the Night Visions of Zechariah', *CBQ* 54 (1992), pp. 249-59, and *idem*, *Haggai, Zechariah, and Malachi* (NCBC; Grand Rapids: Eerdmans, 1995), and Y. Radday and D. Wickmann, 'The Unity of Zechariah Examined in the Light of Statistical Linguistics', *ZAW* 87 (1975), p. 54.

clues suggesting that Haggai and Zechariah are a composite work? C. Meyers and E. Meyers have argued for an envelope construction of language and content that ties together Haggai 1–2 with Zechariah 7–8,[7] and R. Pierce has explored some implications of the interrogative material in Haggai, Zechariah, and Malachi.[8]

Four Interrogative Types in Haggai–Zechariah

'What is a question?' is a question that is sometimes overlooked. It is generally held that questions serve as some type of opening that seeks to be closed, and that they may be placed in either of two categories. One, the information-seeker, is the kind that people in the real world and characters in the narrative world ask routinely when seeking details or explanations. When the Danites look for territory to claim as their own, they send five spies to explore the land around the hill country at Ephraim (Judg. 18.1-2). While at Micah's house, the spies recognize (נכר)[9] the voice of a young Levite and desire to learn more. They ask him three questions: 'Who brought you here? What are you doing in this place? What is your business here?' (v. 3). The answer to this series of questions contains welcome news for the spies: this man is a priest, one able to address questions to, and one assumes get answers from, God (vv. 5-6). A rhetorical question, the second type, is any utterance that invokes the conditions of an interrogative but serves some further

7. C.L. Meyers and E.M. Meyers, *Haggai, Zechariah 1–8* (AB 25B; New York: Doubleday, 1987), p. xlix.

8. Pierce focuses more on patterns broken by narrative interludes than on the rhetorical impact of the questions themselves in 'Literary Connectors' and 'Thematic Development'. He notes that interrogatives appear as a consistent element both before and after Zechariah 9–14, and his analysis leads him to place Zechariah 9–14 as the thematic centerpiece of the Haggai–Zechariah–Malachi corpus. The abrupt shift before and after Zechariah 9–14 helps the reader draw the vivid picture of a flock doomed for slaughter in this focal point. B.O. Long ('Two Question and Answer Schemata in the Prophets', *JBL* 90 [1971], pp. 129-39) has discussed a question-answer schemata in Jeremiah. He finds two types: A (in Jer. 22.8 and parallels) and B (in Jer. 5.19 and parallels).

9. The Hebrew is ambiguous. J.A. Soggin concludes that 'they must therefore have known him well' (*Judges: A Commentary* [OTL; Philadelphia: Westminster, 1981], p. 272). J. Gray determines that 'they either recognised the dialect as of Judah near their home country, or the voice of the individual, which is less likely, or they may simply have heard him at the service and recognised a priest' (*Joshua, Judges, Ruth* [NCBC; Grand Rapids: Eerdmans, 1986], p. 343).

figurative purpose, either assertive or expressive. When Yahweh says to Cain, 'Where is your brother Abel?', Cain takes Yahweh's rhetorical question to be of the information-seeking type and responds by saying, 'I do not know; am I my brother's keeper?' (Gen. 4.9). Both Cain and Yahweh have asked questions, but neither is concerned with the literal meaning of words.

But such a traditional division of questions into two basic types does not do justice to the protean forms of interrogatives that appear in the Bible. In short, the two traditional categories obfuscate the rich variety of rhetoric known to the authors of the Hebrew Bible. At least four types of questions are found in Haggai and Zechariah: rhetorical questions, sequential questions, questions that function primarily to advance the plot, and questions that increase the number of characters in a given scene. (Of course, some of the interrogatives can be placed in more than one of these categories.) Indeed, all four types appear in both books.

1. *The Rhetorical Question*

The first question in Haggai is rhetorical.

> Is-it-time[10] for-you yourselves to-live in-your-finished[11] houses, and-this house is-desolate? (1.4).

No answer is recorded. It is apparent: No, this is not the time for the Yehudites to dwell, content and secure in their homes, while the house of Yahweh remains unfinished and desolate. The question consists of two parts. The A part contains six words; the B part only half as many. The emphasis clearly falls on the houses of the people. The duplication of the pronouns (*you*, *yourselves*, and *your* finished houses) in the A part highlights the lack of responsibility and inactivity of the Yehudites, and

10. I have attempted to maintain Hebrew syntax (hence, the somewhat awkward English constructions) and the original number of words while translating. Single Hebrew words often require more than one English word in translation, and in such instances I use hyphens to join the English words that convey the one Hebrew word. (I attach the word 'and' to the subject, even when the *vav* is conjoined to the Hebrew verb.) P. Trible recommends and follows this procedure in *Rhetorical Criticism: Context, Method and the Book of Jonah* (Minneapolis: Fortress, 1994).

11. Meyers and Meyers, *Haggai, Zechariah 1–8*, pp. 3, 23. The word סְפוּנִים has been variously rendered as 'panelled' (P.R. Ackroyd, *Exile and Restoration* [OTL; London: SCM, 1968], p. 155) and 'ceiled' (H.G. Mitchell, *A Critical and Exegetical Commentary on Haggai, Zechariah, Malachi, and Jonah* [ICC; Edinburgh: T. & T. Clark, 1912]), p. 45.

the repetition drives home the contrast between 'their houses' and the neglected 'this house'. The people do have time for themselves and their projects (you—you—you). Their houses, well-built and decorated, contrast with 'this house', a temple in ruins.

The people had argued that now was not the time for re-building the house of Yahweh (v. 2). The rhetorical question in v. 4 highlights their indifference and lack of fervor in re-building the temple. The issue is not lack of time; priorities are skewed. Their living (lit., 'to sit') in v. 4 contrasts with 'their running' in v. 9, a verse that also contains a question that reinforces the theme of misplaced priorities. Yahweh's house is overlooked amidst the hustle and bustle of daily life. All their activity, at home or away, is undertaken for their own benefit, while religious obligations, epitomized by the temple, are neglected. The near duplication in language, 'this house is desolate' in v. 4 with 'my house is desolate' in v. 9, links the two verses, and the use of double interrogatives reinforces the theme of misplaced priorities. The rhetorical questions are thus woven into the thematic pattern of individual productivity achieved at the expense of communal responsibility.

The initial interrogative in Zechariah, two words in the Hebrew, is also a rhetorical question. It is followed by two additional rhetorical questions in 1.5b and 1.6a.

> Your-ancestors, where-are-they? (1.5a).
>
> And-the-prophets, do-they-live forever? (1.5b).
>
> But my-words and-my-statutes, which I-commanded my-servants the-prophets, did-they-not overtake your-ancestors? And-they-repented and-they-said, Whenever Yahweh-of hosts purposed to-deal with-us according-to-our-ways and-our-deeds, thus he-dealt with-us (1.6).

The answers to questions on the whereabouts of ancestors and prophets are easily supplied: the ancestors have died and of course the prophets do not live forever. The point is accentuated as the prophets are linked here not with God or God's word but with 'the ancestors' in their mortality. The first two rhetorical questions highlight the vanishing nature of human life, and the third conveys the lessons of history on the minds of the audience. The overall rhetorical charge of these three questions contrasts dead ancestors and prophets with enduring statutes that had been commanded by these now dead prophets. In v. 6a, the rhetorical question asks, Did not my words and my statutes overtake your ancestors? The Hebrew word הִשִּׂיגוּ, 'overtake', is a hunting term. Zechariah's question to the hearers is intended to make clear by contrast that God's 'words and statutes' are enduring, unlike one's ancestors or the prophets. The ancestors were overtaken and they 'repented' (שוב), a key word that appears now for the fourth time in a short narrative space (1.3 [×2], 4, 6).

The word of Yahweh is manifest to Zechariah in a series of eight night visions (1.8-17; 1.18-21; 2.1-5; 3.1-10; 4.1-14; 5.1-4; 5.5-11; 6.1-8), and the three rhetorical questions in 1.5-6 rekindle the prophecies of old and also generate these new visions which were anticipated in the 'former' prophecies (Zech. 1.4). For example, the prophecies of the seventy years of captivity in Zech. 1.12 has a parallel in Jer. 25.11 and 29.10; the man with a measuring line in Zech. 2.5 (Eng. 2.1) has a parallel in Ezek. 40.3, and the branch in Zech. 3.8 and 6.12 has a parallel in Jeremiah's righteous Branch (23.5 and 33.15).

The words about the past are put in the form of a question: Did this not happen? A few persons alive just after the return to Israel could remember the history of 597–587 BCE. The exile had been foretold, and even though the prophets died, the words they spoke lived on and would be known even by those not alive at the time of the exile. These words 'overtook' the ancestors. Such words and statutes are portrayed as the overpowering covenant of God with Israel.

Zechariah 3.2 ends with another rhetorical question:

> And-Yahweh said to-ha-satan, may-Yahweh rebuke you, O-ha-satan! And-may-Yahweh rebuke you who-has-chosen Jerusalem! Is-this not a-brand plucked from-fire?

The wood is only partially destroyed; it has survived conflagration. The image of the burned and partially consumed piece of wood conveys the idea of destruction without annihilation. The word used for 'fire' here is אש, and the image is reminiscent of Amos 4.11's reference to the northern kingdom as 'a brand plucked out of the fire' (משרפה). The brand is a charred piece of wood but snatched from the fire it is spared certain destruction. Joshua, the high priest, has been plucked from the exile. His appearance is not unlike the appearance of the wood snatched from the fire. Both are dirty. Joshua is wearing 'filthy clothes' (Zech. 3.3), and the filth may represent the sins of the priest and the people. The angel commands those standing before Joshua to undress him (v. 4). Then they crown him with 'a clean turban' and dress him with 'festal apparel' (vv. 4-5). This change of clothes has a symbolic function: the new, clean appearance symbolizes ritual purity and heralds the advent of the messianic age.

2. *The Sequential Questions (or the 'Pile Up' Phenomenon)*

As the name implies, sequential questions are invoked one after another while the addressee is denied the opportunity of answering. These interrogatives are similar to the rhetorical type, and, indeed, the two types sometimes overlap. The three questions in Zech. 1.5-6, for example, were discussed above under 'rhetorical questions'. With sequential questions, the rhetorical effect is always heightened.

Another series of three questions, one after another, is found in Hag. 2.3.

> Who among-you is-left who saw this-house in-its-former glory? And-how are-you seeing it now? Is-it-not as nothing in-your-sight?

The temple burned down in 587, and the year is now 520 BCE. With this set of three queries, Haggai compares the pre-exilic temple with its present state. The combination functions as a rhetorical device for involving all of Haggai's audience in the continuity-discontinuity tension that characterized the restoration period. A small group of eyewitnesses old enough to remember Solomon's temple are now seventy or seventy-five years old. According to P. Verhoef, some scholars (Mitchell, Koole, Van der Woude) conclude that no one would have attained the age of seventy at this time due to the circumstances of the exile. The question would then be addressed to those who had memories of the temple based on the literature such as Psalm 137 or by means of oral tradition. But Verhoef has argued convincingly that such an assumption is unlikely.[12]

These three questions all contain second person plural references—who among you, how are you, in your sight—and are intended to capture the attention of the audience. The temple is also referred to in each question. The interrogatives are thus conjoined by similar vocabulary and a single image, but they also work independently at the rhetorical level: the first question challenges the oldest members of the returnees, the ones who remember Solomon's temple; the second inquires about the present state of affairs; the third asks about consequences.

The whole affair is defined in terms of 'glory', a word that is ambiguous. The temple may house Yahweh's glory, Yahweh's indwelling holy presence, but the word can also signify physical splendor, such as the beautiful temple described in 1 Kings 6–7 with its ornamentation and

12. P.A. Verhoef, *The Books of Haggai and Malachi* (NICOT; Grand Rapids: Eerdmans, 1987), pp. 95-96 and n. 19.

precious metal before it was demolished by Nebuchadnezzar II in 587 BCE. The 'glory' of Solomon's temple is associated with wealth, and the term also carries economic and political meaning.

The work on rebuilding has just begun and seems to have stalled. The second question creates an antithesis in the minds of the audience between the 'former' (הראשון) and the 'now' (עתה). But the issue at hand revolves not around two temples, but one: the temple before destruction and the temple at this present moment which the people had been admonished to rebuild. The interrogative particle מה is usually translated as the interrogative 'what', but is used here in the sense of 'how' (cf. Gen. 44.16).

The final 'is not' question (הלא) moves the audience to the inevitable affirming response and its rhetorical impact is increased by the two questions that precede it. As the present ruins are compared with the former 'glory', the present ruins are 'nothing' at all. A formulation such as this third question would have forced an affirming response from those in the community dissatisfied with the present state of affairs because the interrogative ה followed by the negative particle suggests a positive answer. Haggai aligns himself with the older generation. Though the building operations are underway, this 'new temple' suffers by comparison with Solomon's magnificent building. The comparative particle כ twice refers to the same object: the present state of the temple. It intensifies the comparison between present desolation and previous glory.

Questions are invoked once again in sequence in Zech. 7.5-7.

> Say to-all-the-people-of the-land and-to-the-priests, saying: When-you-fasted and-mourned in-the-fifth and-in-the-seventh (months), and-this seventy years, fasting, was-it-for-me?[13]
>
> And-when you-eat and-when you-drink, do-you not eat and-drink only-for-yourselves?
>
> Are-not (these) the-words that Yahweh proclaimed by-the-hand-of the-earlier prophets, when Jerusalem was-inhabited and-in-prosperity, and-her-cities around-her, and-the-Negeb and-the-Shephelah were-inhabited?

A delegation from Bethel included Sharezer, Regem-melech, and others. Consistent with the interrogative style of Hag. 2.3, the author formulates

13. On the 'strongest way of asking', see the comments of R. Smith, *Micah-Malachi* (WBC, 32; Waco, TX: Word Books, 1984), p. 221 n. 5a. Cf. also the comments on this elevated discourse in Meyers and Meyers, *Haggai, Zechariah 1–8*, p. 389.

the oracular response in the form of sequential questions. The question in v. 3 originates with the delegation, but the answer is addressed to 'all the people of the land and the priests' (v. 5). The delegation arrived to entreat Yahweh and to ask the priests and prophets if the custom of fasting and mourning in the fifth month should continue. The reference is to the practice of fasting on the anniversary of the temple's destruction, which took place on the fifth month (2 Kgs 25.8-9). (The commemoration of this date by means of a fast is nowhere mentioned in the Bible.) The first oracular response (7.4-7) to the question in v. 3 takes the form of three sequential questions (vv. 5, 6, 7). The lead question—when you fasted and mourned was it for me?—appears to be a rhetorical question, one that stimulates further reflection because the answer is obvious. But one may allow for the possibility that fasts were not undertaken primarily for the benefit of Yahweh. Saul fasted in an effort to help himself communicate with God in 1 Sam. 28.23. The juxtaposition of vv. 5 and 6 in ch. 7 of Zechariah appears to imply that just as eating and drinking benefits the individual, fasting likewise affects the one who abstains. The implied answer to the rhetorical question is: No, it was not for Yahweh.

Eating and drinking (v. 6) are, of course, necessary to sustain life, but they are also part of festal activity, and the reference to priests here along with the people of the land may suggest cultic meals. In sum, vv. 5 and 6 work together to show that the people and the priests do not give proper consideration to God, and v. 7's question confirms that the former prophets did indeed speak in a fashion consistent with the questions articulated in the previous two verses.

3. *Questions that Function Primarily to Advance the Plot*

Another type of question that appears in Haggai and Zechariah serves to advance the plot. In the dialogue between the prophet and the interpreting angel—the angel is a major literary figure in Zechariah's visions—the question-answer format often serves the plot by presenting the vision's subject matter and then its meaning. Take, for example, Hag. 1.9:

> You-have-looked for-much, and-behold, only-little; and-when-you-brought-it to-the-house, I-blew it away. On-account-of what? An-utterance-of Yahweh-of hosts. On-account-of my-house which-is desolate. And-you-are running each-of-you to-his-house.

The two word question, יען מה 'on-account-of what?', appears at the center of this verse. D. Gowan has observed that the יען sentence signals divine speech, spoken either by God or a messenger.[14] Here Yahweh utters both the question and answer, and the response includes an 'on account of my house which is desolate' answer. The questions, admonitions, and curse-fulfillment sayings of the previous verses are now replaced by this tight question-answer framework, and the duplication of יען at the beginning of the answer highlights the point that the temple is still in ruins because of the misplaced fervor of the people who 'run' in their eagerness to build and build up their own houses. As in v. 4, Haggai contrasts 'my house' (Yahweh's house) with 'his house' (the houses of the people). The people have time, energy, and the inclination to build, but their energy is misdirected.

The answer duplicates ideas already expressed. After repeating the first word of the interrogative sentence, 'on-account-of', the prophet continues by repeating what has already been conveyed: Yahweh's house is in ruins; words from v. 4 appear again ('house' and 'desolate'); and the formula 'Yahweh of hosts' concludes the clause in vv. 4-5 and precedes it in v. 9. A form of the second masculine plural pronoun also appears multiple times in vv. 4 and 9, and the contrast is, as in v. 4, between the houses of the Judahites and the house of Yahweh. But 'the house' of v. 4 has become more personalized. It is now 'my house'.

In Zechariah an intermediary figure, the interpreting angel, emerges. In contrast to the visions in Amos, where the prophet has direct verbal and visual associations with Yahweh, the interpreter guides, influences, and even assumes the traditional prophetic prerogatives of intercession and proclamation in Zechariah. Each of the eight night visions is colored by the use of a question-answer schema in the dialogue between the prophet and the interpreting angel. Sometimes the prophet asks the angel about details of the vision (1.9; 2.2 [Eng. 1.19], 2.4 [Eng 1.21]; 2.6 [Eng. 2.2]; 4.4, 11, 12; 5.6, 10; 6.4), while on other occasions the angel inquires of the prophet (3.2; 4.2, 5, 7, 13; 5.2). Both formats are used to draw the reader into the experience of the prophet. A question that advances the plot is voiced in the opening night vision by the prophet.

> And-I-said, What-are-these, my-lord? And-to-me the-angel said, the-one-who-speaks with me, I myself-will-show-you what-they are (1.9).

Many of the questions that Zechariah invokes throughout the night visions serve ultimately to advance the plot, to unfold the meaning of the

14. D. Gowan, 'The Use of *ya'an* in Biblical Hebrew', *VT* 21 (1971), p. 177.

visions themselves. The book opens with a chronological formula (1.1), and the cycle of night visions, which begins at 1.7, is also introduced by a similar expression. But the night vision formula is more precise. It specifies the day and the name of the month taken from the Babylonian calendar. The first vision (1.8-17) opens with a description of a man riding a red horse with horses of other colors behind him. This interpreting angel appears on stage without introduction in v. 9 and offers to show Zechariah 'what they are'. By offering to show—but not to tell—what they are, the interpreting angel projects Zechariah back into the visionary world. But it is the man who rides the red horse who actually answers Zechariah's question in v. 10: 'they are those whom Yahweh has sent to walk to and fro over the whole earth' gathering information to report to God or God's angel (v. 11). This man stands (vv. 8, 10) among the myrtle trees, evergreens whose branches were used in building booths for the Feast of Tabernacles (Neh. 8.15). According to Isa. 41.19 and 55.13, these trees will flourish in the prosperity of the messianic age. Figures from the heavenly counsel do range over the face of the earth and report to God about the conditions of human affairs as in Job 1.6 and 2.1-2. The patrol is inclusive ('all the earth'), and the report is that the earth is dwelling peacefully.

But the image of cosmic peace changes at v. 12 when the angel of Yahweh asks, 'How long will you withhold mercy from Jerusalem, and the cities of Judah with which you have been angry these seventy years?' Zechariah uses this question to elicit a response from God and to call attention to the temple complex in ruins. The first oracle concludes with a message of hope. God will return to Jerusalem with compassion; the temple will be rebuilt and 'a measuring line' will be stretched over the city. God's cities will also be rebuilt, and they 'shall again overflow with prosperity' (v. 17) as Yahweh comforts Zion.

The second night vision continues the thought of the first, and, at the literary level, is linked by the duplication of the interrogative form.

> And-I-said to-the-angel, the-one-who-speaks with-me, What-are-these? And-he-said to-me, These-are the-horns that have-scattered Judah, Israel, and-Jerusalem (Zech. 2.2 [Eng. 1.19]).

Once again and with one word, Zechariah asks the interpreting angel: 'What-are-these?' On this occasion the interpreting angel answers Zechariah's question. The prophet sees four horns and learns from the answer to his question that advances the plot that these four horns 'have scattered Judah, Israel, and Jerusalem'. The interpretation is geopolitical.

'Scattering' is an important theme of this vision, and the horns have brought destruction on Judah and Israel. The vision continues in 2.3 (Eng. 1.20) as Yahweh shows Zechariah four smiths (or artisans).[15] The messenger interprets the horns metaphorically. These horns that have 'scattered' Judah, Israel, and Jerusalem are political-military entities.

In the second stage of this second vision, the question pattern is altered.

> And-I-said, What-are these coming to-do? And-he-said, saying, These-are the-horns that-scattered Judah, so-that-one could-not-raise one's-head. And-these (smiths) have-come to-terrify them, to-strike-down the-horns-of the-nations that-lifted-up horn(s) against-the-land-of Judah to-scatter it (Zech. 2.4 [Eng. 1.21]).

The active participle 'coming' suggests motion, and Zechariah now asks about the significance ('to-do') of these smiths. This question is the only interrogative in the visions that asks about the purpose of the visionary figures. Elsewhere, the questioner asks only about the identity of a figure—such as the horses in vision 1, the lampstand and trees in vision 4, the scroll in vision 5, the ephah in vision 6, the horse and chariots in vision 7, or, as in vision 3, about the place where a figure is going. The departure from the questioning pattern in vision 2 highlights the activity of the workers themselves and draws attention to the smiths' role as direct agents of Yahweh's action.

But as attention turns to Judah alone, the interpreting angel's response in 2.4 focuses more on the 'horns' than the 'smiths'. These horns, political-military entities, have scattered Judah so that no head can be raised. This metaphor suggests total destruction, and the language derives from the battlefield. This metaphor is used in the Bible (Judg. 8.28) and in a number of ancient Near Eastern reliefs where a king's foot is pictured on the head of the defeated enemy. After disclosing that the horns had signified military conquest and total destruction for Judah, Zechariah learns at the end of 2.4 that these 'horns' will 'strike down the horns of the nations that lifted up their horns against the land of Judah to scatter its people'. The horns of destruction have become symbols of protection and restoration: 'but these have come to terrify them'. By means of the interrogative the author points to a coming political reordering, and God is portrayed as one who liberates the people.

15. The term חרשים can designate any craftsperson who works with stone, metal, or wood.

In the fifth vision, the questioning becomes intensive. When the scene opens, the interpreting angel reappears and stirs Zechariah 'as one is wakened from sleep'. The angel asks, 'What do you see?' (Zech. 4.1). This question is the first in a series of seven that will appear in this vision. Once again, the plot advances as a string of interrogatives are invoked.

> And-he-said to-me, What-do you see? And-I-said,[16] I-see, and-behold, a-lampstand-of gold all-of-it, with-a-bowl on-top-of-it and-seven lamps on-it, with-seven spouts[17] on-each-of the-lamps that are-on-top-of-it (4.2).
>
> And-I-answered and-I-said to-the-angel, the-one-who-speaks with-me, saying, What-are-these, my-lord? (4.4).
>
> And-the-angel answered, the-one-who-speaks with-me and-he-said to-me, Do-you-not know what-they are? And-I-said, No, my-lord (4.5).
>
> Who-are-you, great-mountain? Before Zerubbabel, a-plain. And-he-shall-bring-out the-top stone amid-shouts-of grace, grace to-it![18] (4.7).

In this vision, the interpreting angel initiates conversation before Zechariah indicates that he has seen something. In the earlier visions Zechariah had spoken first: I saw a man (1.8); I saw four horns (2.1); I saw a man (2.5); he showed me Joshua (3.1). Now in ch. 4 it appears that the angel is attempting to cause Zechariah to continue the visionary experience. Zechariah reveals that he sees a golden menorah with a bowl on top. The menorah holds seven lamps with seven lips for the wicks. Beside the lampstand are two olive trees, one on the right and the other on the left. The problems and possible interpretations of the gold menorah and two olive trees have been discussed by D. Petersen and need not be rehearsed here.[19] Verses 4 and 12 are the only two instances where Zechariah's questions are answered with a question, and as Zechariah and the interpreting angel converse in this vision, the prophet twice confesses that he does not know what the vision means (vv. 5 and 13).

16. MT reads 'and he said I see'. I follow *qere* and versions that read first person imperfect, 'and-I-said'.

17. Following Meyers and Meyers, *Haggai, Zechariah 1–8*, pp. 227, 235-38.

18. Translation of the Hebrew is difficult. Cf. the translation of Smith, *Micah–Malachi*, p. 203 and the comments of Meyers and Meyers, *Haggai, Zechariah 1–8*, p. 249.

19. D. Petersen, *Haggai and Zechariah 1–8* (OTL; Philadelphia: Westminster, 1984), pp. 217-24.

Zechariah continues the dialogue in v. 4 by asking, 'What-are-these, my-lord?' Zechariah utters the word 'my-lord' on three other occasions when speaking to the angel (1.9; 4.5; 4.13). Such language suggests familiarity between the dialogists, and the fact that three of the four occurrences are found in this fifth vision suggests that it is thematically significant. The sentence is conveyed by two Hebrew words and for the first time Zechariah receives from the interpreting angel a reprimand in the form of a question: 'Do you not know what they are?' This counter question is a rebuke and appears only in the fifth vision (here and in 4.13). In 2.2 Zechariah had asked, 'What are these?' and was immediately told, 'the horns that have scattered Judah, Israel, and Jerusalem'. In the fifth vision, immediately after Zechariah admits his lack of knowledge, the author records two answers spoken by the interpreting angel to Zechariah. The first is a double pronged oracle that enhances the status of Zerubbabel (vv. 6d-7 and 8-10a) and then a more explicit response to the question at hand in v. 10b. It becomes apparent in this question-answer sequence that more work remains to be done despite the encouraging tone of the first four visions. In the course of the oracle, Zerubbabel is depicted as a temple builder par excellence. It is he who is the 'great mountain' (v. 7). A new Solomon, he is the one whose elevation has come not by his own might or power but by Yahweh's spirit (v. 6b). Zerubbabel's elevation is similar to that of Joshua in the previous vision, and their portraits reflect the importance of the dyarchic structure of governor and high priest approved by the Persian authorities.

Two individuals are introduced in the oracle. Zerubbabel receives an endorsement amid shouts of approbation in contrast to the unnamed 'you' in v. 7 ('Who are you?'). The identity of 'you' remains unsolved.[20] The contrasting imagery of v. 7 is, however, clear: Zerubbabel is the mountain and someone else is the plain. Zerubbabel is the one who shall succeed: 'he shall bring out the top stone (to be used in the reconstruction of the temple) amid shouts of "Grace, grace to it!"' (v. 7).

Zechariah asks next about the two olive trees to the left and right of the menorah, and this question is followed by two additional interrogatives:

> And-I-answered and-I-said to-him, What-are-these two olive-trees on-the-right-of the-lampstand and-on-its-left? (4.11).

20. Redditt summarizes the lack of scholarly consensus in *Haggai, Zechariah, and Malachi*, p. 69.

> And-I-answered a-second-time and-I-said to-him, What-are-the-two branches-of the-olive-trees, which-are in-the-hand-of the-two pipes-of gold pouring-out from-upon-them the-gold (4.12).
>
> And-he-said to-me, saying, Do-you-not know what-these-are? And-I-said, No, my-lord (4.13).

The two questions of the interpreting angel in the first part of the fifth vision are now balanced by the two questions that the prophet asks in the second part of the vision (vv. 11, 12). At v. 12, Zechariah asks a question similar to the one invoked in v. 11. The second question is more specific. In this follow-up, he asks about the 'two branches' of the olive trees that pour gold through the golden pipes. The two branches have not been previously mentioned. Again, the interpreting angel expresses dismay at Zechariah's ignorance and answers Zechariah's question with a question: 'Do you not know what these are?' As before, Zechariah must admit that he lacks knowledge and again the angel interprets: the two trees are the sons of the oil who stand next to the Lord of the entire earth. In this fifth vision, more than in any other, the frequent use of the interrogative allows new information to be added to the primary vision.

After the comparatively large number of questions that appear in the fifth vision (4.1-14), one finds only an occasional question in the next three visions. In the sixth vision (5.1-4) the only interrogative appears in 5.2. In the seventh vision (5.5-11) interrogatives are found at 5.6 and 5.10. In the eighth and final vision (6.1-8) the only interrogative appears in 6.4.

> And-he-said to-me, What-do you see? And-I-said, I see a-flying scroll; its-length-is twenty cubits, and-its-width ten cubits (5.2).
>
> And-I-said, What-is-it? And-he-said, This-is the-ephah that-goes-forth. And-he-said, This-is its-iniquity[21] in-all-the-earth (5.6).
>
> And-I-said to-the-angel, the-one-who-speaks with-me, Where-are they-taking the-ephah? (5.10).
>
> And-I-answered and-I-said to-the-angel, the-one-who-speaks with-me, What-are-these, my-lord? (6.4).

21. Following LXX and Syriac. The slight emendation of MT (י to ו) creates a parallel with 'wickedness' in v. 7. But cf. the comments of Meyers and Meyers, *Haggai, Zechariah 1–8*, pp. 297-98.

Each of these questions serves to advance the plot. The fifth vision opens with the narrator's description of Zechariah looking up and seeing a flying scroll. Thereupon, the interpreting angel asks him what he sees. Only in the fifth and sixth visions does the interpreting angel initiate conversation with this question. In all the other visions, the prophet asks the angel 'what are', 'where are', 'what is' questions. The departure in the sixth vision allows the author to emphasize the narrator's report of the 'flying scroll', and to embellish it with a description of its dimensions: it is twenty cubits (approximately thirty feet) wide and ten cubits (approximately fifteen feet) tall. A scroll of twenty cubits in length was not uncommon, but scrolls were usually less than a cubit in height. One ten cubits high would have been unmanageable.[22] This unwieldy scroll corresponds to the vast number of thieves and perjurers (vv. 4-5) and suggests the extent of God's judgement upon them.

At the beginning of the seventh vision, Zechariah is instructed to lift his eyes and see what is coming out. He obeys and immediately asks: 'What is it' (5.6)? This opening question is similar to others Zechariah asks—in the first, second, third, and eighth visions (1.8; 2.2, 6; 6.4)—but it is set apart by the follow-up question in v. 10: 'Where are they taking the ephah?' At the rhetorical level, the opening questions serve to elicit a description of the object, and the interpretation of the object follows after it is identified: 'this (ephah) is their iniquity in all the earth'. After a description of the women with wings who carry the ephah between earth and sky (v. 9), the visionary asks about the destination of the ephah. The interpreting angel answers the question, then supplies more information: 'to the land of Shinar to build a house for it; and when this is prepared, they will set the ephah down there on its base'. This 'where' question accentuates movement of the ephah from Palestine to Shinar, in other words, the land of Babylon.[23] Their 'iniquity' (v. 6) will be sent to the land from which the Judeans have recently been freed under the edict of Cyrus, and the building of a house for a deity in Shinar (v. 11) balances the restoration of Yahweh's house in Jerusalem. Zechariah's eighth and final vision begins at 6.1. He sees four chariots driven by vividly colored horses coming out between two bronze mountains. His 'what are these' question in v. 4 is a request for interpretation; the details of the vision he already knows (vv. 1-3). The interpreting angel immediately responds: 'these are the four winds of heaven going

22. Redditt, *Haggai, Zechariah, and Malachi*, p. 72.

23. The LXX, Syriac, and Targum substitute 'Babylon' for 'Shinar'.

out, after presenting themselves before Yahweh of all the earth' (v. 5). This image encompasses a vast geographic range because the four winds represent the four compass directions, and the explanation in vv. 5-8 creates a sense of confidence in the restored world order under Yahweh's universal realm.

4. *Questions that Increase the Number of Characters in a Given Scene*
The author(s) of Haggai and Zechariah also use questions for a fourth purpose. In this type, yet another dialogic situation whereby prophetic utterances unfold, the number of characters in a scene increases as questions are invoked. On the twenty-fourth day of the ninth month, in the second year of Darius, Yahweh asks for a ruling of the priests.

> If[24] one-carries consecrated-meat in-the-fold-of one's-garment, and-touches with-the-fold the-bread, or-the-stew, or-the-wine, or-oil, or-any-kind-of-food, does-it-become-holy? And-the-priests answered and-they-said, No (Hag. 2.12).

Dialogic situations involving three parties (prophet, priests, and Yahweh in this instance) are quite rare in biblical Hebrew narrative. This question asks if holiness can be transmitted by accidental contact with a person carrying meat (lit., 'holy flesh') in the fold of one's garment. The meat in question is dedicated to the alter for the purpose of sacrifice. The prophet is thus commissioned to ask whether an object becomes holy through indirect contact with holy sacrificial meat (cf. Lev. 6.18). If the fold touches something else, is the sanctity of the holy meat transmitted to the common object? The priests answer in the negative. Indirect contact with the sacred does not make holy what is profane. By means of this question, Haggai brings to the attention of his audience a pragmatic issue and follows with another question, this time about defilement:

> And-Haggai said, If-one-touches an-unclean-corpse[25] with-any-of-these, does-it-become-unclean? And-the-priests answered, and-said, it-does-become-unclean (Hag. 2.13).

24. For this translation of הן, see the comments of H.-W. Wolff, *Haggai: A Commentary* (Minneapolis: Augsburg, 1988), p. 88 n. 12a and Verhoef, *Books of Haggai and Malachi*, pp. 116-17.

25. For the translation of נפש as 'corpse', see the comments of Smith, *Micah–Malachi*, p. 159 n. 13a.

In this second hypothetical case before the priests, Haggai asks about a person who touches a corpse and then contacts the articles of food mentioned in v. 12. Do they become unclean? The priests affirm that the food would indeed be unclean. Such impurity is contagious. The corpse's uncleanness has infecting power and any person who touches it can contaminate food. Any such person who has not been made pure by cleansing rituals defiles the tabernacle of Yahweh and that person shall be cut off from Israel' (Num. 19.13). Anything connected with death has no place before Yahweh.

Holiness, therefore, is not contagious in the way that uncleanness is contagious. The Samaritans were eager to participate in sacrifices and to assist the Jews in rebuilding the temple.[26] The prophet rejects such a coalition on the grounds that the people must trust in Yahweh's assistance and not in any help from the Samaritans (1.13; 2.4b, 5b; cf. 2 Kgs 17.29-41; Ezra 4.2). From this double question-answer scheme, Haggai draws the conclusion: 'so it is with this people, and with this nation before me, says the LORD: and so with every work with their hands; and what they offer there is unclean' (v. 14).

In his discourse on laying the foundation of the temple, Haggai continues to expand the number of characters by referring to 'this people' and 'this nation before me' (2.14). He asks and answers a question in 2.16:

> How-did-you-fare?[27] When-one-came to-a-heap-of-twenty-(measures), there-were-but ten; when-one-came to-the-winevat to-draw fifty measures, there-were-but twenty (Hag. 2.16).

The 'how did you fare?' question refers to the time before the temple was ritually purified and before rebuilding began. The question underscores the plight of the people before work on the temple was begun, and, by asking and answering the question, Haggai exhorts the people to remember their previous distress. The answer is given in two parallel sentences. The previous occasions have been marked by disappointment. When one came looking for a heap of twenty measures, there were only ten, and the person wanting to draw fifty measures from the vat could draw only twenty. Before mentioning the projected day of blessing

26. Verhoef, *Books of Haggai and Malachi*, p. 119.

27. LXX. On the 'incomprehensible' MT's third person plural suffix, see Wolff, *Haggai*, p. 58 n. 16a-a. Cf. also Meyers and Meyers, *Haggai, Zechariah 1–8*, p. 60 n. 16.

(v. 19), Haggai first of all reminds the people of their past circumstances. In this question-answer sequence, Haggai thus constructs an antithesis between the negligence of the people in the past with the projected blessing of Yahweh.

The interrogative form of Hag. 2.16 resumes at 2.19.

> Is-yet the-seed in-the-granary? And-is-it-yet-that-the-vine, and-the-fig-tree, and-the-pomegranate, and-the-olive tree do-not produce?[28] From-this day-on I-will-bless-you.

With these questions we perceive what H.W. Wolff calls 'Haggai's own, familiar, spoken, dialogue'.[29] The prophet again announces an abrupt turn, a new blessing from this day forward. Grapes, wine, figs, pomegranate, and olives—the very staples of Israelite diet—will once again be plentiful. These new images of seed in the granary and fruit on the vine enhance the agricultural picture conveyed by vv. 16-17.

In the midst of Zechariah's first vision, the interpreting angel also increases the number of characters with a question addressed to Yahweh.

> And-the-angel-of-Yahweh answered and-said, Yahweh-of hosts, how-long-will you have-no-mercy on-Jerusalem and the-cities-of Judah, with-which you-have-been-angry these seventy years? (Zech. 1.12).

The interrogative word עד־מתי 'how-long' is often found at the beginning of the individual or communal lament Psalms. By invoking this question, the angel hopes to elicit a response and to call attention to the incomplete temple complex.[30] Rather than record the words of God's response, the narrator reports that Yahweh's response was gracious and comforting (v. 13). Deprived of the words, the audience can only infer their content from the oracles conveyed by the interpreting angel in vv. 14-17. With the city and temple in ruins, it appeared that God had failed to show mercy on Jerusalem, and, with this question, the petitioner addresses a compelling thought directly to God: the time to act has arrived. The question is actually a protest against continued intolerable existence, and, in this instance, it is the interpreting angel, not the prophet, who utters the impassioned plea.

28. The interrogative particle is found with the first question but is not repeated in the second instance. The particle applies, however, to both sentences in the העוד...ועד construction.

29. Wolff, *Haggai*, p. 66.

30. Direct answers to such questions addressed to God are not usually found with this type of lament.

Just before a series of questions in 7.5-7 (discussed above under 'the sequential questions'), an interrogative is voiced about fasting over the destruction of the temple:

> to-say to-the-priests who-were of-the-house-of-Yahweh-of hosts and-to-the-prophets, saying, Should-I-weep in-the-fifth month, restricting-myself,[31] as I-have-done this many years? (Zech. 7.3).

In a fashion similar to the examples above, the invocation of this question increases the number of characters. After the question about mourning and fasting is posed, Yahweh appears manifest in the form of a voice. The question originates with the people of Bethel who are sent as a delegation to ask the priests whether people should continue observing the fast as the temple is being rebuilt. The question is framed in the first person, presumably by one who represents the group and the community who sent them. The petitioner asks if this lamentable period of destruction, punishment, and exile has ended. What sort of rights and attitudes are appropriate for a community that is rebuilding, and at a time when Jerusalem barely exists? Is this a time of grief or hope? This question also provokes a series of sayings on the present spiritual condition of the community, the divine judgement on the ancestors, and a declaration of God's promises for future blessings.

Conclusion

Interrogatives function as literary threads in Haggai–Zechariah. Four different types can be discerned: rhetorical questions, sequential questions, questions that function primarily to advance the plot, and questions that increase the number of characters in a given scene. A sense of unity is heightened in the two books by means of this vivid rhetorical style. The frequent and varied use of interrogatives anticipates the protean forms of interrogatives that pepper certain dialectic forms of instruction evident in rabbinical discourses and are reminiscent of the multiple forms found in the Socratic dialogues.[32]

While one discovers an obvious literary connection among the interrogatives in Haggai–Zechariah 1–8, the pattern does not extend to

31. Following Meyers and Meyers, *Haggai, Zechariah 1–8*, pp. 386-87.

32. K.M. Craig, Jr, *Reading Esther: A Case for the Literary Carnivalesque* (Literary Currents in Biblical Interpretation; Louisville: Westminster/John Knox, 1995), pp. 22, 36-41, 50.

Zechariah 9–14. The night visions conclude at Zech. 6.8, and the remainder of proto-Zechariah (6.9–8.23) is composed of oracles. When reading chs. 9–14, sometimes called second (chs. 9–11) and third (chs. 12–14) Zechariah, one cannot help but be struck by a change in style. More than thirty questions are invoked in the Haggai–Zechariah 1–8 corpus, but only one interrogative appears in Zechariah 9-14 (that is, at 13.6). This shift at the literary level is matched by other changes: Zechariah is never mentioned in the last six chapters; no identifiable person or event is mentioned; the new temple exists in chs. 9–14 (9.8; 11.13; 14.16-21), whereas before it was anticipated; and no visions are reported in chs. 9–14 in marked contrast to the opening chapters. While such discontinuity does suggest a different rhetorical strategy beginning with Zechariah 9, it does not necessarily imply disunity between the two works. However, if one wishes to argue for the unity of Haggai and the fourteen chapters of Zechariah, clues other than the author's predilection for the interrogative must be found.[33]

33. Radday and Wickmann ('Unity of Zechariah') explore this topic from the standpoint of statistical linguistics. R. Mason ('The Relation of Zech 9–14 to Proto-Zechariah', *ZAW* 88 [1976], pp. 227-39) discusses unity as he focuses exclusively on the oracular material in the fourteen chapters of Zechariah. But cf. esp. the discussion at n. 4 above and the articles by Pierce ('Literary Connectors' and 'Thematic Development'). In a subsequent study, one might ask if the many interrogative forms in Malachi fit into the distinct typological scheme of Haggai–Zechariah 1–8.

Zechariah 9–14, Malachi, and the Redaction of the Book of the Twelve

Paul L. Redditt

Malachi 3.22-24 (Eng. 4.4-6) not only closes the book of Malachi, but also casts a glance back at Moses and Elijah. Since neither man is mentioned explicitly anywhere else in the book, scholars have often considered the verses secondary and have entertained the notion that they close the entire Book of the Twelve, if not a larger corpus still. W. Rudolph, for example, points to the references to Moses as God's servant in Deut. 34.5 and Josh. 1.1-2 and argues that Mal. 3.22-24 closes the entire prophetic canon.[1]

Since the verses stand at the end of Malachi and at the close of the Twelve, they do, indeed, occupy a place where redactional activity was highly likely.[2] This paper pursues that activity, particularly as it is

1. W. Rudolph, *Haggai–Sacharja 1–8–Sacharja 9–14–Maleachi* (KAT, 13.4; Gütersloh: Mohn, 1976), p. 291. Cf. the more recent view of D.L. Petersen (*Zechariah 9–14 and Malachi* [OTL; Louisville: Westminster/John Knox, 1995], p. 232), who makes three pertinent observations on this issue. (1) Mal. 4.4-6 is not a summary of Malachi and indeed diminishes the immediacy of some of the diatribes of the rest of the book. (2) Mal. 4.4-6 ties the book to the rest of the canon. (3) Hos. 14.9 (Eng. 14.10), in the epilogue of the first book among the Twelve, functions the same basic way, suggesting that the final editor of the Twelve was responsible for both of those additions.

2. See J.D. Nogalski, *Literary Precursors to the Book of the Twelve* (BZAW, 217; Berlin: de Gruyter, 1993), pp. 12-19. To be sure some scholars, for example, J. Baldwin (*Haggai, Zechariah, Malachi* [Tyndale Old Testament Commentaries; London: Tyndale, 1972], p. 251), B. Glazier-McDonald (*Malachi, The Divine Messenger* [SBLDS, 98; Atlanta: Scholars Press, 1987], pp. 245, 261, 267), and Pieter A. Verhoef (*The Books of Haggai and Malachi* [NICOT; Grand Rapids: Eerdmans, 1978], pp. 163, 337) argue that the verses are authentic. Their arguments, however, do not seem to account for the sudden and unanticipated introduction of Moses and Elijah into the book of Malachi. The eye of the author of 3.22-24 was looking elsewhere than Malachi itself.

observable in Zechariah 9–14 and Malachi. It will offer three proposals with regard to the formation of the Twelve: (1) that the book of Malachi (minus 3.22-24) was originally appended to Haggai/Zechariah 1–8 to explain why the future expected in those books had not yet transpired; (2) that Mal. 3.22-24 was written to conclude a canon including Deuteronomy (if not the whole Pentateuch), the Deuteronomistic former prophets, and the twelve 'named' prophets of the Book of the Twelve, which Book those verses closed; and (3) that with the number of the prophets set at twelve, Zechariah 9–14 was added to the previously existing Zechariah corpus.

I. *A Review of Recent Scholarship on the Redaction of the Book of the Twelve*

The conclusions argued in this paper build upon the work of prior scholars. The first, Rudolph, already mentioned in connection with Mal. 3.22-24, also points out the historical arrangement of much of the collection. Hosea, Amos, Jonah (see 2 Kgs 14.25) and Micah were grouped as prophets from the eighth century; Nahum, Habakkuk, and Zephaniah from the seventh; and Haggai, Zechariah, and Malachi from the fifth. Joel and Obadiah were attached as lead-in and supplement to Amos.[3]

The second contribution is that of Erich Bosshard and R.G. Kratz. In a solo study Bosshard argues that the Twelve parallels the book of Isaiah in content and structure but concedes there is no parallel in the Twelve to the historical narrative of Isaiah 36–39 and the exilic theology of Isaiah 40–55 and thinks Jonah, Zechariah 9–14, and Malachi fell outside the original collection of the Twelve.[4] Bosshard's concessions are telling. On the one hand, he finds no parallel for twenty of the sixty-six chapters of Isaiah (chs. 36–55), and, on the other hand, he argues for a Book of the Ten that is subsequently expanded into a Book of the Twelve.

Bosshard and Kratz develop Bosshard's investigation further by focusing on the book of Malachi. They argue that it was written in three stages, whose relative chronology (and absolute chronology to an extent) can be determined by noting the minor prophets cited at each stage. They think the first stage (1.2-5; 1.6–2.3; 2.4-9; 3.6-12), written during the Persian period, knew Hosea, Amos, Micah, Nahum,

3. Rudolph, *Haggai–Sacharja 1–8–Sacharja 9–14–Maleachi*, pp. 297-98.

4. E. Bosshard, 'Beobachtungen zum Zwölfprophetenbuch', *BN* 40 (1987), p. 36.

Habakkuk, Haggai and Zechariah 1–8.[5] (This conclusion seems to modify Bosshard's earlier argument that the book of Malachi lay outside the original redaction of the Twelve.) The second stage (2.17–3.5; 3.13-21) drew upon the rest of the Book of the Twelve, including Zechariah 9–14. The third and final stage of both the book of Malachi and of the Book of the Twelve included 1.14a; 2.10-12; and 3.22-24. (They omit the obscure text about divorce in 2.13-16).[6] They reconstruct the relative chronology of Zechariah 9–14 and the stages of Malachi as follows: Malachi I, Zechariah 9–13, Zechariah 14 (dated in the Ptolemaic period), Malachi II and Malachi III.[7]

Much of their evidence that Malachi I knew Hosea, Amos, Micah, Haggai, and Zechariah 1–8 consists of single words, sometimes very common, and sometimes used quite differently (for example, the root כבד, which appears as כבודי [my glory], in Mal. 1.6 and as אכבד [I will/may be honored], in Hag. 1.8).[8] They conclude without showing evidence that Malachi I also knew Nahum and Habakkuk.[9] Further, their argument that Malachi II drew upon Zechariah 9–14 reverses the arguments of M. Delchor[10] and J. Nogalski (see below). Also, their dating scheme hinges on the debatable assumption that Zechariah 9–14 was written after the rise of Alexander (see below).

T. Lescow appends his view of the growth of the Twelve to his study of the book of Malachi. Specifically, he distinguishes the books that at least purport to be pre-exilic from the clearly post-exilic works of Haggai, Zechariah 1–8, and Malachi. He thinks that the four prophets with Deuteronomistic superscriptions (Hosea, Amos, Micah, and Zephaniah) anchor the first nine, with Jonah as the pivot. He also argues that Haggai, Zechariah 1–8, and Malachi are built around the theme of Torah. He is correct in connection with Malachi, where the word appears several times in 2.6-9 and 3.22 and details of Torah are debated. In Haggai and Zechariah 1–8, however, the word appears only in Hag. 2.11 and Zech. 7.12, and such issues as the rebuilding of the

5. E. Bosshard and R.G. Kratz, 'Maleachi im Zwölfprophetenbuch', *BN* 52 (1990), p. 29.

6. Bosshard and Kratz, 'Maleachi', p. 29.

7. Bosshard and Kratz, 'Maleachi', pp. 43-45.

8. Bosshard and Kratz, 'Maleachi', p. 33.

9. Bosshard and Kratz, 'Maleachi', p. 36.

10. M. Delchor, 'Les sources du Deutéro-Zacharie et ses procédés d'emprunt', *RB* 59 (1952), pp. 393-411.

temple and the re-establishment of the monarchy appear to have been more important. Lescow is on firmer ground when he points out that Zephaniah, Obadiah, and Amos all treat the subject of the day of Yahweh, as does the conclusion to the Twelve, Mal. 3.22-24.[11]

P.R. House argued that the Book of the Twelve develops a 'comic' plot, that is, it begins on the negative note of sin in Hosea and Joel and concludes with the promise of a new day in Haggai, Zechariah and Malachi.[12] Clearly, Hosea does begin with that prophet's condemnation of sin, and Haggai and Zechariah 1–8, in particular, look toward a better future. However, the 'comic' plot is more characteristic of the individual books, since most have both condemnation for the sins of their contemporaries and a(n added) positive ending, than it is of the Twelve as a whole, especially given the negative perspective of much of Zechariah 9–14 and Malachi.

O.H. Steck argues that late additions to the book of Isaiah and late materials in the Book of the Twelve convey identical theological and temporal perspectives.[13] Specifically, he argues that Isaiah 1–34, 36–39 and Isaiah 40–55 + 60–62, on the one side, and the Book of the Twelve, minus Zechariah 9–14, on the other, already existed in the Persian Period. After Alexander the Great, Zech. 9.1–10.2 was inserted between Zechariah 8 and Malachi 1. Then, between 320 and 315, Zech. 10.3–11.3 was added, followed by additions to Joel (4.16, Eng. 3.16), Obadiah (vv. 15-21), and Zephaniah (3.8, 14-19). Sometime after 311 to 302 (the date Steck ascribes to additions to Isaiah), Zech. 11.4–13.9 was added, followed by Zechariah 14, between 240 and 220. The Twelve reached its present proportions before the time of Sirach, either between 220 and 201 or between 198 and 190, with the addition of the superscriptions in Zech. 9.1 and 12.1, along with Mal. 2.10-12 and Mal. 3.22-24 [Eng. 4.4-6].[14] Steck's reconstruction, like that of Bosshard and Kratz, is

11. T. Lescow, *Das Buch Maleachi: Texttheorie–Auslegung–Kanontheorie* (Arbeiten zur Theologie, 75; Stuttgart: Calwer, 1993), pp. 186-87.

12. Paul R. House, *The Unity of the Twelve* (JSOTSup, 97; Sheffield: Almond Press, 1990). See particularly Chart 2, p. 124.

13. O. H. Steck, *Der Abschluss der Prophetie im Alten Testament; Ein Versuch zur Frage der Vorgeschichte des Kanons* (Biblish-Theologische Studien, 17; Neukirchen–Vluyn: Neukirchener Verlag, 1991), p. 112.

14. Steck, *Abschluss*, esp. pp. 196-98 and 37. Clearly the hymn of the fathers in Sir. 44–50 follows the structure of Torah, Former Prophets, and Latter Prophets, concluding with the Book of the Twelve, and supplies the *terminus ad quem* for the Twelve and for the first two parts of Tanak.

problematic, since it assumes a post-Alexander date for Zechariah 9–14, and it deduces specific dates from obscure allusions.

J. Nogalski has devoted two volumes to the redaction of the Book of the Twelve. In the first volume, he studies catchwords linking the closing of one book with the beginning of the next. The rest of the two volumes draws out the implication of his observations for the redaction of the Twelve. He argues that Hosea, Amos, Micah, and Zephaniah formed a 'Deuteronomistic' corpus, and he agrees with the widely-held view that Haggai and Zechariah 1–8 underwent a common redaction. Both collections were fixed in writing prior to their inclusion in the Book of the Twelve, at which time they received redactional glosses.[15] The existence of these two corpora seems fairly certain.

In the second volume, he argues that the majority of the editorial work in producing the Book of the Twelve occurred in what he calls a 'Joel-related layer', which merged Joel, Obadiah, Nahum, Habakkuk, and Malachi with the Deuteronomistic and the Haggai/Zechariah 1–8 corpora. Subsequently, Zechariah 9–14 and Jonah were added to complete the work.[16] This paper will investigate further the movement from the two short corpora to the Book of the Twelve.

The most recent contribution to the discussion is that of B.A. Jones. He points to the differences in the sequence of books in the MT and the LXX. The first six books in the LXX were, in order, Hosea, Amos, Micah, Joel, Obadiah, and Jonah. Jones concludes that Joel, Obadiah, and Jonah found their position in a series of editions of the Twelve. He posits a Book of the Nine with all of the other books in place, including Zechariah 9–14.[17] A second edition resulted in a Book of the Eleven, with Joel and Obadiah in the places they occupy in the LXX,[18] and a third resulted in a Book of the Twelve, with Jonah at the end. Jones based that conclusion on 4QXII[a], which only includes parts of Zechariah, Malachi, and Jonah. As reconstructed by R. Fuller, the scroll contained writing after the book of Malachi. Fuller argues that the Jonah fragment

15. Nogalski, *Literary Precursors*, pp. 276-82.

16. J. Nogalski, *Redactional Processes in the Book of the Twelve* (BZAW, 218; Berlin: Walter de Gruyter, 1993), pp. 275-79.

17. B.A. Jones, *The Formation of the Book of the Twelve: A Study in Text and Canon* (SBLDS, 149; Atlanta: Scholars Press, 1995), pp. 53-58 and Table 6.2 on pp. 226-27.

18. Jones, *Formation*, pp. 239-40.

represented that additional writing.[19] Jones thinks Jonah was placed at the end of the Twelve as a retrospective commentary on prophetic literature in light of the delay of divine punishment on nations found in much prophetic literature.[20] The fourth edition is that of the LXX, in which the book of Jonah had been accepted as prophetic literature.[21] The final edition of the Twelve was that of the MT.

One of Jones's conclusions may be accepted at once: the overwhelming agreement between the LXX and the MT suggests a common *Vorlage*. A second conclusion, namely that the Hebrew text upon which the LXX was based influenced the MT occasionally, can be evaluated only on a verse by verse basis, which cannot be understaken here. Even if that influence did at times occur, it would not necessarily follow, however, that Jones's sequence of five editions must be right. For one thing, the differences between the LXX and MT order can be explained differently. To cite but one typical example, Eissfeldt thinks the sequence from Hosea through Obadiah was based simply on length, from the longest to the shortest book.[22] Further, Jones's suggestion that Jonah originally stood at the end of the Twelve is based on Fuller's judgement that an unattached fragment of the badly fragmented 4QXII[a] originally stood there. Even if Fuller is correct about that scroll, that is scant evidence for the original placement of Jonah within the Twelve.

This study also builds upon prior studies by this author on Zechariah 9–14 and Malachi, so that work will also be summarized here. Zechariah 9–14 includes four collections of traditional hope (9.1-27; 10.3b-12; 12.1-4a, 5, 8-9; and 14.1-13, 14b-21). These collections were connected by means of revisions best seen as the result of cognitive dissonance, including the so-called shepherd materials (10.1-3a; 11.4-17; 13.7-9), claims for Judah's parity with Jerusalem (12.6-7), and the necessity for cleansing Davidides (12.10-12), priests (12.13-14), and prophets (13.2-9). The author/redactor responsible for these verses is best described as pro-Judah and anti-establishment, though not anti-Jerusalem.[23]

19. Jones, *Formation*, p. 6; see R. Fuller, 'Form and Foundation', in this volume.

20. Jones, *Formation*, p. 238.

21. Jones, *Formation*, p. 238.

22. O. Eissfeldt, *The Old Testament: An Introduction* (New York: Harper & Row, 1965), p. 383.

23. P.L. Redditt, *Haggai, Zechariah, Malachi* (NCBC; Grand Rapids: Eerdmans, 1995), pp. 102-103. See also 'Israel's Shepherds: Hope and Pessimism in Zechariah 9–14', *CBQ* 51 (1989), pp. 632-38; and 'The Two Shepherds in Zechariah 11:4-17', *CBQ* 55 (1993), pp. 676-86.

Of the four collections of traditional materials, ch. 14 is almost universally held to be the latest. It is possible to date that chapter on something like historical-critical grounds. Its view for the future describes the boundaries of Jerusalem using the Benjaminite and the Corner Gates in the badly damaged north wall of the city replaced rather than repaired by Nehemiah. Such a description is far more likely to have been the projection of a prophet before the repairs of Nehemiah than after. The redaction of Zechariah 9–14 would then follow later after a break between Jerusalem and a group of Judeans. The changes brought about by once again making Jerusalem an administrative city and by the conscription of Judeans to inhabit it (Neh. 11.1) suggest that the redaction of Zechariah 9–14 could have followed any time after the city assumed new prominence.[24] A similar date has been calculated by K.E. Pomykala, based on his study of the mention of the Davidic family in 12.10–13.1. Those verses presuppose that the Davidides were the leading family in Jerusalem, a situation he thinks ceased to obtain by the mid-fourth century.[25]

The book of Malachi originated in stages as well. The redactor probably inherited two separate written collections. The first (1.6–2.9; 2.13-16) attacked the priests, while the second (2.17–3.1 + 3.5; 1.2-5 + 3.6-7; 3.8-12; 3.13-15; and 2.10, 12) addressed the laity. The redactor interwove the inherited materials and composed 1.1; 3.1b-4 and 3.16-21 [Eng. 3.16-4.3]. The conclusion (3.22-24, Eng. 4.4-6) was added later.[26] The prophet's use of the term 'Levite' for priests, combined with his concern that people pay their tithes (the collection of which was the

24. Redditt, *Haggai, Zechariah and Malachi*, pp. 94-99. See, for more detail, my 'Nehemiah's First Mission and the Date of Zechariah 9–14', *CBQ* 56 (1994), pp. 664-78. M. Saebø (*Sacharja 9–14: Untersuchungen von Text und Form* [WMANT, 34; Neukirchen–Vluyn: Neukirchener Verlag, 1969], pp. 282-308, 313), likewise, argues that the Shepherd materials derived from the redactor (of chs. 9–13), but thinks ch. 14 is a later addition. Nogalski (*Redactional Processes*, pp. 236-47), likewise, argues that ch. 14 was the last addition in Zechariah 9–14. If they are correct, that means Zechariah 9–14 was complete before Nehemiah's first mission.

25. K.E. Pomykala, *The Davidic Dynasty Tradition in Early Judaism: Its History and Significance for Messianism* (SBLEJL, 7; Atlanta: Scholars Press, 1995), p. 124.

26. Redditt, *Haggai, Zechariah and Malachi*, pp. 152-55. See also my 'The Book of Malachi in Its Social Setting', *CBQ* 56 (1994), p. 249. Bosshard and Kratz included 2.17–3.1a, 5 and 3.13-15 in their second stage, but these verses are better seen as remnants of materials reshaped by a redactor.

responsibility of the Levites), suggests that the prophet was a non-Zadokite Levite. The redactor was probably one of a group of disciples of the prophet pushed to the periphery of Jerusalemite life by the priests.[27]

II. *Towards the Redaction of the Book of the Twelve*

The Book of Malachi and the Book of the Twelve

There is a broad, scholarly consensus that the book of Malachi appeared between 480 and 430 BCE, in other words, just before or during the careers of Ezra and Nehemiah.[28] It is perhaps possible to fit these two proposed stages of the growth of Malachi more precisely within that time frame. The situation Nehemiah faced upon his return to Jerusalem on his second mission (some time between 433 and 423 BCE, cf. Neh. 13.6) was that the Levites had been excluded from their functions in the temple and forced into the countryside (Neh. 13.10).

The Memoirs of Nehemiah, as represented by Nehemiah 13, make it clear that in his second mission (1) Nehemiah opposed the High Priest Eliashib, (2) the High Priest was allied with the Ammonite Tobiah and related by marriage to the Samaritan Sanballat, and (3) Nehemiah befriended the Levites.[29] Hence, M. Smith is correct to argue that

27. Redditt, *Haggai, Zechariah and Malachi*, pp. 151-52; 'Malachi in Its Social Setting', pp. 251-54.

28. Representative dates must suffice. A.E. Hill ('Dating the Book of Malachi', *And the Word of the Lord Shall Go Forth* [ASOR Special Volume Series; Winona Lake: Eisenbrauns and ASOR, 1983], pp. 77-89) prefers a date between 515 and 458 BCE; F. Horst (*Die Zwölf kleinen Propheten* [HAT, 14; Tübingen: Mohr, 1964], p. 263) places the book before Ezra; W.J. Dumbrell ('Malachi and the Ezra-Nehemiah Reforms', *RTR* 35 [1976], pp. 42-52) argues more precisely for 460 BCE; Glazier-McDonald (*Malachi*, p. 17) suggests 460–50 BCE; Rudolph (*Haggai–Sacharja 1–8–Sacharja 9–14–Maleachi*, pp. 248-49) opts for the broader range of 450-20 BCE; Verhoef (*Haggai and Malachi*, pp. 156-60) settles on 433 BCE, between the two missions of Nehemiah. On the other hand, J.M. O'Brien (*Priest and Levite in Malachi* [SBLDS, 121; Atlanta: Scholars Press, 1990], pp. 113-33) argues that Edom could have been destroyed any time between 605 and 550 BCE, so Mal. 1.4 necessitates a date sooner rather than later after Edom's demise. Hence she prefers a date of 515 BCE or earlier. Since the book of Malachi presupposes a functioning temple, however, her *terminus ad quem* is really the *terminus a quo*.

29. Clearly, Nehemiah opposed priests who were willing to cooperate with the duly appointed, ruling powers in Samaria. See R. Albertz, *A History of Israelite Religion in the Old Testament Period* (Louisville: Westminster, John Knox, 1994),

Nehemiah's sympathizers would have included perhaps a few priests, almost all Levites, and [many of] the Jerusalem poor.[30] Further, Neh. 13.10 explicitly notes that Levites fled from Jerusalem back to their lands to make a living. This loss of power by the Levites while Nehemiah was back in Persia might account for a move to the periphery of Judean religious life of the group to which the redactor of Malachi belonged. If the redactor worked during Nehemiah's absence, the prophet of the book of Malachi would have flourished *during* or *prior* to Nehemiah's first mission. Upon Nehemiah's return, his reform efforts included putting a priest, a scribe, and a Levite together in charge of the storehouse (Neh. 13.13), clearly an effort to restore Levites to their position and income. Their return to Jerusalem could have included the group responsible for the book of Malachi, which would account for the return of the redacted book to the city before 423 BCE.

The next question to ask, then, is, How did the book of Malachi came into the Book of the Twelve? Nogalski claims that it was substantially composed to explain the delay of the optimistic future for Jerusalem promised by Zech. 8.9-23 in particular.[31] That would seem to be evidence enough to accept the view that the book of Malachi originally concluded the corpus Haggai/Zechariah 1–8. Instead, Nogalski argues that material in Malachi 3 indicates awareness of a broader context than merely Haggai/Zechariah 1–8/Malachi.[32] His most compelling evidence is the obvious parallel between Mal. 3.11 and Joel 1.4; 2.25. Malachi 3.11, however, could easily have been inserted by the redactor of the Twelve; by itself, it constitutes no proof that the entire book of Malachi was redacted with Joel in view.[33] What Nogalski does show is that

p. 531. It is not clear, however, that Nehemiah succeeded in reforming the priesthood, and it is abundantly clear that an unbroken line of high priests and Davidides continued for generations after Nehemiah's time. See F.M. Cross, 'A Reconstruction of the Judaean Restoration', *JBL* 94 (1975), pp. 4-18, and *Int* 29 (1975), pp. 187-201.

30. M. Smith, *Palestinian Parties and Politics that Shaped the Old Testament* (London: SCM Press, 1987), p. 118. How homogeneous exiles might have been and how much support they might have given Nehemiah may remain open.

31. Nogalski, *Redactional Processes*, pp. 197-200.

32. Nogalski, *Redactional Processes*, pp. 204-10.

33. The relationships between Mal. 1.2-5 and the book of Obadiah mentioned by Nogalski (*Redactional Processes*, pp. 191-93) may also be explained as literary retouching by the redactor of the Book of the Twelve. In addition, of course, they have a common subject, namely the fate of Edom.

Zech. 8.9-23 and Malachi (especially 1.1-14) present *contrasting images* (italics Nogalski's) of the future of Jerusalem,[34] and not the kind of literary interrelatedness he otherwise points out between the end of one book and the beginning of the next.[35] One may argue, then, that the basic redaction of Malachi was made without recourse to Haggai/ Zechariah 1–8 and that the book of Malachi was appended to that corpus for its contrasting function.

The Function of Mal. 3.22-24 in the Book of the Twelve

On the other hand, Nogalski seems correct that Mal. 3.22-24 [Eng. 4.4-6] derives from a redactor of the Book of the Twelve. Elijah is introduced in 3.23 without any prior mention. Further, the superscription in 1.1 suggests that the redactor of Malachi understood the prophet as the messenger and generated a proper name out of the designation 'my messenger'. By contrast, 3.23 speaks of a coming messenger, identified with Elijah. Further, 3.23 contains a quotation from Joel 2.11 and 3.4 [Eng. 2.31]: 'before the great and terrible day of Yahweh comes'.[36] It would appear, then, that the redactor of the Twelve incorporated the entire Haggai/Zechariah 1–8/Malachi corpus at one time by retouching Malachi from Joel and Obadiah and adding 3.22-24.

The redactor of the Twelve, however, had his eye on Moses and Elijah, suggesting that his purview was much broader than Haggai through Malachi or even Hosea through Malachi. Mention has already been made of the literary connections between Mal. 3.22-24 and Deuteronomy 34 and Joshua 1. Of course, Moses was also called God's servant elsewhere in the Pentateuch, so the author of Mal. 3.22-24 may well have had the whole Pentateuch before him. Further, the allusion to Elijah indicates that the redactor expected his audience to be familiar with the traditions associated with Elijah. It is quite possible, then, that he knew the Deuteronomistic book of Kings. Hence, the reference to Moses and Elijah suggests that the redactor composed Mal. 3.22-24 with at least the book of Deuteronomy and the Deuteronomistic corpus of Joshua through Kings in view. Differently stated, he may well have

34. Nogalski, *Redactional Processes*, p. 197.

35. Nogalski, *Literary Precursors*, pp. 20-56.

36. See Lescow, *Das Buch Maleachi*, pp. 186-88. Lescow argues that the concept of the 'day of Yahweh' helps unite the first nine books of the Twelve, and its mention in the editorial conclusion in Mal. 3.22-24 serves to help tie the last three books to the first nine.

written those verses as the conclusion not only to Malachi or the corpus Haggai/Zechariah 1–8/Malachi, but as the conclusion to an emerging canon, opening with the book of Deuteronomy (or perhaps Genesis[37]) and containing the Former Prophets of the emerging Hebrew Bible as well.[38] For this primary redactor of the Twelve, who was also the author of Mal. 3.22-24,[39] the function of the old prophets was to call God's people to remember the law of Moses. Consequently, he prepared a collection of their preaching. Some people both within and without Israel had not heeded the message, however. So, the redactor looked forward to the coming Elijah, who would call those people to repentance.[40]

With the purpose of that redactor in view, it is time to ask what else in the Book of the Twelve would he have included besides Haggai/Zechariah 1–8/Malachi? In view of his apparent interest in Deuteronomistic theology, it seems likely that he would also have been attracted to the 'Deuteronomistic' corpus of Hosea, Amos, Micah, and Zephaniah posited by Nogalski. Further, his retouching of Malachi with citations and overtones from Joel and Obadiah indicates that he at least knew those works and put them in their present place.

Did this same redactor also know Nahum, Habakkuk, Jonah, or Zechariah 9–14? Bosshard and Kratz adduce no parallels between Malachi and Nahum or Habakkuk, though they do cite as a parallel to Mal. 1.6 the hope for Zion expressed in Zech 2.9, 12, which verses in

37. Indeed, the book of Malachi as a whole, not just the redactor, may have known P. See, for example, M. Fishbane, *Biblical Interpretation in Ancient Israel* (Oxford: Clarendon, 1985), pp. 332-34; Glazier-McDonald, *Malachi*, pp. 73-80; and E.M. Meyers, 'Priestly Language in the Book of Malachi', *HAR* 10 (1986), p. 235.

38. J. Miles (*God: A Biography* [New York: Alfred A. Knopf, 1995], p. 16) points out something moderns easily lose sight of, namely that the Hebrew Bible was not at this point a 'book' or a collection of 'books', but a collection of scrolls kept in jars!

39. Jones (*Formation*, pp. 236-37) notes that the LXX places 3.22 after 3.23-24 and argues that 3.23-24 constituted a redactional conclusion to the book of Malachi and that 3.22 was added as the conclusion to the whole Book of the Twelve, evidence of a growing canonical awareness by the editor of the Hebrew *Vorlage* of the LXX. The editor of the MT then moved 3.22 and touched up 3.23-24 to reflect its place in the Twelve. Even so, he sees all three verses as redactional, the only question being which order came first.

40. Glazier-McDonald (*Malachi*, p. 267), quoting S.R. Driver (*The Minor Prophets* [New York: Oxford University Press, 1906], p. 328), notes the natural connection between Moses and the prophet Elijah, who also met God at Horeb.

turn are similar to Hab. 2.14 and Hos. 10.5.[41] Nogalski is more confident that the 'Joel-layer' included both Nahum and Habakkuk. He notes that Mal. 1.1, like Nah. 1.1 and Hab. 1.1, includes the word משא. However, Mal. 1.1 reads much more like Zech. 9.1 and 12.1 (which Nogalski considers later imitations) than like Nah. 1.1 or Hab. 1.1.[42] More definitively, Nah. 1.3, like Joel 2.13 and Joel 4.21, quotes Exod. 34.6. Further, Nogalski argues that Nah. 3.15-17 draws upon the locust plague of Joel 1.4; 2.25 and suggests that Nahum and Habakkuk understand Assyria and Babylon as two of those locusts.[43] It seems likely, then, that Nahum and Habakkuk did indeed belong to the recension of the Twelve that included Joel.

The Book of Jonah and the Book of the Twelve

Nogalski argues that the book of Jonah came in very late. He does so on two bases. First, while he argues for catchword associations between Jon. 2.3-10 and Mic. 1.2-7 and between Jon. 2.9-10 and Hos. 5.15; 6.1-6, he finds no associations with the book of Joel.[44] So, he places Jonah outside the 'Joel-layer', despite arguing that the book's openness to the inclusion of foreigners among the company of God-fearers stands closest in the Old Testament to Trito-Isaiah, Zech. 8.20-23, Mal. 1.11-14, and Zech. 14.16-19.[45] H.W. Wolff thinks, however, that Jon. 3.9a clearly echoes Joel 2.14a and that Jon. 4.2 reads like Joel 2.13.[46] Joel 2.13 borrows originally from Exod. 34.6, of course, but Jon. 4.2 cites that passage even more clearly than Nah. 1.3, which Nogalski does accept as evidence that Nahum belonged to the 'Joel-layer'.[47] Finally, R.B. Salters

41. Bosshard and Kratz, 'Maleachi', p. 33.

42. Nogalski, *Redactional Processes*, pp. 221, 187-89, 136, 99-100.

43. Nogalski, *Redactional Processes*, pp. 175-79, 146-50, 276.

44. Nogalski, *Redactional Processes*, Appendix of Allusions and Citations, pp. 290-91.

45. Nogalski, *Redactional Processes*, p. 272.

46. See H.-W. Wolff, *Dodekapropheten 3: Obadja und Jona* (BKAT, 14.3; Neukirchen–Vluyn: Neukirchener Verlag, 1977), pp. 128, 141.

47. R.C. Van Leeuwen ('Scribal Wisdom and Theodicy in the Book of the Twelve', in L.G. Perdue, B. Scott, and W. Wiseman (eds.), *In Search of Wisdom: Essays in Memory of John G. Gammie* [Louisville: Westminster/John Knox, 1993], pp. 39-46) has shown a pronounced use of Exod. 34.6-7 throughout the Twelve. Joel 2.12-14a, Jon. 3.9 and 4.2, Mic. 7.18-19, and Nah. 1.3a all quote or paraphrase Exod. 34.6-7, while other verses state that Yahweh again showed compassion on his people (Mic. 7.19) or became jealous for them (Joel 2.18). The

notes that Joel 2.13-14 and Jon. 4.2 are the only two passages in the Old Testament that speak of God's repenting of evil.[48] It would appear, then, that the book of Jonah shows several incidences of borrowing from Joel.

Nogalski's second reason for excluding Jonah from the 'Joel-layer' has to do with the date of the book of Jonah, which he dates in the early third century. Such a late date for Jonah cannot be ruled out, of course, but it does not command universal support. A sampling of other suggested dates must suffice. W. Harrelson argues for the exilic period; but more common is the fifth century, nominated by T.E. Fretheim and J. Limburg, or the fourth century, preferred by O.Eissfeldt, G. Fohrer, and R. Lux, who specifies the late Persian period.[49] Also, the strongest evidence for a date in the Greek period is the Hellenistic parallels to the sea episode. Even they do not prove a date after Alexander, however, since Wolff adduces parallels to Jonah from the Greek singer Arion, who flourished ca. 620 BCE.[50]

Nor does Jonah's borrowing from Joel necessitate a late date, since the book of Joel very likely also arose before the career of Nehemiah. Nogalski bases his late date for Joel on 2.9, which he thinks presupposes

connection between Yahweh's 'becoming jealous' for his people and the idea of the day of Yahweh is obvious. Whether Van Leeuwen is correct (p. 36) that the naming and renaming of Hosea's children constitutes a play on Exod. 34.6 may be left open; the influence of the confession on the Twelve is clear, whether Hosea makes allusion to it or not.

48. R.B. Salters, *Jonah & Lamentations* (Old Testament Guides; Sheffield: Sheffield Academic Press, 1994), p. 26.

49. W. Harrelson, *Interpreting the Old Testament* (New York: Holt, Rinehart and Winston, 1964), p. 359; T.E. Fretheim, *The Message of Jonah* (Minneapolis: Augsburg, 1977), pp. 34-37; J. Limburg, *Hosea–Micah* (Interpretation; Atlanta: John Knox, 1988), p. 138; O. Eissfeldt, 'Amos und Jona in Volkstümlicher Uberlieferung', in R. Sellheim and F. Maass (eds.), *Kleine Schriften* (vol. 4; Tübingen: Mohr, 1968), pp. 137-42; G. Fohrer, *Introduction to the Old Testament* (Nashville, TN: Abingdon, 1965), p. 442. R. Lux (*Jona: Prophet zwischen 'Verweigerung' und 'Gehorsam'* [Göttingen: Vandenhoeck & Ruprecht, 1994], pp. 210-11) dated the book in the late Persian period, suggesting that Nineveh was a surrogate for Persia. Thus, the author of Jonah, unlike the author of Joel 2.13, believed that God's mercy was not limited to Israel, so he held out for positive relations with Persian power rather than its replacement by a Messiah. J.M. Sasson (*Jonah* [AB, 24B; Garden City, NY: Doubleday, 1990], pp. 26-28) prefers a date in the exilic or (better) the post-exilic period, though he properly points out that the 'date' of Jonah could cover centuries, from the time the original narratives were told down to its main redaction.

50. Wolff, *Dodekapropheten 3*, p. 86.

the existence of the Jerusalem wall and, thus, the career of Nehemiah.[51] Actually, the verse comes at the end of a lengthy description of the typical battle tactics of the coming army. Their attack on Jerusalem had not yet occurred and even might be precluded if the people repented (Joel 2.12-13); hence, Joel admonished the priests to proclaim a solemn assembly (2.15-17). Joel 2.9 does not, then, presuppose a wall around Jerusalem. The date for the book of Joel hinges, rather, on 4.4-8 [Eng. 3.4-8], generally considered the latest part of the book. That passage threatens Tyre, Sidon, and Philistia with punishment at the hands of the Sabeans, whose power declined seriously after the mid-fifth century. A later date has to treat that warning as unrealistic, a threat against viable peoples in the name of a has-been, far-away country.[52]

It would appear, then, that the book of Jonah can and probably should be dated near the time of Trito-Isaiah, Zechariah 1–8, Joel, and Malachi, sixth and fifth century materials with whose contents it is most closely related, rather than in the third century. Thus, it cannot be excluded from the 'Joel-layer' on the basis of date. Further, since it is all narrative, it seems oddly out of place in the Twelve, which otherwise includes predominantly the sayings of the prophets. One wonders, in fact, if it was not included precisely to bring the number of prophets to twelve. The significance of the number twelve in ancient Israel was so far reaching it seems unlikely a redactor would stop with the 'Book of the Eleven' as Nogalski's (or Jones's) reconstruction with his 'Joel-layer' would have it.

Zechariah 9–14 and the Book of the Twelve

Nor would a Book of the Twelve be expanded into a 'Book of the Thirteen.' The number of the 'minor prophets' was thus fixed at twelve, and the conclusion of the Book of the Twelve, Mal. 3.22-24 [Eng. 4.4-6], closed that book with a look back at Moses and Elijah, the law and the prophets. Hence, Zechariah 9–14 found its home between Zechariah 1–8 and Malachi, not after Mal. 3.22-24. Nogalski points out that it interrupts the connection between Zech. 8.9-23 and Mal. 1.1-14.[53] Specifically, he says that Zechariah 9–11 was incorporated to facilitate the transition to Malachi by sharpening the division between the time of

51. Nogalski, *Redactional Processes*, p. 50. See also, Salters, *Jonah & Lamentations*, p. 26.

52. See P.L. Redditt, 'The Book of Joel and Peripheral Prophecy', *CBQ* 48 (1986), pp. 233-35.

53. Nogalski, *Redactional Processes*, p. 278.

salvation predicted in Zechariah 8 and the circumstances portrayed in Mal. 1.1-14. He also argues that Zechariah 9–14 falls outside the basic redaction of the Twelve in three successive stages: chs. 9–11, 12.1–13.2(3-6), and ch. 14, with the relocation of 13.7-9.[54]

The second of those two conclusions needs further investigation. For one thing, it is far from clear that the materials were simply added serially to Zechariah 1–8 as Nogalski says. As argued elsewhere by this author (see note 17), the political coherence of the Shepherd materials and 12.6-7 and 12.10–13.6 suggests a redaction of Zechariah 9–14 as a whole. Second, Nogalski again opts for a date within the Greek Period for Zechariah 9–14,[55] a date possibly a century later than the date defended by this author (see note 19). If, indeed, ch. 14 arose before Nehemiah's First Mission and the redactor of Zechariah 9–14 could have worked anytime after Nehemiah's first mission, the date of Zechariah 9–14 does not preclude its inclusion by the redactor of the Twelve himself. The question is whether he did so or whether some other redactor added it.

Nogalski finds no allusions to the book of Joel in Zechariah 9–14.[56] Given the existence of such allusions in other books belonging to the 'Joel-layer', it seems unlikely that these chapters were part of the 'Joel-layer'. On the other hand, Zech. 13.9 was written with Hos. 1.9, 2.25, and Mal. 3.2-3 in view, that is with the opening and the closing of the Twelve in view. The point of 13.7-8 was that God would strike (or had stricken) his shepherd, with disastrous consequences for the people: two-thirds of them would be cut off and perish. The thought is complete in itself, but the verses offer the redactor the opportunity to anchor Zechariah 9–14 in the Twelve by picking up the fraction two-thirds (not the fraction one-half which follows in 14.2) and relating it to the first and last books of the Twelve.

With what other canonical materials does Zechariah 9–14 work?[57] A couple of examples will suffice. Within the Twelve, the most obvious

54. Nogalski, *Redactional Processes*, pp. 245-46. See also p. 235 for evidence that Zech. 13.9 knew Hosea and Malachi and pp. 241-44 for evidence that Zech. 14 did as well.

55. Nogalski, *Redactional Processes*, pp. 245-47.

56. Nogalski, *Redactional Processes*, Appendix of Allusions and Citations, pp. 290-91.

57. See the charts prepared by C.L. Meyers and E.M. Meyers, *Zechariah 9–14* (AB, 25C; Garden City, NY: Doubleday, 1993), pp. 40-43.

text is Amos 7.14, which Zech. 13.5 utilizes. Outside the Twelve, Jer. 23.1-4 and Ezek. 34.1-31; 37.15 offer themes reworked by the so-called Shepherd Allegory in 11.4-17. Bosshard (see note 4) and Steck (see note 14) contend that the book of Isaiah offers parallels to Zechariah 9–14. It seems clear, therefore, from even this cursory review that Zechariah 9–14 had a larger corpus in view than the Twelve. It appears to have been written independently of the Twelve and put in its place after the completion of that work, with Zech. 13.9 being the most obvious indicator of that insertion. As an anonymous work from the post-exilic period, and with the number of prophets already set at twelve, it was inserted between Zechariah and Malachi, rather than between the closely related works of Haggai and Zechariah.[58]

If Zechariah 9–14 is the product of a peripheral group exhibiting cognitive dissonance,[59] what would have brought those chapters back to Jerusalem? One way to answer the question is to note what drove the redactor of Zechariah 9–14 and his group to the periphery of post-exilic

58. The attribution in Matt. 27.9-10 of Zech. 11.12-13 (from the Shepherd materials) to Jeremiah might suggest that Zech. 9–14 found more than one position in the prophetic corpus. Of course, it is also possible that the NT author simply cited the wrong prophet.

59. Redditt, 'Israel's Shepherds', p. 640. Four scholars have objected to this conclusion: S.L. Cook, 'The Metamorphosis of a Shepherd: The Tradition History of Zechariah 11:17 + 13:7-9', *CBQ* 55 (1993), pp. 453-66; R.F. Person, *Second Zechariah and the Deuteronomic School* (JSOTSup, 167; Sheffield: Sheffield Academic Press, 1993), p. 154; S.J. De Vries, *From Old Revelation to New: A Tradition-Historical and Redactional-Critical Study of Temporal Transitions in Prophetic Prediction* (Grand Rapids: Eerdmans, 1995), p. 234; and K.J.A. Larkin, *The Eschatology of Second Zechariah: A Study of the Formation of a Mantological Wisdom Anthology* (Kampen: Kok Pharos, 1994), pp. 249, 253. All of these scholars object that criticism of central groups can be made by persons in power and so is not proof that the one offering the criticism is peripheral. Their point is well taken, of course, but incorrect for Zech. 12.10–13.9 for these reasons: (1) The redactor wants to see Judah rank alongside Jerusalem instead of being subservient to it. (2) Members of the Davidic family and the Levitical families are called to repentance, and prophecy (some or all) is held in suspicion. That leadership is responsible for 'piercing' someone the author of 12.10–13.9 holds innocent. (3) The Jerusalem leadership is always spoken of in the third person, never the first, and is blamed for the delay of the eschaton. In short, the redactor's perspective is, thus, that of a victim of the establishment. In fact, when Person finally describes the 'central' group behind second Zechariah (pp. 167-68), he calls them 'disillusioned' and says they became 'more eschatological in light of unmet expectations' and distanced themselves from the Jerusalem leadership. Such a group sounds sectarian!

life. The collection itself points to the 'piercing' of someone as a deed requiring mourning and purification by the Davidides and Levites (Zech. 12.10–13.1). That reference is too vague to explicate today, and the author of those verses held out no hope that the powerful elite would, on their own accord, make amends.

Instead, the denunciation of the leaders of Jerusalem in 12.10–13.9, the reversal of hopes for reunion between Israel and Judah in 11.4-17, and the pro-Judah perspective of 12.6-7 seem so thoroughgoing that one needs to ask what there was about Zechariah 9–14 that might appeal to the community possessing the Twelve. One answer suggests itself immediately. The condemnation of oral prophecy in 13.2-6 implied that written prophecy was all anyone really needed, and such an appreciation for the written word of past prophets clearly lay behind the collection of the Twelve.

Stages in the Growth of the Book of the Twelve

To sum up this part of the essay, the redaction of the Twelve was done in several stages. The first stage involved the 'Deuteronomistic' collection of Hosea, Amos, Micah, and Zephaniah. A second corpus included the two post-exilic prophets from 520 BCE, Haggai and Zechariah, which were probably originally edited by the same hand. At the third stage another hand added the book of Malachi to Haggai/Zechariah 1–8. The fourth stage included the combination of those two corpora and Nogalski's 'Joel-layer' (Joel, Obadiah, Nahum, and Habakkuk), plus the book of Jonah, bringing the total number of 'prophets' to twelve.[60] The fifth stage was the addition of Zechariah 9–14.

III. *Organizational Principles Underlying the Book of the Twelve*

What were the organizational principles behind the Book of the Twelve? For the MT the most obvious answer is that offered by Rudolph: chronology. Eighth century prophets (Hosea, Amos, Jonah and Micah) come first, seventh century prophets (Nahum, Habakkuk, Zephaniah) next, and post-exilic prophets (Haggai, Zechariah, and Malachi) at the end. The superscriptions of Hosea and Amos relate both books to the

60. Clearly the number of prophetic voices in the collection far exceeds twelve, but their messages are collected under twelve names supplied in superscriptions. Even this comment presumes that 'Malachi' in Mal. 1.1 was intended as a proper name, at least by the time of the final redactor.

reign of Jeroboam II.[61] Further, 2 Kgs 14.25 identifies Jonah as a prophet during the days of that same king, so he is placed after them but before Micah, who is dated during the subsequent reigns of the southern kings Jotham, Ahaz, and Hezekiah.[62] Among the seventh century prophets, Nahum belongs to the Assyrian period, and Habakkuk could be read that way: the coming of the Babylonians (1.6) is future. Zephaniah is clearly dated during the reign of Josiah. The post-exilic corpus Haggai/Zechariah 1–8/Malachi would have come last.

What clearly falls outside that chronological framework, then, are the books of Joel and Obadiah. Their placement among the eighth century prophets by the redactor of the 'Joel-layer' was due to a second organizing principle, namely the alternation of prophets who flourished in Israel and Judah: Hosea (Israel), Joel (Judah), Amos (Israel), Obadiah (Judah), Jonah (Israel), Micah (Judah).[63]

What caused the redactor of the 'Joel-layer' to adopt that principle of alternation may have been, among other things, an interest in Edom. Outside of Joel and Obadiah, Edom is mentioned elsewhere in the Twelve only in Amos and Malachi. Malachi looks back on the fall of Edom, and thus it is later than Joel and Obadiah, which predict (if only after the fact, which is not a necessary conclusion) the fall of Edom.[64]

61. The superscription of Hosea includes later kings than Jeroboam, while that of Amos does not, so the duration of Amos's career is limited by the superscription to no more than two years. While critical scholars routinely date Amos's career a few years earlier than Hosea's, the redactor may have thought Hosea's career not only lasted later but also began earlier.

62. See Nogalski, *Redactional Processes*, p. 270.

63. See Van Leeuwen, 'Scribal Wisdom and Theodicy in the Book of the Twelve', p. 34. Rudolph (*Haggai–Sacharja 1–8–Sacharja 9–14–Maleachi*, p. 298) cites scholars advocating this view but rejects it on the grounds that Amos was from Judah.

64. Similarities between the book of Obadiah and other books is clear. For example, Nogalski (*Redactional Processes*, pp. 71-74) notes similarities between Obad. 16, 17-21 and Amos 9.11-15, between Obad. 15a, 16-21 and Mic. 1.1-7, and both Nogalski (p. 70) and J. Ward (*Thus Says the Lord* [Nashville: Abingdon, 1991], p. 245) point to similarities between Jer. 49.14-16 and Obad. 1-4 on the one hand and Jer. 49.9-10 and Obad. 5-6 on the other. Of importance to this essay is the relationship between Obad. 17 and Joel 3.5 (Eng. 2.32). Joel 3.5 seems to quote Obad. 17, concluding with the phrase 'as Yahweh has said'. If so, one may conclude that the book of Obadiah, mosaic as it may have been, is older than Joel. That conclusion is not novel, obviously, but if Joel can be dated between 515 and 445 BCE (see Redditt, 'Book of Joel', p. 235), Obadiah must be dated earlier. A date in the

How much Edom material is authentic to Amos is debatable. Edom appears in Amos 1.6, 9 as the recipient of slaves, in 1.11-12 as the object of God's punishment, in 9.11-15 as a people whose land the future Judah would possess, and in 2.1 as the people the bones of whose king were burned to lime. The authenticity of all but 2.1 has been challenged, but that verse alone would have provided a reference for a later redactor to build on. Of the contested references, the one in the oracle against the Philistines (1.6-8) is most often accepted,[65] and S.M. Paul accepts them all.[66] The redactor builds on the reference(s) to Edom which he finds in Amos, perhaps adding some of them himself. He places the book of Joel, with its contrast between the futures of Judah and Edom in 3.4 and 3.19-20, before the book of Amos and the book of Obadiah, with its contrast between the futures of Judah and Edom (especially in v. 17) after the book of Amos. Malachi 1.2-5 then shows that God had indeed kept his word which he gave to Joel, Amos, and Obadiah and can be relied upon to keep his word about the two peoples in the future.

It may have been precisely because Joel and Obadiah stand outside of the chronology that the LXX order differed, an order that may well have been secondary, instead of primary as Jones argues. It is easier to explain the changes in that direction. The key is the movement of the book of Micah for the sake of chronology. Given the 'Deuteronomic' editing of Hosea, Amos, and Micah (along with Zephaniah), placing Micah with the other two clearly eighth century prophets was natural. If the order of the MT was original, that change would leave Jonah standing next to Nahum, bringing their differences into even sharper relief. Joel was moved next to Obadiah, which was left in its old place, perhaps because the sequence of the last six books seemed firm and Jonah provides a fitting contrast to Nahum.

exilic period for Obadiah seems about right, but the early post-exilic period cannot be excluded.

65. See, for example, Eissfeldt, *Old Testament*, p. 400; Fohrer, *Introduction*, pp. 434, 436; and H.-W. Wolff, *Joel and Amos* (Hermeneia; Philadelphia: Fortress, 1977), pp. 157-58.

66. S.M. Paul, *Amos* (Hermeneia; Philadelphia: Fortress, 1991), pp. 16-27, 288-89.

IV. *The Sequence of Prophets within the Book of the Twelve*

Hosea to Obadiah

The order of the books within the MT Book of the Twelve requires further discussion. The redactor of the 'Joel-layer' inherited a Deuteronomic corpus that opened with Hosea. Nogalski helps understand the juxtaposition of Hosea and Joel with his observation that the antecedent for the pronoun 'this' in Joel 1.2 ('Has this happened in your days or in the days of your father?') is the series of blessings promised in Hos. 14.4-7.[67] The implied answer is 'No'. The redactor announces with the book of Joel that the blessings have been delayed, even for Judah and Jerusalem, but promises God will eventually send them. He uses the book of Amos to explain that the blessing did not come to the northern kingdom because of its sin. Nor did the blessings come to Judah and Jerusalem. The oracle predicting their destruction, whether Amos's creation or that of a redactor, had also come true.[68] The addition of 9.11-15 promises that the blessings would eventually come in connection with Judah's possession of the land of Edom, a theme explored in more detail in the book of Obadiah. L.C. Allen, in fact, called Obadiah 'a virtual commentary on Amos 9.12'.[69]

Jonah to Nahum

The connections between Jonah, Micah, and Nahum also warrant mentioning. Nogalski notes that nothing in Jon. 1.1-17 shows traces of revision in light of Obadiah.[70] Perhaps that is because with Jonah a new subject is introduced, namely, the fate of Assyria and its capital city Nineveh in particular. To be sure, Hosea had referred to Assyria in 5.13; 7.11; 8.9; 10.6; 11.5; 11.11; and 12.1, but neither Joel, Amos, nor Obadiah mentioned it. In Jonah, Micah, and Nahum, Assyria is first pardoned, then threatened with subjugation by Judah's shepherds (Mic. 5.5-6), and finally condemned to undergo God's retributive vengeance (Nah. 1.2 and frequently). The clear contrast between the perspective of the book of Jonah (as opposed to the prophet himself) and the book of

67. Nogalski, *Redactional Processes*, p. 16.

68. House, *Unity*, p. 206. House notes further that Hosea, Amos, and Obadiah point to the future when the exiles come back.

69. L.C. Allen, *The Books of Joel, Obadiah, Jonah, and Micah* (Grand Rapids: Eerdmans, 1976), p. 129.

70. Nogalski, *Redactional Processes*, p. 270.

Nahum is, thus, ameliorated by the presence of the book of Micah. The redactor's reading of history would seem to be something like this: repent though Nineveh might have done at the urging of Jonah, she apostatized by the time of Micah and deserved all the punishment Nahum envisioned.

The redactor explores these dealings of God with Assyria and Israel in light of the confessional statement found in Exod. 34.6-7, as Van Leeuwen demonstrated (see note 41). This self-description of God to Moses establishes once and for all the nature of Yahweh's relationship to his own people, and Joel 2.13 quotes part of the confession as the basis for Judah's returning to God: 'he is gracious and merciful, slow to anger and abounding in steadfast love, and repents of evil' (NRSV). Jonah complains (4.2) that since God is so gracious Jonah knew God would pardon Nineveh itself and, hence, had refused God's original command to preach to the Ninevites.

With regard to the people of Judah, Mic. 7.18 asks: 'Who is a God like you, pardoning iniquity and passing over the transgression of the remnant of your possession?' Slow to anger in the first place, he also 'does not retain his anger forever...'[71] Hence, the future looked bright for them.

God's fidelity to Israel, however, also necessitated punishing Assyria for its continued (or renewed) sins against Israel. In the opening verses of Nahum, a semi-acrostic poem that Nogalski argues was composed for the book's insertion in the Twelve,[72] one reads in v. 3: 'The Lord is slow to anger but great in power, and the Lord will by no means clear the guilty'. This verse picks up phrases from Exod. 34.6-7, and it joins them with the phrase 'but great in power'. Nahum 1.2 picks up on the treatment of the guilty and joins it with a quotation from Exod. 34.14, with the following result: 'A jealous and avenging God is the Lord, the Lord is avenging and wrathful; the Lord takes vengeance on his adversaries and rages against his enemies'. The motif that God was jealous appears as well in Joel 2.18, where God is said to have become jealous for both land and people, and in Zech. 1.14 and 8.2, where God is said

71. This quotation is followed by a comment that Nogalski (*Literary Precursors*, p. 153) thinks points to the book of Jonah as the referent for the phrase in Mic. 7.19b: 'You will cast all our sins into the depths of the sea'. It is difficult to image a person who had just read Jonah not thinking of his misfortune when reading Mic. 7.19.

72. Nogalski, *Redactional Processes*, pp. 101-11.

to have become jealous for Jerusalem. In the Zechariah verses, God is also said to feel great wrath toward the enemies, presumably the Babylonians, thus carrying the use of the 'jealous and avenging God' motif through the exile.

Nahum to Zephaniah

The placement of Habakkuk and Zephaniah needs less explanation, but two comments are apropos. (1) They fit chronologically with Nahum since all three can be read as messages from the late Assyrian period. The place of Nahum was probably secured by its relationship to Jonah. (2) The redactor of the Twelve was working with the 'Deuteronomistic Corpus', which opened with Hosea and closed with Zephaniah. Given the breadth of destruction portrayed by Zephaniah 1 and 2 (from Ethiopia to Assyria, if not the whole 'face of the earth' as 1.2-3 proclaims), Zephaniah served as a fit climax both to the four-book 'Deuteronomistic Corpus' and the expanded nine-book compilation of the pre-exilic section of the Twelve. Hence, the redactor placed Habakkuk within that framework, in other words, during the Assyrian period, but after Nahum and before Zephaniah.

Zephaniah to Malachi

All that remained was to add the post-exilic corpus Haggai/Zechariah 1–8/Malachi. He did so by appending 3.18-20 to the book of Zephaniah. Those verses contain God's promise to deal with Zion's oppressors and bring home her exiles. They also provide an introduction to the book of Haggai.[73]

V. *Conclusion and Implications*

This paper has offered three proposals with regard to the formation of the Book of the Twelve: (1) that the book of Malachi (minus 3.22-24, Eng. 4.4-6) was originally appended to Haggai/Zechariah 1–8 to explain why the future expected in those books had not yet transpired; (2) that Mal. 3.22-24 was written to conclude a canon beginning with Deuteronomy (if not the whole Pentateuch), the Deuteronomistic former prophets, as well as closing with the Twelve; and (3) that with the number of the prophets set at twelve, Zechariah 9–14 was added to the

73. Nogalski, *Literary Precursors*, pp. 201-15.

previously existing Zechariah corpus. What do these conclusions imply for reading the Twelve?

House speaks of the 'implicit narrative' within the Twelve, which he thinks employs a comic plot.[74] At least with regard to Jerusalem and Judah, it would be more accurate to speak of a 'double plot' with comic elements (in which the righteous are rewarded) and tragic elements (in which the sinful are punished).[75] For Assyria too the plot is double, though ultimately tragic, and for Edom it is unwaveringly tragic. Further, the implicit narrative is clearly historical, as this study shows and as House indicates.[76] More to the point of this study, however, is that the plot should be seen from the perspective of the post-exilic redactor, the author of Mal. 3.24-26.

As mentioned several times above, his overarching perspective, revealed in those three verses, reached back to Moses and Elijah. Glazier-McDonald rightly draws Deut. 18.15-16 and 2 Kgs 17.13-14 into the discussion of Mal. 3.22-24. Moses, conceived of in Deuteronomy as a prophet, gave the law; and the prophets, personified by Elijah, called the people to remember it.[77] These verses not only close the Twelve, but they provide one perspective from which to read the entire collection, namely backwards!

From this perspective, Haggai/Zechariah 1–8/Malachi (1) expressed hope for the future centered on the temple (Haggai/Zechariah 1–8), with the functions of Zerubbabel already handed over to Joshua (Zech. 3.8; 6.11), and (2) explained the delay in fulfilling that hope (Malachi). The redactor probably understood the 'God-fearers' addressed in Mal. 3.16-18 as the whole post-exilic community or a major part of it, rather than

74. House, *Unity*, pp. 122; citing N.K. Gottwald, 'Tragedy and Comedy in the Latter Prophets', in J.C. Exum (ed.), *Tragedy and Comedy in the Bible* (Semeia, 32; Decatur, GA.: Scholars Press, 1984), p. 84.

75. See the discussion about 'double plot' in apocalyptic rhetoric by S.D. O'Leary, *Arguing the Apocalypse: A Theory of Millennial Rhetoric* (Oxford: Oxford University Press, 1994), pp. 66-92. Larkin (*Eschatology of Second Zechariah*, p. 218) points out that the eschatological notes in Hos. 2.2, 16-17; 3.4-5 function to express hope alongside the message of doom in the opening chapters of the Twelve.

76. House, *Unity*, p. 161.

77. Glazier-McDonald, *Malachi*, pp. 266-67. One should note that she translates על in 3.24 'together with' instead of 'to' (p. 243). Elijah 'will turn the heart of the fathers together with that of the children, And the heart of the children together with that of their fathers…'

as a righteous minority. Looking further back, Habakkuk and Zephaniah anticipated the fall of Jerusalem as the result of sin. Necessarily, the sinful city of Nineveh met the same fate (see Nahum and Hab. 1.5-11, if the redactor thought of the 'wicked' as Assyria). Earlier still, Micah, Amos, and Hosea had warned the people, predicting the fall of Jerusalem and Samaria before it. Even so, within those earlier books, with the exception of Jonah, he uncovered or added passages of hope for the righteous in Jerusalem and Judah: for example, Zeph. 3.11-20; Hab. 2.2-5 and 3.13; Nah. 1.15; Mic. 4.1–5.15 and 7.8-29; Obad. 17-21; Amos 9.11-15; Joel 2.18–4.21; Hos. 1.11 and 3.5. The exception, the book of Jonah, speaks of the restoration of Nineveh, providing in concert with the book of Nahum a parallel 'double plot' of reward and punishment for that city also. A second parallel plot was the opposing futures of Judah and Edom.

Read this way, the Book of the Twelve is a historical review justifying God's past dealings with Israel and the nations. God dispensed punishment for sins, punishment concerning which the prophets had given ample warning. God also promised a new day beyond the fall of Jerusalem in the books of Joel, Obadiah, Micah, Habakkuk and Zephaniah, in addition to Haggai/Zechariah 1–8/Malachi. The readers of the Twelve would be blessed if they remembered the law and heeded the prophets, cursed if they did not.

MALACHI'S DUAL DESIGN: THE CLOSE OF THE CANON AND WHAT COMES AFTERWARD

Donald K. Berry

Malachi is not the end, at least not finally and exclusively. It may or may not have been the last book written among the twelve.[1] If it were the last, it does not present itself as a straightforward closing chapter of Yahweh's prophetic work. One clue to this exists in the word 'my messenger'—a figure promised in the book. Of course, Malachi is not the beginning either. 'Behold I send my messenger' seems to introduce God's last great work. Yet the conclusion of Malachi makes it clear that the messenger is yet to come. The Malachi who narrates the message is a figure who, like John the Baptizer, offers verbal tokens of future, if imminent events. Yet, by referring to Malachi as 'like John the Baptizer', we have reversed history. The gospel writers understood that John was the messenger returned, heralding a final solution which itself would prove a lengthy interim between prophecy and apocalypse.

For the Christian interpreter, the figure of the Christ remains distinctive, for he did not limit himself to announcements regarding what God was 'about to' do. Jesus carries unique status for Christians due to his claim that the final chapter of history had actually begun with him. Jesus embodied a mysterious anachronism: he seized the throne, acting as agent of the future. Previous messengers, like Malachi, stood at the threshhold of the eschaton. That eschaton carried either the hope of paradise or the threat of perdition, most often both. In similar fashion, all the protagonists of the Hebrew Bible, from Abraham to Moses, Elijah, and David, propel the people of God through wilderness toward death or Eden. What then represents Malachi's distinctive? Malachi marks the end of the historical depiction of this pilgrimage. Before Malachi, there

1. See B.A. Jones, *The Formation of the Book of the Twelve: A Study in Text and Canon* (SBLDS, 149; Atlanta: Scholars Press, 1995), for a plausible discussion considering Joel, Obadiah, and Jonah as the last works added to the twelve.

are prophets and this is primarily Malachi's role. After Malachi, only apocalyptic conveys Israel's vision of the future. If all Israel's messengers stood at the threshhold, Malachi's unique contribution involved a last sentimental look back at covenant and priesthood as well as unusual hints of God's final acts.

Older Traditions

This consideration of Malachi as an inclusive appendix to the Book of the Twelve and to prophecy in general begins with a comparison of the contents of the book with other segments of the canon (see Table 1). Except for the relative brevity of Malachi, this would be an impossible task. The sheer number of allusions (or instances of intertextuality) complicates the task. Such a survey faces a legitimate challenge on the basis of a cosmic theology fallacy. With such a wide sample of literature, are not coincidental parallels inevitable? Little is gained by collecting bits and pieces of every tenuous claim ever made for Malachi's relationship with other books and overwhelming the reader by the weight of accumulated evidence.

Table 1

Allusions to Canonical Traditions in Malachi

Malachi	*words or themes*	*possible sources*
1.1	משא	Isaiah 13–30 (throughout); Nah. 1.1; Hab. 1.1; Zech. 9.1; 12.1
1.1	word of the LORD	Jer. 1.2; Ezek. 1.3; Hosea (throughout); Joel (throughout); Jonah (throughout); Mic. 1.1; Zeph. 1.1; Haggai (throughout); Zech. 1.1; 8.1; 9.1
1.1	מלאכי	also 3.1; Exod. 23.20-33
1.2	I have loved you	Deut. 7.7-8; Isa. 5.1-7; Hos. 11.1
1.2	Esau/Jacob	Gen. 25.25–33.16; Obadiah
1.2-3	loved-hated	Deut. 7.9-10; 21.15; Amos 5.15; Mic. 3.2
1.4	Edom	Isaiah (5 mentions); Jeremiah (9); Ezekiel (8); Obadiah
1.8-9	show favor, gracious to us	Num. 6.25-26

Malachi	*words or themes*	*possible sources*
1.10	shut doors	Isa. 1.13; Ezek. 44.1-2; Amos 5.21-22
1.10	offering rejected	also 1.13; 2.13; 3.10; Gen. 4.1-5; Isa. 1.13; Hos. 9.4; Amos 5.21-23; many others
1.11	pure offerings from gentiles	Mic. 4; Zeph. 3.9-10 (pure speech)
2.2	curse and blessing	Deuteronomy, DtrH; Num. 5.18-27; 22.6–24.10; Neh. 13.2; Zech. 5.3; 8.13
2.3	rebuke offspring	Lev. 21.17-23
2.3	dung	Ezek. 4.12, 14-15; Nah. 3.6; Zeph. 1.17
2.4-9	covenant of Levi	Num. 18.21-32; Deut. 33.8-11; Jer. 33.21; Zech. 12.13
2.6	instruction	Lev. 10.11
2.10	God as father	also 1.2; Deut. 8.5; 14.1; 32.6
2.11	marriage to other god	Hosea
2.17	wearying God	Mic. 6.3
2.17	theodicy	Hab. 1.2-4, 13
3.1	messenger	Exod. 23.20-21; 2 Chron. 36.15-16; Obad. 1; Nah. 2.14; Zech. 1–6; 12.8
3.1	preparing way	Isa. 40.3
3.5-6	sorcerers, adulterers, swear falsely, oppressing workers/ widows/orphans/aliens	Exod. 22.17; Deut. 22.20 Decalogue; Deut. 18.10; 24.14-15; 26.12-13
3.7	return [to the LORD]	Isaiah (throughout), Jeremiah (throughout); Ezek. 43.1-9; Hos. 1–3; 14.12; Amos 4.6-11; Hag. 2.17; Zech. 1.3-4; 8.3
3.10	storehouse	Neh. 13.10-14
3.11	locust	Joel 1.4; 2.25; Amos 4.9; 7.1; Nah. 3.15-17
3.12	nations... happy	Gen. 12.3; Isa. 61.6-9
3.12	land of delight	Isa. 62.4-5
3.16	book of remembrance	Exod. 17.14; 24.7; 32.32-33; Deuteronomy; Joshua; 2 Chronicles; Nehemiah

Malachi	*words or themes*	*possible sources*
3.19	the 'day'	also 3.23; Joel 2.1-12; Amos 5.18; Obadiah; Zephaniah
3.22	Moses	Deut. 18.15-18; 34.10-12
3.23	Elijah	1 Kgs. 18.17-40; 19.8-18
use of questions		Jer. 13.12-14; Ezek. 18.1-29; Amos 3.3-7; Hab. 1.2-3; Hag. 1.4

Some of the points of contact between Malachi and other books reveal patterns. Most of these patterns have been noticed if not elaborated by previous prophetic studies. Yet the accumulation of a number of these parallels can show much about the special nature of Malachi. Every point of correspondence means something. The interpretation of the evidence offers the possibility for advances in understanding. For our purposes, all reflections of canonical theology in Malachi indicate to a greater or lesser degree (1) the book's dependence on scripture or (2) the book's awareness of scripture or (3) the awareness by the producer(s) of the book of the general situation reflected in writings of the same age as Malachi. If it is true, as I claim, that Malachi reveals intentional design for the purpose of closing a chapter in the development of canon, then the broader and more diverse the reflection of previous writings, the stronger the confirmation of the claim.

The interests of current readers of Malachi include not only historical ties to former traditions, but also the canonical interconnections of biblical books. None of the claims of the book's dependence on former writings can be finally proven. Instead, Malachi's evaluation takes place in its canonical context. Whether or not the writer, editor, or redactor intentionally encoded each allusion, each correspondence to biblical texts merits acceptance as part of a network of images orienting the message of Malachi within its 'position' as a part of the Christian scriptures, the Hebrew Bible, the minor prophets, and any specialized section within these divisions. For such purposes, concepts from the domain of comparative literary studies, such as dependence, influence, allusion, and intertextuality, serve as essential tools.[2] Malachi's influences include Zechariah, Haggai, other books of the Twelve, the major prophets, the

2. Much of the motivation for this study is owed to H. Marks's suggestion that 'intertextual echoes' (from both law and prophets) reflect Malachi's canonical position ('The Twelve Prophets' in R. Alter and F. Kermode [eds.], *The Literary Guide to the Bible* [Cambridge, MA: Harvard University Press, 1987], p. 229).

former prophets, and the Torah. Ezra and Nehemiah are important because their careers are so close to the time of Malachi's original oracles.

The use of rhetorical questions also requires some attention. Jeremiah 13.12-14 makes use of a single question involving dialogue between the prophet and hearers. Their question, 'Do you think we do not know that every wine-jar should be filled with wine?' (13.12b) leads to the prophetic announcement that God is preparing to 'fill' the land with his wrath. This question serves as a prophetic device very similar to those of Malachi. Some even more striking parallels appear in Ezek. 18.1-4, 19-32. God questions the people and voices their questions in a prophetic dialogue similar to Malachi. The people are asked why they quote the 'sour grapes' proverb in v. 2. The dialogues introduced with 'yet you say' suggest direct influence on the form of the Malachi dialogues.

> Yet you say, 'Why should not the son suffer for the iniquity of the father?' (v. 19)

> Yet you say, 'The way of the Lord is unfair.' Hear now, O house of Israel. Is my way unfair? Is it not your ways that are unfair? (v. 25, repeated in v. 29)

The questions in Mal. 2.17 also seem to relate to the issue of God's justice. The rhetorical questions in Amos 3.3-7 are proverbial and are scarcely related to the message of Malachi. Yet their message, like Malachi's, involves God's punishment of his people. Malachi's view of a judgement by fire could well be influenced by this and other passages from Amos.

Rhetorical questions also serve as a major structuring device in other minor prophets.[3] Haggai contains several and 1.4 provides the basis for the entire message of the prophet. 'Is it a time for you yourselves to live in paneled houses, while this house lies in ruins?' Habakkuk also begins with questions, this time regarding God's justice (1.2-3).

Numerous prophetic studies suppose that the book of Malachi was originally the last of three oracles beginning in Zechariah 9. Blenkinsopp suggested that all three began as anonymous supplements[4] because of the similarities of the inscriptions of Zech. 9.1; 12.1 and Mal. 1.1. On the other hand, some scholars argued that Zech. 9.1 was modified to include

3. See K.M. Craig, Jr, 'Interrogatives in Haggai-Zechariah: A Literary Thread?', in this volume.

4. J. Blenkinsopp, *Prophecy and Canon: A Contribution to the Study of Jewish Origins* (Notre Dame: University of Notre Dame Press, 1977), p. 108.

the word משׂא 'burden' and Zech. 12.1 was inserted by an editor or author who placed the word at the head of Malachi.[5] The word משׂא appears commonly in the prophets, most often in Isaiah 13–30, but also in the introductions to Nahum and Habakkuk. Whether the work of author or redactor, the presence of the word constitutes an important connection with previous traditions on the level of a direct literary influence.

The 'burden' of the messenger is described as the 'word of Yahweh' (Mal. 1.1). This phrase serves as a broad, if weak, allusion especially to the past work of the prophets which includes prophets who, like Moses, mediated God's word in terms other than oracles. Yet the term is especially common as an introduction to speeches by the latter prophets. Both they and Malachi use it as a general allusion which reinforces their message by connecting it to widely acknowledged sacred communication. Malachi also uses the phrase to mark the immediacy of the communication by announcing its divine origin. So the phrase, 'word of the LORD' serves to emphasize both the authority of static documents and the transcendent voice of God.

The message of the book is fittingly conveyed by מלאכי (1.1 and 3.1). A second occurrence in 3.1 involves the construct state with the word 'covenant' as its antecedent (מלאך הברית). The issue of whether Malachi is a proper name or not remains unsettled. If it is read as the name of an individual, one must ask why the identical word in 3.1 should not be read that way. The question with regard to מלאכי in 1.1 involves more than an either/or choice. It could be an appellative without naming an individual prophet. This would help to account for both the LXX reading (ἀγγέλου αὐτοῦ 'his angel') which renders the word as though it were not a proper name and the addition of the Targums, '...who is Ezra the scribe'. The word itself begs for further identification since it designated divine emissaries and the prophets as such.[6] The same can be said of Elijah in 3.23. His introduction uses terms almost identical to the introduction of the מלאכי of 3.1 and Elijah's role, like that of the

5. W. Rudolph, *Haggai–Sacharja 1–8–Sacharja 9–14–Malachi* (KAT, 13.4; Gütersloh: Gütersloher Verlagshaus Mohn, 1976), pp. 168 n. 1(a), 253; J. Nogalski, *Redactional Processess in the Book of the Twelve* (BZAW, 218; New York: de Gruyter, 1993).

6. P.R. House, *The Unity of the Twelve* (Sheffield: Almond Press, 1990), p. 186. House claimed that the Book of the Twelve assumes the identity of the prophet as messenger.

messenger, is to prepare for a divine visitation. Admittedly, all these cross connections fit together loosely, yet, in its present canonical shape, such shadowy intertextuality provides much of the distinct message of the book.

In a similar fashion, the words 'I have loved you' recall the touching illustration following God's declaration of love in Hos. 11.1. This constitutes a more subtle, though less puzzling, allusion to the prophetic canon. The idea of God's love as motivation for his relationship with Israel also serves as the controlling theme of Isaiah's song of the vineyard (5.1-7). In Malachi, God's love is conveyed through election. That love motivated his choice of Israel and his rejection of Esau. Esau represents a host of others (for example, Cain, Lot, and Saul) who played out the tragic role of proximity to but exclusion from God's blessing. Malachi's use of the word שׂנא provides a key to this interpretation. It can designate not only literal hatred but also the misfortunate circumstance of being the second choice.[7] Deuteronomy 21.15 uses שׂנא to designate the wife less favored by her husband than another wife. God's personal choice of Israel constituted a mystery interpreted as both challenge and blessing by Israel's historians. How could one take for granted or respond casually to such good fortune? Continued emphasis on the human response to divine covenant throughout Malachi places prominent emphasis on this theme.

The word pair שׂנא/אהב occurs in Amos 5.15 and in Mic. 3.2. Both place the vocabulary within the framework of moral choice and both use the terms 'good' and 'evil' as the objects of the verbs. Amos presents the imperative construction, 'Hate evil and love good!' This completes a chiasm begun with 'Seek good and not evil' in 5.14. The unit displays a tight construction indicating its usefulness as a summary of Amos's message. The first half of the chiastic structure occurs at the precise center of the book of Amos.[8] Micah 3.2 uses the word pair in a relative clause, 'who hate the good and love the evil'. Such an affront to logic designates perverseness to the point of nonsense. The people's question

7. M.E. Tate proposed that 'hated' actually designated one less loved. In this passage in Malachi, he suggested the term love indicated a sort of international covenant. So God shows his 'love' by hating/destroying Edom, in other words, acting in good faith to honor covenant ('Questions for Priests and People in Malachi 1:2–2:16', *RevExp* 84 [1987], pp. 394-95).

8. See F.I. Andersen and D.N. Freedman, *Amos* (AB, 24a; New York: Doubleday, 1989), p. 504.

in Mal. 1.2, 'How have you loved us?' constitutes a similar breach of logic and similar perverseness. God has loved his people and destroyed their adversaries. The text of Malachi indicates that his people had not followed suit by 'loving good' and 'hating evil' as his prophets commanded.

Mentions of Edom (1.4) are especially common in the major prophets. The name occurs five times in Isaiah, nine times in Jeremiah, and eight times in Ezekiel. Its frequent mention is easily understandable in terms of the historical circumstances of the rival kingdoms. Jeremiah 49.7-22 and Ezek. 25.12-14 present oracles against Edom which promise the sort of destruction Malachi envisions. Among the minor prophets, of course, Obadiah presents the strongest interest in Edom. Obadiah's vision of God's punishment of Edom involves the day of the LORD (vv. 15-18). The related images of fire in Mal. 3.19-21 differ in that the source of the fire in Obadiah is God's people while in Malachi fire symbolizes the day of the LORD itself. Whereas Obadiah looks forward to the escape of 'Jacob and Joseph', the content of Malachi considers the punishment of unfaithful Israelites and the vindication of the faithful from other nations (with the probable exclusion of Edom).

The portion of the dialogue in Mal. 1.6–2.9 seems a parody of the priestly blessing of Num. 6.23-27. Malachi negates the blessing in both content and style. This is a case of direct literary influence. The book employs the ironic restatement of the components of the blessing as illustration of the disruption of divine order and blessing. The irony is heightened in that the loss of blessing is a direct result of the corruption of the priestly office.[9] (See further below.)

The words 'shut the door' have some parallels in the prophetic literature. Isaiah 1.13 similarly calls for a halt to all worship until justice is employed in Israel. In a related vein, Ezekiel's vision of the temple contains a provision that the eastern gate, through which Yahweh has entered, remain shut (44.1-2). The issue, as in Malachi, involves consecration and defilement. In Ezekiel, the gate is holy due to God's presence. In Malachi, all the gates are to be shut to protect the sanctuary from impure offerings.

Amos 5.21-23, like Isaiah, connects the unaccepted worship to the unacceptable lifestyles of the worshipers. God hates what they offer and refuses to accept it. The refusal of offerings recurs four times in the book

9. M. Fishbane, *Biblical Interpretation in Ancient Israel* (Oxford: Clarendon Press, 1985), pp. 332-34.

of Malachi (1.10, 13; 2.13, and 3.10). The programmatic example of the rejected offering in the Hebrew Bible is God's rejection of Cain's offering in Gen. 4.1-5. It would not have gone unnoticed by the producer of Malachi that Cain's offering was rejected without cause, while the rejection of the offerings of the restoration community was induced by improper attention to cultic regulations. If Yahweh rejected Cain's offering due to his connection with the Canaanites, conversely, he rejected his people's offering in Malachi because they were his people. Cain possessed no distinct obligations, while the members of the community of Malachi were unfaithful to their covenant obligations. In Isa. 1.13 and Amos 5.21-23, the motivations for God's rejection of the offerings are moral rather than cultic. In Malachi, the object of injustice is not the poor or disenfranchised, but Yahweh himself. Perhaps the distinction is less important than it seems to the contemporary interpreter since both social obligations and ritual performance were regulated by the same code.

Amid such cultic concerns, it is most surprising to discover Malachi advocating multinational Yahwism. The nations offer 'incense' and 'a pure offering' (1.11), by implication, a purer worship than the Levites. This expression may depend on Zephaniah's eschatological vision (3.9-10):

> At that time I will change the speech of the peoples
> to a pure speech,
> that all of them may call on the name of the LORD
> and serve him with one accord.
> From beyond the rivers of Ethiopia
> my suppliants, my scattered ones,
> shall bring my offering.

The 'pure speech' corresponds to Malachi's 'pure offering' as indicated by the mention of an offering in the last line of 3.10. In Zephaniah, this reverses the effect of Babel. Perhaps the author of Malachi assumes Zephaniah's hope fulfilled in the days of the new temple community. This can only be partially true since Malachi's view of the present seems otherwise so caustic. An even more important correspondence with Malachi's 'pure offerings' appears in the fourth chapter of Micah.

> In the days to come
> the mountain of the LORD's house
> shall be established as the highest of the mountains,
> and shall be raised up above the hills.
> Peoples shall stream to it,
> and many nations shall come... (Mic. 4.1-2a)

The connection with Micah 4 assumes even more importance when Micah is considered the center of the Book of the Twelve. It is the sixth book and perhaps the fourth chapter, with its emphasis on the restored temple as a site for the worship of all peoples, which marks the precise center of the Twelve.[10] The 'all peoples' motif occurs in numerous late prophetic passages. It is difficult to understand its role in Malachi's message which otherwise involves priestly sectarian interests. Yet many other features of Malachi suggest an indiscriminate selection of unrelated themes combined to achieve synthetic comprehension rather than thematic uniformity.

Malachi 2.2 reflects the less universal concerns of the priesthood. It employs the blessing and curse terminology common to the Deuteronomistic History. The phrase 'curse your blessing' is unique. Malachi uses familiar ideas common to Israel's populace but places them within the framework of demonic (in other words, negative) imagery. Curse and blessing were well understood, but Malachi interprets such cultic practice in foreign ways intended to shock his readers. The suggestion that God will reverse the Deuteronomic blessing indicates that the deity has drastically changed the rules. Such vacillation can only be explained as the result of anger due to extreme provocation. Perhaps there is slight influence from the oath of the woman accused of unfaithfulness in Num. 5.18-27. Her oath results in a curse if she has been dishonest. Similarly, Yahweh's grant to Israel of land, dwellings, and vineyards which they did not work for (Deut. 6.10-11) was complemented with the threat that God could also grant Israel's accomplishments to their enemies due to disobedience (Amos 5.11). Balaam's 'curse' of Num. 22.6–24.10 serves as a compelling mirror image of the passage in Malachi. According to both the passage in Numbers and a later notation in Neh. 13.2, Balaam's intended curse turned into a blessing whereas the restoration community's blessing would be transformed into a curse. In contrast, Zechariah uses references to curses and blessings traditionally. The flying scroll of Zech. 5.3 presents a curse on those who steal or who swear falsely in God's name. Zech. 8.13 promises God's blessing in compensation for the curse they previously endured as his punishment. This almost directly opposes the perspective of Malachi.

The reference to God's humiliation of his people through the use of dung (2.3) offers an even more shocking description of his retribution. According to the image, God soils his own hands with the unclean stuff.

10. J.D.W. Watts, 'Introduction to Malachi', *RevExp* 84 (1987), p. 379.

Such an action on God's part would certainly have been incredible for the priests whom the text addresses. The dung of the sacrificial animals is never referred to in quite this way. The only references to dung in the Torah involve its inclusion in bodies of animals burned in a clean place outside camp (Exod. 29.14 and Lev. 4.11). Ezekiel was asked to cook with human dung (גל) and instead was allowed to use cow's dung (4.12, 14-15). Nahum's 'filth' is thrown at the inhabitants of Nineveh as though they are prostitutes subject to public humiliation. Nahum's שקצים 'filth', like Malachi's פרש 'dung', is cultic terminology. It designates unclean things including such diverse items as food and idols. Most likely the objects thrown in Nahum are household garbage. The use of the word גל 'dung' in Zeph. 1.17 evokes the stronger image of the people's flesh scattered like dung as the result of a horrible battle. This entails no special cultic reference or vocabulary. Again, Malachi employs familiar images in strange ways. This is also true of the rebuke of offspring (also in Mal. 2.3) which may be related to the banishment of the deformed from the rite of sacrifice (Lev. 21.17-23). God treats their children as though they are unclean.

In this passage, the cultic references support the Syriac and Targums reading, 'put you out of my presence' rather than the MT, 'lift you to it'. The idea seems to be that God considers them defiled and will consequently exclude them from his presence. Dung in and of itself would not do this, but the symbol of humiliation shows them unfit to offer sacrifices. God makes use not of the offerings themselves, but of their dung in another demonic reading.

The covenant of Levi discussed in 2.4-9 accords with no single covenant or ceremony elsewhere in the Hebrew Bible. It displays some connection with Num. 18.21-32, which describes the tithe and landholdings with which the Levites are rewarded for their service in the tent of meeting. Yet the passage contains no mention of special cultic responsibilities such as those implied in Mal. 2.4-9. Deuteronomy 33.8-11 contains some stronger parallels, but it scarcely involves a covenant. The blessing of Levi fits in with the blessings of the other tribes by Moses. The tribe of Levi is given the responsibility for the Urim and Thummim in return for faithfulness in the wilderness. Their responsibility for instruction is mentioned in Deut. 33.10. Priestly instruction serves as an important theme in Malachi and is alluded to in Mal. 2.6. This may be compared to Aaron's responsibility to teach Mosaic laws (Lev. 10.11). The tribal blessing of Deuteronomy also includes a reference to their burning incense and offering whole burnt offerings. The pattern of Malachi's intertextual connection with the Torah shows a looser affiliation with the content of the law than with the content of the prophets. Malachi's contents often parallel the statements of the Latter Prophets but tend toward vague allusions to the books of the Torah. The reference to Levi is one of these bland allusions. Among the Latter Prophets the name Levi occurs only in Malachi and Zech. 12.13, where 'the house of Levi' names one of the families who will be in mourning at the eschaton. If the reference has priestly overtones, they are not apparent. Only the Deuteronomist, among the Torah, describes the 'sons of Levi' as priests (Deut. 21.5; 31.9). Mention of the levitical priest as the messenger of Yahweh seems to relate to traditions common to the restoration period, yet before Ezra. By the time of the Chronicler, the offices of priest and Levite were clearly separated (1 Chron. 23).

The 'covenant with the wife of your youth' elaborated in 2.13-16 along with the mention of the marriage with 'the daughter of a foreign god' in 2.11 calls to mind the relationship between Hosea and Gomer in Hosea 1–2.[11] Seemingly, the divorce involves a Hebrew wife who was consequently left without advocacy in the community. This may narrow the reference to 'father' in 2.10 to the creation of Israel as a people rather than the creation of all humans. It is not surprising that Hosea's divine directive to marry an immoral woman is not reflected here. Hosea's experience was exceptional and symbolic of God's love for unworthy Israel. The book of Malachi encourages the general populace to follow Hosea's example of maintaining the relationship with a first wife. The influence of Hosea especially applies to the importance of proper social relations in the milieu of the divine covenant.

This covenant background surely informs the concept of 'wearying God'.[12] The question itself is almost directly borrowed from Mic. 6.3:

> O my people, what have I done to you?
> In what have I wearied you? Answer me!

11. T. Collins, *The Mantle of Elijah: The Redaction Criticism of the Prophetical Books* (Biblical Seminar, 20; Sheffield: JSOT Press, 1993), p. 66. Collins saw the influence of Hosea also in the reference to God as father in 2.10 (p. 81).

12. The verb employed in Malachi is יגע and the verb employed in Micah is לאה. They are near synonyms with the slight difference that the verb of Malachi connotes weariness as the result of labor while לאה indicates weariness from hardships of other sorts as well (such as frustration). See *BDB*, pp. 388 and 521. לאה also occurs with God as object in Isa. 7.13.

Malachi 2.17 simply reverses the subject and object of the action:

> You have wearied the LORD with your words. Yet you say, 'How have we wearied him?' By saying, 'All who do evil are good in the sight of the LORD, and he delights in them'. Or by asking, 'Where is the God of justice?'

The verse in Micah is the opening question of a divine lawsuit against the people. It involves two important elaborations: first, God's deliverance from Egypt, specifically mentioning the Balak–Balaam incident, and second, the people's empty ritual due to moral corruptness. In Malachi the question concerns theodicy. This could be linked with the people's failure to live up to covenant ideals. 'Since God shows favor to the evil, why bother to do good?' Or, 'If the God of justice disappears, no one holds us accountable for fairness.'

If the passage matches the vocabulary and rhetoric of Mic. 6.3, a closer match with respect to theme occurs in Habakkuk. Habakkuk 1.2-4 expresses concern for God's inactivity in response to violence. 'The law becomes slack and justice never prevails' (Hab. 1.4) shows a despondency similar to that assumed in Mal. 1.17. Malachi, unlike Habakkuk, allows no debate on issues related to theodicy. In this verse, claims of unfairness are dismissed as empty excuses and evidences of the pattern of rebellion the prophet condemns. The people have denied one of the central tenets of Malachi's prophecy. God punishes the disobedient. The book of Habakkuk counsels patience on the part of the worshiper. The tone of Malachi implies that divine patience is exhausted perhaps because speculations on injustice have led to desperate breeches of law and order. There is some indication of this in Mal. 1.13, which uses the noun תלאה 'weariness' to describe the people's attitude toward sacrifice. Their skepticism does not serve Malachi's purpose of consolidation.

The introduction of the messenger/angel of Mal. 3.1 plays a pivotal role in Malachi's design and message. The messenger is introduced with phraseology that shows direct influence from Exod. 23.20-21:

> I am going to send an angel in front of you, to guard you on the way and to bring you to the place that I have prepared. Be attentive to him and listen to his voice; do not rebel against him, for he will not pardon your transgression; for my name is in him.

The implications are discussed in the following section of this article. At this point it suffices to claim that the messenger of Mal. 3.1

comprehensively names the prophet, the divine visitor of Exodus, the levitical priest, and the eschatological prophet who is Elijah.

Nahum 2.14 may provide some of the background of Malachi's theology of the messenger/angel. If so, Nahum's assumption that the human messengers who protect the community are cut off leads to Malachi's suggestion that a divine messenger will appear to introduce God's last judgement and eschatological hopes. (Cf. the Chronicler's claim that Israel repeatedly ignored the warning of God's messengers/prophets, for example, 2 Chron. 36.15-16.) Malachi promises one last messenger to prepare for God's last work. A stronger tie occurs in the angel who mediates the divine message in Zechariah 1–6. Nogalski suggested that the storyline running from Haggai through Malachi is interrupted by Zechariah 9–14.[13] The messenger of Mal. 3.1 could reflect not only the angel of Zechariah 1–8 but also the introduction of the visitations of Zechariah 9–14. Zechariah 12.8 claims that the house of David will play the role of the guiding angel of God in wars. Assuming that Malachi responded to the eschatology of Zechariah 9–14, Malachi indicated that before these events God himself would send a messenger to warn all and guide the obedient. This messenger mysteriously combines the roles of prophet and angel. Yet the central role of this figure is to prepare for God's direct intervention (Isa. 40.3). In many ways the strongest tie between Malachi's messenger and previous prophetic literature is the messenger of Obad. 1. Like Malachi's messenger, the figure in Obadiah introduces the Day of the LORD. The book of Malachi very likely presumes this background and further defines the nature of Obadiah's 'day'.

Concerning the judgement accompanying the divine visit, Malachi cites codes of conduct in the Torah. The legislation involves injunctions against sorcerers, adulterers, and those who swear falsely, as well as those who oppress workers, widows, aliens, and orphans. The legal material on which these are based is shared by Deuteronomy and Exodus: the Decalogue; Exod. 22.18, 20-23; Deut. 18.10; 24.14-15; 26.12-13. Though the references come directly from the Pentateuch, they do not seem to play a strong role in the distinctive work of Malachi.

The emphasis upon the people's return in 3.7 comes from the prophetic literature. The theme is so important for Isaiah and Jeremiah that their numerous mentions cannot be listed. Ezekiel emphasizes the special theme of God's return to the temple (43.1-9). Although the

13. Nogalski, *Redactional Processes*, p. 204.

terminology is different, Mal. 3.1 mentions God's return. Malachi regards the event with awe equal to that of Ezekiel, but Malachi's emphasis goes beyond Ezekiel's vision of the renewed temple.

Among the minor prophets, Hosea 1–3 emphasizes God's wish that Israel return to Yahweh. The closing verse of the unit mentions this explicitly (3.5). Malachi complements Hosea's call for return by indicating that God had forsaken his people and would not return until they did. The closing chapter of Hosea also summons Israel to return (14.2). Amos 4.6-11 lists five catastrophes God had sent to induce their return. In each case their failure to return is recorded. Haggai 2.17 seems to allude to Amos 4.9 through the use of the word pair 'blight and mildew'. Malachi similarly depended on Zech. 1.3 for the statement 'return to me and I will return to you'. Zechariah 8.3 reiterates Ezekiel's message that God would return to Jerusalem, though Zechariah fails to mention the temple. Malachi 3.1 indicates God's return to the temple. On the side of the people's response, Mal. 3.7 hopes for the return to covenant law which somehow constitutes the return to God. This context for 'return' is especially important in Zech. 1.3-4.

The reference to the temple storehouse recalls a passage in Neh. 13.10-14. Due to the lack of tithes, the Levites were working in the fields for their livelihood instead of attending to their temple duties. In Nehemiah, this is not tied to the lack of blessing of Yahweh's community, but the logic followed in Malachi is not difficult to grasp. Malachi considers the withholding of tithes a matter of robbing God which brings a corollary curse. Complying with the rules regarding temple donations would yield immediate blessing.

Malachi 3.10-11 also reflects emphases in Haggai and Joel.[14] Haggai 2.18-19 connects the blessing of the community with the building of the temple. Joel 1.16-17 mentions storehouses, albeit the storehouses of the people, which are empty on the verge of the day of the LORD. Joel 2.23-25 combines showers and locusts with a similar emphasis on God's blessing as evident in the presence of the former and the absence of the latter. Joel discusses (ch. 1) and Malachi implies that Yahweh's displeasure is communicated through locust and drought. References to locusts also appear in Amos 4.9 and 7.1 as implements of God's destruction. Locusts serve as a symbol of the destruction of battle in Nah. 3.15. When God rebukes the locust, the nations will account Judah happy.

14. As noted by Nogalski, *Redactional Processes*, pp. 205-206.

There is something of a reiteration of Abraham's blessing here (Gen. 12.3), in spite of the fact that the word used here is אשׁר 'to pronounce happy' rather than ברך 'to bless'. The eyes of all the nations are upon Israel, beholding the blessing mentioned in 3.10. Malachi's understanding of the blessing resulting from faithfulness bears an intertextual relationship with the vision of Isa. 61.1-9. Verse 9 places special emphasis upon the restored community's standing in the eyes of the nations.

Closely related to the theme of the nations' recognition of their good fortune is the description of Israel as a land of delight. Another close parallel exists in Isaiah. Isaiah 62.4 attaches the name 'My Delight is in Her' (among other names) to the land. Perhaps Malachi uses this literature to paint the strongest possible picture of the blessing that results from obedience.

One of the most interesting features of Malachi is the mention of the book of remembrance in 3.16. It is impossible to say precisely what type of document is intended. The book may refer to a recorded copy of a covenant which would have included the signatures or names of the parties involved. Perhaps this is what Moses meant by asking to be blotted from the book that God had written (Exod. 32.32). The book of the covenant appears in Exod. 24.7. It seems to contain God's demands of his people who respond by pledging their loyalty. In Exod. 17.14 a book records God's promise to annihilate Amalek. Like the mention in Malachi, its record 'reminds' God to eradicate 'their remembrance'. Such books apparently either offered God's life or death. The book of remembrance in Mal. 3.16 promises life. The books of Deuteronomy and Joshua as well as those of 2 Chronicles and Nehemiah contain repeated references to the 'book of law'. These references tend to combine the theme of blessing and curse with the theme of covenant. The book of remembrance in Malachi does not seem limited to a list of names. The book was written 'before him *to* or *for* those fearing Yahweh and thinking of his name'.

Beyond the traditional references implied by Malachi's 'book of remembrance', the book suggests some of the radical views of present and future contained in apocalyptic. Though Malachi as a whole is scarcely apocalyptic in any sense, some of its images could be used to lay the groundwork for an apocalyptic message. These include the divine messenger, the day of the LORD, the promise of Elijah, and most importantly the mention of this book of remembrance. Apocalyptic arose partly from the birth of sects. Malachi 3.16 offers the kind of concept which readily appealed to such groups. All that remained was for a group to identify themselves with the exclusive community of God identified in the 'book'. Given the prophetic understanding of Malachi, it is hard to imagine such a writing as the 'book of remembrance' would have remained unknown. Many of the hints and allusions of other prophets came to life in the worlds 'created' by the apocalypticists. This is not to suggest such a community can be identified directly with the message of Malachi. The point is that Malachi lends itself to such a reading due to its mysterious references to future occurrences.

An additional reference to such occurrences is the mention of the day of the LORD in 3.19. This concept holds great importance for several books of the Twelve, but it is less important elsewhere, indeed, scarcely mentioned outside the Latter Prophets. Malachi 3.19 associates two images of fire with the day. First, it envisions an oven (one thinks of Daniel's companions) which will destroy the evildoers. Second, it presents the rising sun under whose light the righteous enjoy life. Malachi 3.23 adds the association of Elijah with the day of the LORD. Joel 2.1-12 depicts the day of the LORD with both fire and battle. Joel presents the day as an entirely demonic event. The day of the LORD brings catastrophe avoided only by repentance (v. 12). Joel mentions not the sun of righteousness, but the darkening of the sun as characteristic of the day. Amos's view of the day of the LORD in 5.18 is also negative although it is clear that his contemporaries understood the day differently. Like Joel, Amos presents it as a day of darkness which appears total. The darkness of Egypt during the plagues comes to mind.

In Obadiah, the day heralds divine intervention rather than the march of Israel's armies against foes. Obadiah saw the day as a sort of final act of God on a par with his aid to the nation in past history. Its result would be Israel's repossession of all the promised land. Various verses describing what Edom did 'on the day' provide the motivation for divine action. The image of fire in v. 18 refers to Jacob and Joseph's burning of Esau (like stubble, as in Mal. 3.19). The day of divine visitation is introduced by 'a messenger'. It seems that Malachi 3 depends on Obadiah for the demonic side of the day of the LORD imagery, but Malachi has changed the texture of the day by applying it principally to Israel.

The day of the Lord as conceived by Zephaniah begins with utter devastation. God's own people receive the brunt of the punishment due to worship of foreign gods. The day brings principally war and darkness (whether figurative or literal, 1.15). Hope remains for the 'humble of the land' (2.3; 3.12). The fire of the day of the LORD is associated with God's anger in 3.8. In spite of the negative picture of the day, it results in purification and a new obedient community purged of the unrighteous. So, Zephaniah may provide the background for the two sided nature (reward and punishment) of the day presumed in Malachi.

Careful design on the part of editor or redactor brought about the reference to Moses which supplements the message of Malachi. It should be read as an integral part of the work, in part because of the references to Mosaic legislation throughout Malachi. Two counterposed messages from Deuteronomy inform the allusion to Moses. The first promises the succession of Moses by another prophet like him (Deut. 18.18). This clearly indicates Joshua, but biblical references to the future are rarely fixed by later history. Since the passage does not identify Joshua by name, the promise remains open for future fulfillment. The second passage could actually loosen the association between Moses and Joshua assumed by the first. It proclaims that Israel has never known a prophet like Moses with whom God spoke person to person (Deut. 34.10). For reasons more fully explained later, the reader may understand Malachi to refer to an eschatological figure as well as the prophet Moses. God's revelation to Moses at Horeb came through fire (Deut. 5.1-5). Similarly, God met Elijah at Horeb and displayed his power in fire before speaking to him (1 Kgs 19.8-18). Links such as this suggest that Moses and Elijah serve as future as well as past figures.

In Malachi, Elijah plays the specific role of preparing Israel for the day of the LORD. The association of the day of the LORD with the general theme of theophany, concomitant with Elijah's experiences (1 Kgs 18.17-40; 19.11-18), and its association with the destruction of Baal worshipers in Zeph. 1.4 suggest Elijah's strong ties with the day of the LORD.[15] B.S. Childs elaborated several connections between Elijah and Malachi:

> Like Malachi, Elijah addressed 'all Israel' (1 Kings 18.20). The people of Israel were severely fragmented by indecision of faith (18.21). A curse had fallen on the land (18.1 // Mal. 3.24, EVV 4.6). Elijah challenged all Israel to respond to God by forcing a decision between the right and the wrong (// Mal. 3.18). He did it by means of the right offering (// Mal. 3.3) and a fire which fell from heaven (// Mal. 3.3, 19).[16]

15. Y. Hoffmann, 'The Day of the Lord as a Concept and a Term in the Prophetic Literature', *ZAW* 93 (1981), pp. 44-45.

16. B.S. Childs, *Introduction to the Old Testament as Scripture* (Philadelphia: Fortress, 1979), pp. 495-96.

Elijah is not mentioned elsewhere in the Latter Prophets. This makes his appearance at the conclusion of Malachi even more compelling. It seems unlikely that the Elijah character of Malachi designated any particular person of Malachi's age.[17] Instead, his appearance would mark the end of history as humans know it. John, the Elijah figure of the New Testament, fills precisely this role. His appearance marks the beginning of the end.

Some correspondence with the combination of Moses and Elijah exists in Zechariah 3–4. In Zechariah the priest, Joshua represents the law and Zerubbabel serves as the prophetic figure. Otherwise, the affiliation with Malachi is loose. The actions of Zerubbabel in receiving the prophetic word and Joshua in atoning for the people's sin relate more to the present community than the future. Yet the promise of the Davidic ruler suggests stronger ties to the future than may otherwise be apparent.

Key Themes

Among the themes identified in the foregoing section several appear as organizing media in Malachi. Standing over and above all the rest is the issue of covenant. This organizing theme best accounts for the whole of the book. Malachi does not define covenant, but it assumes it. The concept of covenant present in Malachi draws from various segments of the canon of law and prophets. Some sections receive more attention in Malachi, but it seems safe to assume that Malachi's messages developed within the milieu of a relatively full canon. Because of all the assumed tradition 'behind' Malachi, the eclectic style of the book appears somewhat incoherent. On the other hand, by elaborating more fully some of the traditions behind the work, Malachi's messages take on more clarity. We cannot presume to give clear definition to all the features of Malachi, but we can attempt to understand the general motivations behind many of its more ambiguous allusions.

It has already been noted that elements of Mal. 1.6–2.9 reflect awareness of the Aaronic Benediction (Num. 6.22-27):

17. W.J. Dumbrell ('Malachi and the Ezra-Nehemiah Reforms', *RTR* 35 [1976], p. 52) suggested that the original Elijah character was Ezra. When hopes in Ezra went unrealized, the later prophetic community looked forward to God's personal intervention in history.

> The LORD spoke to Moses, saying: Speak to Aaron and his sons, saying, Thus you shall bless the Israelites. You shall say to them,
> The LORD bless you and keep you;
> the LORD make his face to shine upon you and be gracious unto you;
> the LORD lift up his countenance upon you, and give you peace.
> So they shall put my name on the Israelites, and I will bless them.

Malachi 1.6–2.9 in many ways parodies the content of the priestly blessing. It employs a vocabulary and style that negate the blessing in both content and style. Malachi's ironic restatement of the blessing illustrates the disruption of divine order and blessing owed to the corruption of the priestly office.[18] For example, 1.8 discusses the possibility that God will show his people favor in light of their improper offerings. The benediction's 'lift up his countenance' reflects Malachi's 'show you favor'. Further, 1.9 uses the very words of the blessing—'be gracious [to us]'. Marks noted the following shared elements: (1) despising rather than conferring God's name, (2) curses instead of blessings, and (3) kindling altar fires rather than making God's face to shine.[19]

Malachi's use of the Aaronic Benediction constitutes dependence of a special type, as if the ritual offenses of Malachi were an overlay which took shape against the backdrop of the priestly blessing. At each turn, God's response to priestly work negates the blessing. The priests were to confer God's blessing on the people by the use of the benediction, but their intended blessing turns out to be a profane curse because God has rejected the priests and their message. Actually, the curse falls upon the priests for their poor example.

At first investigation, the Aaronic Benediction appears to be a major theme of Malachi. In actuality, it serves as an elaborate concrete illustration of the general problem of the corrupt priesthood. The priests' own liturgical literature becomes the means for their condemnation.

Other than the single passage from Numbers, nearly all other references to priestly duties presuppose Deuteronomy. Jeremiah 33.21-22, like the Deuteronomistic literature throughout, make 'Levites' and 'priests' equivalents. The book of Jeremiah described the covenant with Levi, so essential to the message of Malachi, as an everlasting covenant. Jeremiah 33.21-22 affixed the theme of the covenant of Levi to the more integral theme of the Davidic covenant. In this way, the priestly hegemony rested upon the shoulders of Davidic promises (33.25-26). If

18. Fishbane, *Biblical Interpretation*, pp. 332-34.
19. 'The Twelve Prophets', p. 230.

this is the passage from which Malachi borrowed the language, Malachi developed it according to the full range of priestly responsibilities and in connection with the complete range of Israel's history. Malachi is immersed in Deuteronomic theology.

Connections between Malachi and Deuteronomy begin with the first verse of each. Both are addressed to Israel, even though Malachi's words are primarily directed to those of the temple area. Perhaps there is an inclusio of features from the Deuteronomic History. Malachi begins with the beginning of Deuteronomy and concludes with references to Moses and Elijah.[20] Its Deuteronomistic nature is incontestable. The position of Malachi among the twelve may have exercised some influence on its particular Deuteronomistic bent.[21] The editor used the closing book to sum up many of the far reaching concerns of the unit. Malachi becomes the principal secondary source for those valuing Deuteronomistic theology in the mid fifth century. The redactor who appended the reference to Moses in 3.22 understood and affirmed this. Deuteronomy 18.18 implied that all future prophets would resemble Moses. Though the context of 18.18 mentions only the rejection of other gods, Fishbane is correct in seeing a reference to covenant legislation in the verse.[22] It is precisely the mediation of the law that indicates the divine use of Moses and by which the future prophet would resemble Moses. This invites the testing of all prophets on the basis of the legislation of the Torah. A prophet 'like Moses' would not challenge the basic Torah and Mal. 3.22 immortalizes this claim. The concern for priestly instruction in ch. 2 can also be read against these issues.

20. Dumbrell, 'Malachi', p. 49. Perhaps Malachi's ties to former priestly traditions are moderated through the reforms of Ezra and Nehemiah. According to Dumbrell, the book constituted 'a last prophetic protest against...developing tendencies towards total priestly control' (p. 43). If this is true one would expect more general condemnations of priests and less emphasis on the purification of priests. Instead, the content resembles that of an apology for the Levitical priesthood.

21. Collins, *Mantle of Elijah*, p. 62. Whoever was responsible for producing the text of the twelve (Collins presumes it was done as a whole) shared the concerns of the Deuteronomistic writers. Malachi espouses D theology 'in general'.

22. *Biblical Interpretation*, p. 536.

Table 2

Ritual Offenses Indicated in Malachi

Verses	*Charge*
1.7-8, 13-14	offering polluted food
1.12	saying the LORD's table is polluted
2.8	corrupt instruction
2.10-12	foreign worship in sanctuary
2.15-16	divorce
3.5	sorcerers, adulterers, false oaths; oppressing workers, widows, and orphans.
3.8-10	withholding tithe
2.17; 3.13-15	denying God's justice (theodicy)

Malachi provides a remarkably comprehensive list of ritual offenses (see Table 2). All, it seems, are ritual offenses in that Torah legislation forbids them. Yet some have little to do with cultic performance and relate to the justice and monotheism of the community. The three most important examples of this are the statements regarding divorce (2.15-16), the list of social crimes (3.5), and the skeptical statements regarding justice (2.17; 3.13-15). Malachi, like the Deuteronomist, is interested in the complete range of law. Malachi emphasizes total obedience rather than concentrating on a few priestly concerns.

No simplistic reading of Malachi can account for this breadth of material. Achtemeier's view that the book presents the lawsuit of a Levitical priest who acts as messenger of the covenant in the temple is compelling enough.[23] Yet the book evades such easy classification. The lawsuit form could account for the shape of 1.1–3.18, but leaves 3.19-22 unaccounted for. Achtemeier claimed that 3.17-21 was the verdict, but the escahatology of vv. 17-21 does not fit the court scene. Whatever the precise shape of the book, one must look for the answer in the figure of the messenger/angel. The emissary plays a multi-dimensional role in the narrative. The messenger functions as priest (2.7), and the messenger assumes the role of prophet (3.1). The messenger acts as the divine emissary (angel) announcing God's advent. The term is used as fully as possible. It embodies the specific work of this prophet and the full range of canonical concerns emphasized by the book. The messenger/angel serves as a summary figure to conclude the Twelve, but he implements innovation as well as tradition.

23. E. Achtemeier, *Nahum-Malachi* (Interpretation; Atlanta: John Knox, 1986), p. 172.

Even these global descriptions cannot account for all of Malachi's uses of the messenger/angel theme. The description of the angel in Exod. 23.20-21 contains several themes which Malachi implies. First, the divine messenger will direct them to the future (prepare the way). Second, the messenger allows no rebellion. This impatience is perhaps even amplified in Malachi. Third, the messenger embodies the cultic name. The general emphasis on obedience and blessing looks like Malachi 1–2. Clearly, along with the Aaronic Benediction, the description of the messenger provides a backdrop for a significant degree of our understanding of Malachi. Can we understand the new messenger of Mal. 3.1 as Malachi himself, or Elijah redivivus? In the first place, the angel prepares the way quite literally. The figure identifies the road through the wilderness. The later Elijah instead shows the way to the future. This suggests an eschatological role. God's coming in Mal. 3.1 is no less than a second Sinai intended as a final revelation of the divine will. In 3.23, God enters history not to reveal his will, but to enforce it. Torah suffices and will not be replaced or changed but obedience/ disobedience will be noted. The altars will be purified. Yet the altars are impure because of the people, so pure altars indicate the purification of the people. Such wholesale changes loom well beyond the historical experiences of the fifth century community. For this reason, the prophet Malachi himself serves as messenger only in a partial or temporary sense. The role of the prophet Elijah also involves the introduction or identification of the messenger who acts in more of a divine than human role.

Through such themes the idea of the day of the LORD is woven into Malachi's message. The day of the LORD primarily indicates a theophany. When God appears, punishment and reward are meted out. References to 'the day' in Malachi generally build in intensity from the first mention in 3.2 to the final mention in 3.23. The first reference remains fairly ambiguous. 'The day of his coming' (3.2) does not specify what will come with it. It will be an important day, for the messenger will prepare for it. Even the statement, 'who can endure?' and the reference to refining and whitening do not provide especially strong descriptions. In 3.17, 'the day when I act' includes God's sparing the faithful. At this point the day begins to take shape. Images of burning are involved in the descriptions of 3.19 and 3.21: (1) the day is coming, burning like an oven; (2) the day that comes shall burn them up; and (3) the day when I act (identical to 3.17, except for the added idea that the righteous will tread on the ashes of the wicked). With 3.19, one feels the full fury of the day.

It is finally described in the strongest terms in 3.23—'the great and terrible day of the LORD'. This time the day receives an introduction from none other than the fiery prophet himself—Elijah.

The book of Malachi uses the concept of the day of the LORD to tie all the Deuteronomic interests together. One cannot conclude that the day of the LORD is the most important theme of Malachi. It would seem instead that the earliest theme assumes the most prominent attention—Deuteronomic obedience on the part of the priests and the people. Even prior to this theme, though less prominent in the vocabulary of the book, the related theme of covenant predominates. Covenant provides the broadest frame of reference and actually encompasses all the law and prophets (at least all portions emphasized by Malachi). The theme of obedience both informs the notion of covenant and serves to underpin it. All the concerns for proper ritual and conduct stand within this context. The specific (albeit not singularly defined) emissary of this obedience is the messenger who will enable a reestablishment of tribal consolidation prior to and consummated by the day of God's intervention. The day of the LORD is actually a narrow focus within the book, yet it stands as *the* event which affirms the rightness of the Torah.

Why does the book of Malachi use such a variety of traditions? Is its purpose to relate several distinct traditions from key time periods, as though dealing with all the history related to the book of Isaiah? If so, Malachi attempts to do so without three major divisions but instead combines all interests into a single short writing. The simplest solution would be to disavow the unity of the book and understand the latest redactor (or a series of editors for that matter) as hopelessly eclectic.

As affirmed above, Malachi's ties to previous traditions provide the key to the book's structure. The book refers to past traditions through the references to Jacob and Esau (1.2-3; 3.6) and the covenant with Levi (2.4). It refers to 'days of old' (3.4) and 'days of your ancestors' (3.7). I could add to these explicit references to the past, the traditions cited throughout the work. When Malachi looks to the present, it notes rebellion and sin. Malachi does not see this as a new problem, yet the work holds to the ideal of faithful individuals and small groups past and present. When Malachi looks to the future, it identifies the ultimate solutions to the problems of past and present. The messenger will come. The day will come. Elijah will come. Yahweh will come. And the people are ultimately asked to do only one thing in preparation. 'Remember the teaching of...Moses.' The motif of faithful readiness contributes much to the unity of Malachi. Up to chapter three, Malachi uses references to the past (obedience or rebellion) to emphasize the rebellion of the present. Beginning with chapter three, Malachi alludes to future acts with an emphasis on present rebellion. The only exception to this trend is 3.16-17. This passage actually reinforces the scheme, for it records the renewal of covenant fidelity. The book of remembrance leads the community which the book addresses toward the eschaton. It is the eschaton which resolves the religious and moral issues central to Malachi.

Malachi's approach to history distinguishes it from apocalyptic literature. Malachi foregrounds the present, not the past. The past is often 'predicted' in apocalyptic. Apocalyptic tends to explain the past through the historical events it contains. Malachi instead centers interest on the future, stemming from the uncertainty and dissolution of the present. The book does not present enigmatic language to be deciphered by the believer, but a clear message of warning directed to the believer. Later apocalypticists (especially Daniel) had to some extent given up hope in history. History simply served as the paradigm through which God communicated an otherworldly message. Malachi, like the Deuteronomist, blames all the shortcomings of history on human disobedience. Hope exists for the restoration of order precisely because humans hold the blame for the world's ills. Even here, the hope does not rest primarily in the conception of a new world order which makes friends of God's enemies. Malachi expresses the more practical view that the laxness of the covenant community itself must be abolished. So, the blame and the hope lie with those who call God 'Father'. This serves as a natural conclusion to the law and prophets. The redactor who placed Malachi in its present position (or for that matter, the community which provided the basis for Malachi's view of canonical traditions) determined that it would not do to end the prophetic canon with apocalyptic.

Such suggestions contrast only slightly with Fishbane's understanding that the reference to Moses at the end of Malachi served the purpose of maintaining social order in an era anticipating a new age. The eschatological view of history could lead to laxness with regard to the current political and moral system.[24] When compared with the content of the entire book, however, 3.22 seems less unusual or distinctive in that regard. The concern for moral and political order drives much of the message of Malachi. If we assume that for a later redactor Moses' authority outweighed the authority of the prophetic writings, the

24. *Biblical Interpretation*, p. 524.

addition of the name of Moses to the book would reinforce its authority. The name consolidates the various covenant concerns of the book by anchoring them to the scriptures of the times.

God formerly revealed himself to Moses in a most direct and powerful way. It was sufficient even for the exiles in Babylon to look back to this face-to-face revelation. But with the loss of morale at the time of Ezra, references to a sacred history so distant from the present despondency no longer sufficed. They needed a new revelation, so enter eschatology, enter Moses, enter Elijah who passes the mantle of hope to future generations. Both were consummate prophets. Both had seen God. Both 'died' in extraordinary ways.

Without the temple, it was sufficient to live in hope that at its rebuilding the community would be rejuvenated. Perhaps the function of Malachi's messenger conflates with that of Haggai's messenger (1.13) and all Malachi's message relates to hopes for and disappointments in the temple from the later perspective. Perhaps precisely because of the building of the temple and the failure of this event to transform Israel to success and obedience, Israel began to push its hopes beyond the future. If the motivation for faithful service could not be found in the hope and morality of the present, it could surely be found in God's future redemptive acts or in the accompanying threat of destruction. Due to the concluding references to Moses and Elijah which authenticate Israel's history and due to the references to the day of the LORD, it can be claimed that the book functions on the precipice of history. Beyond Malachi lies the oblivion of apocalyptic, yet most of the book expresses one last hope for history.

The Structure of Malachi

Malachi's interest in Torah (3.22) was not bookish. As Wellhausen recognized, the prophetic authority was not secondary to a written Torah.[25] Instead, the prophets offered oral Torah. This living interpretation of the Law gave the Law its dynamic relevance. Verses 22 and 23 belong together in that 23 follows the reference to Torah with expectation of prophetic revelation. The relationship between Moses and Elijah in these verses stands as a symbol of the dual design of the final form of the book. Malachi serves as a summary-conclusion to the prophetic books

25. J. Wellhausen, *Prolegomena to the History of Ancient Israel* (1878; repr. Gloucester, MA: Peter Smith, 1983), p. 399.

(and the prophetic era) and as an introduction to the day of the LORD. This enables the book to function as a canonical bridge between two very different perspectives on history. Moses represents the Torah and traditions of nascent Israel. Elijah represents prophecy as well as its eschatological vision.

The special structure of Malachi necessarily plays upon the distinction between law and prophecy. 'Free prophecy made possible the survival of the normative order [Torah] by opposing the tendency for that order to be assimilated to current institutional patterns.'[26] This helps to explain Malachi's opposition to the priests. Malachi views the Torah as ultimate in authority so that the priestly claims appear relatively transient. No inherent authority exists in title, position, even election. Malachi sees a vast gap between scripture (and other forms of divine disclosure) and the human order. From Malachi's perspective, the human order values scripture but cannot displace its role as the benchmark determining the validity of divine claims.

Gottwald suggested that references to Torah in the prophets were taken to refer to the canonical Torah by later readers/redactors.

> Such a 'canonical consciousness' worked to assimilate elements of Law and Prophets to one another and to facilitate use of passages from any part of the the two great collections to affirm a common message of adherence to law piety as read in conjunction with prophetic admonition and consolation.[27]

Accordingly, 'Moses' represents all the legislation of the Pentateuch. Malachi has certainly made a practice of gathering various materials from the segments of canon. Similarly, the reference to the book of remembrance in 3.16 recalls the books of Torah and the covenants they contain.[28] The future orientation of the context surrounding the reference is remarkable. These covenant makers are marked for mercy on the day that God acts. They will be remembered because they have remembered their faithfulness to the covenant.

From another perspective, Malachi engages in 'inner biblical aggadic exegesis'.[29] Malachi aims to incite full commitment to the Mosaic

26. Blenkinsopp, *Prophecy and Canon*, p. 6.

27. N.K. Gottwald, *The Hebrew Bible: A Socio-Literary Introduction* (Philadelphia: Fortress, 1985), p. 468.

28. I follow Dumbrell on this point by reading the verse as a reference to a covenant ('Malachi', p. 50).

29. Fishbane, *Biblical Interpretation*, p. 408.

covenant. Such interpretations of history may stress (1) continuity with the past (for example, ritual offenses), (2) discontinuity with the past (for example, rejection of offerings), or (3) the remembrance of some determinative point in history.[30] Malachi stresses continuity with the past and historical remembrance in chs. 1 and 2. On the other hand the forward looking warnings in ch. 3 employ discontinuity by emphasizing a new work of covenant making. All three chapters of Malachi show ties with the past, but the future element of ch. 3 is entirely absent in chs. 1–2.[31]

Several of the themes of the book of Malachi help to illustrate the dual nature of its structure. A sort of 'thematic doubling' is evident in the recurrence of certain themes in ch. 3. For instance, the theme of blessing and curse of 2.2 reappears in 3.9-10. In 2.2 the curse is principally a threat, but in 3.9-10 the curse is a reality resulting from the withholding of tithes. The former occurrence implies the blessing of election and covenant which adds to the understanding of the curse in 3.9-10. The latter names 'the whole nation of you' as the culprit. When read in conjunction with 2.2, this also implies covenant, yet in 3.9 the curse appears in the context of eschatological judgement. The curse in 2.2 instead calls for cultic reform.

A similar, yet stronger, thematic doubling occurs with the mention of the messenger in 3.1. This word (מלאכי) is identical to the word in the superscription (1.1). In this case, the theme helps to construct a sequence for the work. It ties together the messenger of 1.1 and the covenant of Levi in 2.4-5 with the reference to both the messenger/angel and the messenger of the covenant. Based on my thesis, that the introduction to the future-oriented portion of Malachi is 3.1, the cumulative nature of its contents is no accident. The verse acts as a springboard which propels the reader from interest in the traditional covenant to a covenant of the future which includes the assent of the people (3.16) and the radical intervention of Yahweh.

Such thematic doubling also appears in the opposing thematic clusters dealing with dirt, filth, and uncleanness in chs. 1–2 and dealing with

30. Fishbane, *Biblical Interpretation*, pp. 409, 412.

31. The division of the book into two parts at the juncture of 2.17 and 3.1 relies completely on thematic considerations. This involves no challenge of the continuation of the dialogical pattern into ch. 3, nor that ch. 3 marks the addition of an editorial unit. Cf. F. Prose, 'Malachi' in D. Rosenberg (ed.), *Congregation: Contemporary Writers Read the Jewish Bible* (San Diego: Harcourt Brace Jovanovich, 1987), p. 279.

purity and sanctity in ch. 3. The first cluster relates to the sin and guilt of the people. In one occasion, the uncleanness relates to God's reaction to their unfaithfulness (2.3). The second cluster attests to God's conveyance of purity as a final solution to the people's rebellion, but in this case the disobedient experience rejection preliminary to restoration. This accords quite well with the cultic notion of purity: the separation of the clean from the unclean is the first act of purification whether the object is mineral or vegetable or animal. Ultimately, the human stewards of sanctity must be separated on the same basis. This final solution occurs in part B of Malachi, while part A involves a historical call to purity.

Behind many such smaller themes lie macrostructures through which various elements of the book are related either to the final acts of Yahweh or to the earthly times of the prophet. These do not clearly associate the present with either the past or the future but share the present (which one can understand either as the time of the final redaction of Malachi or as one of various times in the history of its redaction) as associated either with past or future. One such larger thematic structure involves the continuum of Torah and prophecy. Torah primarily relates to the past and is emphasized in (though not limited to) the first two chapters of the work. Prophecy primarily depends on Torah as the means to determine Yahweh's will for the present. It is not that Torah cannot belong to the present without the advocacy of prophecy. Prophecy serves as a reminder of the claims of Torah and interpreter of its relevance. Using Torah as the platform for ch. 3 provides a secure basis for the innovative and radical claims of eschatology. Whereas chs. 1–2 deal with God's withdrawal due to inattention to Torah, ch. 3 announces God's return for purification and consolidation of the faithful. The announcement of God's displeasure is a Torah concern. The heralding of his return to complete the work of covenant in a new way belongs to prophecy. Both share an immediate concern for the present state of affairs.

Two related macrostructures are (1) the emphasis on impurity (chs. 1–2) and purity (ch. 3) treated above and (2) the interest in rebellion in part A and the companion interest in obedience or destruction in part B. The second of these related macrostructures deals with the people as a unity in chs. 1–2 and separates them in ch. 3. Thus part A reflects the hope for repentance while part B recognizes an end to the call for repentance. This marks the division between the expectation of redemption in history and the expectation of redemption beyond history. Even the eschatological portions of Malachi are saturated with warning. One could say that ch. 3 gives a stronger warning than chs. 1–2, since it introduces the expiration of the era of divine mercy. Prophetic judgement (before the execution of the 'sentence') involves the hope of a proper response to discipline. The new age involves a separation offering hope only to those who are currently faithful. The day of the LORD served as an ominous rhetorical tool for the prophet who intended to evoke the response of repentance and obedience. Yet 'the day' as Malachi sees it is clearly more than a figure of speech. If the prophet could bring his audience to the understanding that Yahweh's day of vengeance existed as an imminent historical reality, he could effect remorse in all but those most stubbornly rebellious.

Malachi's concept of God's final intervention involves no messianic imagery. The gospel writer conflates Malachi's day of the LORD with the dawn of the gospel age. Yet Elijah was not expected to precede the messiah, but the world's end. The identification of Elijah as the pre-messiah figure may be a later misreading of the gospels. John the baptizer does indeed announce the coming of Jesus, but his principal message is one of repentance (Mt. 3.2, 7-10; Mk 1.4; Lk. 3.3-14). According to Luke's view of history, Jesus' coming signaled the final chance for human response before the world's end. Jesus functioned like a prophet sent to avert judgement that was sure except for the condition of repentance. Certainly, Jesus' identity involves much more than the features contained in Malachi or in John's preaching (as recorded by the Synoptics). Yet the Elijah figure of Malachi served to restore the tribes of Jacob. This interpretation of 3.24 receives support in Sir. 48.10.[32] Further support comes from Malachi's absolute preference for Torah and priestly traditions rather than monarchical traditions. Elijah is the only figure from the former prophets who receives attention in Malachi and his ties to the monarchy were entirely negative. One should not engage in too much deduction based on this argument from silence. At the least, the book as a whole is not likely to favor messianic imagery, since its vocabulary and structure highlights only Torah. For Malachi, the Elijah figure precedes not a consummate ruler (messiah), but the

32. D.E. Orton, *The Understanding Scribe: Matthew and the Apocalyptic Ideal* (JSNTSup, 25; Sheffield: Sheffield Academic Press, 1989), p. 33. Sirach 48.10 contains the earliest known reference to Elijah's coming (approx. 200 BCE) according to Orton. This would challenge the connection of Elijah to the coming of the messiah.

LORD himself. This interpretation certainly falls within the parameters of the gospel writers' view of Jesus. To state the stages in clearer terms, the Elijah figure precedes God's appearance on the last day, which in turn occurs proleptically in the person of Jesus the Christ.

How important was the content of Malachi to the final editor(s) of the the twelve? Blenkinsopp indicated that the number 12 was the goal of the editors, and Malachi's message was secondary to the need to make a twelfth book out of the third משא oracle (Zech. 9.1; 12.1; Mal. 1.1).[33] It is difficult to judge the intention of an unknown editor. The importance of the number 12 and the connection of the three oracles notwithstanding, in its present position and with its present ending, the prophecy of Malachi presents claims that relate to the whole of prophecy. The Masoretic tradition clearly identified Malachi as the final book of the twelve as does the Septuagint. Although Jones cited one possible exception, very little evidence exists for important lists which place Malachi elsewhere.[34] Disregarding the supposed intentions of editors or redactors, Malachi completes the Twelve and in doing so also completes the prophets. Because this is true in terms of sequence, a canonical perspective invites investigation into the formal elements in the book that reflect its summary character. Malachi's dual design provides one connection between its canonical placement and its message.

The mention of the book of 3.16 may also relate to the canonical position of Malachi. Nogalski claimed such books typically concerned the future and in this case referred to the Book of the Twelve as orienting the reader toward the future.[35] Although I find no evidence to confirm the identity of Malachi's book with the Twelve, the theory offers some important implications. The twelve prophets speak of God's judgement affecting the righteous and the wicked. In the Book of the Twelve those who feared Yahweh saw the difference, which is to say that the message of the minor prophets is an elaboration of this difference. If the 'book' of 3.16 is in fact the minor prophets, then the entire message of Malachi calls for a special reading as the recapitulation of the

33. He linked this to the mention of 'fathers and children' in 3.24. In light of Sir. 48.10, this referred to some sort of 'restoration' of the twelve tribes (*Prophecy and Canon*, pp. 120-22). Nogalski favored the view that Malachi was first placed at the end of the Twelve and Zechariah 9–14 was added later (*Redactional Processes*, p. 211).

34. See Jones, *Formation*, pp. 1-18 for a full discussion of evidence.

35. *Redactional Processes*, pp. 208-209.

message of the prophetic books. This presents an appealing option, but it overreaches the concerns of the present thesis.

The allusions to the figures of Moses and Elijah offer more consequence for canonical concerns than the book of remembrance. It is easy for the current reader to conclude that because the Torah was previous to the prophets that prophecy was canonized as commentary on Torah. Yet prophecy survived as the catalyst for Torah and seemingly provides the framework without which the Torah would be consigned to irrelevancy. The figures of Moses and Elijah not only represent the law and the prophets, but also give ascendancy to prophecy. At the very least, prophecy and law work in tandem. Yet without prophecy, the destiny of God's people which may be implied by law is not realizable. The fact that after the close of the canon 'law and prophets' was a common reference to the Jewish scriptures shows the canonical interest involved in Malachi. Late works such as Malachi were instrumental in shaping this perspective. However, for the first century community and for us, 'law and prophets' are both written texts. This is not necessarily the case for the original prophecy of Malachi, yet certainly by the time of these supplemental passages (3.22-24) the canon consisted primarily of written texts. The living tradition of the late prophet is 'fixed' by the allusions to canon at the close of the Book of the Twelve.

One further concern involves the role of Malachi in the unity of the Twelve. Once more the dual design of the book receives prominent attention. According to House, the plot of the Twelve is 'u' shaped. Israel's experience in the minor prophets involves tragic movement in the first portions of the Twelve and takes a comedic turn after Habakkuk. Malachi opens with a positive theme and in spite of castigation for sins looks forward to the ultimate restoration.[36] Due to its historical nature, I would describe the Book of the Twelve as an open-ended epic without characterizing it as either comedy or tragedy. This epic parallels the historical epic of the Former Prophets and reiterates the epic narrative of the Torah. Arguments for a sequential unity seem unconvincing. Still, the unity of the basic message of the Twelve deserves strong defense, for the Twelve presents: (1) Israel as God's elect; (2) the nature of the people as subject to rebellion and punishment in the past and present; and (3) God's ideal community (covenant) as a conception of the future. God's purification of the sons of Levi in Mal. 3.3 represents the preparation of the sometimes disobedient elect

36. House, *Unity of the Twelve*, pp. 123, 159-60.

for the future community. Other prophets look to this future, but only in Malachi is this future so neatly applied to the past and present. The depiction of the final resolution of these prophetic concerns begins in Malachi at the juncture where the question, 'Where is the God of justice?' (2.17) meets the promise-warning, 'I am sending my messenger' (3.1). The epic continues toward a vaguely predictable, future resolution.

So Malachi sums up the message of the twelve and prepares for the future. One vision of the way Malachi's future plays out is the vision of Christianity. In Christian scriptures Malachi serves as a 'bridge' between prophecy and the fulfillment of the prophecy in the person of Jesus.[37] The link between prophecy and the Christian interpretation of its fulfillment is the figure of Elijah. The interpretations of Elijah provided in Mt. 11.7-15; 17.10-13; and Mk 6.14-16 can be added to others already cited. 'Elijah must come first' (Mt. 17.10) because he is the messenger whom the last verses of the prophetic canon tell the reader to expect before God's last intervention.

If the book of Malachi assumed its position as the last book of the Twelve by accident, it was a happy accident. If one supposes that the author of Malachi or a later redactor were attempting a conclusion to all the holy writings of the time, how could this person achieve such an epilogue? First, the author would fill the book with as many images as possible, perhaps limited by the needs of historical circumstance. Second, a debate style would serve this purpose well, so as to include the peoples' own statements of their rebellion. Another benefit ensues from the lively nature of this style of writing, which leaves plenty of room for invective. Third, instead of primarily re-presenting past demands it would behoove the producer to incorporate present events and anticipate future events. The stronger the images of the divine message to the present community and the stronger the images of God's future activity, the more compelling the message. Fourth, drop names of historical figures widely recognized by readers, like Jacob and Esau, Levi, Moses, and Elijah. Omit contemporary figures whose claims of divine authority have not survived the test of history (Ezra). If this is a fanciful summary, in the end Malachi trumps all such efforts at propaganda by introducing...theophany!

With such strong images, Malachi mixes concern for both openness and closure. It seems to mark the cessation of a group of writings. At the same time, it introduces a future entailing so many possiblities that

37. Watts, 'Introduction', p. 374.

even though the actor (God) and the event (day of LORD) are clearly named, its accomplishment means that all future beyond the event will be basically discontinuous with the traditions that give it meaning. Up to this point (beginning with 3.1), the book's commitment to openness/closure reveals a cyclical or a reciprocating pattern. Standing in tension are the blessing and the curse of the covenant, the reward and the punishment of the day of the LORD. Both of these cycles are conditional upon the obedience and the disobedience of the people. Yet the reciprocations of retribution cease with the dawn of the future envisioned by Malachi and the new beginning offers more for the imagination than for the satisfaction of reason. It is this openness which makes it so terrible and wonderful.

The relationship of Malachi 1–2 with Malachi 3 can be expressed in metaphorical terms as book ends. The book ends are not identical, nor are they exact opposites. One book end corresponds to the other in that it is the representation of a companion subject. Arranging them according to the direction in which English speakers read, the book end on the left depicts the subject: yesterday and today. The book end on the right depicts the subject: today and tomorrow. The special shape of each reveals the nature of past and present from the perspective of the prophets at the time of the close of the prophetic canon.

BIBLIOGRAPHY OF WORKS BY JOHN D.W. WATTS

1948 'The Heavenlies of Isaiah' (ThD dissertation; Southern Baptist Theological Seminary [unpublished]).

1952 '"For My Name's Sake"—A Study of the Phrase in Ezekiel XX', *The Fraternal* 85: 13-17.

1954a 'Biblisches Geben', *Der Gemeindebote* 32: 105-108.

1954b 'Note on the Text of Amos V:7', *VT* 4: 215-16.

1954–55 'The Origin of the Book of Amos', *ExpTim* 66: 109-12.

1956a 'An Old Hymn Preserved in the Book of Amos', *JNES* 15: 33-39.

1956b 'The People of God', *ExpTim* 68: 232-37.

1957 'The Song of the Sea—Ex. XV', *VT* 7: 371-80.

1958a *Vision and Prophecy in Amos* (Leiden: Brill).

1958b 'Elements of Old Testament Worship', *JBR* 26: 217-21.

1958c 'The Knowledge of God in the Old Testament', *RevExp* 55: 155-64.

1959a *Lists of Words Appearing Frequently in the Hebrew Bible* (Leiden: Brill, 3rd edn, 1968).

1959b 'Remarks on Hebrew Relative Clauses', *Akten des 24. Internationalen Orientalisten Kongresses, München '57*: 190-91.

1960 'The Methods and Purpose of Biblical Interpretation', *SWJT* 2: 7-16.

1961 'Jeremiah—A character study', *RevExp* 58: 428-37.

1962 'Infinitive Absolute as Imperative and the Interpretation of Exodus 20:8', *ZAW* 74: 141-45.

1965a 'Jahweh Malak Psalms', *TZ* 21: 341-48.

1965b 'Today's Man of God', *RevExp* 62: 361-66.

1966a *Studying the Book of Amos* (Nashville: Broadman).

1966b 'Amos, the man'. *RevExp* 63: 387-92.

1966c 'Amos—The man and his message', *SWJT* 9: 21-26.

1969 *Obadiah: A Critical Exegetical Commentary* (Grand Rapids: Eerdmans).

1970 'Deuteronomy', *Broadman Bible Commentary*. II. *Leviticus-Ruth* (Nashville: Broadman): 175-296.

1971a *Basic patterns in Old Testament religion* (New York: Vantage; Jameson Press, 2nd edn, 1978).

1971b (with J.J. Owens and M.E. Tate) 'Job', *Broadman Bible Commentary*. 4. *Esther-Psalms* (Nashville: Broadman): 22-151.

1972a 'A Critical Analysis of Amos 4:1ff', *SBLSP* (Missoula, MT: Scholars Press): 489-500.

1972b 'Zechariah', *Broadman Bible Commentary*. VII. *Hosea–Malachi* (Nashville: Broadman): 308-65.

1972c Review of D. Balzer, *Ezechiel und Deutero-jesaya*, *JBL* 91: 252-53.

1974a 'The Authority of the Old Testament', *Foundations* 17: 364-70.

1974b 'The Historical Approach to the Bible: Its Development', *RevExp* 71: 163-78.

1975 *The Books of Joel, Obadiah, Jonah, Nahum, Habakkuk and Zephaniah* (CBC; Cambridge: Cambridge University Press).

1976 'Higher Education in Southern Baptist Foreign Missions', *Baptist History and Heritage* 2: 218-31.

1977a 'The Deuteronomic Theology', *RevExp* 74: 321-36.

1977b 'Exodus', *Theological Educator* (Fall 1977): 58-68.

1978a *Study Outlines of Old Testament Books* (South Pasadena, CA: Jameson).

1978b 'The Formation of Isaiah Chap. 1: Its Context in Chaps. 1–4', *SBLSP 13* (Missoula: Scholars Press): 109-19.

1981 'Current Issues in Old Testament Interpretation', *SWJT* 23.2: 7-19.

1983 'Preaching on the Narratives of the Monarchy', in J.W. Cox (ed.), *Biblical Preaching: An Expositor's Treasury* (Philadelphia: Westminster Press).

1984 'Psalms of Trust, Thanksgiving, and Praise', *RevExp* 81(3): 395-406.

1985 *Isaiah 1–33* (WBC, 24; Waco, TX: Word Books).

1986 'The Characterization of Yahweh in the Vision of Isaiah', *RevExp* 83.3: 439-50.

1987a *Isaiah 34–66* (WBC, 25; Waco, TX: Word Books).

1987b 'Introduction to the book of Malachi', *RevExp* 84: 373-81.

1987c 'The Vision of "the Ideal" in Isaiah', *Theological Educator* 35: 84-90.

1988 'Babylonian Idolatry in the Prophets as a False Socio-Economic System', in A. Gileadi (ed.), *Israel's Apostacy and Restoration: Essays in Honor of Roland K. Harrison* (Grand Rapids: Baker): 115-22.

1989 *Isaiah* (Word Biblical Themes; Dallas: Word Books).

1991a 'Reading Isaiah in a New Time', *RevExp* 88: 131-36.

1991b 'Resources for Preaching from the Book of Isaiah', in J. Cox (ed.), *The Ministers Manual* (San Francisco: Harper, 1992 edn): 267-72.

1992a 'Baptists and the Transformation of Culture: A Case Study from the Career of William Carey', *RevExp* 89: 11-21 (reprinted in *EvRTh* 17 [1993]: 329-41).

1992b 'A Canonical Model (Hab. 2:4)', in R. Bailey (ed.), *Hermeneutics for Preaching* (Nashville: Broadman): 53-76.

1992c 'Images of Yahweh: God in the Prophets', in R.L. Hubbard, R.K. Johnston, R.P. Meye (eds.), *Studies in Old Testament Theology: Historical and Contemporary Images of God and God's People* (Dallas: Word Books): 135-47.

1993 Autobiographical essay in *How I Have Changed My Mind: Essays by Retired Professors of SBTS* (Louisville: Review and Expositor): 124-34.

1994 'The Spirit in the Prophets: Three Brief Studies', in M.W. Wilson (ed.), *Spirit and Renewal: Essays in Honor of J. Rodman Williams* (JPTSup, 5; Sheffield: Sheffield Academic Press, 1994): 84-91.

1995a 'Amos: Across Fifty Years of Study', *RevExp* 92: 189-93.

1995b 'Isaiah', in W.E. Mills *et al.* (eds.), *Mercer Commentary on the Bible* (Macon: Mercer University Press): 565-613.

1996 *Vision and Prophecy: Expanded Anniversary Edition* (Macon: Mercer University Press).

INDEXES

INDEX OF REFERENCES

OLD TESTAMENT

NEW TESTAMENT

OTHER ANCIENT LITERATURE

INDEX OF AUTHORS

JOURNAL FOR THE STUDY OF THE OLD TESTAMENT
SUPPLEMENT SERIES

110 Niels Peter Lemche, *The Canaanites and their Land: The Tradition of the Canaanites*
111 J. Glen Taylor, *Yahweh and the Sun: Biblical and Archaeological Evidence for Sun Worship in Ancient Israel*
112 Leo G. Perdue, *Wisdom in Revolt: Metaphorical Theology in the Book of Job*
113 Raymond Westbrook, *Property and the Family in Biblical Law*
114 Daniel Cohn-Sherbok (ed.), *A Traditional Quest: Essays in Honour of Louis Jacobs*
116 Hugo Gressmann, *Narrative and Novella in Samuel: Studies by Hugo Gressmann and Other Scholars 1906–1923*
117 Philip R. Davies, *Second Temple Studies: 1. Persian Period*
118 Raymond Jacques Tournay, *Seeing and Hearing God with the Psalms: The Prophetic Liturgy of the Second Temple in Jerusalem*
119 David J.A. Clines and Tamara C. Eskenazi (eds.), *Telling Queen Michal's Story: An Experiment in Comparative Interpretation*
120 R.H. Lowery, *The Reforming Kings Cult and Society in First Temple Judah*
121 Diana Vikander Edelman, *King Saul in the Historiography of Judah*
122 Loveday Alexander (ed.), *Images of Empire*
124 Baruch Halpern and Deborah W. Hobson (eds.), *Law and Ideology in Monarchic Israel*
125 Gary A. Anderson and Saul M. Olyan (eds.), *Priesthood and Cult in Ancient Israel*
126 John W. Rogerson, *W.M.L. de Wette, Founder of Modern Biblical Criticism: An Intellectual Biography*
127 Diana Vikander Edelman (ed.), *The Fabric of History: Text, Artifact and Israel's Past*
128 Thomas P. McCreesh, OP, *Biblical Sound and Sense: Poetic Sound Patterns in Proverbs 10–29*
129 Zdravko Stefanovic, *The Aramaic of Daniel in the Light of Old Aramaic*
130 Mike Butterworth, *Structure and the Book of Zechariah*
131 Lynn Rosemary Holden, *A Motif-index of Abnormalities, Deformities and Disabilities of the Human Form in Traditional Jewish Literature*
132 M. Daniel Carroll R., *Contexts for Amos: Prophetic Poetics in Latin-American Perspective*
133 Roger Syrén, *The Forsaken Firstborn: A Study of a Recurrent Motif in the Patriarchal Narratives*
134 Gordon Mitchell, *Together in the Land: A Reading of the Book of Joshua*
135 Gordon F. Davies, *Israel in Egypt: A Reading of Exodus 1–2*

162 Heather A. McKay and David J.A. Clines (eds.), *Of Prophets' Visions and the Wisdom of Sages: Essays in Honour of R. Norman Whybray on his Seventieth Birthday*

163 J. Cheryl Exum, *Fragmented Women: Feminist (Sub)versions of Biblical Narratives*

164 Lyle Eslinger, *House of God or House of David: The Rhetoric of 2 Samuel 7*

166 Martin McNamara and Derek R.G. Beattie (eds.), *The Aramaic Bible: Targums in their Historical Context*

167 Raymond F. Person, Jr, *Second Zechariah and the Deuteronomic School*

168 R. Norman Whybray, *The Composition of the Book of Proverbs*

169 Bert Dicou, *Edom, Israel's Brother and Antagonist: The Role of Edom in Biblical Prophecy and Story*

170 Wilfred G.E. Watson, *Traditional Techniques in Classical Hebrew Verse*

171 Yair Hoffman, Benjamin Uffenheimer and Henning Graf Reventlow (eds.), *Politics and Theopolitics in the Bible and Post Biblical Literature*

172 Volkmar Fritz, *An Introduction to Biblical Archaeology*

173 M. Patrick Graham, William P. Brown and Jeffrey K. Kuan (eds.), *History and Interpretation: Essays in Honour of John H. Hayes*

174 Joe M. Sprinkle, *'The Book of the Covenant': A Literary Approach*

175 Tamara C. Eskenazi and Kent H. Richards (eds.), *Second Temple Studies 2. Temple and Community in the Persian Period*

176 Gershon Brin, *Studies in Biblical Law: From the Hebrew Bible to the Dead Sea Scrolls*

177 David Allan Dawson, *Text Linguistics and Biblical Hebrew*

178 Martin Ravndal Hauge, *Between Sheol and Temple: Motif Structure and Function in the I-Psalms*

179 James G. McConville and John G. Millar, *Time and Place in Deuteronomy*

181 Bernard M. Levinson (ed.), *Theory and Method in Biblical and Cuneiform Law*

182 M. Patrick Graham and Steven McKenzie (eds.), *The History of Israel's Traditions: The Heritage of Martin Noth*

184 John C. Reeves and John Kampen (eds.), *Pursuing the Text: Studies in Honor of Ben Zion Wacholder on the Occasion of his 70th Birthday*

185 Seth Daniel Kunin, *The Logic of Incest: A Structuralist Analysis of Hebrew Mythology*

186 Linda M. Day, *Three Faces of a Queen: Characterization in the Book of Esther*

188 Robert H. O'Connell, *Concentricity and Continuity: The Literary Structure of Isaiah*

189 William Johnstone (ed.), *William Robertson Smith: Essays in Reassessment*

190 Steven W. Holloway and Lowell K. Handy, *The Pitcher is Broken: Memorial Essays for Gösta W. Ahlström*

192 Henning Graf Reventlow and William Farmer (eds.), *Biblical Studies and the Shifting of Paradigms, 1850–1914*

193 Brooks Schramm, *The Opponents of Third Isaiah: Reconstructing the Cultic History of the Restoration*

194 Else Kragelund Holt, *Prophesying the Past: The Use of Israel's History in the Book of Hosea*
195 Jon Davies, Graham Harvey and Wilfred G.E. Watson (eds.), *Words Remembered, Texts Renewed: Essays in Honour of John F.A. Sawyer*
196 Joel S. Kaminsky, *Corporate Responsibility in the Hebrew Bible*
197 William M. Schniedewind, *The Word of God in Transition: From Prophet to Exegete in the Second Temple Period*
198 T.J. Meadowcroft, *Aramaic Daniel and Greek Daniel: A Literary Comparison*
199 John Eaton, *Psalms of the Way and the Kingdom: A Conference with the Commentators*
200 M. Daniel Carroll R., David J.A. Clines and Philip R. Davies (eds.), *The Bible in Human Society: Essays in Honour of John Rogerson*
201 John W. Rogerson, *The Bible and Criticism in Victorian Britain: Profiles of F.D. Maurice and William Robertson Smith*
202 Nanette Stahl, *Law and Liminality in the Bible*
203 Jill M. Munro, *Spikenard and Saffron: The Imagery of the Song of Songs*
204 Philip R. Davies, *Whose Bible Is It Anyway?*
205 David J.A. Clines, *Interested Parties: The Ideology of Writers and Readers of the Hebrew Bible*
206 Mogens Müller, *The First Bible of the Church: A Plea for the Septuagint*
207 John W. Rogerson, Margaret Davies and M. Daniel Carroll R. (eds.), *The Bible in Ethics: The Second Sheffield Colloquium*
208 Beverly J. Stratton, *Out of Eden: Reading, Rhetoric, and Ideology in Genesis 2–3*
209 Patricia Dutcher-Walls, *Narrative Art, Political Rhetoric: The Case of Athaliah and Joash*
210 Jacques Berlinerblau, *The Vow and the 'Popular Religious Groups' of Ancient Israel: A Philological and Sociological Inquiry*
211 Brian E. Kelly, *Retribution and Eschatology in Chronicles*
212 Yvonne M. Sherwood, *The Prostitute and the Prophet: Hosea's Marriage in Literary-Theoretical Perspective*
213 Yair Hoffman, *A Blemished Perfection: The Book of Job in Context*
214 Roy F. Melugin and Marvin A. Sweeney (eds.), *New Visions of Isaiah*
219 Gerald Morris, *Prophecy, Poetry and Hosea*
220 Raymond F. Person, Jr, *In Conversation with Jonah: Conversation Analysis, Literary Criticism, and the Book of Jonah*
221 Gillian Keys, *The Wages of Sin: A Reappraisal of the 'Succession Narrative'*
222 Norman Whybray, *Reading the Psalms as a Book*
223 Scott B. Noegel, *Janus Parallelism in the Book of Job*
224 Paul J. Kissling, *Reliable Characters in the Primary History: Profiles of Moses, Joshua, Elijah and Elisha*
228 Volkmar Fritz and Philip R. Davies (eds.), *The Origins of the Ancient Israelite States*
230 Kevin J. Cathcart and Michael J. Maher (eds.), *Targumic and Cognate Studies: Essays in Honour of Martin McNamara*